Desert
 *Songs*

SUNY Series, The Margins of Literature
Mihai I. Spariosu, editor

Desert

Songs

Western Images

of

Morocco

and

Moroccan Images

of

the West

 *by John Maier*

State University of New York Press

Published by
State University of New York Press, Albany

For information, address State University of New York Press,
State University Plaza, Albany, N.Y., 12246

Production by Marilyn P. Semerad
Marketing by Fran Keneston

Library of Congress Cataloging in Publication Data

Maier, John R.
    Desert songs : western images of Morocco and Moroccan images of
the West / John Maier.
        p.   cm. — (SUNY series, the margins of literature)
    Includes bibliographical references and index.
    ISBN 0–7914–3017–0 (hardcover : alk. paper). — ISBN 0–7914–3018–9
(pbk. : alk. paper)
    1. Morocco—Foreign public opinion. 2. Europe—Foreign public
opinion, Moroccan.   3. United States—Foreign public opinion,
Moroccan.   4. East and West.   I. Title.   II. Series.
DS317.M255   1996
964—dc20   96–4822
                                                                    CIP

10 9 8 7 6 5 4 3 2 1

Contents

Preface

D*esert Songs: Western Images of Morocco and Moroccan Images of the West* examines a wide variety of modern Western, mostly American, and Eastern texts in a series of cultural studies. The East in this case is at first the Middle East of Orientalist fascination, an East described from the outsiders. Then the voices of the Middle East and North Africa are heard. Including the cultural "other," especially the voices of Arab-Muslim women, adds another dimension to the study of colonial and postcolonial cultural production. By juxtaposition the Western and Eastern texts illuminate one another.

Desert Songs is unusual in juxtaposing very different forms of cultural production: modern and postmodern fiction and folktales, advertising copy and oral histories, travel literature and ethnographic studies. Well-known classics are set next to stories that are rarely heard. *The Aeneid*, for example, is followed by film versions of the popular musical, *The Desert Song*. Jane Bowles and Paul Bowles are considered along with the nonliterate storytellers Paul Bowles recorded and translated. Many academic disciplines are also juxtaposed—literature and literary theory, linguistics, history, psychoanalysis, sociology, film studies, women's studies, and anthropology—largely because they have themselves been transformed by the cultural questions raised here.

The decision to concentrate on texts generated by Americans and Moroccans, both of whom are seen as marginal to the historically deep traditions that formed West and East, is quite deliberate. Seeing America on the margins of the West may surprise many readers, who are accustomed to thinking of the United States as the powerful leader of a mostly European alliance, but his first study, of Virgil's *Aeneid*, establishes the center of that tradition, whose power runs largely in a line from Rome through Paris to London. For its part, Morocco is almost by definition—as the "farthest west"—on the border of the Arab-Muslim world. The margin often provides a strikingly clear, if necessarily distorted view of the center. Both are relatively new nations and have had to struggle for identity within the dominant culture. Morocco has also been of Arab-Muslim nations the most "accessible" to European visitors, scholars, and political interests. That is an important consideration for these studies, which raise the question of access to the cultural other.

It may be worth mentioning certain personal experiences that led to this book. Exposing cultural stereotypes is one thing. Attempting to negotiate between cultures and between subcultures is notoriously difficult, as illustrated by the intense debate in the United States over cultural diversity. I would like to see in this work the beginning of an approach that involves the analysis of texts, since texts at least lend themselves to analysis, and one reading can be joined to another. The approach is suggested in the studies that follow and is addressed directly in the Conclusion. The result I would like to see is neither the traditional goal of winning a contest—that my reading will win out over its rivals—nor a string of comments, like those attached to *hadiths*. The readings are not complete enough to win, but they are detailed enough to elicit a response.

In the case of the United States and Morocco, it is not a question of need. Morocco does not need the United States in the way it needs the Arab league and the European community. The United States does not need Morocco, however useful its friendship has been. The Rogerian approach taken here, it is hoped, may be useful in other bicultural and multicultural settings, to remove some of the wariness with which one faces another. For most Americans, the Arab-Muslim world is a complete mystery, known only through headlines that emphasize the latest international crisis, almost always political, usually violent. For many of my students in the Middle East and North Africa, America is well-known, but often in such a distorted way that it appears a dream world, a whore more often than I would have liked to hear, but a most seductive one nonetheless. Tamar Liebes of the Hebrew University in Jerusalem ran a study to determine how different groups interpreted what once was an international icon of America, the television series

"Dallas." She discovered that Israeli Arabs, Moroccan Jewish immigrants, kibbutz members, and Russian Jewish immigrants all decoded the text in different ways, according to the collective understandings they brought to it (Tannen, 207). If not "Dallas," what of our more subtle works?

The point was brought home to me on the first occasion of "entering" a Syrian family. I had been invited, by chance, to eat with an acquaintance from the first of what so far have been three extended stays in the Middle East and North Africa. (Fulbright fellowships have enabled me to teach at universities in Syria, Jordan, and Morocco.) My reasons for going to Syria were not entirely innocent. Like Paul Rabinow, when I was completing a dissertation in medieval and Renaissance studies in the late 1960s, I had become quite dissatisfied with my obsessive concern with Western civilization. If there is a "center" to that historical-cultural, it is the Renaissance; and my research, on the English poet Edmund Spenser, required a very far-ranging knowledge with the sources that influenced him, Judeo-Christian and classical. Having been saturated with the West, I wanted to know if our most basic concepts of literature, authorship, interpretive communities, and the like were entirely Western and therefore mainly hidden to us. Could they be used to read texts that could not have been influenced by the West—in this case, ancient Sumerian and Akkadian literature written in cuneiform? It turned out that I was not alone in calling into question the assumptions with which those of us engaged in literary study had become comfortable. The late 1960s saw a change in virtually all areas of literary study, a change that is now well documented. Mine was only a rather odd way to proceed.

I had gone to Syria, then, because a very important cache of cuneiform texts had been discovered within a few miles of Aleppo, where I would be teaching. With no Arabic and only a sketchy idea of Syria, I blundered through all the well-known phases of culture shock. Eventually, I ran through something like Rabinow's series of informants. Though the idea had been only half-formed at the time, I did want to know more than the foreign community in Syria and more than the Westernized (and often disaffected) educated elite. To be invited by a Syrian into his home—that is, his family—was, of course, an important moment. The details of the meal will be recognized by anyone who has known Middle East hospitality. The younger men of the family served me; the women who had prepared the meal kept out of sight and could only be heard chuckling in the next room. (I knew even then what it meant when Elizabeth Warnock Fernea was told by a Moroccan friend that the French may have controlled the land, but they were not invited into Moroccan households.)

Once the leisurely dinner was completed, I was given an unexpected opportunity—to meet the father of the family, who was off in another room in the apartment. The meeting was correct and formal, the father gracious and reserved. My Arabic, limited to a few phrase-book greetings, quickly failed me. I could not help but notice what the father was watching on the television: an episode of "the Love Boat." If "Dallas," then the rage, was problematic, what did this traditional Syrian paterfamilias make of "the Love Boat?"

Teaching in Aleppo, Amman, and Fez raised more and more questions not only about Arab-Muslim culture but about what it is to be an American, the translocation of ethnicity discussed in chapter 6. It, too, is a well-known phenomenon. Americans in particular do not like being considered part of a group, and it comes as a shock that, as an American, the individual is immediately seen as a representative of larger collectives. This was particularly true in Aleppo. I was the first American the vast majority of my students, who were often the first in their families to be literate, let alone university students, had seen in "real life." The Syrians of Aleppo were used to many languages and many cultures in their midst—Arabs, Kurds, Armenians, Turks, Circassians, a few French and Russians. But Americans like me, my wife, and my son were completely strange.

After some years of struggling with Modern Standard Arabic and Moroccan Arabic, I had gotten to the point where a story told (in English) by the renowned Moroccan scholar, Mohammed Abu-Talib, to an audience of Moroccan teachers of English gave rise to yet another question. As with earlier questions, it formed so slowly that I was unable to pose it at the time. Mohammed Abu-Talib is a remarkable figure in Morocco. A scholar who is deeply interested in his own traditions, a poet who writes in English as well as in Arabic, a gifted teacher, Abu-Talib is probably the most cosmopolitan Moroccan I met in that country of polyglots. He was the first to study in Mexico. He has traveled throughout the world and has taught in the United States a number of times. He not only founded English departments in the Moroccan university, but also he established Spanish and German departments as well. (Of course his French is fluent, a given among the intellectuals of his country.)

What at first bothered me about the story he told was the unmistakable note of pain that pervaded it. He may himself have been the victim of the incident he reported.

According to Abu-Talib, a high-ranking American businessman, perhaps the head of the World Bank, was invited to Morocco. There his host treated him to a great feast. Hundreds of the host's family and colleagues were present. Animals were slaughtered to provide the banquet. Naturally there was no talk of business. That would come later. The American enjoyed the pleasures of a large estate.

Later, when the Moroccan was invited to the United States, he received rather different treatment. The American met him at an airport in New York, delivered him to a hotel, invited the visitor to avail himself of the city, left the driver with him, and promptly left. At 12:30 the next day, as scheduled, the Moroccan met the American for an hour-and-a-half lunch at a first-rate restaurant. Their business concluded, the men parted.

To all the Moroccans I spoke with who had heard the story, the American's behavior was deplorable. I had been around the Middle East and North Africa enough to know at least some of the rules of hospitality, and I could understand the Moroccans' dismay. What only came later, though, was a very American response. If the businessman in the story was such a powerful person, and if the Moroccan was cultivating the relationship for reasons of business, the American's actions, though they did not show much concern with Moroccan traditions, could be interpreted in a different way. For most Americans, the chance to visit New York with carte blanche and even a driver is seen as an opportunity—the freedom to make the best use possible of a limited time in the city. It is assumed that an individual would want to organize his or her time according to the individual's interests and desires. The restaurant lunch means good food—and a chance to have the banker's ear entirely to himself for a good part of the busy man's day. There is nothing of family here, nothing of public display, no extra time—just two individuals for whom, the American suspects, time is money. My guess is that the banker had no thought of insulting the Moroccan. He was simply projecting the extreme individualism onto the contextualized self of his

Moroccan colleague. However, the insult made it all but impossible for the Moroccan (and his audience) to see the incident from an American point of view.

More often than not the images of one culture produced by another are not intended for the "natives" at all, and there is relatively little needed to deconstruct the stereotypes in the image, to show how images represent the desire and/or aggressiveness of the producer. Magazine advertising of consumer products is a case in point. Two ads that appeared in national magazines in the United States provide examples that could stand for many, except that they seem so carefully managed and, in one case, puzzlingly complex.

One Orientalist ad consists of a photograph that dominates the top half of the page. Below the photograph is a great deal of white space and three messages. One, the least obvious, encourages the purchase of a certain line of clothes for males: the fashions promise a "socially spirited experience in men's clothing." A second, in tiny print, says something to Americans rather than to Moroccans (or anyone who has actually visited the place): "Destination Casablanca." Casablanca is the largest city in Morocco and the one closest to a Western industrialized city, the least Moroccan, very little like the Humphrey Bogart hangout. In fact, Casablanca is almost entirely the product of Western modernization. The French saw the advantage of a large port where, in the early nineteenth century, a scant three to five hundred people lived.

The third message appears in bold print, and its ambiguous message is pure Americana: TURN LOOSE.

What is to be turned loose? The photograph is visually striking and more complicated than seems necessary. Two sets of human figures are set against that background of brilliant light (from the direction of "Casablanca") on a large swell of white sand. Moving to the crest of a dune is a Western man holding the hand of a fully veiled woman. Presumably, he is leading the woman, who is known to be young and beautiful (only because the eyes are visible), to "Casablanca." She gazes at him with an expression that seems a mixture of fascination and fear. He does not look at her. Rather, the tall, blonde male, hand casually in his pocket, wearing "socially spirited" Western-style clothing (including a band around his tousled hair), looks impassively away from her and toward the sun. On the other side, below the first group of figures, and cast mainly in shadow, is a Western woman, immobile, looking peevishly at the man and the veiled woman moving away from her. Next to the Western woman is a sexless lump of clothes. The body beneath the black djellaba and headpiece entirely obscures the age, strength—even the sex—of this native. All we see is that the lump's head is downcast. Little wonder the woman, who is going nowhere, is upset. *Her* Moroccan is tiny, faceless, weak, and immobile.

One of the Moroccans is certainly an attractive young woman. In what way is she to be turned loose? (Remove the veil? the *djellaba*? Lose her religion? the traditions that tied her to this land?) The other Moroccan is not going to be turned loose. The Western woman is a study in anger and envy. She is clearly stuck with a depressed clump of body. Is the Western Woman unable to move a Moroccan man? a Moroccan woman?

For a magazine ad that, on average, would be scrutinized for less than half a minute, the humiliation of the Moroccans may bring comfort to the readership, which is overwhelmingly Western. Even so, what is gained by glamorizing the Western man at the expense not just of the Oriental but also of the Western woman? Exactly how this is a figure for a socially spirited experience is difficult to guess. (One wishes there were a comic appeal, but it is not evident.)

At least the ad did not base its appeal on one of the more persistent images that has fascinated the West, the mysterious and erotic Oriental woman hidden beneath the long, shapeless garments and the veil. Another full-color magazine ad for a travel magazine turned the fascination around. In something like an earth-colored tent, eight women are bunched together. Seven of them are fully clothed and fully veiled. Their eyes look out directly at the viewer. The seven surround (three standing, four sitting or squatting) a much taller, blond Western woman. She is dressed in a two-piece bathing suit, and her arms are draped with a diaphanous yellow scarf and jewelry to give her at least something of an Oriental look. Moroccans would consider her naked. As this robust beauty dominates the cluster of Eastern women and the photograph, the copy proclaims, "Jerry Hall's swimwear may have raised a few eyebrows in Morocco. But no one's really sure." In fine print, the ad comments on a line of swimwear "inspired by the glamour of old Hollywood." The magazine says it is more interested in the "unveiling of Hall" and sampling the "glamour of old Marrakesh" than in the swimwear. The magazine offers its readers "the insider's guide to the outside world."

Jerry Hall, then, turns around the very old Orientalist fantasy of the Eastern woman, the femme fatale. Many of the images of the exotic woman derive from the ancient world, from the depiction of Cleopatra especially, a Cleopatra seen by usually hostile Roman eyes. *The Aeneid*, as chapter 1 will show, is a key text in that tradition. (Shakespeare's Cleopatra represents something of a transvaluation of the figure.) Virginia Allen has argued that the femme fatale, the "dark half of the dualistic concept of the Eternal Feminine—the Mary/Eve dichotomy" (vii)—is rooted in deep antiquity, the goddess figures of the Mediterranean and the Near East. But, she argues, the femme fatale is mainly a nineteenth-century creation. The Astartes, Liliths, Salomes, beautiful but devouring the men who fall under their magic, become more fatal, more evil, and more erotic at the very time that the West was penetrating the East. The Eastern woman attracted men and women, Allen suggests, because she was powerful, independent, sexually free, and pleasure-seeking. She was "one of the few role models for women in the nineteenth century that combined freedom with fascination and erotic intrigue" (191).

While Orientalism, at least, has been discussed as a historical phenomenon and as a matter of stereotyping, this is a work in what is called the "new historicism," and in dealing with stories rather than ethnographies or historical archives, it follows the convolutions of texts. Texts do not merely reflect the history and culture in which they participate but help to make them.

As stories, they rather ask that the audience respond. And the hope of the author of this book, which contains a number of initial responses, is that it will stimulate others to respond. The analyses do not pretend to be exhaustive; rather they are part of a Rogerian approach (after psychologist Carl Rogers) to the texts about or by the cultural other. In a Rogerian approach to texts, meaning is not only "truth," meaning as it were in itself, but useful, meaning for the other, for "understanding." The approach parallels linguist George Lakoff's theory of metaphor, one that attempts to avoid the excesses of the Western philosophical tradition that has tended, since the seventeenth century, to take either an objectivist or a subjectivist tack (195–213). The first step in negotiating the meaning of the text is to state the interpretive problems in a way that is acceptable to the other—in much the same way that mediators in a labor dispute first attempt to get the opponents to accept the position of the other side in language the two will grudgingly agree to.

This often requires, to change the metaphor, something like colorizing a black and white film, intervening in order to bring out features that may not have been anticipated by the director. (The director, after all, constructed the film with an eye that discounted those background features.)

Two figures dominate the chapters that follow because the book is engaged in finding a cultural self through the "detour," as Paul Ricoeur would have it, of the cultural other. The two figures are the path and the mirror. One seems inevitably, and perhaps endlessly, in search of an identity that cannot be known immediately, through introspection. Even Paul Bowles's fictional wanderers, often impossibly obtuse, negotiate by the roadsigns constructed by the natives. The quest for the other is as often as not a quest for the self; in these studies, though, both self and other are called into question. It may be that neither can be known, simply exchanged.

The second figure is the mirror. Jacques Lacan's "mirror stage" that inaugurates the human infant into culture, that is, the symbolic order, is particularly useful because Lacan notices the distortion that all mirrors offer. The image viewed in the mirror may be the surest guarantee that the "I" exists. The I enters language and assigns itself a name. But that I is just as much a construct of the other, of language. And the image in the mirror distorts by presenting to the fragmented body a unified and completed self. (Lacan noted the "flutter of jubilant activity" in the infant who, incapable of holding itself erect, struggles to right itself, to become what it will, in fact, later be.) The mirror in this book evokes the recognition of an "East" as a distorted image of the Western cultural self, an image that nonetheless constructs a self as if it had always existed.

The East has been important for a Western self-understanding at least since the Greeks.

While I would not be quite as skeptical of introspection as a way to find one's own culture as Edward T. Hall is, I do think his formulation of the principle on which he based his book *Beyond Culture* (1977) can be taken (with apologies for the sexist language that was still in use in the 1970s) as a principle for the cultural studies that follow in *Desert Songs*.

> An INDIVIDUAL cannot thru introspection and Self-examination understand himself or the forces that mold his life, without understanding his CULTURE. CULTURES won't change unless everyone changes. There are: neurological-biological political-economic-historic and CULTURE-PSYCHODYNAMIC reasons for this. CULTURE is **dictatorial** unless *understood and examined.* "It is *not* that MAN must be in sync with, or adapt to his CULTURE but that CULTURES grow out of sync with MAN." When this happens PEOPLE go crazy and THEY DON'T KNOW IT. In order to avoid mass insanity PEOPLE must learn to transcend and adapt their CULTURE to the times and to their biological organisms. To accomplish this task, since introspection tells you nothing, man needs the EXPERIENCE of other CULTURES. I.e., to survive, all CULTURES need each other. (281–83)

One might find in Hall's effort to go "beyond" culture by experiencing other cultures the larger hope that as ancient a division as East and West might yet be overcome.

Acknowledgments

This book is the product of much reading and some immediate experience. The authors of the many fine studies listed in the Bibliography are, necessarily, immediate contributors to this book, and I acknowledge my debt to them and apologize if I have misread their works. The State University of New York Press readers of this manuscript have made invaluable suggestions. Many other people, in the United States, England, Syria, Jordan, and especially Morocco have provided me with insights along the way. I mention only the ones whose contributions are not obvious but proved to be important: Mohammed Abu-Talib, Hassan Mekouar, A. Tazi Saoud, Driss Ouaouicha, Moha Ennaji, Fatima Sadiqi, Ahmed Saber, Bahanou Akabouch, Abdurahman Hakim, Fatima Bennouiss, Mohamed Ouakrime, Fatima Mouaid, Khadija Loummou, Jilali El Koudia, Lahcen El Yazghi Ezzaher, Abdellatif Khayati, Ahmed Radi, Abdnaby El Helouwi, Hamid Eddijli, Amina Hayani Fakhri, Fatima Mernissi, Leila Abouzeid, Roger Allen, Sharon Spencer, Priscilla Roberts, Robert Gilliam, Jeanne Saraceni, Alison Baker, Susan Slyomovics, Joan Undeland, Richard Undeland, Edward H. Thomas, Leila Thomas, Jerome Bookin-Wiener, A. B. Yehoshua, Anton Shammas, Walid Ikhlassy, Yehya Abu-Risha, Ahmed Hussaini, Assem Faress, Zayneb El Abed, Jamil El Abed, Fayez Iskandar, Mohammed Shaheen, Eid Dahhayyat, Denys Johnson-Davies, Elizabeth Warnock Fernea, Riane Eisler, and especially Susan Schaefer Davis, for permitting me to reproduce segments of her unpublished transcription of an interview with "Zahrah."

I also acknowledge the following editors/publishers for allowing me to reproduce materials:

Reprinted from Virgil, *The Aeneid*, translated by W. F. Jackson Knight, copyright © 1956. By permission of Penguin Books Ltd.

Reprinted from *Middle Eastern Muslim Women Speak*, edited by Elizabeth W. Fernea and Basima Q. Bezirgan, copyright © 1977. By permission of the editor and the University of Texas Press.

Reprinted from Elizabeth Warnock Fernea, *A Street in Marrakech*, copyright © 1980. By permission of Watkins Loomis.

Reprinted from Jane Bowles, *My Sister's Hand in Mine*, copyright © 1978. By permission of the William Morris Agency.

Reprinted from *The Aeneid of Virgil*, translated by C. Day Lewis, copyright © 1952. By permission of Sterling Lord Literistic Agency.

Reprinted from *Arabic Short Stories*, translated by Denys Johnson-Davies, copyright © 1983. By permission of Quartet Books Limited.

Reprinted from *The Philosophy of Nietzsche*, copyright © 1954. By permission of Random House, Inc.

Reprinted from *Reflections on Fieldwork in Morocco*, copyright © 1977. By permission of University of California Press.

Reprinted from *Doing Daily Battle: Interviews with Moroccan Women* by Fatima Mernissi. Translated by Mary Jo Lakeland. Copyright © 1986 by Fatima Mernissi; English translation copyright (c) 1988 by Mary Jo Lakeland. By permission of Rutgers University Press.

Reprinted from Clifford Geertz, *Islam Observed*, copyright © 1968. By permission of Yale University Press.

Reprinted from Vincent Crapanzano, *Tuhami, Portrait of a Moroccan*, copyright © 1980. By permission of the University of Chicago Press.

Reprinted from Paul Bowles, *The Spider's House*, copyright © 1955, and *Let it Come Down*, copyright © 1952. By permission of Black Sparrow Press.

Several chapters have appeared previously in journals, and I thank the editors for allowing me reproduce material:

Reprinted from Jilali El Koudia, "Rolling Rubber," *Collages & Bricolages* II (1990). By permission of Marie-José Fortis.

"Asia under the Sign of Woman: The Feminization of the Orient in *The Aeneid*," reprinted from *Works and Days* 18 (1991): 89–116. By permission of David B. Downing.

"Silence and Ecstasy: Watching the Sufis Dance," reprinted from *Journal of Ritual Studies* 4 (1990): 41–64. By permission of J. W. Traphagan.

"Elizabeth Fernea's Moroccan Pilgrimage," reprinted from *MELUS, Journal of the Society for the Study of Multi-Ethnic Literature of the United States* 15 (1988): 76–81. By permission of Joseph T. Skerett, Jr.

A segment of "New English Stories in Morocco," reprinted from *The Maghreb Review* (1993). By permission of Mohamed Ben Madani.

"Two Moroccan Storytellers in Paul Bowles's *Five Eyes:* Larbi Layachi and Ahmed Yacoubi," reprinted from <*Postmodern Culture*>, *An Electronic Journal of Interdisciplinary Criticism* 1 (1991): MAIER 591. By permission of John Unsworth.

Still photographs from *The Desert Song:*

1929. DS-283 and DS-346. Courtesy of George Eastman House. © 1929 Turner Entertainment Co. All Rights Reserved.

1943. DS-167 and DS-119. Courtesy of Warner Bros. Archives, School of Cinema-Television, University of Southern California. © 1943 Turner Entertainment Co. All Rights Reserved.

1953. 781-86 and 781-41. Courtesy of The George Eastman House. © 1952 Warner Bros. Pictures, Inc. All rights reserved.

Introduction

ORIENTEERING

Commodore Hawser Trunnion, the retired naval officer in Smollett's satiric novel *The Adventures of Peregrine Pickle* (1751), was so unsteady on land that he led his wedding party on horseback across a field in zigzag fashion, tacking to take advantage of the wind while ignoring the road that ran directly to his destination. His bizarre maneuver did not go unnoticed:

> "Lord, Sir," said the valet, "what occasion have to you go zig zag in that manner? Do but clap your spurs to your horses, and ride straight forward, and I'll engage you shall be at the church porch in less than a quarter of an hour." "What! right in the wind's eye?" answered the commander; "ahey! brother, where did you learn your navigation?" (Walter Allen 67)

Studies that cross cultures almost inevitably require metaphors of travel, and they seem increasingly to follow Commodore Trunnion's lines. Facing unfamiliar territory, the traveler is ever forced back upon whatever navigational devices the traveler knows best—at the risk of looking ridiculous when a destination is actually reached. (The way is a little easier if a valet—an insider—is at the traveler's side and can be understood.) *Desert Songs: Western Images of Morocco and Moroccan Images of the West* is such a study, and it has not escaped the Trunnion mode of indirection. "Images" in the title of the book are much like buoys, signs warning the reader that the journey is not straight forward into the wind's eye.

Scouts learn a form of orienteering on land not far removed from Trunnion's navigation. Take a fix on the destination by sighting not just the place itself but by knowing exactly where you are and by reference to a third point in the landscape. Critics of twentieth century narratives, suspicious of straightforward storytelling, do not read the "thing itself," *what* is represented, without considering the point of view from which the thing is seen, and the instability of signs as well—a form of critical triangulation such as is practiced here.

The "orient" of orienteering is not an arbitrary trope for this study of Moroccan and American texts that somehow implicate one another. Edward Said's masterful *Orientalism* (1978) removed whatever innocence the study of an East by a West could claim. Said showed that even the most scientific, objective, and dispassionate scholarly treatment of the Orient rests upon often unspoken assumptions about the scholar and the society that cooperate in producing the scholarly text. What try to pass as straightforward histories of the Middle East or descriptions of Arabic or handbooks of Islam rarely escape imperial or hegemonic designs: by knowing to control the subject. Rana Kabbani's study of travel literature, *Europe's Myths of Orient* (1986), and Martin Bernal's massive *Black Athena: The Afroasiatic Roots of Classical Civilization* (1987, 1990) are but two of many challenges to the earlier innocent views in the wake of Said's work.

Much of this book reinforces the dangers of an unselfconscious Orientalism. Since *Desert Songs* examines a wide variety of texts, from products of high culture to advertising and popular advertising and storytelling, Orientalism at its worst involves crude stereotyping of supposedly inferior primitive peoples. Somewhat more frequently, the Orient is imaged as a backward place in need of modernizing and civilizing—in the direction, of course, of the West.

Where this book differs from earlier accounts of Orientalism is, first, the variety of texts and, second, the attention given to texts produced by the "Orientals" themselves. If one were to concentrate on the first half of this century, the earlier views of Orientalism would certainly be adequate. The situation since around 1967 is much different, much more complicated, and one almost wishes to think, more hopeful. Texts produced in the last twenty-plus years are allowing us to *hear* the many voices of the East in a way that was virtually impossible before.

Ancient Mesopotamia and Egypt performed elaborate rituals for "opening the mouth" of gods. Today we have subversive genres that are opening the mouths of peoples who seemed to be silent because they did not write, because they were isolated and inaccessible behind window grills and protecting walls—because we could not hear them. Anthropologists, linguists, feminists, fiction writers, translators, editors, and publishers East and West are providing access where there was little before.

The Orient of the not so distant past was thought to be massive, unchanging, dark, and mysterious. It was thought at least to be well defined and well placed. What may come as a surprise in this study is the extent of dislocation not only in the East, under enormous pressure to adjust to modern life, but also in the West. The figures whose lives and works best represent that displacement are the expatriate American fiction writers Jane and Paul Bowles.

Consider Jane Bowles's first response to Morocco. In a letter written in July 1948, while Jane was staying in Tangier at the Hotel Villa de France, she describes to Paul her delight at what she has seen and whom she has met. "The view of the Arab town from my window is a source of endless pleasure to me. I cannot stop looking and it is perhaps the first time in my life that I have felt joyous as a result of a purely visual experience" (*Out in the World*, 81).

Jane Bowles's pleasure in looking at the strange, new place was matched by a profound unease as she pushed herself to meet the women of the marketplace.

> I said my first words yesterday after Cherifa sneaked behind the stall and I suppose I said them in desperation. The older dyke was there, thank God (she comes to the market irregularly), so I walked over to her and somehow spoke. Just a few words actually, but immediately some old men gathered around me and everyone nodded happily. They said to each [other] that I spoke Arabic. I am slow and stupid but determined. (81–82)

We have in English a powerful trope for this kind of displacement and the giddiness it causes. Eric Partridge reminds us of the rich associations that have developed from the Latin *oriens* (itself clipped from *sol oriens*, the sun rising), the East. Disoriented, we look east to orient ourselves. In this we are always necessarily west of the sun rising, the place of "origin" and of "aboriginal" peoples (457). Our orientation, social and sexual, requires in some way a positioning in space.

That the orientational trope in English has a long historical connection with a Greco-Roman civilization that saw itself as "West" as opposed to "East" is important here. The Greeks saw themselves as culturally, not just geographically, different from the "Asia" that began, they thought (as we do) with the area just east of the Greek mainland, modern Turkey. The first dramatic tragedy to be preserved, Aeschylus's *The Persians* already maintained the "otherness" of the luxuriant East. What is possibly the single most important narrative in the Western tradition—important in the sense that it shaped subsequent narratives and formed the basis of a Western literary-critical theory—the *Aeneid* encoded a now-familiar division of human experience into a Western masculinity and an Eastern femininity, the one embodied in the hero Aeneas, the other in his temptress Dido.

A more recent example, from a different cultural register, is the 1930 Paramount film *Morocco*, directed by Josef Von Sternberg. *Morocco* starred Marlene Dietrich as singer Amy Jolly, Adolphe Menjou as Monsieur La Bessiere, a wealthy "citizen of the world," and his rival for Amy, Gary Cooper, playing Tom Brown, an American serving in the foreign legion. The film has elicited much response, especially from feminists who are disturbed by the dehumanizing cinematic gaze on the body of Marlene Dietrich. The Orientalism of the film, not unrelated to its treatment of women, has received less attention.

Morocco begins with a magnificent framing device: after a map to establish the scene, the film begins with a native having a difficult time trying to get a donkey moving. In the background, first the sounds, then gradually the sight bring the foreign legion into the foreground. The forces penetrate a gate, forcing the natives roughly to the side. Women are seen, one with upper torso nude. The natives, in very close quarters, are pushed ever deeper into the city by the movement of the troops.

Von Sternberg returns at the end of the film to the troops moving again, this time out of a town through an elaborate gate, a group of women scrambling to follow after the troops—all of them Moroccan except for Amy Jolly, who chooses to run after Tom Brown. She abandons her high-heeled shoes in the sand in order to catch up with the other women.

Amy Jolly had gone to Morocco at least in part to sing in a very elegant cafe theatre, clearly a mark of the Western presence in a backward land. There she meets both the "citizen of the world" and (in a humbler gallery) the ordinary legionnaire, Tom Brown, too poor to pay for the apple she offers him, a man forever borrowing money. Tom Brown is *the* American presence in the film, and it is as important that he speaks little. He is the inarticulate American, and when he does speak, he uses unadorned American English. Amy, especially when she is with him, also does not have to speak much. A great deal of the film depends on silence and gestures rather than speech. Elegant, elaborate public speech, in British English and in French, is entirely associated with the wealthy, sophisticated people in charge of "protecting" Morocco.

In a key scene, Amy is seen alone, preparing her performance in the cafe dressing room. Dressed in male garb (tuxedo, without the coat), holding a mirror, she sings in French. Later she performs in top hat and tails. While she sings, Amy smokes a cigarette. When she finishes her song, she lavishes her attention on a woman in the audience, taking a flower from the woman and kissing her full on the lips. As if by accident, she tosses the flower to Tom.

Still later in the same sequence, Amy is seen backstage with the cafe owner. She carries a huge white feather boa and shows off her legs in a skimpy outfit like a one-piece bathing suit.

In a much-discussed 1977 study, "Visual Pleasure and Narrative Cinema," Laura Mulvey draws upon the psychoanalytic concept of "the gaze" to explain the peculiar character of the look in film, which she claims demonstrates "the way the unconscious of patriarchal society has structured film form" (412). One of her most telling examples from the history of film is *Morocco*. Where there are usually three "voyeuristic-scopophilic" looks that constitute filmic pleasure, Von Sternberg's film intensifies the male gaze upon the beautiful woman, involving the viewer directly. The three different looks are those of the camera, the audience, and the characters. By convention, the first two are subordinated to the third, the way the characters turn their gaze upon the erotic object. In *Morocco*, however, Von Sternberg "produces the ultimate fetish" by subordinating the male protagonist's gaze to that of the audience. "The beauty of the woman as object and the screen space coalesce; she is no longer the bearer of guilt but a perfect product, whose body, stylized and fragmented by close-ups is the content of the film and the direct recipient of the spectator's look" (422–23).

Mulvey's aim is to examine "patriarchy" with "the tools it provides," psychoanalysis as articulated by Freud and Jacques Lacan. She looks forward to an alternative cinema that might break the hold of mainstream film, which "coded the erotic into the language of the dominant patriarchal order" (414). Freud's notion of 'scopophilia', where looking is itself pleasurable, is important here. As early as his 1905 *Three Essays on Sexuality*, Freud "associated scopophilia with taking other people as objects, subjecting them to a controlling and curious gaze" (415). The pleasure one takes in turning the filmed woman into an object of desire is related to the threat of castration, which the woman symbolizes.

Woman, then, stands in patriarchal culture as signifier for the male other, bound by a symbolic order in which man can live out his fantasies and obsessions through linguistic command, by imposing them on the silent image of woman still tied to her place as bearer of meaning, not maker of meaning. What appears simple enough, the innocent delight of the spectator deep in the darkness of a theater watching the brilliant play of images on screen, is tied to something so deep in the culture that the "control" involved in the gaze is overlooked or denied.

To understand the fascination of the spectator with the male protagonist, typically the active character in the film narrative, Mulvey calls upon Lacan's idea of the "mirror phase," when a child first recognizes its own image. The pleasure in identifying with the film's protagonist derives from this first moment, when the child "imagines his mirror image to be more complete, more perfect than he experiences his own body. Recognition is thus overlaid with misrecognition: the image recognized is conceived as the reflected body of the self, but its misrecognition as superior projects this body outside itself as an ideal ego" (417).

The fascination with the woman, with the object of erotic desire, is then a "function of the sexual instincts," while the interest in the dominant male is one of "ego libido" (418). As often as not in film, looking at the woman freezes "the flow of action in moments of erotic contemplation" (419).

Less often considered in *Morocco* is the way Moroccan natives are shunted off when they are no longer useful to the story. Amy Jolly is a *chanteuse* who chooses to follow the American legionnaire. Her decision places her on the level of the poor Moroccan women who follow their men. Before she makes that decision, however, Amy finds Tom in a cafe much smaller and shabbier than the one where she had worked. Tom is surrounded by his admirers among the native women. The Moroccan equivalent of Amy sings a plaintive song in the background—a song that the film does not bother to translate.

If Amy decides to follow the poor American instead of the wealthy man of the world, Tom will abandon his Moroccan women for his one true love, like him a Westerner.

Desert Songs provides many examples of the Orientalist gaze. More than that, the book wants to find the song that has been ignored.

Looking at the cultural other is always important. People in the East *look different*, and the Orientalist tradition in the West appreciates those differences, especially because it is difficult to see the people, especially the women: people living in compounds that are not open to outsiders; women veiling their hair (and sometimes their entire bodies); Bedouins in tents. Even today, visitors to Fez have difficulty finding maps of the old city. Swarms of "guides" attach themselves to the hapless traveler who only wants to have a look at the largest walled medieval city in the world. The streets are so narrow in places, there are so many dead ends, and the paths meander through such unplanned city neighborhoods that the guides wait for the unwary visitor to become lost.

MOROCCO FOR EAST, AMERICA FOR WEST

Desert Songs concentrates on Morocco for images of the East. Morocco may seem at first an inappropriate choice, since few in the Arab-Muslim world see that North African nation as central to its world. Egypt, the Levant, Iraq—perhaps even the gulf states—have been historically and remain in a position to influence the region in religious, political, and economic terms. Morocco, whose name in Arabic means the "farthest west," is actually farther west than any country in western Europe except for Ireland. Many of the customs and foods that are known every place in the East that fell under the influence of the Ottoman Turks are unknown to Morocco, which resisted Turkish overlordship.

However, Morocco looks like the East, as many of the fabled cities such as Damascus, Beirut, and even Jerusalem do not. (Later we will see why this is so.) Towering palm trees and minarets, walled cities, fast camels, a large part of the population still in traditional dress—these images are carefully used by the Moroccan Department of Tourism and are actually quite common throughout the land. Morocco can be used to film almost any Eastern site, including the Holy Land and its neighbor Algeria in the film version of *The Sheltering Sky.*

Most important is that Morocco, though on margin of the Arab-Muslim world, is accessible to the West. Morocco was often the first stop for any western European traveler and made lasting impressions on artists such as Matisse.

Not that Moroccans could not hold its secrets. In subtle ways the people kept the French, who "protected" the country from 1912 to independence in 1956, from penetrating the family homes. But Morocco was nearby, usually inexpensive, and for the most part "pacified," as this book will illustrate. It was, and is, available to the Western gaze.

Such access has meant that Morocco is not the East as such (whatever than may be) but stands in such a relation to the West that it provides an even better glimpse of Orientalist thinking than do areas considered more central to the Arab-Muslim world.

However, the images of the West in *Desert Songs* are provided almost entirely by Americans. Since America played a rather small role in the great drama of empire during the nineteenth and early twentieth centuries, the United States is in some respects far less representative of the West than would be Great Britain, France or even Spain, Italy, or Germany. Spain and France held vital interests in Morocco, where the United States did not. It may come as a surprise to Americans to realize that the United States and Morocco have had, on the whole, cordial relations for over two hundred years—a surprise because Morocco is still far more a French-speaking (and Spanish-speaking) country than one following the British Empire and using English.

One might argue—as I do here—that studying a landscape from its borders is as useful as studying it from the center, that the very marginality of the United States and Morocco provides an unusual, if eccentric, perspective on East and West. From a supposed center, each country has been called "marginal." However, marginalization has a certain covert power to see what is too brightly lit in the center, the way a city can be seen at night from hills around it, though the hills are too dark to be glimpsed from the interior. And the border areas are usually less bound to the traditions that hold in the center—and so are often the scene of violent play.

Within the historical and geographical reach of Western civilization the United States is the "wild" West. (Tom Brown in the French foreign legion is an extension of the American cowboy.) More than two hundred years after its birth, the United States is still the first postcolonial experiment in the West. Sociolinguistic histories of the English language have noted that the movement to speak a distinctly American English—H. L. Mencken argued it was a separate language by the early twentieth century—began as early as the War of 1812. Nearly half a century as a "superpower," a role that coincided with the collapse of European imperial claims on the third world, has not reorganized the West with the United States as a center. Powerful and influential, yes, but an experiment nonetheless, on the margins of the Western world.

Morocco does not control the holy places of Judaism, Christianity, or Islam. It has not produced the art and literature of the Arab-Muslim world to the extent that a distinctly Moroccan art or, perhaps more important, a Moroccan literature is recognized apart from Arabic literature or from the Francophone literature of the Maghreb. The oldest university in the world, still in operation (though with only a small group of students in religious disciplines), is to be found in Fez, but its younger offspring in Egypt and in Europe are better known in the East and the West. In Morocco today one can study Moroccan Arabic and even can find newspapers written in that dialect. (The newspapers consist largely of cartoons and jokes.) But the Moroccan who wants to write must choose Modern Standard Arabic, not the dialect, or French—or in a few cases, as we shall see, English.

Consider the plight of the nonliterate Moroccans, the vast percentage of whom are women. Their first language may be Berber. They will, except in very isolated areas of Morocco, learn Moroccan Arabic. If they are not schooled, they will have trouble understanding the Modern Standard Arabic used on radio and television. They will not have ready access to government services, since French is still widespread in the vast bureaucracy. Moroccan sociologist Fatima Mernissi has sought to change that by publishing a series of Moroccan folktales in French, Modern Standard Arabic, and Moroccan Arabic. So far only one of the tales, chosen because they hold particular interest to women, has been published, and it is not yet selling well.

Nonliterate Moroccan women, usually in the most traditional settings, are the most marginalized of persons in the East. They are almost
by definition inaccessible to the outsider. (Most of the women depicted
in Orientalist paintings were prostitutes, far from being socially acceptable. They were the only native women accessible to the Western
artists, diplomats, soldiers, and scholars, who were, until quite recently,
men.) One of the main objectives of *Desert Songs* is to show how this
most marginalized group, the ultimate cultural other, is finally gaining a
hearing.

This inaccessibility of the other is at the heart of *Desert Songs*, and it
is another reason for choosing cultures marginal to both East and West
to represent those cultural constructs. Cultural studies, as David
Bathrick has pointed out, have "come to suggest a remapping of the
humanities as a whole around new contents, new canons, new media,
and new theoretical and methodological paradigms" (320). Edward
Said has argued that even those engaged in cultural studies are sometimes trapped by limiting their study to prestigious "literary" forms.
Rather, a "broad range of social writings, symbolic formations, and systems of representations" (Bathrick 326) should be considered. The theoretical principles of *Desert Songs* are discussed in the Conclusion.
Instead of confronting the theory at the outset, the reader is encouraged
to read first the chapters that deal with a great variety of texts, canoni-
cal and popular, well-established literary genres; and new, subversive
oral genres (like oral histories and folktales), then read the implications
of this new historicist study.[1]

However, the inaccessibility of the other does require a comment
on the one who is looking at and listening to the other, the constructor
of this book. Cultural studies do not simply appear, without a context.
The one who is looking is situated historically and located in a different
culture than is the subject. Anthropologist Paul Rabinow distinguishes
between a personal self and a cultural self, and to the extent such a distinction can be maintained, it is really the cultural self that falls under
the "I" of this extended narrative. While someone—Jacques Berque, for
example, who has done it—may have the expertise in languages and the
grasp of a variety of cultures to produce a *Cultural Expression in Arab Society
Today* (1974), that person is not the compiler of this work.

As an American, male, with but a tenuous grasp of the languages
encountered in the East (in Morocco, Modern Standard Arabic,

Moroccan Arabic, French, and Berber), certainly with no claim to fluency (and no knowledge of Berber at all), I entered Morocco without the specialists's knowledge and training that give them ready access to texts and people. I entered, in middle age, to teach English at Sidi Mohamed Ben Abdellah University under the generous provisions of a Fulbright Senior Lectureship, as I had a decade earlier spent a year in Aleppo, Syria, and Amman, Jordan. The French I had studied in college was, as the Foreign Service kindly puts it, asleep. The subtleties of written and spoken Arabic are notoriously difficult for the outsider to grasp. Study of Modern Standard in Amman and Moroccan Arabic in Fez did not produce an Arabist. (Previous study of an ancient Semitic language related to Arabic, Akkadian, proved useful to see how the triliteral roots of Semitic languages work, but the languages are far from interchangeable.)

It has become clear to me that programs like Fulbright-Hays and the Peace Corps, while they are not exactly unique, are yet an important part of a distinctly American search for different experiences. Gilles Deleuze and Félix Guattari see American society as a relentless decoding—in the sense of the breaking down of codes—of cultural constructs (260), and I am inclined to agree with that assessment. No sooner is one institution established than it is disestablished; programs are broken, transformed, abandoned the way city neighborhoods are treated. Is it any wonder that the ubiquitous law-and-order television shows invariably include a violation of the law—at least a traffic violation—by the law itself? Americans living in Morocco study Moroccan Arabic, as often as Standard Arabic, to speak with "the people," carrying out a program that American linguists during and after World War II initiated—to codify what many Arabic-speaking people do not consider a "real" language, the ordinary language of conversation.

Many aids are available to help translate a culture before a person travels. Especially useful are books and articles by specialists in the region. One entering, like the Fulbrighter, through official channels finds a host of contacts, Americans and Europeans who have lived or still live in Morocco and Westernized Moroccans. The Moroccans are particularly important, but they, like the Fulbrighter, bring a certain cultural burden to any conversation. Usually they have studied in France, England, or the United States. That experience makes them conscious of cultural differences and takes away a certain unselfconsciousness that others in the culture share. Even if they have not lived in the West, their very education, steeped as it was in Western thought, sets them apart from their fellows. An American who was asked about the curious prohibition of "telling on" people—tattling—might find it difficult to explain it to an outsider, especially if the American had been trained to reflect on American culture, where another who just uses the rule without thinking much about it may, by example or story, bring the point home directly.

In a homosocial society like Morocco's, men and women, except for the Western-educated, do not easily talk to one another. When the stranger from America appears, gender differences are very clear, but at the same time difficult to grasp, and the male will find it all but impossible to reach the other. To give a fairly obvious example. My academic background is mainly in English and American literature and literary criticism. Two Moroccan colleagues were delighted to hear that I was looking for short fiction in Arabic written by Moroccans. They had already collected a number of pieces and had begun to translate them into English. When I asked if the collection included women writers— by that time I had read of several—the men were puzzled. It had not occurred to them to think about gender and writing; they could not recall any women writers and found my question, routine by now in American literary circles, very odd.

READING HISTORY

Morocco is a much older country than the United States. Its roots are as deeply set in the East as America's are in the West. *Desert Songs,* as the subtitle makes clear, is not a history of two regions but is, rather, a kind of Trunnion history, a study of interreflections with a historical character. Morocco, like the East as a whole, is seen not in itself but in relation to a more familiar narrative, a story of the West. The West provides a third point on the landscape by which the historian navigates.

Without imposing a false teleology, the record of twentieth century images of East and West suggests a pattern to that interaction. The early history of Morocco is, in a strange way, reflected in one of the most famous, certainly most prestigious narrative poems produced in the West, Virgil's *The Aeneid,* the focus of the first major study in this book (chapter 1). A brief sketch of Moroccan history is given here to provide background to that chapter and to provide a bridge between the ancient and the modern worlds.

Moroccan history conventionally opens in 788 A.D., when a descendent of the Holy Prophet Muhammad, Idris, arrived and Islam was accepted by a Berber tribe, the Awraba.[2] Before that was simply *jahiliya*, darkness. (This is rather like beginning American history with Columbus. Morocco before Idris, of course, has been reconstructed by archaeologists and historians.) It is a matter of some pride to the Moroccans that Morocco was the first country to recognize the American republic when, in 1777, protection was given to American ships in Tangier by Sultan Mohammed III. By declaring independence of England, Americans had lost the treaty protection of British vessels. In 1786 Morocco became the first nation to recognize the independent United States. (Correspondence between George Washington and Mohammed III antedates the French recognition of the United States, usually thought to be the first official recognition of the new country.)

Long before Idris I and Mohammed III, the Moors were known to the West. North Africa and the Moors enter Western literature in a decisive way with *The Aeneid*.

The most imposing ancient site in what is now the nation-state of Morocco is the Roman city of Volubilis, located in the interior not far from Meknes. By 40 A.D. the Moorish kingdom of Mauretania, an area that corresponds roughly to the modern Maghrib, had come under Roman control. Volubilis and Tangier belonged to the westernmost third, Mauretania Tingitana.[3] During the time Virgil was writing *The Aeneid*, left unfinished at his death in 19 B.C., the kings of Mauretania were largely faithful to Rome. But the princes divided their loyalties between Caesar and Pompey, and with the defeat of Pompey in 46 B.C., the way was paved for Juba I, who had backed Caesar. North Africa was increasingly Romanized—Westernized—even to the extent that the ancient Phoenician deities such as Baal and Tanit were assimilated to Roman gods and goddesses.

Juba's successor, Juba II, was given power in 25 B.C. Brought up in Rome and an enthusiastic Hellenist and scholar, Juba II would seem to have been the perfect client of the Roman state. One decision, though, eventually brought Rome into rule directly, and the decision involved the very Orientalism we will see occupying Virgil's vision of history. Juba II married Cleopatra Selene, daughter of Antony and Cleopatra.

The reign of Juba II was peaceful and prosperous, but the Romans still feared the now-legendary Cleopatra and her descendants. In *The Aeneid* Cleopatra's opposition to Caesar was seen as the latest in a long historical conflict between East and West, a struggle that went back to the Trojan War and the Phoenician Queen Dido. The historical Dido may have committed suicide to avoid falling under the control of Iarbus, the Berber ruler of the land that had included the new city of Carthage. However, Virgil tells rather a different story.

In what quickly became the most popular part of *The Aeneid*, Dido commits suicide when the Trojan prince, Aeneas, leaves her to fulfill his destiny of forging an alliance of Trojans and Latins to establish what would become the great Roman imperial state. Before she dies, Dido curses Aeneas. From that curse, Virgil suggests, arose the enmity between Carthage and Rome, three Punic Wars, and a new world order that finally emerged when Augustus was able to defeat the East. Readers today may find it odd that Virgil could so easily link a Phoenician queen from Tyre who founded Carthage to an Egyptian queen from Thrace, Cleopatra, centuries apart, as the great symbol of opposition to the West. *The Aeneid* is not the earliest Orientalist fantasy, but it is the most important in antiquity. Dido is for that reason the first Oriental woman, and Iarbus, the Berber chieftain, the first Oriental male in Western literature. In them the East became feminized as shown in chapter 1.

Juba II's decision to wed Cleopatra Selene eventually led Caligula to have Juba's successor, Ptolemy, murdered, and North Africa came under the direct rule of Rome. To a certain extent, Latinized Berbers prospered under Roman rule. One, Septimus Severus, became emperor. Long before the Arab invasion of the seventh century A.D. that brought Islam to the Maghrib, the world had become divided conceptually into West and non-West, and the "farthest West"—the meaning of *Al-Maghrib Al-Aqsa*⁴—had become part of the East and had experienced the "protection" of the West. Abdallah Laroui puts it succinctly.

In the eyes of the Carthaginians, the subjected Libyan was opposed to the unsubjugated Numidian; in the eyes of the Romans, the African, or Romanized Numidian, was opposed to the subjugated Numidian within the *limes* [fortified frontier], and both to the independent Moor. If Moor means western, the meaning is sociopolitical, for the center of the world was the Mediterranean, and the Atlantic Ocean was the wall behind which there was nothing. The Moor was the untractable man of darkness; first localized in the region of Volubilis, he reappeared in the fourth century A.D. in eastern Algeria, and in the sixth century before the walls of Carthage. (63–64).

Morocco is a constitutional monarchy, a country of some 25 million people, with certain historical and cultural connections with its neighbors in the Maghrib (Tunisia, Algeria, and Mauretania). Arabic is the official language, and Sunni Muslims make up officially 99.97 percent of the population. It is thus clearly an Arab and Muslim country. But as the nearest point of entry to the East from Europe—a short ferry ride from Spain—Morocco was often taken as the prototypical Arab-Muslim society. (Its proximity to Europe and the years of the French Protectorate led some of the nationalists to suggest that Morocco belonged more to Europe than to the Arab league. Even now, for economic reasons, it would like to join the European community.)

Like the United States to the West, Morocco is marginal to the complex Arab-Muslim world. It is the "farthest West."

Combining historical and anthropological perspectives, Clifford Geertz reads Moroccan history in terms of its distance from the center of Islam. Of course, Islam is the same everywhere, but the way its principles are translated into local cultures can lead to some very different emphases. Geertz did fieldwork at the two geographical extremes of the Islamic world, Morocco and Indonesia. In *Islam Observed* (1971), he wrote surely the most unusual book about Islam, one that contrasts the Indic-influenced Indonesia with popular Islam in Morocco. He notes that different reform-minded Moroccans have sought to purge the country of what they consider un-Islamic practices. But a final image in the book provides Geertz with a symbol of the Moroccan Muslim today, trying to negotiate between East and West. He tells of seeing

> a Moroccan student, a highly educated, French-speaking, but traditionally raised *evolué*, as the sour vernacular of French colonialism would call him, on an airplane bound for New York, his first trip away from home, where he will study at an American university. Frightened, as well he might be, by the experience of flying (as well as the thought of what awaits him when he lands), he passes the entire trip with the Koran gripped in one hand and a glass of scotch in the other. (116–17)

The particular isolation of Morocco from even the rest of the Maghrib permitted what Geertz calls the "classical style" of Moroccan

Islam to develop. Quite unlike the "national archetype" of the Indonesian peasant—"the settled, industrious, rather inward plowman of twenty centuries, nursing his terrace, placating his neighbors, and feeding his superiors" (9–10), his Moroccan counterpart is the "restless, aggressive, extroverted sheikh husbanding his resources, cultivating his reputation, and awaiting his opportunity." The classical style in Morocco is dominated by the *murabit*, which the French turned into Marabout. Geertz thinks Moroccan history is figured in three "complexes," a *siyyid* complex associated with dead saints and the tombs in which they are buried; a *zawiya* complex centered in the religious brotherhoods commonly known as "Sufis"; and the *maxzen* complex, the term for a central government (49). The Moroccan monarchy, for example, whose latest dynasty, the Alawites, dates from the seventeenth century, is not merely a secular power. The king derives much of his authority from the claim that he is, like many of the saints, a *sherif*, a descendant of the Prophet. The saints may possess *baraka*, power or grace, from Allah; the *sherif* claims it by descent. Often the two are fused in the same person.

Geertz's method is to identify and then unpack a complex symbol that will open up the system of significance by which a culture operates. For Indonesia he chooses a meditative prince, Sunan Kalidjaga, who learned Islam like a Buddhist, without having seen a Qur'an. For Morocco Geertz sees in the well-regarded seventeenth-century saint Sidi Lahcen Lyusi the symbol of Moroccan Islam. One of the Lyusi stories tells of Lyusi's gaining baraka after many years of searching. At an oasis deep in the desert he finds a Sufi master who is so ill his disciples will not tend to his needs. Lyusi washes the foul nightshirt of the master and drinks the water he used to wash it. He emerges, "his eyes aflame, not with illness, for he did not fall sick, but as though he had drunk a powerful wine" (32).

The initiation of Sidi Lahcen Lyusi, though, pales before his confrontation with the most famous of the early Alawite kings, Sultan Moulay Ismail, who reigned from 1672 to 1727. This powerful figure rivaled his French counterpart, Louis XIV. Today Moulay Ismail is known mainly for the gigantic fortress city in Meknes, the ruins of which are visible throughout the old city today. Moulay Ismail acted on a grand scale. He put together an army of 40,000 blacks to put down tribal rebellions. Thousands of Christian slaves were forced to work on the imperial palace. At one time some 50,000 slaves, servants, and eunuchs served a royal family of 500 wives and 1500 children there. The story of a confrontation between the fiery saint and the larger-than-life sultan, then, captures the essence of Moroccan history and culture, according to Geertz.

The Sultan invited the scholar-saint to Meknes. While he was being hosted, Lyusi noticed the cruel treatment of the slaves that were building the wall around the city. One man who fell ill while he was working was simply sealed into the wall. Lyusi attracted the Sultan's attention by systematically breaking all the dishes he could find, the clay vessels alluding to Allah's creation of his vessels, the humans who have been mistreated. To avoid the Sultan's wrath, Lyusi removed himself to a cemetery outside the walls.

> "Tell him," Lyusi said, "I have left your city and I have entered God's."
>
> Hearing this, the Sultan was enraged and came riding out himself on his horse to the graveyard, where he found the saint praying. Interrupting him, a sacrilege in itself, he called out to him, "Why have you not left my city as I ordered?" And Lyusi replied, "I went out of your city and am in the city of God, the Great and the Holy." Now, wild with fury, the Sultan advanced to attack the saint and kill him. But Lyusi took his lance and drew a line on the ground, and when the Sultan rode across it the legs of his horse began to sink slowly into the earth. Frightened, Mulay Ismail began to plead to God, and he said to Lyusi, "God has reformed me! God has reformed me! I am sorry! Give me pardon!" The saint then said, "I don't ask for wealth or office, I only ask that you give me a royal decree acknowledging the fact that I am a sherif, that I am a descendent of the Prophet and entitled to the appropriate honors, privileges, and respect." The Sultan did this and Lyusi left, still in fear for his safety, fleeing to the Middle Atlas forest, where he preached to the Berbers (and against the king) and ultimately died, was buried, and transformed into a *siyyid*, a man around whose tomb an elaborate devotional cult has developed. (34–35)

What is most remarkable is perhaps what is left unsaid by Geertz. The story resembles early Christian saints' lives in many ways, with the secular authority challenged by the saint fierce in his belief. Of course what is different is that both the sultan and Sidi Lahcen Lyusi claim descent from the Prophet, and the story is about the confirmation of the saint's power, or baraka. The odd turn is that although the saint's wrath was kindled at the treatment of slaves, the story does not end with any change in the treatment of those slaves. Lyusi takes his decree and flees, sensibly, to the forest, for the story in no way suggests that the *sherif*, Moulay Ismail, has any interest in changing his practices.

The Sufi saints of Morocco have, until quite recently, had relatively little to do with the Western image of the East—except as evidence of the alleged "fanaticism" that was foisted upon Islam by an increasingly secular modern West. (The renewed interest by Americans and Moroccans in the mystical and psychic practices is a major part of this book. Here it need only be pointed out that, since World War II especially that interest has gone far beyond the curiosity seeking of earlier days. An overview is given in chapter 2.)

If the saints have not gotten much attention until recently, sultans have. Voltaire cited Moulay Ismail in his satiric attack on the gross abuses of power. In *Candide*, written at the time in the Enlightenment when Western intellectuals were identifying the features of "civilized" life—in contrast to barbarity, savagery, atrocity and superstition—and denouncing slavery as the most heinous of the crimes against civilization, Moulay Ismail is not just condemned for his excesses. The sultan—and by extension, the society that produced him—came to symbolize everything that was wrong with despotic and "primitive" rule.

Hassan Mekouar has pointed out that Americans did not necessarily rush to visit Morocco when Mohammed III recognized the independence of the United States; but they did write quite a bit about the area. The "Barbary-inspired" novels, plays, and poems Mekouar takes as a subgenre of the Orientalism that was popular in Europe. What Orientalism allowed, the femme fatale, for example, was a socially acceptable form of erotic and often violent fantasy—acceptable since the Orient was removed and primitive, not modern and enlightened. Flaubert's *Salammbô* is perhaps the most remarkable of these Orientalist works, since the eroticism and cruelty are raised to a degree seldom seen before the twentieth century. (*Salammbô* inspired many costume parties in Paris and other intellectual circles, not surprisingly.) In America, as early as Susanna Haswell Rowson's play *Slaves in Algiers* (1794), an "Arabesque" tradition was forming. Among the Americans writing in the tradition, Mekouar lists not only Poe and his fellow romantics, but also Washington Irving, Royall Tyler, James Kirk

Paulding, Peter Markoe, John Howard Payne, and others (260). Mekouar found that the Barbary-inspired literature has "only one subject (the plight of Americans 'enslaved in Barbary') and one aim (to whip up patriotic fervor in American readers)" (261–62).

Typically in the Arabesques an American, usually young, is captured by Barbary pirates and must face a fate that is most at odds with the American way of life: a free citizen suddenly finding himself or herself enslaved. Mekouar sees the fascination with these tales in the insecurity of a new nation projected upon a North Africa of "exoticism, heat, cruelty and violence, scimitars and bowstrings, despots and harems, fierce whiskers, slave drivers, poverty, ignorance, and disease" (266–67).

The Enlightenment, then, identified the Orient not only with the arbitrary, capricious, and irrational rule of despots in the home and in the state, but with the primitive.

The specific American concern—perhaps obsession—with the free individual drove the American image of Morocco through the nineteenth century. That obsession, though, has taken some unexpected turns in the twentieth-century relations between the United States and Morocco. One example is an event early in the century that has been refigured in popular culture. In 1902 a Greek-American businessman, Ion Perdicaris, was kidnapped by Ahmad Raisuli, a Moroccan. After angry protests from President Theodore Roosevelt, the captive was released (though not before the ransom was paid).

A 1975 film directed by John Milies, *The Wind and the Lion*, romanticized the event. For one thing, the businessman is transformed into a widow (Candice Bergen) with a young, innocent son and daughter. While the kidnapper and the woman do not exactly become lovers, they come to a meeting of minds, and she ends up freeing *him* when a group of machine-gun-wielding Germans has him trapped. Although this was filmed long after the world wars, the addition of Germans adds to the story a totally insensitive representative of European imperial designs on a society about to be crushed by the modern West, imaged in the machine-gun.

Another change is that Teddy Roosevelt is changed into a rough-riding caricature who sends the marines into Tangier harbor, where they terrify the ruler, even though Roosevelt must brush aside the illegality of sending such a force. (No such appeal to arms was actually used.)

However, *The Wind and the Lion* is instructive in its portrayal of the dashing Raisuli (Sean Connery) as a noble savage. His is a tribal world of swords and horses. The Germans with their machine guns represent the brutality of modern warfare, killing at a distance. Teddy Roosevelt (Brian Keith) is a rifleman and cowboy; the rifle gives him a kind of kinship with Raisuli, also skilled with the rifle. The American and the Moroccan thus mediate between a primitive land sure to be lost and the modern state, which is just as sure to prevail.

In fact, the United States in the early twentieth century was trying to thwart European designs on Morocco. The United States played a role, for example in the 1906 Conference of Algeciras that, according to Abdellatif Benabdeljelil, is one of the highpoints of United States–Moroccan relations, since it helped protect Moroccan sovereignty for at least a few years (1–4). In 1912 France established the Protectorate in Morocco that held until independence in 1956. The United States did not recognize the Protectorate until 1917 (the time of Edith Wharton's visit to Morocco, taken up in chapters 2 and 3).

Even after France had established its control over Morocco, the United States on different levels maintained an anticolonial sympathy for the Moroccans. One reason for the popularity of the curious musical, *The Desert Song*, is that it romanticized a rebellion among the Riff tribes against the French and the Spanish. Jamâa Baida discovered that American sympathy for the rebels was widespread because of two audacious American journalists who managed to penetrate the Riff to report the story: Vincent Shean and Mowrer Paul Scott (183–96). That may account for the importance of journalists in even the earliest versions of *The Desert Song*.

The 1920s was also a period of significant anthropological work in Morocco, such as Edward Westermarck's fieldwork and the American Carleton Coon's study of Arabic and Berber cultural traits in the Riff tribes (Bouasla 224–25).

More significant for binational relations, at a meeting between Franklin Roosevelt and Sultan Mohammed V at Anfa, January 22, 1943, Roosevelt is said to have advised the sultan to resist French overlordship. As John Damis claims,

> The President also discussed with the Sultan the assistance in technical and economic aid which the U.S. would be able to provide Morocco

after the war. There can be little doubt of the importance of this meeting for Mohammed V; it opened vast horizons to the Sultan and perhaps did more to cause him later to demand independence than the urgent entreaties of Moroccan nationalists. For the moment, after noting in what distrust both Roosevelt and Churchill, who was also present, held French Resident-General Auguste Nogues, the Sultan's relations with France could never quite be the same. (4)

Benabdeljelil agrees, calling the meeting "an event undeniably significant for the independence of Morocco" (2).

The 1943 version of *The Desert Song* reflects this sympathy almost as much as it expresses an anti-Nazi sentiment. A shift *away* from this anticolonialist stance is evident in the 1953 version of the musical. Baida accounts for the postwar shift by the cold war. The United States, by then a major actor internationally, could not take the chance that Moroccan nationalists would swing to the Communist side. Related to it was a rapproachement between the United States and France, the result of French cooperation in setting up NATO air bases in Morocco. (The Moroccans were not even consulted.) When the French had finally decided to withdraw from its colony, the United States tried to delay independence to protect the air bases (188–93).

By 1959, cordial relations between the two countries had been restored, and they have been maintained since. An indirect result has been the favorable treatment American institutions like the Peace Corps and the Fulbright programs have received. Anthropologists have been permitted to work in Morocco when they have been denied access to other Arab-Muslim countries.

The postwar, postmodern turns in the stories Americans and Moroccans tell form the substance of this book, so comments here will be brief. One moment is worth noting, though:

> I left Chicago two days after the assassination of Robert Kennedy. My apartment in Chicago was practically bare. I had finished packing and had sold most of my furniture, leaving only the bed and a coffeepot. I had been mildly anxious about leaving, but the news of the murder had buried those feelings under a wave of revulsion and disgust. I left America with a sense of giddy release. I was sick of being a student, tired of the city, and felt politically impotent. I was going to Morocco to become an anthropologist. (1)

The anthropologist completed his fieldwork and then set about demystifying it. The result was a brilliant essay in the hermeneutics of the cultural other. Paul Rabinow borrowed from Paul Ricoeur the aim of the anthropologist, "the comprehension of the self by the detour of the comprehension of the other" (ix). What Rabinow takes us through in his "reflections" on his own fieldwork in Morocco is the complex investigation that never lets us forget the cultural mediation and the historical situation of the investigator.

Rabinow wanted to enter Moroccan village culture, and he traced his successes and failures through six informants, increasingly close to the profoundly other he wanted to understand (155–59). The first informant was a Frenchman he called "Maurice Richard," a hotel keeper on the very edge of Moroccan society. The second was Ibrahim, a kind of professional guide to the society, through whom Rabinow gained his first "break-throughs of Otherness." His third, Ali, Rabinow called an "insider's outsider," an adventurous soul who irritated and manipulated the villagers—and Rabinow.

These first three informants were all marginal figures. Three others, within the community (of Sidi Lahcen), moved him closer and closer to the object of his study. Malik, the last, was fairly close to the center of the community, a real insider. But it is interesting that the person who had what seemed to be the key to an insider's view of the society, Driss ben Mohammed, refused to become the anthropologist's informant. Driss ben Mohammed was deeply within the cultural and historical situation Rabinow wanted to enter; he looked, for example, to his forefather, a seventeenth-century saint, for direction in the modern world. That he was a Muslim who "maintained a belief in the ultimate and unconditional superiority of Islam" became the absolute barrier between Rabinow and the Other. Ironically—or, better, paradoxically—the one who refused to become the informant became the friend.

> But our friendship tempered our differences. Here we had come full circle. There were now two subjects facing each other. Each was the product of an historical tradition which situated and conditioned him. Each was aware of a profound crisis within that tradition but still looked back to it for renewal and solace. We were profoundly Other to each other. (161)

RECENT FIGURATIONS

To consider the history of Morocco, not from the inside but from the point of view of a fledgling United States trying, as postcolonial societies seem to do, to establish an identity apart from the empire to which it had been attached, there were at first a few actual contacts— Morocco recognizing the new nation, for example—but for the most part no history at all. Morocco was simply too remote, too little involved in the politics and the economy of the United States to claim much attention. The Arabesque literature of the nineteenth century sees Morocco through the haze (or veil) of romantic Orientalism, as an unchanging, rather lawless territory of Barbary pirates and cruel despots, the utter antithesis of enlightened reason, order, and law. Morocco and the Barbary coast were merely extensions of the larger Orient that stretched back to the Greeks and periodically involved the West but seemed to remain static even when Islam transformed the entire region. In that sense, to Americans, contemporary Morocco was as remote as ancient Persia and offered just about the same measure of cruelty, oppression, and luxury as those old opponents of the hardy and "modern" Greeks.

The twentieth century presents a much more complicated image of Morocco, as the early chapters in *Desert Songs* will detail. After the first chapter, "Asia under the Sign of Woman: The Feminization of the Orient in *The Aeneid*," deals with the ancient world, the chapters turn to the twentieth century and follow roughly a chronological course. *The Aeneid* is a useful start because, until quite recently, it could lay claim to being the single most important literary work in the West, the one text for anyone (until recently, mostly men) claiming to be educated, that is, literate. *The Aeneid* is important as a heroic narrative, the very model of epic literature with its celebration of the "phallic self." The tendency today to consider the epic as a kind of "master" narrative to be decoded, broken, and subverted as a way of deconstructing patriarchal orders is testimony to its importance. More than any other text, *The Aeneid* maintained its prestige through centuries of change in the West. It virtually defined the literary canon and shaped the "kinds" of literature that writers and readers in the Renaissance, for example, shared. It directly influenced many writers, whose anxiety over being influenced by the father-poet was never so great as to obscure the connection with the great ancestor. However different from *The Aeneid The Faerie Queene* might seem, for example, the epic conventions lead the reader directly back to Virgil and, through Virgil, to Homer.

What is important for this study is that *The Aeneid* already elaborates the Orientalist portrait of a fascinating but oppressive regime that produces a certain kind of Oriental man and a certain kind of Oriental woman, even a kind of space within which these characters prey upon one another.

Subsequent chapters in *Desert Songs* present a variety of symbolic formations generated in the twentieth century from World War I until the early 1990s. The texts fall into three large movements, though perhaps too much weight should not be given to the categories. The first, from World War I until the early 1930s, might be considered a classic phase, a continuation of the Arabesque tradition with one important difference. The Civilizing Mission of the West enters American discourse about Morocco. Its best representative is, not surprisingly, an American with an international theme, Edith Wharton (chapter 3).

That early period, though, already shows an interesting ambivalence not only about the Civilizing Mission but about civilization itself. The musical that provides the title for this book, *The Desert Song*, was staged first in 1927, and by 1929 was turned into the first all-talking, all-singing feature film. The popular musical would be transformed again during World War II (with anti-Nazi themes) and yet again during the cold war, when Morocco was trying to gain independence from France. The musical operates like a folktale in these various retellings. Ironically perhaps—ironic because the 1920s versions on stage and film make little attempt to give a real "look" at Morocco, although the later film versions try to get the settings right—the earliest versions are the most sympathetic to Moroccan attempts to throw off the imperial burden. Freud's critique of civilization, that is, seeing civilization itself as repression, is largely responsible for this surprising development. The popular American tradition of supporting the underdog is part of the challenge to a patriarchal order in the early versions of *The Desert Song*.

The 1930s film *Morocco*, mentioned already, is part of the first phase, as are anthropological, folkloristic, and linguistic studies of Moroccan Arabic carried out by Edward Westermarck in *Marriage Ceremonies in Morocco* (1914), *A Short History of Marriage* (1926), and *Wit and Wisdom in Morocco* (1931).

The Desert Song of 1943 and probably *Casablanca* of the same year are evidence of a different, skeptical phase, where suspicion of all authority coexists with the immediate terror of the Third Reich but more generally an almost existential dread. Paul Bowles's terrifying short stories, "A Distant Episode" (1945) and "The Delicate Prey"

(1948), upon which his reputation as a fiction writer still depends, are the best known representations of Morocco from this period, which runs from about 1939 through the year of Moroccan independence, 1956. The earliest of Paul Bowles's short stories in his *Collected Stories, 1939–1976*, "Tea on the Mountain," is set in Morocco, as are the vast majority of those collected stories and his major novels. Several chapters in this study involve Paul Bowles. The concentration will be on his lesser-known and later works, but it is clear from the better-known pieces that Bowles was not an expatriate American like Hemingway, Fitzgerald, and Henry Miller, for whom the foreign landscape and the people who happened to live there were as often as not a mere backdrop for Americans who carried their culture with them unexamined. With Paul Bowles—and with Jane Bowles in "East Side: North Africa" (1951), later turned into the brilliant short story, "Everything Is Nice"— personal identity and cultural identity are exposed as constructs over the abyss. In the fiction of Paul and Jane Bowles, Moroccans are for the first time as fully realized as the Westerners. If anything, they are more confident in their culture than are the alienated Westerners; but they are never romanticized into noble savages. The period was already seeing Moroccan writers gaining a position in Arabic literature, as is evidenced in 'Abd al-Majīd Ben Jallūn's "A Stranger" (1947).

The third film version of *The Desert Song* (1953) falls into this period, and it provides a caution against imposing too rigid a historical frame upon the texts. As the Moroccans were increasingly demanding independence and the French were increasingly willing to give it, the United States found itself in the odd position of opposing—or at least slowing down—independence. Moroccan independence appeared to threaten U.S. interests because of Communists and NATO bases within Morocco. Independence could mean that the United States would lose a convenient cold war ally. That did not happen, as it turned out, but the cold war version of *Desert Song* is respectful of the French protectors and suspicious of the Moroccans—a complete reversal of the earliest versions.

The third phase is postmodern and polyvocal. From anthropologist Clifford Geertz's *Islam Observed* (1971) to the present mix of American and Moroccan writers—especially women writers—that make up the last five chapters of *Desert Songs*, the assumptions of earlier phases are called into question. The international unrest through which

Paul Rabinow traveled to conduct fieldwork in Morocco coincided with the 1967 war, the single event that more than any other shocked the Arab-Muslim world. Anthropology questioned its assumptions about studying the other; literary studies at the same time turned increasingly theoretical, undermining earlier confidence in literary history and in the new criticism. And the tape recorder, which had revolutionized American linguistics by making it possible to analyze massive data about spoken language, had come to Morocco.

The most obvious use of the tape recorder in recent years has been in eliciting oral histories. Americans such as Vincent Crapanzano and Susan Schaefer Davis and Morocco's Fatima Mernissi have given the nonliterate Moroccan a chance to speak to the West and to the Western-educated outside the region. Elizabeth Warnock Fernea, who began as a journalist, has become a leader in promoting the study of women in the Arab-Muslim world, in such books as *Middle Eastern Muslim Women Speak*, which she edited with Basima Qattan Bezirgan (1977), in films, and in accounts of her own life in the East. *A Street in Marrakech* (1980) records her experiences of a year in Morocco.

Folklore and literature, once separated by a kind of iron curtain, are increasingly blurred (as are fiction and oral histories), and that blurring has allowed the nonliterate a hearing. Highly educated writers such as Mohammed Barrada and self-educated writers such as Mohammed Chukri author stories in Modern Standard Arabic that are earning them a reputation in the Arab world. Folktales, like the ones collected by Inea Bushnaq, Daisy Hilse Dwyer, and Fatima Mernissi, are taken more seriously today than in the past. And Paul Bowles, who first saw Morocco in the 1930s and has not lived there for over forty years, has made available the stories of the cafe storytellers such as Ahmed Yacoubi and Larbi Layachi.

Paul Bowles was interested in the nonliterate storytellers as early as the late 1940s, when he took up residence in Tangier. It was 1956, when the tape recorder arrived, that he began to record their performances—and many years later to translate the tapes into English. His preoccupation with the Moroccans upset Jane Bowles, who thought Paul was not giving as much attention to his own fiction. By the early 1960s, from which one can date the emergence of the "later" Paul Bowles, his short stories were more and more like Moroccan folktales or attempts to get into the heads of the Moroccans with whom he lived.

From stories such as "He of the Assembly," "The Time of Friendship," and "The Wind at Beni Midar" until very recent works, such as "The Eye" (1983) and "New York 1965" (1988), Bowles has pursued cross-cultural themes in a way that is unique among American authors.

Recently, Moroccans have begun to write, not only scholarly works but also creative pieces in English. For the educated Moroccan Arabic was always a possibility, and French allowed access to a very different audience. Moroccans writing in French do not appear in *Desert Songs*, not because they are not worthy of study, but because they deserve a volume to themselves. For Mohamed Abu-Talib to pursue the writing of poetry in English and Jilali El Koudia to write fiction in English requires a far different literary milieu than one would have found in the earlier periods.

Mention of poetry again points to an area than has been neglected in this book. For Arabic writers, poetry is still more prestigious than fiction, as Egyptian Najib Mahfouz made clear when he wondered, upon becoming the first writer in Arabic to receive the Nobel Prize for Literature, why the award was not given to a poet. It is the prestige of narrative in the West than accounts for the neglect here. A Moroccan might well navigate the literary landscape in a very different way than is encountered here.[5]

With the exception of *The Aeneid*, then, the texts presented in these chapters fall into three periods of the twentieth century: (1) a classical phase, when the Civilizing Mission of the West and civilization itself were matters of concern, from World War I until the beginning of the Depression; (2) a skeptical phase, suspicious of authority but tied to America's emergence as protector of the Western alliance, from World War II until the time of Moroccan independence in 1956; and (3) a postmodern phase, from the mid-1960s to the present. Jane and Paul Bowles dominate the second phase. Paul Bowles's own works, mainly essays and fiction, change under the influence of nonliterate Moroccan storytellers, whose stories Bowles translates for an English-speaking audience. Journalists, film makers, anthropologists, and folklorists give the West access to more Moroccan voices, especially to the nonliterate women about whom the West had held only the narrowest of stereotypes. And Moroccans writing fiction in Arabic came gradually to be recognized in the Arab-Muslim world and in the West.

The chapters of *Desert Songs* do not divide quite as neatly as the three phases might indicate. While the chapters follow roughly a chronological sequence, the texts are presented to the Western reader from the most accessible to the least accessible; from West to East; and from male voices to female voices. That organization reflects the historical situation and cultural location of the author, a middle-aged male who studied literature—mainly Western literature, at first—through the changes that have completely transformed English, American, and comparative literature. From the early 1960s, under the influence of civil rights, the women's movement, pressures of the third world, and critiques of modernity, the study of literature has become increasingly self-reflective and theoretical. The place of the text in culture and history is seen through a new historicist lens in these studies, as will become clear. The concluding chapter makes explicit the theoretical principles unfolded in the earlier chapters.

Schematically, then, *Desert Songs* begins with the text with which the literate Westerner is most comfortable, *The Aeneid*, and ends with oral histories of Moroccan women, as mediated by American anthropologists.

Desert Songs is an appropriate, if slightly ironic, title for this series of essays. The first four chapters look at texts that look upon Morocco from the outside. Chapters 5 through 10 gradually reverse the perspective. Together the chapters constitute a Trunnion navigation of cultural landscapes. Paul Bowles stands at the center, seen from various angles in a number of chapters, but the focus of chapter 5. Bowles's introduction to his novel about Morocco on the eve of independence, *The Spider's House* (1955), provides a convenient signpost toward which and then away from which this textual orienteering proceeds.

Bowles's main character, John Stenham, like Bowles an American writer, follows a Berber guide through the dark streets of Fez's wandering medina. Stenham thinks he knows his way through the maze of narrow alleys, and he resents his host for insisting on a guide. The circuitous route taken by the guide puzzles Stenham, but in one way he is delighted:

> Stenham smiled: unaccountable behavior on the part of Moslems amused him, and he always forgave it, because, as he said, no non-Moslem knows enough about the Moslem mind to dare find fault with it. "They're far, far away from us," he would say. "We haven't an inkling of

the things that motivate them." There was a certain amount of hypocrisy in this attitude of his; the truth was that he hoped principally to convince *others* of the existence of this almost unbridgeable gulf. The mere fact that he could then even begin to hint at the beliefs and purposes that lay on the far side made him feel more sure in his own attempts at analyzing them and gave him a small sense of superiority to which he felt he was entitled, in return for having withstood the rigors of Morocco for so many years. This pretending to know something that others could not know, it was a little indulgence he allowed himself, a bonus for seniority. Secretly he was convinced that the Moroccans were much like any other people, that the differences were largely those of ritual and gesture, that even the fine curtain of magic through which they observed life was not a complex thing, and did not give their perceptions any profundity. It delighted him that this anonymous, barefoot Berber should guide him through the darkest, least frequented tunnels of the city; the reasons for the man's desire for secrecy did not matter. (6)

Bowles has always maintained a certain skepticism about knowing the other. But as a writer of fiction that regularly subverts the traditional Western notion of the 'self' (and with it much of what confidently provides a Western identity) Bowles remains the American most impelled to understand the other. The extreme form of the quest for identity in Bowles's fiction is somewhat obscured by his relentlessly dark vision. In that quest he pushes to an extreme certain themes of Western literature. He reveals the gap between Americans on the border of the great tradition and the European center, where the Western sense of self still resides.

The deconstruction of a particularly modern and Western view of the self is the most prominent feature of this book. Against the atomistic self, the autonomous ego that is so important to the emergence of the novel in the West, the Moroccans themselves are now countering with *homo contextus*, a very different social construct. The final chapter of *Desert Songs* takes up that theme explicitly. The chapters that attempt to look at the East from the inside, chapters 6 through 10, are necessarily indirect in their approach to the other, even less able to travel in the wind's eye than the earlier chapters.

Chapter 6, Elizabeth Fernea's account of the year she and her family spent in the old city of Marrakech, contains the most explicit attempt of an American to "encounter" the lives of Moroccan women. Her account involves what I call a "translocation of ethnicity." The more Fernea involves herself in the lives of her Moroccan friends and acquaintances, the more she must confront the culture that she has carried with her unselfconsciously before. Like many foreigners who come to look and to listen, Fernea had thrust upon her the role as representative of her culture. The more personal her contacts with the women of Marrakech become—a process that eventually falls under the sign of pilgrimage to the sacred locus of the others, carefully hidden away from the gaze of the foreigner—the greater the resistance to and finally the acceptance of her own otherness.

Pain is everywhere evident in the Moroccan texts discussed in chapter 7. There, five short stories by very different writers are considered. With the exception of the last and most recent of the stories, Jilali El Koudia's "Rolling Rubber" (1990) they were written originally in Arabic. (El Koudia's was written in English.) In my experience, when Moroccans are asked to name their important authors, they invariably mention Driss Chraibi and Tahar Ben Jallūn, neither of whom is included in *Desert Songs*. Both write in French and are considered important because they have been recognized by the French. As Leila Abouzeid, whose story "Divorce" (1989) is one of the five considered in chapter 7, points out, for the generation of Moroccans that has grown up since independence, when the school curriculum was increasingly Arabicized—a process was only completed in 1990—the language of preference is Arabic. From 'Abd al-Majīd Ben Jallūn's strongly anticolonialist "A Stranger" (1947) to the postmodern complexities of Mohammed Barrada's "Life by Instalments" (1979) and Mohammed Chukri's "Flower Crazy" (1979), the Arabic language is necessary to understand the society from within.

Paul Bowles's increasing interest in the oral storytellers of Morocco is evident in chapter 8. Among other considerations that arise from the study of stories first performed then translated into English is the problem of authorship. To what extent is Ahmed Yacoubi's tale "The Night Before Thinking" an original piece? Could it just as easily be considered anonymous, as so many folktales are designated? However, Larbi Layachi's "The Half-Brothers" appears to borrow from the Western literary tradition certain conventions of "realistic" fiction that blur the boundaries of the two cultures even for the nonliterate Moroccan. Finally, the role of the translator in translating cultures makes authorship in the modern Western sense problematic.

The Moroccan material moves in chapter 7 from recognizably literary texts to the hybrid genres of oral texts, folktales, and life stories. The stories by public storytellers do not provide the same problem as the last few narratives. Larbi Layachi, Ahmed Yacoubi, and Mohammed Mrabet tell stories; Paul Bowles records them and translates them. The result is a hybrid text in English with no "native" readers. However, the stories by women require a special sort of intervention. One is a folktale that was transcribed in Moroccan Arabic in order to study the dialect; translation into English came much later. But the life stories of Zahrah Mohammed and Habiba correspond to no recognized literary or oral tradition in Arabic. They are life stories elicited by Western or Western-educated social scientists. In one sense, they are necessarily bicultural. In another sense, they could not have been elicited by a man. They could hardly have existed without the international concern about the status of women.

American anthropologist Susan Schaefer Davis and Moroccan sociologist Fatima Mernissi have found nonliterate Moroccan women who will talk about their lives (chapters 9 and 10). The hardships of those lives are readily apparent, almost predictable given the homosocial society in which they were raised. The power of such women is less evident and certainly less predictable. Only through the intervention of the women could the power of, particularly, a Moroccan so deeply rooted in tradition and almost entirely free of Western influence be displayed. At that remove from the West, Aisha Qandisha regains the mythical force that may derive from a Phoenician goddess the historical Dido could have known.

One conclusion is certain to emerge in this collection of readings. The pretense that the reader of an exotic literature is selfless, valueless, a presuppositionless observer of the literary scene has to be dropped. Just as the anthropologist, whose aim is to understand the cultural other, must always keep himself in the picture; the student of literature must not pretend that hers is a purely scholarly activity. The anthropologist may want to know people, and the critic may want to know texts, but the cultural barriers in either case must become known, the process examined, the limits explored and, if possible, recognized.

From my point of view, culture, as represented (and culture may always have to be represented, or continually presented, exhibited), is recursive, to use a term popularized by the generative linguistics of Noam Chomsky. That is to say, a limited number of cultural themes (images, symbols) recur in an infinite series of distinct, original performances (expressions, exhibitions, texts). These performances are a combination of themes. The hermeneutical task consists of entering the system (as within a culture one is already "in," an insider, but must enter a text, by reading it). Entrance is always disruptive, painful, dislocating. As Paul Rabinow points out,

> Interruptions and eruptions mock the fieldworker and his inquiry; more accurately, they may be said to inform his inquiry, to be an essential part of it. The constant breakdown, it seems to me, is not just an annoying accident but a core aspect of this type of inquiry. Later I became increasingly aware that these ruptures of communication were highly revealing, and often proved to be turning points. At the time, however, they seemed only to represent our frustration. Etymology comes to the rescue again; e-ruption, a breaking out, and inter-ruption, a breaking in, of this liminal culture through which we were trying to communicate. (154)

Reading a text of another culture requires an analogous eruption and interruption—with the burden always that what we try is never an innocent operation. The essays in this book follow a pattern, from the texts most accessible to an American of this historical situation to those least accessible. The book begins at the center of the Western tradition (chapter 1), then moves abruptly to a popular image of the East in the twentieth century, a product of confidence that the West is civilized and the East primitive (chapter 3). Chapters 3 through 6 trace a movement in American perspectives on the East from one that accepts this civilizing mission (chapter 3) through increased questioning of the Western sense of self and therefore of its mission in the third world (chapters 4–6). The cultural other, at first an object of exotic fascination, becomes increasingly important to subvert old certainties and to at least begin Ricoeur's "detour."

Chapters 7 through 10 attempt to understand Eastern texts. They, too, begin with the most accessible, stories written in Standard Arabic, texts that nonetheless owe much to Western-invented modes of fiction writing. Beyond the "official" literature of Morocco, though, are more complicated, less accessible forms—products of oral tradition, products of those who have had no official voices, the poor, the nonliterate, the unschooled, particularly women. These texts are not produced spontaneously, in most cases, since they do not meet traditional needs of their society. Rather they are increasingly elicited by the very Western adventurer/seeker who leaves home and penetrates the other in quest of a new and subversive sense of the self. In the process they are producing new genres, especially of self-disclosure.

One major hope—I can hardly call it an objective—of this book is that it will be taken up by readers in the Middle East and North Africa. Moroccans may find much of this book offensive or obvious, but these studies of Orientalist and (sometimes) Occidentalist texts aim only at developing a critical community. After his many months in Morocco, Paul Rabinow said, "I had a strong sense of being American. I knew it was time to leave Morocco" (148). These Trunnion navigations should lead the Western reader to a recognition much like Rabinow's, but one which invites, as the reading of texts allows, a response from the other.

Chapter One

Asia under the Sign of Woman:

The Feminization of the Orient in The Aeneid

Consider the heroic narrative, intensely "literary," ancient, "classi-cal," quintessentially prestigious in the Western tradition of litera-ture—and an Orientalist fantasy. The overwhelming *gravitas* of Virgil's *The Aeneid* and the impact it had on the West guaranteed that, until very recently when the Latin classics lost much of its hold on the humanities, its way of looking at the world would be passed along through the gen-erations and might even be taken as true. The West created an East as a kind of distorting mirror that helped define "us" by what "we" are not. Virgil did not initiate that move, but his work did more than any other to maintain an image of the East that persists to this day. The East—that is, what is now called the "Middle East and North Africa"—is usually taken as a place where men dominate women to the point of secluding them. Ironically, the East has come to be seen under the sign of the fem-inine, and *The Aeneid*, because of its prestige, played an important role in that signification.

The Orientalism of Virgil includes a complex of factors: the Asiatic origin of Phrygian Great Mother worship and the Bacchic rites; the historical connection between the Trojans and the Phoenicians (and its development into the Aeneas/Dido, Roman/Carthaginian contact and then hostility); an East that could include things as far afield as the effeminate dress and behavior of the Phrygians (derived from the worship of Cybele) and the luxury of North African desert tribesmen. Of greatest importance was the association between the East and the Woman. Otherwise unrelated images of uncontrol and chaos, of passion, anger, love, ecstasy, bestiality, fire, and madness are coded feminine and oriental. Dido is the great embodiment of them all, just as Aeneas embodies a wide array of masculine images, the ones that have been repeated endlessly in the Western literary tradition.

If the gods represent a higher plane of existence for Virgil, to which humans can only approximate, the exchange between Juno and the great Jupiter, who recognizes the importance of destiny, is paradigmatic of the female in the patriarchal order. While Juno has a great deal of freedom to act in human affairs, when the smiling Jupiter declares it over, her activity stops. In her terrible anger she is yet able to make a deal, a clever way of allowing Aeneas to win the heroic battle and yet lose his Eastern culture—his garments and his language—as the noble Trojan stock is introduced into the manliness of the Latins.

From this angle it is easy to see the importance of the Oriental woman, Dido, to the heroic destiny of Aeneas. Following her, in the vision of history advanced by Virgil, was the contemporary threat of yet another Oriental woman, Cleopatra. At other times in the emergence of a Western civilization the East has been perceived as a threat, most notably during the Crusades and during the fall of Constantinople to the Muslims, as Edward Said and a growing body of scholarship have shown. In modern times, from Napoleon's penetration of Egypt through the Western imperialist operations in the Middle East and North Africa, the East was no longer a military or a political threat. But a threat did remain, a seductive East of the imagination, an exotic dreamscape peopled with fierce Arab chieftains and inscrutable women, dangerous desert lands where hashish (or even un-Islamic alcohol), violence, and sex tempted the Christian to give into base, if fascinating, urges; a land at once soft and harsh; a land of fierce individualism and lawlessness—yet dominated by cruel despots and filled with slaves.

In her survey of the changing image of Cleopatra from antiquity to the present, Lucy Hughes-Hallett indicates just how widespread the perception of a "feminine East" has become since the nineteenth century: "The image of an Eastern country as a woman and of a Western male—whether military aggressor, mystic, scholar or tourist—as her heterosexual lover is one so commonplace as to pervade all Western thinking about the East" (207). Raymond Schwab, in passing, noted the importance of *The Aeneid* in establishing a notion of the "people of the dawn" and a *res orientales* essentially different from a West (1). Edward Said's *Orientalism* demonstrated that the perception is much older than Virgil, at least as early as Aeschylus' *The Persians* (56). From Martin Bernal's *Black Athena* we have learned that the East was by no means dismissed by the Greeks, who recognized that many of their intellectual achievements derived from the Egyptians and the Phoenicians. (It is Bernal's thesis that the denigration of the East, including the denial that the Greeks could have learned anything important from the East, is a product of romanticism and its attendant science of antiquity on the one hand and the European conquest of the East on the other [30–31].) Although *The Aeneid* was not the first to raise the problematic, I will argue that the specific association of the East with the feminine is articulated fully in *The Aeneid* and that the historical importance of Virgil's epic contributed to the continued acceptance of that association.

It will become evident in the analysis that follows that this chapter shares Stephen J. Greenblatt's new historicist theory (or antitheory) that history and literature are both "textual," that is, made up by particular texts, and it shares his desire to "subvert the tendency to think of aesthetic representation as ultimately autonomous, separable from its cultural context and hence divorced from the social, ideological, and material matrix in which all art is produced and consumed" (429). It will also become clear that the patriarchal ideology of what Toril Moi has called "traditional humanism," especially the notion of a self-contained, powerful "phallic self," the "seamlessly unified self—either individual or collective—which is commonly called 'Man'" (8) is embodied in the work for which Virgil is most praised. Virgil and his creation, Aeneas—not to mention the Augustus of literature/history—are examples without equal in the West of that humanistic phallic self.

In what is perhaps the most thorough and multifaceted collection of statements and responses to ancient (mainly biblical) texts, *Reasoning with the Foxes: Female Wit in a World of Male Power* (*Semeia* 42 [1988]), one of the essayists, Esther Fuchs, identified three major narrative strategies that reinforced the patriarchal character of ancient storytelling.

Fuchs studied the story of Rachel (Genesis 31) and discovered a number of "narrative gaps," insufficient indices of authorial judgment, suppression of motivation, and the lack of closure when women were part of the story (68), even when women came to be praised by the tradition. These strategies would not be quite so obvious in the Homeric-Virgilian epic tradition, which eschews narrative gaps. Dido, to whom much of this chapter is devoted, is not slighted in any of the three ways Fuchs found in the story of Rachel; but Cleopatra, perhaps the "real" subject of *The Aeneid*, is so treated. (The Battle of Actium, Hughes-Hallett noted, formed a kind of "miniature" in the larger narrative of *The Aeneid* [62–63], but Virgil's contemporaries would have been reading the slighted Cleopatra into the more explicit story of Dido.)

Simone de Beauvoir stated the case for a large-scale shift in antiquity when *Homo faber* dethroned the Great Mother. As humans discovered a world of tools, including of course those intellectual tools of logic and mathematics, a very different way of looking at the world, one in which women and the religion of woman were central, was overthrown. "The religion of woman," she maintained,

> was bound to the reign of agriculture, the reign of irreducible duration, of contingency, of chance, of wailing, of mystery; the reign of *Homo faber* is the reign of time manageable as space, of necessary consequences, of the project, of action, of reason. . . . It is he who makes the crops grow; he digs canals, he irrigates or drains the land, he lays out roads, he builds temples; he creates a new world.[1]

De Beauvoir's thesis has been extended by Riane Eisler, who has surveyed the archeological and historical evidence for the change. The earliest literature that has yet been discovered, written in cuneiform Sumerian from the third millennium B.C.E., would seem already to confirm the shift.

Sumerian stories of the god Enki contesting with the great goddesses of the Sumerian pantheon deal with virtually all of the areas de Beauvoir cited.[2] The Sumerians were noted for the control of agriculture through the management of floodwaters—by canal digging and irrigation systems—and for road building and enormous temple complexes such as de Beauvoir considered as evidence of *Homo faber*. In this regard, Eisler noted that the key words for agriculture used by the Sumerians (the words for farmer, plow, and furrow, for example) were not Sumerian in origin, and the terms signifying craftsmen, who in Sumerian times were thought to have a special relationship to the male-imaged Enki—the crafts of the weaver, tanner, basket maker, smith, mason, and potter—were taken over from the goddess-worshiping peoples living in the areas the Sumerians came to dominate.[3]

Because of its great prestige in the West, *The Aeneid* has been in a position to influence thinking about two apparently unrelated images—the feminine on the one hand, and the East on the other—that are brought together in a particularly striking way in Virgil's poem. At the center of this complex is the tragic heroine Dido, certainly one of the most noteworthy characters in Western fiction, an Eastern queen. The tragedy of Dido will be considered at some length here, for in her famous portrait the feminization of the Orient is most artfully figured. After a brief notice of the way Dido's tragic death is set against Aeneas's manly resistance to feminine passion, a series of related images will be presented. Then Dido's tragedy will be taken up again.

To understand the full impact of Dido's tragedy, one must trace the connections between the divine world, on the one hand, and the historical world of humans, on the other. Dido mediates between Juno and Cleopatra, the other important characters that feminize the Orient. On three levels, then, woman is marked as Eastern and therefore unable or unwilling to control herself. The results in the heavens, in the heroic world of the past, and in the recent Roman past (Augustus's battle with Cleopatra) are always the same: chaos and the need for male (marked "Western") intervention. To display these levels operating in *The Aeneid*, the argument here will move from Dido's tragedy to:

1. the impact of "Eastern" religions on a "West" that was coming to define itself in opposition to those very "Eastern" cultures imported through increasingly popular religions (not the least of which would be Christianity). The opposition, which is now called "Orientalism," is almost as old as Western literature itself; but Homer's even-handed treatment of East and West gave way quickly to what will appear full grown in Virgil;

2. the way in which Jupiter resolves Juno's passionate demand that Phrygian culture be stripped from the Trojans even as they triumph over the Latins will be shown to play out the conflicts between East and West, female and male, on a cosmic plane;

3. on the human level the charge of Phrygian effeminacy is glimpsed in the conflict between Ascanius and Numanus;
4. in a related note, an "Eastern" male, Iarbus, ironically redoubles the feminization of the Orient by presenting a corrupt image of a male who objects to Dido acting like a man;
5. Dionysian madness, genuine or feigned, intensifies the identification of destructive passion and the feminine (in Dido and in the allegory of Allecto); and, finally,
6. Cleopatra's battle against Virgil's master, Augustus.

TRAGEDY IN *THE AENEID*

The Aeneid contains elements of "tragedy," which again until recently was assumed to be the only form of narrative in the West to carry the prestige of the epic. Since a woman, Dido, is the tragic hero of the work, one might assume that this raises rather than diminishes her stature. Virgil's narrative incorporates tragedy but goes beyond the tragic. *The Aeneid* swallows the tragic—W. F. Jackson Knight's term for the *misera*[4] of Dido's death,

> *nam quia nec fato, merita nec morte peribat,*
> *sed misera ante diem subitoque accensa furore* (IV.696–97)[5]
>
> ("She perished neither by destiny nor by a death deserved, but tragically, before her day, in the mad heat of a sudden passion." Knight, *Aeneid* 118)

in the larger, though no less moving, action of the epic. The West would come to value such *misera* for its own sake, as Renaissance and modern narratives became more and more interested in the psychology of the tragic hero. Barbara J. Bono has shown, for example, how the *Aeneid* "establishes subtle typological ties between its foreground tragedy, the story of Aeneas and Dido, and the historical event that occasioned its composition, the defeat of Antony and Cleopatra by Octavius Caesar at Actium."[6] She argues that Virgil's Orientalism, in typologically relating Dido to Cleopatra, understands the history of Antony and Cleopatra "as the domestication of a rich, evocative, barbaric culture to Roman values" (86). In turn, the Renaissance would turn "Dido's tragedy into Cleopatra's triumph"—the transvaluation of the story into its "romantic apotheosis" (87).

But this happens much later in the West. The gap between the attitude of the ancients and that of the moderns was noted explicitly at least as early as John Dryden's *An Essay of Dramatic Poesy* (1668). In that work, one Eugenius argues for the superiority of Shakespeare's "excellent scenes of passion" to even the great classical tragedies,

> for love-scenes, you will find few among them; their tragic poets dealt not with that soft passion, but with lust, cruelty, revenge, ambition, and those bloody actions they produced; which were more capable of raising horror than compassion in an audience: leaving love untouched, whose gentleness would have tempered them; which is the most frequent of all the passions, and which, being the private concernment of every person, is soothed by viewing its own image in a public entertainment. (101–2)

Earlier, though, such a "mad heat" of "sudden passion" was the mark of woman's nature, and its value was to a great extent lessened by that association.

The feminization of an "Orient" was accomplished in large measure by two women, Dido and Cleopatra. Although it has suffered something of an eclipse by Homer in the twentieth century, Virgil's *The Aeneid*, left unfinished at the author's death in 19 B.C., became the single most important narrative (excepting the Bible) in a line of continuous readings from antiquity to only recently and can lay claim more than any other work to defining a "Western" literature. The epic and its only serious rival, tragedy, were emulated for centuries. The feminization of the Orient came about largely because of the successful portrait of the Roman hero who was able to overcome the dangers imaged in the Oriental woman.

Roman "manliness" (*virtus*, from which we derive the word *virtue*, everything excellent, especially moral worth) is embodied in the hero Aeneas. Aeneas is not the stereotypical macho womanizer or bully. He falls in love. He weeps when occasion demands it. He feels deeply about those around him. And while he represents the ideals of Stoicism,[7] he is not perfect. The rational control of the passions that is his most admirable quality—the ability to accept his grand destiny, the establishment of what would become the Roman Empire, though it earns him little joy; the ability to conquer fear, especially the fear of death—stays with Aeneas until the very end of Virgil's long epic. The outrage his enemy Turnus committed against Aeneas' friend Pallas is simply too great for him to bear with his usual equanimity.

> Aeneas' eyes drank in the sight of the spoils which revived the memory
> of his own vengeful bitterness. His fury kindled and, terrible in his rage,
> he said: 'Are you to be stolen hence out of my grasp, you who wear spoils
> taken from the one whom I loved? It is Pallas, only Pallas, who by this
> wound which I now deal makes sacrifice to you; he exacts this retribu-
> tion, you criminal, from your blood.' Saying this and boiling with rage he
> buried his blade full in Turnus' breast. His limbs relaxed and chilled; and
> the life fled, moaning, resentful, to the Shades.[8]

With his hero's victory, and his loss of control, the "war-weary" Virgil
ends his battle-filled narrative. If the demonic passion links Juno,
Dido, Allecto, and Turnus—as studies of the "fire" image in the poem
have shown—finally with Aeneas, the end of the epic is all the more
disturbing.[9]

Still, Aeneas is as close to a model of "masculine" control as can be
found in Western literature. In the one episode of *The Aeneid* that has
received perhaps more attention than any other, he walks away from
the woman he loves, the Carthaginian queen, Dido, in order to fulfill
his great historical destiny. No literary work of antiquity better exem-
plifies the phallic self than *The Aeneid* does in this episode.

The despairing Dido, in trying to keep Aeneas with her, is willing
to give him anything in exchange only for a little more time, time to
give her "mad mood a breathing-space and a rest" until she could be
taught "submission and the art of grief" (1:424, 426; Knight, *Aeneid* 110).

> Such was Dido's entreaty; and her poor, unhappy sister carried the tear-
> ful messages between them. But all these appeals left Aeneas quite
> unmoved. He was deaf to every plea, for destiny barred the way and a
> divine influence checked his inclination to listen kindly. He stood firm
> like a strong oak-tree toughened by the years when northern winds from
> the Alps vie together to tear it from the soil, with their blasts striking on
> it now this side and now that; creaking, the trunk shakes, and leaves from
> on high strew the ground; yet still the tree grips among the rocks below,
> for its roots stretch as far down towards the abyss as its crest reaches up
> to the airs of heaven. Like that tree, the hero was battered this side and
> that by their insistent pleas, and deeply his brave heart grieved. But his
> will remained unshaken. The tear rolls down, but without
> effect.(IV.437–49)[10]

While Dido and her people are now, in the words of Philip
Hardie, "set on an irreversible course of decline" (280), Aeneas is recov-
ering "the path toward ultimate control of the vertical axis." Hardie

notes the "extremes of up and down" caught in the same simile, where the ancient mountain and tree, battered by the winds, remain unmoved—the tree whose roots reach toward the Underworld but, like the world tree so conspicuous in Ancient Near Eastern poetry, whose branches reach toward the heavens.

Virgil and Eastern Religions

Why, though, connect the despairing Dido with the East?

In his important work *Orientalism* Edward W. Said observes that as early as Aeschylus, the Greeks, so important in the development of a "Western" identity, were drawing a line between East and West. The earliest extant Athenian play, *The Persians*, celebrates the destruction of the Persian armies under Xerxes by the Greeks (56). Asia is a hostile "other," defeated and distant, while Europe is "powerful and articulate" (57). Yet Asia remains a threat, a danger because the "excess" of the East threatens Western rationality. Robert M. Grant calls his chapter on the post-Homeric influx of Eastern deities and rites "Mediterranean Religions Westward."[11] Certainly it is difficult to distinguish East and West in the intensity of that movement west and in the generally syncretistic religious centers like Hellenistic Alexandria. But as Grant points out, when Mark Antony proclaimed himself a new Dionysus paired with the new Isis, Cleopatra, the Romans did not take to "this sort of behavior" Dio Cassius thought was "alien to the customs of his country" (39).

Said has made clear the dangers of Orientalism, not as a representation of a certain place in the world or even as a nefarious plot to keep Eastern peoples subject to the West.

> It is rather a *distribution* of geopolitical awareness into aesthetic, scholarly, economic, sociological, historical, and philological texts; it is an *elaboration* not only of a basic geographical distinction (the world is made up of two unequal halves, Orient and Occident), but also of a whole series of "interests" which, by such means as scholarly discovery, philological reconstruction, psychological analysis, landscape and sociological description, it not only creates but also maintains; it *is*, rather than expresses, a certain *will* or *intention* to understand, in some cases to control, manipulate, even to incorporate, what is manifestly a different (or alternative and novel) world. (12)

The Orientalism of *The Aeneid*, because of the profound influence of the work in the Western literary tradition, exaggerates a tendency already centuries old but not so evident in Virgil's models for the epic.

Homer seems to have avoided the distinction. The evenhanded-ness with which the enemies that fought at Troy are treated by Homer—perhaps as much a reflection of the techniques of oral compo-sition as of any intention to give equal treatment to both sides in the dispute—has often been remarked. Both sides in the conflict know the same gods and share the same culture. In Aeschylus, both sides name the same gods, but the cultures are very different on either side of the line. By the time of Virgil, the distinction between East and West had hardened. The "Teucrian" line of the Trojans (from an ancestor of Aeneas, Teucer) may have produced the pious Aeneas, the ideal of virtue, but the Trojans were as often as not in *The Aeneid* "Phrygians," effeminate followers of the Oriental goddess, the Phrygian Mother Cybele.

While there may be no simple concept of a Trojan "culture" oper-ating in *The Aeneid*, there is a notion of the *res Asiae Priamique...gentem immeritam* (III.1–2), Knight's "Asian empire and Priam's breed of men."[12] Any unified concept is obscured by Virgil's use of a great variety of fixed epithets, formulas imitative of Homer (and imitative of the oral tradi-tion): "Phoenician woman," "Phrygian bonnet," and the like. So many names tie the narrative to Greek literature, on the one hand, and to the history of Rome, on the other, that the modern reader, having lost the foundations of a humanistic education, Greek and Roman literature, is often bewildered by the many allusions. If it is not driven by a simple concept of the East, however, *The Aeneid* nevertheless displays a cluster-ing of epithets and motifs that suggests that Asia is not just a geograph-ical designation and that the East has become a cultural other that is important in defining the West, Hesperia, which, like the East, is not just a geographical designation.

Asian, Oriental, Teucrian, Phrygian, Phoenician, Tyrian—the con-nection between Carthage, a Phoenician city founded by exiles from Tyre—set off different aspects of the East within the Trojan "people." (Bono details the "Asiatic richness" of Dido's kingdom, which she inter-prets as "a temptation to lawless indulgence."[13]) The Asiatics are certainly not charged with the negativity that, say, medieval narratives (e.g., "Saracen" in *The Song of Roland*) carry when they distinguish between good and evil realms. The two features that most readily identify the Trojans as orientals, the garments they wear and the language they speak, are ultimately stripped from them, even as they are victorious.[14]

Juno and Phrygian Culture

The episode in which Trojan (Teucrian/Phrygian) culture is given up includes the most obvious statement of the patriarchal order that, for Virgil, holds both for human society and for the cosmos. The statement is all the more important because it deals with the gods, with the relationship between the great gods, Jupiter and Juno. Dido and Cleopatra (the one representing the already legendary past, and the other representing a very present danger to Rome in Virgil's time) are, after all, merely humans. What happens to Juno validates the patriarchal order in human society. The problem is not seeing the god under the sign of woman as weak or passive.

The two goddesses most prominent in *The Aeneid*, Juno and Venus, are anything but passive, and they are treated in a positive way by the poet.[15] They act at their own initiative, and they act forcefully again and again, to help or hinder Aeneas in the fulfillment of his destiny. But the patriarchal cosmos, of which imperial Rome is a reflection, is revealed in the figure of Jupiter, "king of all-powerful Olympus," who has finally had enough of the bickering of the two goddesses. In the final book of *The Aeneid*, Jupiter invites the goddesses to yield to his "persuasions:"

> My wife, how shall it end now? . . .
> Then yield to my persuasions, give up the long feud now at last!
> No more of the hidden rancour that so consumes you, the sullen
> Recriminations your sweet lips have troubled me with so often!
> This is the end, I say. You had power to harry the Trojans
> All over lands and seas, to kindle accursed war,
> Bring tragic disgrace on a king's name and drape a betrothal
>   in mourning.
> I forbid you to carry the feud any further. (XII.793–806;
>   Lewis 634–44)

Knight translates the last line, "Further effort I forbid" (334). Juno must yield, but she does not accept the decision without striking a bargain with her consort.

> Do not command the indigenous Latins to change their ancient
> Name, to become Trojans and to be called the
> Teucrians: Allow them to keep the old language and their
>   traditional dress:
> Let it be Latium for ever, and the kings be Alban kings:
> Let the line be Roman, the qualities making it great be Italian.
> Troy's gone; may it be gone in name as well as reality.
> (XII.823–29; Lewis 644; cp. Knight, *Aeneid* 334)

Jupiter is amused by Juno's passionate demand, and he grants what she asks, though not without a comment on her overly emotional address.

> The creator of man and of all things replied to her with a smile:—
> Jove's sister you are indeed and the second child of Saturn,
> So powerful the tides of wrath sweeping within your breast!
> But come, there was no need for this violent emotion; calm
>   yourself.
> Willingly I grant what you ask: you have won me over.
> The Italians shall keep their native tongue and their old traditions;
> Their name shall not be altered. The Trojans will but sink down in
> The mass and be made one with them: I'll add the rites and usage
> Of Trojan worship to theirs. All will be Latins, speaking
> One tongue. From this blend of Italian and Trojan blood shall
>   arise
> A people surpassing all men, nay even the gods, in godliness.
> (XII.830–39; Lewis 643–44)

(Note: Knight translates Juno's request as, "Let there be the Roman breed drawing power from Italian manliness," and in Jupiter's response, he prefers, "The Trojans shall only blend, absorbed, in the Italian breed.")

Phrygian Effeminacy

Since few today in the West trace their ancestry to the Phrygians, no one mourns the loss of those Trojan rites and customs. What the Trojans would be asked to give up can be glimpsed, though, in a brief episode involving Aeneas's son, Ascanius (Iulus). Numanus tries to draw the young man into battle with the taunt of effeminacy. The Teucrians were also Phrygians. The Phrygian garments, soft and beautiful, were associated with the gentle arts and rituals of Cybele, the Phrygian goddess. Note the references to pipe, timbrels, and boxwood flute used in the service of the Great Mother. Already the East is associated with softness and luxury, idleness, music, dance, and the worship of the Mother.[16]

> Twice-captured Phrygians, are you not ashamed to be this second time beseiged and imprisoned behind a stockade, relying once again on walls to fend death from you? . . . We are by our birth a hard race. We carry our baby sons down to a river as soon as born and toughen them by the water's icy cold. Our boys go sleepless for their hunting and never do they let the woodlands rest. . . . And our young men work and endure and are trained to privation; constantly they harrow and master the land; or set towns quaking in warfare. At every age we are bruised by iron. To goad our bullocks' backs we use a spear reversed. . . . But you, your garments are embroidered in saffron and ablaze with purple dye. You love best a life of idleness, and indulgence in the dance is your joy. Why, your tunics have sleeves and your bonnets strings to tie! You are women of Phrygia, not Phrygian men. Go running over Dindyma's height, to the music of a twin-bore pipe of reed, for which indeed you are trained. The Mother of Ida's Berecyntian tabors and boxwood flutes are the tools of your trade. But leave arms to men; lay not claim to steel. (IX.598–620; Knight, *Aeneid* 244)

To the extent that "Asian" had come to be associated with the feminine, the loss of garment and speech could be seen as another triumph of the masculine, Latin virtues. A few of the more obvious examples will serve for a host of other, often quite subtle associations.

A Moorish Man's Lament

A somewhat more complicated instance combines Phrygian effeminacy with the worship of Bacchus/Dionysus. Aeneas' only serious rival for the hand of Dido is Iarbus. Furious at Dido and Aeneas, Iarbus laments to Jupiter Ammon,

> O Jupiter Almighty, to whom now the Moorish (*Maurusia*) nation, banqueting on divans of rich-coloured weave, pours Bacchic (*Lenaeum*) offering in your honour, do you see what is done? . . . For a woman, a vagrant,

> . . . has rejected my marriage-suit, and accepted Aeneas. . . . So now this
> second Paris, wearing a Phrygian bonnet (*Maeonia . . . mitra*) to tie up his
> chin and cover his oily hair, and attended by a train of she-men (*cum semi-*
> *viro comitatu*), is to become the owner of what he has stolen."
> (IV.206–17)[17]

For Iarbus, Aeneas in his Phrygian bonnet and oily hair and surrounded
by his half-men is deserving only of contempt. However, his own
Moorish nation is itself characterized by Oriental luxury and softness,
"banqueting on divans of rich-coloured weave," and pouring out offer-
ings of the oriental god of intoxication, Bacchus. The image of an Asian
chieftain—since North Africa is as much the East as is Asian Minor—
arrogant in his wounded male pride and yet wearing the trappings of
unmanly softness will manage to persist through centuries of Orientalist
fantasies. Note as well the very different way Iarbus considers Dido:
while Aeneas shares a romantic atttachment with Dido, Iarbus considers her merely a possession. Aeneas, from his point of view, has simply
stolen what was Iarbus's right to hold. Iarbus is simply ignored there-
after, unmotivated, without even the dignity of authorial judgment, his
story simply dropped.

Dionysus in the West

The reference to Bacchic rites is a reminder that the Bacchus/Dionysus
was another of the Oriental gods whose cult had invaded the West.
Immensely popular, especially with women, the religion was marked by
ecstatic rites quite different from the religion of the Olympians. When
Bacchic rites are described in *The Aeneid*, they are associated with madness and bloodlust. Dido herself rages like a Maenad in Bacchic frenzy
(IV.300–303).[18] When the "fire" of madness enters the great Latin hero,
Turnus, he makes just the kind of mistakes that will enable Aeneas to
defeat him (Clausen 46).

   The story of madness entering Turnus is told by Aeneas in an elaborate allegory of the demonic Allecto (book VII).[19] The irrationality
caused by Allecto and spread through the women keeps the leaders of
the opposing camps from negotiating a peaceful settlement of their differences. *The Aeneid*, which ends in terrible war, could otherwise have
been the story of a peaceful settlement of Trojans in Italy.

The story of Allecto and Queen Amata, in brief, is this. Juno seeks to destroy a proposed marriage that would unite the warring factions once Aeneas is in Italy. The great goddess sends the monster-demon Allecto to drive Queen Amata mad. Allecto's power is seen as fire that destroys reason. To save her daughter from marrying a Trojan, Amata hides the daughter in the mountains, where a wild, Bacchic frenzy is unleashed. While Virgil writes that Amata "pretends" the *numen* of Bacchus is upon her (*simulato numine Bacchi* (VII.385), it is difficult to see where pretense ends and the Dionysian madness begins.

> She even went out into the forests in her flight, pretending that the power of Bacchus was upon her, and so venturing on a still graver, wilder sin. . . . The news flew fast; and every mother's heart now blazed with this same hysterical passion to look for a new dwelling-place. Quickly they forsook their homes, with necks bare and hair left free to the winds. Others, dressed in fawn-skins and carrying spear-shafts of vine, filled the sky with quavering holloas. In the centre of them was Amata, who feverishly held high a blazing pine-brand and, turning all about her her reddened eyes, sang the wedding-song for her daughter and Turnus. Suddenly she roared like a beast: "Mothers of Latium! Hey! Hear me, each one of you, wherever you may be! If you still have any sympathy for poor Amata in your faithful hearts, or any prick of conscience for a mother's claims, untie the bands around your hair and take to the wild rites with me!" (VII.373–404; Knight, *Aeneid* 187)

These Bacchic rites belonged to a group of religions—along with Mithraism, Judaism, and Christianity—that were thought to have come from "the East," and which did derive, for the most part, from that part of the world we now consider the Middle East. Virgil might, of course, have known about the Bacchic rites firsthand. That the religion had come from the East, and that it was in some way fused with the orgiastic and ecstatic rites of Cybele, was something he could have found in the literary tradition of the Greeks. The "Oriental" origin of Dionysus was made explicit in Euripides's *The Bacchae* (Guthrie 151–59). The syncretism that involved the Great Mother of Phrygia, Cybele with her ecstatic rites, and the Thracian Dionysus was clear as early as the fifth century B.C.

The Trojans, having lost at Troy, attempted a return to their ancient mother, but are advised in a dream from the gods to seek their "true home," what the Greeks call "Hesperia," the "western land," Italy.

The deflection of Aeneas from his goal, the tragic episode of his love affair with the Tyrian Dido, is the major stumbling block to the fulfilling of his destiny. And the episode involves the conquest of the inner man—or woman.

Augustus versus Cleopatra

Of Cleopatra, there is more than a little irony in the way Shakespeare was able to make her appear worthy of tragic *phobos*. His portrayal of the Egyptian queen, as Shakespeare scholars have been telling us for some time, is as the embodiment of "things Eastern" in contrast to the Roman leader who was able to resist her. Less studied these days is the important passage in *The Aeneid* (VIII.678–713) that sets the Oriental woman against the noble Roman male. Michael Grant put it succinctly. Cleopatra was "regarded as the epitome of un-Roman-ness" (Michael Grant 296; see Hughes-Hallett 45–48). There is no obvious *historical* connection between Cleopatra in Egypt; a Macedonian playing the role of the new Isis to Antony's new Dionysus; and the earlier Dido, a Phoenician, founder of Carthage. That is, of course, the point of working out a complex network of poetic images that symbolically link heterogeneous figures to an "other" Asian culture opposed to things Roman. Chaos, the demonic, passion, luxury, the feminine oppose the jovial, the rational, the male.

   To set off the contrast between the heroic leader and his chaotic opponent, it is useful to cite a verse translation of the passage in which Virgil describes the naval encounter between Cleopatra and Virgil's patron, Augustus. C. Day Lewis captures the formal features of the verse that highlight order versus chaos.

> On one side Augustus Caesar, high up on the poop, is leading
> The Italians into battle, the Senate and People with him,
> His home-gods and the great gods: two flames shoot up from his
>   helmet
> In jubilant light, and his father's star dawns over its crest.
> Elsewhere in the scene is Agrippa—the gods and the winds fight
>   for him—
> Prominent, leading his column: the naval crown with its miniature
> Ships' beaks, a proud decoration of war, shines on his head.
> On the other side, with barbaric wealth and motley equipment,

> Is Anthony, fresh from his triumphs in the East, by the shores
>   of the Indian Ocean; Egypt, the powers of the Orient and
>   uttermost Bactra
> Sail with him; also—a shameful thing—his Egyptian wife.
> (VIII.678-88; Lewis 641-42)

Committed, as he had to be, to the high style, appropriate to the epic (rather than breaking the style to present Cleopatra as a modern writer might, in a style more representative of ordinary life),[20] Virgil insinuates the corruption at the heart of the un-Roman East. While Augustus is brilliant in light and aided by the (right) gods (*Penatibus et magnis dis*, VIII.679), Antony brings with him into battle the uncivil horde (*ope barbarica variisque*, VIII.685). Virgil even intervenes with a comment—*nefas*, "O shame!"—on Antony's Egyptian wife.

Once the fleets converge, there is terrible slaughter. The military tactics are of less importance to the narrative than the image of Cleopatra.

> In the midst, Cleopatra rallies her fleet with Egyptian timbrel,
> For she cannot yet see the two serpents of death behind her.
> Barking Anubis, a whole progeny of grotesque
> Deities are embattled against Neptune and Minerva
>   And Venus....
> Viewing this, Apollo of Actium draws his bow
> From aloft: it creates a panic; all the Egyptians, all
> The Indians, Arabians and Sabaeans now turn tail.
> You could see the queen Cleopatra praying a fair wind, making
> All sail, in the very act of paying the sheets out and running.
> The Fire-god had rendered her, pale with the shadow of
>   her own death,
> Amid the carnage, born on by the waves and the westerly gale;
> And, over against her, the Nile, sorrowing in all its length,
> Throws wide the folds of its watery garment, inviting the
>   conquered
> To sail for refuge into that blue, protective bosom.
> (VIII.696-713; Lewis 642)

What could be more grotesque than the demonic figures of Egyptian religion pitted against the Roman gods Neptune, Venus,

Minerva: *omnigenumque deum monstra et latrator Anubis*, "monstrous gods of every form and barking Anubis" (Virgil 2: 108-109)? The panic and terror that cause the crowd of Orientals to flee, the unseemly haste of Cleopatra to run away from conflict, even the strangely haunting image of the Nile, her watery garment opened to receive the vanquished—all images are of a rowdy, uncontrolled, and uncontrollable rabble, led by an unstable woman and barbarous gods to destruction. In contrast, Augustus, the victor, leads his people "in triple triumph" through the streets of Rome. "The conquered peoples move in long array, as diverse in fashion of dress and arms as in tongues" (*quam variae linguis, habitu tam vestis et armis*, VIII. 723; Virgil 2:109–11).

THE WOMAN AND THE SWORD

The most important figure in *The Aeneid* to represent both the feminine and the Oriental is, the queen of Carthage herself, Dido. We see her first in her city.

Knight's "The Holy City of the East" drew heavily on the Eastern tradition, as far back as ancient Sumer, to show that Virgil, much more than Homer, conceived of the city as sacred. For the Greeks, the city was the secular space of the public square. Virgil revived, rather, the old Eastern ideas of the sacred city.[21] The walls of the city in early Italy were holy or magical; the city was often identified with an important temple and with "in personification . . . goddesses of the cities' defence"; and attacks on cities are manipulated by supernatural agencies (293–94), among other elements of the Ancient Near Eastern city.

The sacrality of the city is reflected in Virgil's treatment of Dido, for she is, as Philip Hardie has demonstrated so well in his study of Virgilian hyperbole, identified with her city. The identification of a queen with her subjects and her city is an example of what Northrop Frye called the "royal metaphor." The vertical dimension of sacrality enables Carthage to be seen cosmologically as well as historically the enemy of Rome, and the destruction of Carthage in 146 B.C., the working out of a struggle on two levels of existence. It prepares for the third dimension, recent history, Cleopatra.

> The most important type of power struggle here is that which opposes the forces ranged along the vertical axis, the powers of good and evil, of light and darkness, of heaven and hell. The themes of Roman imperialism in fact

bind human and divine power struggles in an inextricable unity; the
growth of Roman power is also the history of the the victory of the gods of
the upper heaven over the forces of the Underworld. (Hardie 268)

The tragedy of Dido, however moving it is as a human love story, participates in the larger cosmological and historical orders of Virgil's
story.

The identification of Dido and her city makes the otherwise puzzling detail—that work stops in the city when Dido is moved by the
passion of the *hieros gamos* (another ancient Oriental theme) arranged by
the goddesses. The neglect of usual occupations is a *topos* of ancient love
poetry, as Hardie points out, but the *topos* does not account for the *city's*
neglect of productive activity (271). The destruction of Dido prefigures
the destruction of the city in its struggle with Rome (284). The notion
of the sacred city also makes sense of the remarkable pyre in the center
of a temple-like palace, a pyre "of gigantic proportions, reaching
towards the sky" (282).

When Aeneas is given his first glimpse of Dido's Carthage, he sees
"fortunate people" whose "city-walls are already rising" (Knight, *Aeneid*
41). Dido is acting vigorously, the way a ruler should.

> Aeneas looked wonderingly at the solid structures springing up where
> there had once been only African huts, and at the gates, the turmoil, and
> the paved streets. The Tyrians were hurrying about busily, some tracing
> a line for the walls and manhandling stones up the slopes as they strained
> to build their citadel, and others siting some building and marking its
> outline by ploughing a furrow. And they were making choice of laws, of
> officers of state, and of councillors to command their respect. At one
> spot they were excavating the harbour, and at another a party was laying
> out an area for the deep foundations of a theatre; they were also hewing
> from quarries mighty pillars to stand tall and handsome beside the stage
> which was still to be built. It was like the work which keeps the bees hard
> at their tasks. (I.421–30; Knight, *Aeneid* 40)

Where there had been only "African huts," there now could be seen
the emergence of civil order, at least those aspects of civilization most
valued by the Romans: paved streets, a carefully engineered citadel, harbor and theatre, institutions of law and politics. Collapsed in these few
lines are the marks, not of a sprawling Oriental despotism, but of the *civitas*—the regime of *Homo faber*, as Simone de Beauvoir defined it.

This is not so much an admiring glance at Rome's—and the poet's—enemy, dreaded Carthage, as it is a measure of Dido's fall when once passion overwhelms her. The story of Dido is certainly moving. Even in antiquity this was so. Augustine, long after he had turned against the literature he had loved so long, could recall "weeping the death of Dido for love to Aeneas."[22]

But there is no question that Dido's passion for Aeneas overrules reason, and the city suffers for it immediately: "Meanwhile the partly built towers had ceased to rise. No more did young soldiers practise arms. The construction of harbours and impregnable battlements came to a stop. Work hung suspended on gigantic, menacing walls, and the sky-high cranes were still (IV.86–89; Knight, *Aeneid* 99).

What makes the story of Dido's tragic fall so moving is Virgil's ability to describe the rich interior life of the passionate woman. The increasing isolation of Dido from her queenly rule, from her sister and confidant Anna, and finally from Aeneas is captured in a series of interior monologues (IV.533–53, 586–629, 651–71).[23] Virgil's mastery of the interior monologue is brilliant. The very interiority of Dido, so valued in later Western literature, is used to condemn her.

In their study of soliloquies and monologues as devices for characterization, Robert Scholes and Robert Kellogg analyzed Dido's first soliloquy (IV.533–53). They point out that the speech begins, as many others in the tradition of Greek literature, in a traditional rhetorical fashion. As Dido's passion intensifies, however, Virgil represents the movement of the tortured mind itself. In "the disjointedness of the last sentences, the hopping from topic to topic and thought to thought" (287), Virgil turns the piece into a very effective psychological exploration of a character in deep distress.

Dido prepares a bizarre setting for her suicide. She builds a setting for the event furnished with the symbols of her interior life:

> Presently the pyre had been built with logs of holm-oak and pine. It was vast, rising to a great height, and it stood in the centre of the building. The queen had festooned the hall with flower-chains, and wreathed the pure with the greenery of death. On it was the bed, and there she placed a sword which Aeneas had left, with garments which he had worn, and a portrait of him, knowing all the time what was to be. (Knight, *Aeneid* 112)

Tormented, and no longer able to speak even to her sister, she speaks to herself, "communing with herself in her heart:"

There! What is there for me to do? Risk mockery by returning to my former suitors, sound their feelings, and plead humbly with some Numidian
to marry me, though time after time I have scorned to think of one of
them as a husband? Or instead should I sail with the Trojan fleet and sub-
mit to Trojan orders however harsh? Am I so sure that they are pleased
with the aid and relief which I gave them, that they remember, and that
their gratefulness for what I did then is still alive? But indeed, even
granted that I wished it, would they let me come, and welcome me to
their ships? They are arrogant, and hate me. Lost fool, can you not see?
Can you even now not realize how treacherous Laomedon's nation can
be? Besides, if I sail with these mariners, who are so triumphant now at
their departure, do I go alone, or do I take with me all my Tyrian friends,
thronging round me when I go to join the Trojans? If so, how can I order
them to spread their sails to the winds and force them to voyage once
more out onto the ocean? It was all that I could do to uproot them from
their former city, Sidon. No. You have deserved death and you must die.
Only the blade can save you from the agony. . . . O Anna, I have been
mad; but it was you who first laid on me this load of suffering, for you
gave way to my tears, and set me at the mercy of my foe. If only I could
have been allowed to pass my life free from reproach as the wild animals
do, without any wedding, and in no danger of anguish like mine. . . . And
the vow which I made to the ashes of Sychaeus is broken too. (Knight,
Aeneid 113–14)

The first long series of questions does not show the movement of
the mind as much as a movement of appropriate thoughts. When Dido
turns, though, to comment, "They are arrogant, and hate me," and when
later she turns again—"No. You have deserved death and you must
die"—her feelings are forcing an utterance that sounds something like
the mind thinking. "Language in its formal dress—words artfully
deployed so as to move the reader or audience by focusing on him and
his responses" is what ancient rhetoric sought to produce, and the first
part of Dido's utterance is rhetorical. She turns, though, to "words
deployed in patterns referrable not to verbal artistry but to actual
thought, focusing not on the audience but on the character" (Scholes
and Kellogg 185). Historically, the turn in Dido's soliloquy from rhetor-
ically appropriate speech to something like the emotional utterance of a
person in pain is most important, and Virgil had countless imitators in
the West. The gain would seem to be in psychological realism.

That such a narrative technique, long the formula followed by romancers, has become hackneyed in the centuries since Virgil should not obscure Virgil's achievement. A thousand imitators should not diminish the model. However, Virgil's success in moving the reader should not obscure the message of gender implied in the passage. For classical antiquity such passion (and the lack of control it represented) was clearly the mark of the woman, not the man. Clausen explains Aeneas's curious reluctance to tell Dido of his love, for example, as a constraint of the epic tradition. A man's passionate love could be expressed in comedy, elegy, or pastoral, but not in the epic.[24]

Not surprisingly, Scholes and Kellogg present for the study of ancient monologues mainly female characters—Medea in *The Argonautica*, Dido, Myrrha in Ovid's *Metamorphoses*, Chloe in Longus's *Daphnis and Chloe*.[25] They notice that in Homer, the interior monologues of the great male heroes—Odysseus, Menelaus, Agenor, Hector, and even Achilles—typically move "from unworthy or unsuitable considerations or feelings to worthy or suitable ones"—from fear of battle, for example, to courageous thoughts (179, 284–92). There is much less interest in presenting a man driven by desperate and "unworthy" emotions.

People falling in love, mainly women, utter the most moving psychological monologues in ancient literature so often that Scholes and Kellogg are prompted to remark, "The inner life of the female of the species contemplating her erotic situation has been a focal point of narrative concern with the psyche from Medea and Dido to Anna Karenina and Molly Bloom. The emphasis on the feminine psyche in ancient times was due, no doubt, to the prevailing view that women were more passionate than men" (183). No doubt. In Virgil, psychological and moral problems need to be resolved before the hero can proceed to the real work of the hero, action. What Dido represents is danger not just of a historical sort (accounting for the long hostility between Carthage and Rome) but psychological. When she is "ablaze" with love (Virgil's leitmotif for intense passion),[26] she can govern neither herself nor her city. Even her "good name" was no longer a bar to her passion (*nec famam obstare furori*, IV. 91). True, Venus and Juno contrive to bring Aeneas and Dido together; and true, their union is imaged as a *hieros gamos*. But Virgil is careful to note that the relationship is mortally flawed because of Dido's lack of control:

> Dido and Troy's chieftain found their way to the same cavern. Primaeval Earth and Juno, Mistress of the Marriage, gave their sign. The sky con-

nived at the union; the lightning flared; or their mountain-peak nymphs raised their cry. On that day were sown the seeds of suffering and death. Henceforth Dido cared no more for appearances or her good name, and ceased to take any thought for secrecy in her love. She called it a marriage; she used this word to screen her sin.[27]

Ever more desperate, Dido tries her magic, and she utters two more interior monologues, cursing Aeneas, speaking her last words to her "sweet relics." She kills herself by falling, appropriately enough, on Aeneas's *ferrum*, his sword. If the sword is, as Quinn maintains, the sword she had given Aeneas and left by him when he abandoned Carthage,[28] the motif of dying on the enemy's weapon is doubly ironic. Quinn maintains that Aeneas wore it "as one of the symbols of consortship" (148), and his abandonment of that most masculine of symbols—the symbol also of their relationship—is another example of Virgil's care to draw the clearest distinction between male and female roles.

Even in the underworld, where "Phoenician Dido" (VI.450) is grouped in the fields of mourning with those (women) who "have pined and wilted under the harsh cruelties of love," Dido is still blazing in anger at Aeneas. Though he tries to mollify the shade—"imperiously forced by that same divine direction which compels me now to pass through the shadows in this world of crumbling decay under deepest night"—she flings herself away from him and returns to the shadows with her former love, Sychaeus. Aeneas gazes after her a long time, "with tearful eyes and pity for her in his heart" (Knight, *Aeneid* 160–61).

On either side of the appearance of Dido in the underworld Virgil gives us catalogs, first of women, then of men. Dido belongs to the first group, of course, the ones who "gained death for themselves by their own hand" (Knight, *Aeneid* 160) and those in the fields of mourning: Phaedra, Procris, Eriphyle, Evadne, Pasiphae, Laodamia, Caeneus. After Aeneas sees Dido, he moves through the fields "thronged by those glorious in war." Tydeus, Parthenopaeus, Adrastus, the Dardanids, Glaucus, Medon, and the like. The division of a male and female consciousness could not have been made more clear.

That feminine consciousness is, as well, presented as an Eastern trait. Clausen captures it best when he remarks that "Dido is no Roman matron, although she is sometimes judged by that severe standard; she is a Phoenician, "Phoenician Dido," as Aeneas reminds her in a terrible moment (IV.348), exotic and passionate—hence something of her fascination for the father of the Roman people" (43). Aeneas's fear of and fascination with the passionate queen owes much to her embodiment of feminine ways—but also much to Aeneas's heritage, which he will have to abandon.

The exaggerated masculine images of traditional heroic stories and poetry should not obscure the way the Oriental enemy has been feminized.

Eugene Delacroix's *Death of Sardanapalus* (1827) is the masterpiece of nineteenth-century Orientalist painting. In Sardanapalus (the historical Ashurbanipal, king of Assyria) the Oriental male, a cruel despot, propped up on an enormous bed looks impassively upon a scene of excessive wealth, slavery, and gratuitous violence—the utter antithesis of rational control in the individual and in society. The viewer, like the painter, looks on with much the same impassive gaze but also with some guilt that we enjoy the scene.

Much of the East is still seen from without, but Moroccan sociologist Fatima Mernissi sees it from within. *Beyond the Veil* is subtitled *Male-Female Dynamics in a Modern Muslim Society*. While the focus is on women and gender differences, Mernissi suggests that the major impact of modernization (from the West, of course) has been an effect of castration as the functions traditionally exercised by the father (protection and economic security for women, and education) have been taken over by the nation state. Women earning money outside the home exacerbates the problem (171). The Western penetration of the East, demonstrated by Said and Bernal, involved more than military and political control. Scholarship and the arts developed and maintained an exotic other that now looks back upon the West in dread.

Americans remain deeply ambivalent about the primitive. (The heroic posture of the cowboy owes almost nothing to modern warfare, while the modern cowboy—Dirty Harry, Rambo—may avail himself of sophisticated weaponry.) Since the Civil War, the heroic fighter, using fists, knives, perhaps a handgun, has been set against the machine gun and other long-distance weapons. The twist that estranged the Arab Muslim in the Gulf War (1990–1991) was the wholehearted acceptance of a sanitized technologically sophisticated battle against an irrational and primitive enemy.

Against the high-tech image of modern warfare. Saddam Hussein employed a traditional heroic imagery to rouse his people. The image has its basis, according to Raphael Patai, in the tribal ethos of "collective responsibility expressed in such institutions as the blood feud, raiding, and the inviolate laws of hospitality and sanctuary, as well as just concepts as honor, *wajh* ('face'), and nobility" (19). The image has been preserved in a long tradition of Middle Eastern heroic poetry, both written and oral. The "mother of all battles" and the warrior "wading in the blood" of his enemies brought only ridicule from the Western media.

The *Aeneid* is, of course, firmly within the ambit of the literate, far from "primitive," oral heroic poems. However close Homer may be to oral tradition, Virgil is on the other side of the divide. Walter J. Ong put it well:

> "As orality diminishes with writing and print, the epic irresistibly changes shape despite the author's best intentions and efforts. The narrator of the *Iliad* and the *Odyssey* is lost in the oral communalities: he never appears as "I." The writer Virgil begins his *Aeneid* with "Arma, virumque cano," "I sing of arms and the man." (159)

Still, the epic is primarily oral, and the heroic rhetoric of Saddam Hussein was enough to condemn him in the West.[29]

The rhetoric of *The Aeneid* is, of course, nowhere near the bloodless abstractions of rational defense intellectuals.[30] The epic is ages away from killing at a distance and technostrategic language. Battles, games, and crowd scenes are quickly personalized, always humanized. History and the cosmos are seen in hierarchical human-social terms. Individuals, approaching the ideal of the phallic self, remain in focus throughout—an advance, perhaps, from oral tradition.

But the phallic self and its rhetoric of control (self, control, reason, mastery), if not detached from the human life world, anticipates modern technostrategic thought.

The more Sardanapalus and the "primitive" Arab chieftain came to be celebrated in nineteenth-century Orientalist art, the more the ultramasculine qualities reversed into its opposite: the luxuriant, emotional, cruel, static, exotic, irresponsible and fantastic qualities of the Oriental despot come to characterize as well the femme fatale—and a Western perception of the feminine, reminiscent of Virgil's Dido, Cleopatra, Juno, Venus.

The Egyptians with their "bestial" (i.e., their theriomorphic) gods and their weird music were never so un-Roman as when they submitted to a woman ruler. Dio Cassius thought the Orientals, "ruled by a woman, are effeminate," as Hughes-Hallett noted (49). The one man who lost out absolutely to Dido was Iarbus. (Jerome wrote that Dido preferred to "burn rather than marry.") Ironically, the Oriental male is treated by Virgil in a manner that recalls the biblical treatment of women: without adequate motivation, authorial motivation, or closure.

Orientalism produced noteworthy art and literature in the West. Shakespeare's Cleopatra is a particularly good example, since it reverses—transvaluates, in Barbara Bono's term—the very complex Virgil had prepared so carefully. Flaubert's masterful reconstruction of Carthaginian religion of Tanit in *Salammbô* (whose heroine was based in part on ancient records, in part on a Turkish courtesan Flaubert encountered in Upper Egypt) is more modern and more disturbing. In a sense the fantasy allowed the mind to wander in a primitive and amoral world, the better to steel it in its civilizing enterprise around the world. The beauty and the dangers of this kind of doublethink are clear in the popular arts today as well as in the great works of antiquity that encouraged the development of an East that awaited penetration by the West.

Stereotypes of Arabs common today in the West—that they are emotional and irrational, primitive and tribal, strong and insensitive, violent but cowardly, confusing fantasy and reality, and sexually aggressive (Shipler, 182–234)—are then already prefigured in the feminized Asia of *The Aeneid*. The Oriental woman is already seductive, and even if, as goddess or woman, she possesses great power apart from her sexual allure, her inability to control her passions causes her to lose that power. For his part, the Oriental male, in spite of his instant call to arms when his honor is slighted, fritters away his chances in bursts of ineffectual rhetoric. In the grave business of leading men into battle, organizing a state, and maintaining order, they are easily bested by the rational man.

By the time of *The Aeneid* (and through the prestige of that influential work) the East had come to be regarded as feminine: alluring, mysterious, penetrable, and ultimately powerless before the male who found his weaknesses and fears mirrored in the cultural projections of the East. In the long event that constitutes Western history and culture, whose axis runs through Rome, Paris, and London, and only very recently to New York and Washington, the maghrib or farthest western margin of that cultural complex, the interest taken by Americans in the East could be at a comfortable distance. Through its first century the United States had no vital national interests in a region so far removed from its shores. The romantic images of an exotic East could persist without challenge.

The next chapter will focus on a spectacle that in some ways reinforced romantic images of the East, a form of mysticism popular in Morocco, as viewed by a series of Americans. In its public form, the trance dancing of Moroccan Sufis and the self-mutilation of the Sufis in ecstasy could easily reinforce the ancient stereotype of the primitive savage, wildly emotional and intensely irrational. The Western observer, at first comfortably civilized and rational, increasingly takes those spectacles seriously. Americans such as Jane and Paul Bowles, influenced by Western depth psychology and challenges to rationality and the civilized world, find the repressed in themselves projected in the mystics. Only in the third phase, shown in the next chapter in the observations of Elizabeth Fernea, would the opposition to civilization be overcome in a way that connected mystical ecstasy to ordinary reality. The discovery that Moroccan women have a rich life of religious concern, including mystical ecstasy, opens a new avenue to the cultural other. It required an American woman to notice that religious activity among Moroccan women, since it is largely carried on well away from men's eyes. Fernea's observations of Moroccan women—and her participation in their lives—will seriously qualify the ancient stereotypes of the Oriental woman. The way Fernea writes about women's religious life anticipates a more detailed study of her writing in Chapter 6.

Chapter Two

Silence and Ecstasy:

Watching the Sufis Dance

Insiders, as anthropologists have been fond of pointing out, are likely to interpret an event, a performance, in a way far different from outsiders who happen upon the scene. Even within a community of believers there may be sharp differences of opinion. Among people who identify themselves as Christians, for example, the handling of snakes, the appearances of the Virgin Mary, and the swallowing of the Host can be met with revulsion in one camp and taken as profoundly moving in another. What the Islamic tradition knows as *hadra*, or trance dancing, provides another example. Anthropologists who have studied Morocco routinely refer to the still very popular rituals of the Hamadsha, the Jilala, the Gnawa, the Wazzaniyya, and a host of other religious brotherhoods. The 'Isawa, for example, beat their chests raw during a certain dance, while the Wazzaniyya say a dhikr and pray to Allah, Jesus, Moses, Mohammed, and others (Crapanzano, *Tuhami* 92–93).

No one denies the popularity of such trance dancing, but Islamicists rightfully protest when outsiders interpret what many Muslims find embarrassing or even scandalous. There is, of course, the danger Edward Said has detailed in his masterful *Orientalism*, the far-from-innocent way the West has, from as far back as the Greeks, seen in the "East" a dangerous cultural "other," one that deserved the domination the West periodically attempts to throw over, especially, the Muslim Middle East. But there is also a danger that the non-Muslim will misinterpret a matter of some controversy among Muslims themselves.

That danger was brought home to me vividly when I invited a colleague, a distinguished Islamicist, as well as his class and mine, to view a film directed by Elizabeth Warnock Fernea, *Saints and Spirits*. The film documented the religious life of Moroccan women, a subject still very little known in the West. The film largely confirmed what Clifford Geertz argued in *Islam Observed: Religious Development in Morocco and Indonesia*, that the "classical style" of Moroccan Islam was heavily influenced by "Sufism" and involved, among others, a "*siyyid* complex" (the cult of saints, pilgrimages to the tombs of dead holy men and women, and a great interest in descent from the holy prophet Mohammed) and a "*zawiya* complex" (involving the religious brotherhoods) (49). What Fernea filmed demonstrates that women, too, made pilgrimages to the tombs of the saints, and that they, too, participated in the ritual dancing. In a particularly vivid scene, a young woman dressed like a bride, is led by the music into a trance state and touches a garment bloodied by the sacrifice of a lamb.

My colleague was so upset by the film that he insisted the two groups meet more than once to discuss what he considered was completely un-Islamic about the filmed rituals. His argument was not so much that the film was made by an outsider. Rather, he was particularly worried about the shedding of blood in an otherwise holy setting. His plea, sensible enough, that we understand Islam in the "right way," has been repeated by those who seek an understanding of Sufism from within Islamic tradition. No one would deny that Sufism is a mystical tradition within Islam, that Sufis are "those Muslims who have most sought for direct experience of the Divine," as John Alden Williams puts it (122). Also, no one denies that perhaps the best known of the ecstatic Sufis, Jalal al-Din Rumi, allowed a form of trance dancing (Chittick 325–28). Still, many of the practices of Moroccan Sufis, male and female, are seen as excessive by other Muslims. Seyyed Hossein Nasr is perhaps the most eloquent of those who worry that the West's increasing interest in Sufism runs the danger of highlighting the very features of Sufi practice that are most excessive and least in line with the legitimate spiritual practices of Islam (11–16).

The four Western writers discussed here are outsiders in almost every way. Of them, only Isabelle Eberhardt claimed to be a Muslim and a Sufi. (She dressed like a man in order to travel freely through North Africa, and she was initiated into a Sufi brotherhood.) Born and raised in Europe, Eberhardt tried more than anyone else to crush every trace of Western Christianity in her and to become a North African Muslim. The other three are Americans, and this chapter argues that they provide, in their responses to the ecstatic rituals they witnessed in Morocco, an index to an important change in American attitudes toward the Islamic world. Edith Wharton, Paul Bowles, and Elizabeth Warnock Fernea do not claim at all to speak as Muslims or to speak for Muslims. They are writers who turn what they see into literary forms that can be understood in the community of Western readers. In an important way, though, they do show a tendency to understand the rituals from an insider's point of view.

The complexity of their responses should be seen first in a Western context, then in encounters with an alien East. *Ecstasy* is a notoriously difficult term to define, and the attempt here will be to define it in the context of the four Western witnesses to ecstatic performance. Trance dancing and ecstatics are known from ancient Mesopotamia, and there is an open question—which cannot be taken up here—if certain ecstatic practices in Morocco are vestiges of pre-Islamic rituals (e.g., vestiges of ancient Canaanite rituals brought to the territory by the Carthaginians). What is not questioned is that ecstasy in some form is very ancient both in the East and in the West and that the fascination with ecstasy in the skeptical modern West is an important, if not well-understood, feature of the modern world.

Since Richard F. Hardin has pointed out the highly inadequate way literary criticism has made use of "ritual," often perpetuating assumptions (e.g., about relations between myth and ritual, between ritual and drama) that have been long repudiated by the anthropologists who first proposed them (846–47), it is important to state what assumptions about ritual are operating here. Hardin appears to prefer Victor Turner's definition of ritual, "prescribed formal behavior for occasions, not given over to technological routine, having reference to beliefs in mystical beings or powers" (851), to René Girard's, that "Ritual is nothing more than the regular exercise of 'good' violence" for the sake of preventing the spread of violence through the community (856).

Hardin thinks Girard's identification of ritual with sacrifice (and the scapegoat) too great a narrowing of the scope of ritual (857). Nevertheless, he finds in Turner and Girard more adequate views of ritual than had been proposed in the past.

Richard Schechner also acknowledges the importance of Turner and Girard. For Schechner,

> One of rituals's main functions is to keep people from thinking "too much." Individual and collective anxieties are relieved by performances whose qualities of repetition, rhythmicity, exaggeration, condensation, simplification and spectacle stimulate the brain into releasing opium-like endorphins directly into the bloodstream.(12)

He emphasizes that, though ritual shares much with art, especially with theater, "ritual is efficacious; it claims a direct and measureable effect on the world. Theater is entertainment" (16).

For the purposes of this chapter the Sufi trance-dancing rituals retain the character of anonymous, unreflective, unchanging repetitions, not because they are, in themselves, unchanging, but because they are observed by outsiders, the Western witnesses who turn them into literature, self-conscious, modern, individualistic.

Before the rituals themselves are considered, the term *ecstasy* should be defined. Ecstasy, through much of the Western tradition of mysticism a much sought for state of surrender to—or rather, annihilation into—the other, has lost much of its ontological cast. Once the single term that best captured the religious mystic's desire to break through the constraints of the ego, to abolish the self, ecstasy has taken a familiar turn in modern English, away from the plane of the real toward the rhetoric of interior states. From the magnificent paradoxes of John Donne's "Ecstasy" (already troubled by a very modern swerve from the soul and God to a rhetoric of human love)[1] to the definitions in a twentieth-century dictionary, the drive to psychologize religious language has been completed. Now, according to *The American College Dictionary*, for example, the term *ecstasy* means "overpowering emotion or exaltation; a sudden access of intense feeling"; "rapturous delight"; "the frenzy of poetic inspiration"; and finally a vestige of its older meaning, "mental transport or rapture from the contemplation of divine things."

Consider the experience Nietzsche described:

That decisive section [of *Thus Spake Zarathustra*], "Old and New Tables," was composed during the arduous ascent from the station [in Nice] to Eza, that wonderful Moorish eyrie. When my creative energy flowed most freely, my muscular activity was always greatest. The body is inspired: let us leave the "soul" out of consideration. I might often have been seen dancing; I used to walk through the hills for seven or eight hours on end without a hint of fatigue. I slept well, laughed a good deal—I was perfectly vigorous and patient. (*Ecce Homo* 898–99)

Nietzsche did not hesitate to describe "what poets of a more vigorous period" than his own, the late nineteenth century, called "inspiration" (Nietzsche 896–97). In describing his own experience writing *Thus Spake Zarathustra*, he emphasized the "instinct for rhythmical relations."

One hears—one does not seek; one takes—one does not ask who gives: a thought flashes out like lightning, inevitably without hesitation—I have never had any choice about it. There is an ecstasy whose terrific tension is sometimes released by a flood of tears, during which one's progress varies from involuntary impetuosity to involuntary slowness. There is the feeling that one is utterly out of hand. . . . There is an instinct for rhythmical relations which embraces an entire world of forms (length, the need for a widely extended rhythm, is almost a measure of the force of inspiration, a sort of counterpart to its pressure and tension). Everything occurs quite without volition, as if in an eruption of freedom, independence, power and divinity. The spontaneity of the images and similes is most remarkable; one loses all perception of what is imagery and simile; everything offers itself as the most immediate, exact, and simple means of expression. (*Ecce Homo* 896–97)

If Nietzsche thought nineteenth-century poets were growing reticent about ecstasy and inspiration, twentieth-century writers are likely to be embarrassed by what might, after all, turn out to be an "altered state of consciousness," available to the writer after a few pipes of kif, as easily as it might be a summons to participate with the divine. Recently, Frederick Turner has called for an "ontological criticism" of literature, one that recognizes the way literature is grounded in orality, and oral composition is grounded in ritual performance, especially the rhythmic driving involved in chanting (78). His explanation draws more on endorphins and right-brain/left-brain synchrony than on the ascent to truth, but Turner is particularly good at seeing the "archaic genetic armature of mammalian/primate ritual" at the heart of human artistic performance (72). He sketches something of the "long event"—to use again Fernand Braudel's term—of human art.

Since at least 1910, when Rudolf Otto began his famous journey to the East in North Africa and came back to declare that "the sacred," the *numinous*, manifested itself, among other ways, in the inspiration of poets (186–89) and the frenzies of the "savage mind" (133–34), Western travelers through the Islamic world have found something genuine in the violent dances of the Sufis. Among witnesses to the Sufi dancing, a ready index to changing attitudes in the West, Wharton, Bowles, and Fernea demonstrate a peculiarly American response to the cultural other—a sympathy that is remarkable and puzzling. Together they provide evidence of the change in American attitudes toward the East that falls into three phases.

FIRST PHASE: EDITH WHARTON

The contrast between Edith Wharton's response to the Sufis (during World War I) and Elizabeth Warnock Fernea's response (after World War II, when American anthropologists were engaging in a great deal of participant observation of Moroccan society) suggests that a very important cultural shift has taken place in the United States in relation to the cultural other. Sufi dancing is part of an ancient tradition,[2] deeply Islamic though no doubt influenced by other traditions.[3] The increasing sense that "we" in the modern West are cut off from ancient traditions, and "our" inability in a time when traditional Judeo-Christian orthodoxy is increasingly marginalized, has increased the distance between us and popular Islamic practices. In this Fernea occupies ground midway between Wharton and Paul Bowles.

On her 1917 journey through Morocco, Edith Wharton was permitted to witness religious dancing, an aspect of Moroccan Islamic practice that is, if anything, more controversial among Muslims now than it was earlier in this century.[4] One way to capture the sacred force known as "baraka" was for the religious brotherhoods to dance into unconsciousness. In many cases, the dancers lacerated themselves in order to demonstrate the spirit's conquest of the body and the working of baraka in the ceremony. The way in which Western observers react to this mys-

tical trance dancing is a fair index of their sympathy for Moroccan culture. Wharton's response was one of mounting horror at the sight of it.

Wharton tells us she had heard the chanting of the Aissaouas
before, as they celebrated "their sanguinary rites" (51). At the holy city
of Moulay Idriss, though, she was able to see the rite of another group,
the Hamadshas (or Hamadschas), and her account is one of the most
riveting sections (50–58) of the book. However horrified she might
have been, she was disappointed when her entourage had to leave
before the end of the ritual (57–58). The dance, she claimed, had not
been seen by a foreigner more than a year before she was able to see it,
and she considered herself lucky to have seen it.

The dance took place in a beautiful setting, with a "blessed air of
unreality" about it, a beauty that "redeemed the bestial horror." What
she saw were the Hamadshas swallowing thorns and hot coals, slashing
themselves with knives, and rolling on the ground in fits. The music and
the strange order to the dance fascinated her. On the one hand the
dancers, with "fixed eyes and a grimace of comic frenzy" "rocked and
circled with long raucous cries" about a holy man, "a tall grave person-
age in a doge-like cap." The leader, who remained calm, directed the
dance, stimulating some, restraining others. "There was something far
more sinister in this passionless figure, holding his hand on the key that
let loose such crazy forces, than in the poor central whirligig who
merely set the rhythm of the convulsions" (55–56). As the dancers
hacked at their own skulls and breasts, she noticed that many of them
simply chanted; "most of the bleeding skulls and breasts belonged to
negroes" (56). The explanation of this disparity comes later. The saint,
Hamadsh, had a faithful slave, who killed himself in despair at his master's death. "The self-inflicted wounds of the brotherhood are supposed
to symbolize the slave's suicide; though no doubt the origin of the ceremony might be traced back to the depths of that ensanguined grove
where Mr. Fraser plucked the Golden Bough" (57).[5] The strange beauty
of the scene is not enough to balance the outsider's disgust with "primitive" ritual: the "bestial horror," "grimace," and "comic frenzy," the "raucous cries" and "crazy forces." The calm demeanor of the *moqaddam* is
merely "sinister," the leader himself "passionless." The division between
the leader and the frenzied blacks is for Wharton further confirmation
that the people have not been civilized: the distinction between master
and slave persists and is carried out in a racist way. Even the allusion to

Sir James Fraser's *Golden Bough*, in later writers—Joseph Campbell, for example—a suggestion that the antiquity of a tradition in some measure validates it, in Wharton is merely a slam. The "ensanguined grove" is no better than this "bestial horror" (see also chapter 3).

SECOND AND THIRD PHASES: PAUL BOWLES

In *Let It Come Down* (1952) an American, Nelson Dyer, anxious to break free of the "cage" his life as a bank teller in New York City has become, leaps at the chance to relocate in Tangier—and ends up driving a nail into the skull of the only Moroccan he had come to know, a man named Thami. The paranoia that led him to destroy Thami was partly induced by smoking kif, a drug to which Dyer had only just been introduced.

To a certain extent, the two men share a condition Bowles's characters seem fated to, a marginality that makes them outsiders almost everywhere, even in their own communities. Dyer is alienated from his United States, especially his own family; and Thami is a high-born Moroccan, the favorite of his impressive father. Thami's dissolute life and a bad marriage—one not sanctioned by his family—have set his brothers against him. The American and the Moroccan meet in the International Zone, before Moroccan independence a kind of border town and a perfect setting for intercultural intrigue. Both men escape the city to the far less Westernized Spanish Morocco, and although each distrusts the other, in spite of their smoking kif together, only the American acts in a violent manner. While Dyer suspects that his Moroccan "friend" has designs on Dyer's money and person, the reader has no inkling at all that Thami is a violent man. For Dyer, the journey from New York to Tangier and from Tangier to the "primitive" place where he kills Thami is the journey "farthest out," away from all things familiar and comforting. For Thami, the journey is, one that takes him back to his extended family and actually offers the possibility of a reconciliation with his past and his community. Thus the two men, in many ways so much alike, take separate paths in the story.

Dyer's fear of the cultural other grows increasingly intense in the final kif-distorted days of the novel. The narrative of Dyer's fantasies (275–85), after he swallows majoun (kif in a candied form)—"the magical substance"—is a beautifully crafted surrealistic nightmare rarely to be met in fiction. As they approach the climax, each man in his own way is "irrevocably delivering himself over to unseen forces which would take charge of his life for the hours to come" (275).

Dyer stumbles around the village[6] in the darkness as the kif gains more and more hold on him. He picks up the instruments he will use to kill Thami, a hammer and a "big nail," when the shopkeepers leave their shops to engage in a dispute. The confusion in Dyer's mind is reflected in his inability to concentrate without great effort. "What were the hammer and nail for?" he asks himself. "To fix the door. What door? The door to the cottage, the rattling door that kept him from sleeping. And where was the cottage, how was he going to get there?" (273–74).

Richard F. Patteson has emphasized the architectural metaphors Bowles uses in his fictional presentations of the "outsidedness and root-lessness" so prominent in twentieth-century life and literature (*A World Outside* x). In Bowles's fiction, the problem of the expatriate, the out-sider, is central, for the world is "unremittingly *outside*" (x), and shelters of all kinds are flimsy and collapsing. The shelters include not only cot-tages with rattling doors, but structures humans build "to humanize the nonhuman, to make the great outside seem bearable, the mysterious intelligible" (15)—structures of family, society, religion, and art. Not surprisingly, Patteson turns almost immediately to the structures Dyer forms to keep the outside at bay, the windowless house Thami takes Dyer to and the memory of the sky-mother who comforted him as a child (16).

Patteson has also demonstrated, brilliantly, the tension in Bowles's narratives, again using spatial metaphors, between "enclosure," a cen-tripetal movement that brings a narrative to closure in the manner of a traditional novel, and "exposure," a centrifugal movement that resists closure. The final section of *Let It Come Down* is perhaps the best illustra-tion in Bowles of the tension. On the one hand, Bowles's story is marked by a conscious shaping of materials (sequence, pace, point of view, character)—Patteson calls it the story's "shapefulness"—and on the other hand, the plot is not neatly "tied up." Gaps are not filled, and the pace changes (90–92). The surrealist method, with its brilliantly clear images in a nightmare landscape of altered consciousness, serves Bowles particularly well in the last section of this novel.

There is no need to detail here Bowles's concatenation of images intensifying in the mind of Dyer, who has completely lost his cultural moorings and has thrown himself open to the effects of kif. Moon, night bird, fire, snippets of Dyer's long-concealed memories, messages in Arabic script on the walls, and Thami's body combine, collapse, and recombine in a way that Poe's invention, "phantasmagoric," best describes. Dyer need not open his eyes.

> His lids had become transparent. It was a gigantic screen against which images were beginning to be projected—tiny swarms of colored glass beads arranged themselves into patterns, swimming together and apart, forming mosaics that dissolved as soon as they were made. Feathers, snow-crystals, lace and church windows crowded consecutively onto the screen, and the projecting light grew increasingly powerful. Soon the edges of the screen would begin to burn, and the fire would be on each side of his head. (278)

Dyer's paranoia rises with the inability to seal up the windowless cottage. He makes his way unsteadily through the "magic room." He knows vaguely there is something he must do: nail shut the rattling door. The "knobless door" kept sending out to him "its ominous message. It was not sure, it could not be trusted. If it opened when he did not want it to open, by itself, all the horror of existence would crowd in upon him" (282). Ironically, he mistakes Thami's body for the door he must somehow nail shut, and in driving the nail into the ear of the other man, Dyer keeps urging himself to remember that he exists: "I must remember that I am alive" (284). Of course, this terrible mistake is no mistake at all if he is attacking not only Thami and his sky mother but the outside in every form—when silence comes, the fire is out, and "inhuman night had come into the room" (284).

What is even more remarkable than this paranoid, violent act by the American is a moment when he is not yet so intoxicated with kif but is wandering through a village where he knows no one, knows nothing of the languages spoken there, is terrified at being caught with a large amount of stolen cash, and has no idea of the danger he might be in. The man who has been characterized through the novel as one incapable of connecting with others suddenly finds himself watching a bizarre ritual that, indeed, draws him out—to the other. What follows is Paul Bowles's finest description of a Sufi dance (268–71).

Trying to lose a man Dyer thinks is a policeman, Dyer finds a lighted building and pushes into it. He finds himself in a small cafe, crowded with men wearing white turbans. Drummers are playing for someone in the room, at first to Dyer only "a formless mass that quaked, jerked, shuddered and heaved." In the phrase that gave the section of the novel its title, Dyer hears in spite of the loud drumming "another kind of silence" in the air, "an imperious silence that stretched from the eyes of the men watching to the object moving at their feet."

As the dim light and confused figures gradually give way to something like clear vision, Dyer sees a man, hands locked together, writhing and twisting on the floor, "an expression of agony on his tortured face." As the ritual (incomprehensible to Dyer, who has never experienced anything like this) continues, the audience joins with "rhythmical calls of 'Al-lah!'" When he looks around him, Dyer sees in the audience the "utter absorption in the dance, almost adoration of the man performing it." Calmed by a pipe of kif offered him by the group, Dyer is gradually taken up by the spectacle. The sweet odor of incense, and the music and chanting have a profound effect on Dyer (and the description of them on the reader).

The dancer pulls a large knife out of the garment he is wearing and begins to cut his bare arm, again and again. "And again and again, until the arm and hand were shining and black." The ecstatic slashes his other arm and licks the blood:

> With the shortening of the phrases, the music had become an enormous panting. It had kept every detail of syncopation intact, even at its present great rate of speed, thus succeeding in destroying the listeners' sense of time, forcing their minds to accept the arbitrary one it imposed in its place. With this hypnotic device it had gained complete domination. (270)

The dancer begins hacking at his legs, and the "music's volume swelled." As the ritual reaches its climax, Dyer is thrown into a "kind of participation" he had been unable to reach in any other way, including the sexual experiences recounted in the novel and mentioned as part of Dyer's past.

> Dyer was there, scarcely breathing. It could not be said that he watched now, because in his mind he had moved forward from looking on to a kind of participation. With each gesture the man made at this point, he felt a sympathetic desire to cry out in triumph. The mutilation was being done for him, to him; it was his own blood that spattered onto the drums and made the floor slippery. In a world which had not yet been muddied by the discovery of thought, there was this certainty, as solid as a boulder, as real as the beating of his heart, that the man was dancing to purify all who watched. When the dancer threw himself to the floor with a

despairing cry, Dyer knew that in reality it was a cry of victory, that spirit had triumphed; the expressions of satisfaction on the faces around him confirmed this. (271)

The musicians then help the man to recover. Conversation among the men in the cafe begins again. The dancer kisses each of the musicians on the forehead. "Then he pushed his way through the crowd, paid for his tea, and went out" (271) The detail of the performer ironically paying for his own tea makes it clear, of course, that the ritual was not a money-making stunt. It also confirms what countless witnesses to such scenes of self-laceration have stressed, that the Sufis show a remarkable capacity for regenerating after the performance. Paul Rabinow noted, for example, that his informant, Ali, a rather corrupt fellow but still a *wlad siyyed*, a descendent of a saint and a member of a religious lodge, danced "quite deep in trace, slashing his forearms with his fingernails" (55). "Although that night his arms were covered with blood, the next day he mysteriously had only minor scratches." (However, Ali was, quite fatigued by it and "complained of a severe headache.")

From Nelson Dyer's ambivalent response to the dancer one might guess that Paul Bowles's is a rather more complex response than the nihilistic denouement of the novel, the murder of the other, might indicate. The "rapture" of the dancer, his triumph of the spirit over the body, takes a troubling turn indeed in Dyer's bizarre state of mind; but Bowles's description is so enticing that the dancer's ecstasy promises more than appears to be realized in Dyer's paranoid fantasies (see also chapter 5).

When Paul Bowles first approached Morocco, he was seeking "wisdom and ecstasy" (*Without Stopping* 125). At least that is what he claimed later, reminiscing about his first glimpse of the land that would hold the American expatriate for over forty years. The rhetoric in which he casts the reminiscence, though, tends to undercut, in the ironic manner so pervasive in the twentieth century, the language of spiritual pilgrimage.

> Like any Romantic, I had always been vaguely certain that sometime during my life I should come into a magic place which in disclosing its secrets would give me wisdom and ecstasy—perhaps even death. And now, as I stood in the wind looking at the mountains ahead, I felt the stirring of the engine within, and it was as if I were drawing close to the solution of an as-yet-unposed problem. (125)

Since T. E. Hulme, "romantic" is almost automatically adolescent and laughable, and paired with intuitions "vaguely certain," raises more than a little suspicion that this is just another arch dismissal of what older, more primitive times and peoples took seriously, but "we" do not. Still, Jeffrey Bailey used the phrase *wisdom and ecstasy* to introduce his interview of Bowles to the readers of the *Paris Review* (63). And the "magic" that attracted Bowles—"a secret connection between the world of nature and the consciousness of man, a hidden but direct passage which bypassed the mind" (*Without Stopping* 125)—persists as a great deal more than what it has come to mean today, an advertising byword for low-level fantasy. Bowles hangs onto Tangier because "so far it has been touched by fewer of the negative aspects of contemporary civilization than most cities of its size" (366), but also because it remains, for him, a magic place.

> I relish the idea that in the night, all around me in my sleep, sorcery is burrowing its invisible tunnels in every direction, from thousands of senders to thousands of unsuspecting recipients. Spells are being cast, poison is running its course; souls are being dispossessed of parasitic pseudo-consciousness that lurks in the unguarded recesses of the mind. (366)

Magic, sorcery, spells, and poison repeatedly appear in Bowles's fiction, especially in the novels and short stories set in North Africa. Such a preoccupation with the occult is not all that incompatible with the thoroughgoing nihilism that one of Bowles's critics, Johannes Willem Bertens, considers the unifying theme in his work (7). Whatever destroys the ego, at least temporarily, and connects consciousness with nature in the "visceral" way that "bypassed the mind," is consonant with Bowles's desire to "destroy the world," to "destroy the establishment," to purify it, as he told Daniel Halpern (170). Breaking through the "pseudo-consciousness" of modern civilized life is one more form of "attacking" what Bowles dislikes.

About some esoteric matters the normally forthright Bowles falls silent. He translated and introduced a selection of Isabelle Eberhardt's writings, *The Oblivion Seekers*, and while he did not connect his own thinking with that most intriguing figure, a woman who dressed like a North African male in order to travel freely, alone, through the least Westernized parts of Algeria and Morocco to join a Sufi brotherhood, Bowles provides a clue to his preoccupation with Sufi activities—and his own silences. In describing that "extraordinary singleness of purpose and an equally powerful nostalgia for the unattainable" in Eberhardt, a spiritual pilgrimage that took her from "simple escape" through an "obsession with total freedom" to "a quest for spiritual wisdom through the discipline of Sufism," Bowles makes a simple but profound observation about her: "As to Sufism, even if the doctrine had not been a secret one, she had too much humility to consider herself anything more than a neophyte, and so she kept silent about it" (7).

It is, perhaps, too easy to psychologize the fascination with trance dancing that, as many a Western observer in Morocco has found, turns violently self-lacerating. Isabelle Eberhardt admitted to a "strange desire to suffer" (9), and she sought out the difficult ascetic practices of the Sufis, not to watch and study, but to participate in the rites and write about the "natives" from an insider's view. Others, like Edith Wharton, could barely admit to themselves that they were mesmerized by a ritual they had to condemn as uncivilized. After World War II, though, American writers—journalists, religionists, anthropologists, fiction writers—have sought out the Sufis and tried to describe what they experienced from a point of view that fell short of active participation but with a deep sense that something important was going on in the rites. Still they often keep silence about exactly what significance the rituals hold for them.

Bowles, ever the careful craftsman, has admitted to having been influenced by the twentieth century surrealists[7] as much as by Poe,[8] and that might account for his continued interest in altered states of consciousness, in kif-inspired and automatic writing, for example. He completed the final section of *Let It Come Down*, "Another Kind of Silence," in much the same way as Nietzsche, deep in the "absolute silence of the mountain nights" in another Moorish eyrie, Xauen, near Tangier. There he "shut off the controls and let *Another Kind of Silence* guide itself, without supplying any conscious direction. It went as far as it could go, then stopped, and that was the end of the book" (8). Whether he was inspired in the Nietzschean sense or not, giving up control in the surrealistic manner produced one of the most gripping and bizarre episodes in post–World War II American fiction.

It might be useful to recall that Bowles's novel (1952) was published a year before the cold war version of *The Desert Song* (1953). Clearly, not everyone in the United States was prepared to alter the view that such Eastern practices were simply primitive irrationalism.

In Paul Bowles, the most important description is probably Dyer's response to the Sufi dance described earlier (*Let It Come Down* 268–71). The episode plays against an earlier moment in the last section of that novel, when Dyer, having escaped both the United States and French Morocco, in the security of a boat Thami has found for them, comes close to connecting with the real.

> There was no question of sleeping; he was much too alert for that, but as he lay there in a state of enforced inactivity, thinking of nothing at all, he found himself entering a region of his memory which, now that he saw it again, he thought had been lost forever. It began with a song, brought back to him, perhaps, by the motion of the boat, and it was the only song that had ever made him feel really happy. "Go. To sleep. My little pickaninny. Mammy's goin' to slap you if you don't. Hushabye. Rockabye. Mammy's little baby. Mammy's little Alabama coon." Those could not have been the words, but they were the words he remembered now. He was covered by a patchwork quilt which was being tucked in securely on both sides—with his fingers he could feel the cross-stitching where the pieces were joined—and his head was lying on the eiderdown pillow his grandmother had made for him, the softest pillow he had ever felt. And like the sky, his mother was spread above him; not her face, for he did not want to see her eyes at such moments because she was only a person like anyone else, and he kept his eyes shut so that she could become something much more powerful. If he opened his eyes, there were her eyes looking at him, and that terrified him. With his eyes closed there was nothing but his bed and her presence. (228)[9]

Dyer is the archetypal American, representative of the spiritual malaise the character Richard Holland talks about in *Let It Come Down*—a character Bowles admitted was a self-portrait, or rather a caricature of himself (9). At a party Holland talks at length about the mistake of modern man that will surely bring about the destruction of the species (128–9). "There's nothing wrong in the world," Holland maintains, "except that man has persuaded himself he's a rational being, when really he's a moral one. And morality must have a religious basis, not a rational one. Otherwise it's just play-acting" (128). Dyer misreads virtually everything about Thami and the Moroccans except the one element common to both cultures, the obsessive desire for money and the accompanying dishonesty it engenders (121). The one opportunity to discover something authentic in the cultural other is Dyer's experience of the trance dance. Having no way to translate the religious experience into anything meaningful in modern Western thought, Dyer's experience turns inward, regressive, wild, and madly violent.

Bowles found a kindred spirit in Isabelle Eberhardt, a Westerner who managed to find the truth inside Islam. In the introduction to his translation of a number of her writings, Bowles noticed in her the "powerful nostalgia for the unattainable," the "obsession of total freedom," and the "quest for spiritual wisdom through the discipline of Sufism" (*Oblivion* 7). In "The Breath of Night" (ca. 1904), for example, Eberhardt describes the Aissaoua brotherhood:

> As the night grows perceptibly cooler, the members of that enlightened brotherhood, the *khouan*, pound on the tambourine and draw strident sounds from the oboelike rhaita. They also sing, slowly, as if in a dream. And they dance beside the flaming pots of charcoal, their wet bodies moving to an ever-accelerating tempo. From the fires rise intoxicating fumes of benzoin and myrrh. Through ecstasy they hope to reach the final target of unconsciousness. (76)

(This is the second of two moments in "The Breath of Night." Earlier, Eberhardt discerns sounds, a dance. Then she describes the Aissaoua. Later, even deeper in the night, the "heat of rut," she discovers the rebirth of desire.)

Besides *Let It Come Down* and his translation of the Sufi Eberhardt, Bowles elsewhere wrote of the dancers. In "The Wind at Beni Midar" (1962), a soldier, Driss, enters into the world of magic, *djenoun*, ecstasy. In a small cafe he sees "shameful things" (327); but as the story moves along, Driss becomes caught up in those very things. At first he grumbles to himself,

> Shameful things happened there. Several times he had seen men from the mountains get up from the mat and do dances that left blood on the floor. These men were Jilala, and no one thought of stopping them, not even Driss. They did not dance because they wanted to dance, and it was this that made him angry and ashamed. . . . A Jilali can do only what the music tells him to do. When the musicians, who are Jilala too, play the music that has the power, his eyes shut and he falls on the floor. And until the man has shown the proof and drunk his own blood, the musicians do not begin the music that will bring him back to the world. (328)

Driss is told that the land is changing, and Bowles need not tell his readers that the change is toward modern, Western, rational thought. With
children going to school, soon there will be no more *djenoun*. Women
will not use magic against their husbands, and the Jilala and the
Hamatcha and others "would stop cutting their legs and arms and
chests" (328). "He sees a man in a yellow turban, and Driss does not
want to look at him. The man dances and pulls out his knife, cutting
himself above the eyes, and Driss is forced to watch" (330). Days later
he sees another dance. Driss is supposed to enlist the aid of the dancer,
so he waits until the man is licking blood from his arms to make a
demand of the Jilali. Driss's action takes him into the world of djinn and
afreet, a "dangerous" world he had not wanted to enter.

Bowles also wrote about the brotherhoods in his autobiography
and in his essays. Paul reported on Jane Bowles's first experience of the
Aissaoua. After a steep climb through scrub forest and around boulders,
in a place near Marrakech, she said

> some thirty men were suddenly running full tilt down the mountain
> toward them, their eyes staring like marbles, their mouths wide, scream-
> ing, their faces and garments red and wet with blood. "Oh, my Gawd!"
> said Jody. Jane said nothing at all. . . . The men were Aissaoua who had
> just gone through the ceremony of eating a live bull; in their altered psy-
> chic state they probably did not even see the two Nazarene women cow-
> ering there among the boulders. (285–86)

The storyteller Bowles encouraged more than the others, Mohammed
Mrabet, is a Jilali. In *Without Stopping* Bowles tells of a party given by one
of the Westerners that included Jilali musicians to entertain the group.
For the Europeans, it was only music; for the members of the brotherhood, "it [was] a sequence of explicit choreographic instructions, all of
which [were] designed to bring about a state of trance, or possession"
(363). Mohammed Mrabet began to dance, at first casually, then in
earnest. Before long he was in a "deep trance." When the Westerners
spotted Mrabet with a long knife in his hand, they tackled him.

> As for Mrabet, the psychic shock of being interrupted in his ritual was
> such that it took him about an hour to recover consciousness and begin
> once more to function. It is doubtful that he would have returned to his
> normal state without the aid of the musicians, who consistently played
> the necessary music for him until he was awake and able to speak. It

seemed unthinkable that anyone should have dared to interfere with a Moslem in the state of trance. (364)[10]

In 1959 Bowles traveled through Morocco on a grant from the Rockefeller Foundation to record indigenous music. He recorded some sixty hours of music in twenty-three villages. The most conspicuous result was a set of two recordings, *Music of Morocco*, for the Library of Congress (L 63/64). In 1961, at Sidi Kacem, south of Tangier, he observed the festival at the tomb of the saint, Sidi Kacem, including an Aissaoua ceremony. Bowles noted the controversies that continue to surround the Sufi orders in Morocco:

> The Aissaoua have been prohibited from practicing their rites in public since the late 'thirties. There is some justification for the ban on the cult, since an Aissaoua ceremony can become a very bloody spectacle. Educated Moroccans consider the Aissaoua imperfectly converted Moslems; they have retained and incorporated pre-Islamic (animist) elements in their worship. Persecution of the dancing cults such as the Aissaoua, Hamatcha, Djilala, Haddaoua, Derqaoua and Guennaoua has been perceptibly lessened during the past year. (LC 12,017A)[11]

In "Africa Minor" Bowles suggests that the heterodox practices of Moroccan Muslims, including "gigantic pilgrimages" (*moussems*), women and men dancing together—"the height of immorality, the young puritans tell you" (27)—derives from the Berbers. More shocking than the dancing itself, though, is the mixing of blood and Islamic practice. "Self-torture, the inducing of trances, ordeal by fire and the sword, and the eating of broken glass and scorpions are also not unusual on such occasions" (27). To this Bowles adds his explanation for the fascination the spectator feels in such displays. "To me these spectacles are filled with great beauty, because their obvious purpose is to prove the power of the spirit over the flesh" (28). The spectacles gave him the opportunity for what is probably Bowles's most explicit statement on the meaning of the dance for him. Elsewhere he maintains a wise silence.

> The sight of ten or twenty thousand people actively declaring their faith, demonstrating *en masse* the power of that faith, can scarcely be anything but inspiring. You lie in the fire, I gash my legs and arms with a knife, he pounds a sharpened bone into his thigh with a rock—then, together, covered with ashes and blood, we sing and dance in joyous praise of the saint and the god who make it possible for us to triumph over pain, and

by extension, over death itself. For the participants exhaustion and ecstasy are inseparable. (28)

THIRD PHASE: ELIZABETH WARNOCK FERNEA

A Street in Marrakech (1980) is a far different account of Moroccan life than Wharton's *In Morocco*. It represents a sensibility conditioned by participant observation, the fieldwork so important in American anthropology since World War I. (Fernea spent the academic year 1971 through 1972 with her husband, Robert, who was doing anthropological research in Marrakech.) The religious experiences of the Moroccans are taken seriously; Fernea remained a "Nazarene," a Western outsider in the neighborhood until the women of the *zanka* admitted her into their religious life. As Fernea's subtitle suggests—*A Personal Encounter with the Lives of Moroccan Women*—the lives of women in an Arab-Muslim homosocial society remain hidden to outsiders. Until recently, most visitors to Morocco, including anthropologists, were men, and they had little access to the lives of ordinary women. Even Edith Wharton, though given a glimpse of upper-class Moroccan life, came away with a very superficial sense of women's lives (see also chapter 6).

The first hint that religion is indeed important to the women of the *zanka* comes at the beginning of part 3 of *A Street in Marrakech*, when Fernea learns that one of the women, Fatima Henna, is joining a *zawiya*, a religious sisterhood equivalent to the Sufi brotherhoods that visitors to Morocco have written about so frequently. (According to Clifford Geertz, Morocco had some twenty-three brotherhoods at the outset of World War II, to which nearly one-fifth of the male population belonged [51–52]). Fernea had not known *zawiyas* for women existed (233). The woman who is her friend, Aisha, visits the *murabits*, the tombs of *sidis*, or saints. Since the *murabit*, in Morocco, is forbidden to non-Muslims, Aisha is faced with a problem when Fernea indicates a desire to visit one.

When Aisha takes her to one of the holy places, Fernea is introduced by Aisha as "her friend, she is Christian but she wants baraka [the power, grace] from Allala Arkiya, believe me, she is in need of baraka, and who knows, she may need it more than we do, since she is a Christian" (239).

Another stage in her understanding is reached when she is taken to Mul el Ksour (the fifteenth-century mystic, Sidi Abdallah el Ghezwani, one of the seven patron saints of Marrakech). There she enters the shrine and observes the *zawiya*, including the mystical trance dancing others have witnessed among the Sufi brotherhoods. Inside the holy place, a girl, just having entered puberty, dances herself into a trance (289):

> I could see the whole scene from my new vantage point: The drummers, in white, with pale blue scarves tied around their heads, were seated inside the circle of spectators; and a girl danced alone, a dark-haired girl just entering puberty, one might have said, from her immature body, her legs too long for the short skirt she wore under her blue nylon school smock, a *tablier* just like [her daughter] Laura Ann's. . . .
>
> The dancing girl looked to me as though she had reached a state of trance and was almost out of control, her head lolling back and forth, her arms limp. An older woman in a gray djellaba and hood stood close behind, clutching the back of the girl's tablier, keeping her on her feet, or the girl, it appeared, would have fallen to the ground. At that moment the dancer's head dropped forward onto her chest, the drummers ceased abruptly, and the woman in grey grabbed the girl under the armpits. The drums began another beat, slower, softer. Although she seemed to have collapsed in the older woman's arms, the dancing girl gradually straightened up and began to move to the new beat, not in the jerky, lolling manner of before, but simply and gracefully. (289)

Others join the dance, but B. J. is unwilling—or unable—to join them. She learns from Aisha that "it is bad to dance to the wrong tune, the wrong beat, one's spirit becomes confused" (296). Each person has his or her own "beat." Aisha's manner in this episode is quite intimate: "Never had Aisha become so personal with me" as she was when explaining the *zawiya*"(296).

After Fernea witnesses the dance and returns to the family's home, her patronizing acquaintance, Abdul Lateef, proceeds to explain her experience to her. He is taken aback when what he describes as a "serious, psychological experience . . . deep and important," struck her as "pleasant" (294) "I knew that this kind of dancing and music session had often been described as therapeutic, cathartic, full of intensity and drama, but my whole impression of the occasion had been that all were in a gay and lighthearted mood and enjoyed themselves thoroughly. 'It was fun, Abdul Lateef'" (294).

This is not to say that Fernea did not discover the complexity of the notion of 'baraka,' which is what the dancers (and the witnesses) seek. Indeed, the joy she finds in one of its more dramatic manifestations is a sign that she has seen a great deal in it. Most descriptions are, like Abdul Lateef's, intense and serious. Geertz, for example, defines the term, which means "blessing" or "divine favor," in a complex description:

> Spreading out from that nuclear meaning, specifying and delimiting it, it encloses a whole range of linked ideas: material prosperity, physical well-being, bodily satisfaction, completion, luck, plenitude, and, the aspect most stressed by Western writers anxious to force it into a pigeon-hole with mana, magical power. . . . "Baraka" is personal presence, force of character, moral vividness. Marabouts have baraka in the way that men have strength, courage, dignity, skill, beauty, or intelligence. (44)

The point of many popular Islamic practices is to receive baraka, not necessarily to demonstrate the triumph of spirit or even to make contact with ultimate reality, which many of the dancers would find blasphemous. However, those who take the mystical tradition seriously caution against reducing the ecstasy or "annihilation" (*fana'*) the Sufi seeks to a psychological state.[12] Idries Shah, for example, sees rapture as a threat to genuine mystical experience.

> The ecstatic condition, when the human being feels himself at one with creation, or a Creator, rapture, something like intoxication; when he feels that he has entered paradise; when all senses interchange or become one sense—What is considered by the individual to be a blessing is in fact a flooding-out of potentiality. It is as if a flood of light has been shone into the eyes of someone who was until recently blind. It has a glory and a fascination. But it is of no use, because it dazzles. (335)

This false *tajalli* stands opposed to the "access of knowledge," a "permanent increase in intuitive knowledge" (336). However, mystical union with the Supreme Reality (*fana' fi-l-haqq*) is not necessarily the aim of those who participate in the Sufi rites. Among the Hamadsha, for example, the rites are usually performed for the purpose of "curing an individual who has been struck by the devil or is possessed by one" (Crapanzano, "Hamadsha" 343). Most often there is something to be gained through the mediation of a saint—baraka in the form of good fortune, good health, appeasement of a spirit.[13]

AMERICAN ATTITUDES TO THE IRRATIONAL

What separates Edith Wharton from the later observers is her confidence in Western civilization and the progress it brings to unenlightened primitive peoples. She was, after all, invited to Morocco by Resident General Lyautey himself, who was anxious to show off the positive changes that had been made in only a few years of French overlordship. She was accompanied on her travels by French military personnel and was permitted access to places and persons an ordinary tourist would not be given. The elements of Moroccan life that fascinated her, especially the ritual dancing, did not shake her faith in the great, perhaps unreconcilable, gap between the civilized West and its "Oriental" other. Indeed, she was even more intense in the defense of colonial rule than was Lyautey himself. Her time in Morocco was brief, a pleasant sojourn in the midst of a grim world war.

Wharton's visit during World War I was much earlier than Paul Bowles's first visit. Elizabeth Fernea's stay in Morocco (1971–1972) was already later than the change in Paul Bowles, the only one of the three who lived in the country for an extended period. Many of Bowles's best works were written from the late 1940s until 1967, which according to Wayne Pounds (32–33) saw a turning point in Bowles's relationship with the people among whom he was living. (North African characters came then to dominate his fiction; he adopts their point of view and is much influenced by nonliterate storytellers.) More and more he encouraged the storytellers, especially his Jilali friend, Mohammed Mrabet, to tell their stories, and he devoted his time to translating them. The skepticism he expressed earlier—the inability of anyone from the West to know the Muslim North African—gave way to an unexpressed confidence in his ability to speak for the other. More than the other Americans his fascination with the dance is a way to ecstasy.

Ecstasy may seem an odd accompaniment to the nihilism that critics such as Bertens find in Bowles, nihilism that is always related to American culture and the West (8). More than any other critic, Ihab Hassan has seen just how much the ironic pilgrim/prey, the solitary adventurer, is part of the mainstream of American fiction, from Poe, Melville, and Hawthorne through the postmoderns ("Quest" 125–27). And the mysticism involved in what Hassan calls the "New

Gnosticism," a participation in universal consciousness (Palmer 372–73), is part of a complex Richard Palmer has labeled "postmodernity." Among the ten features of postmodernity Palmer includes transcending technological rationality, the movement "beyond Western forms of reality," and a nonperspectival and holistic "new consciousness" (369–79).[14]

In *A Street in Marrakech*, Elizabeth Warnock Fernea never suggests that Western civilization is superior to Eastern. Ever sensitive to cultural differences, she represents a healthy, scientific curiosity that looks first and evaluates later and never denigrates the culture she sought to understand. Her response to the ritual dancing is engaged, sympathetic, and increasingly informed, as she questions others in the culture about *their* responses to such performances. She did not plan to stay in Morocco longer than a year. Her understanding of popular Islam is always set in the context of the West's very slight knowledge of Islamic women. Witnessing the dance is as close as she can approach to the religious life of the women she came to know, and it represented the deep acceptance she gained in her friendship with Aisha.

THE QUEST FOR THE OTHER

Since the quests in Bowles's fiction are as often as not unconscious and end badly, as is Dyer's in *Let It Come Down*, where the pilgrim is unable to return home, one might not think that recourse to the mystical and the mythical would be very appropriate to Bowles and his work. Yet we can find Bowles's ironic turns in Hassan's summary of a very unique American style of quest:

> Still, we can plausibly conclude that the historic experience of America proved singularly congenial to the spirit of quest. That experience conjoined energy and wonder, violence and sacrament, alienation and reverse, in unique measure. It is as if the "complex fate" of which Henry James spoke at the turn of our century really entailed, more than a confrontation between Europe and American, a spiritual adventure into the uncharted wilderness of both the New World and of the Old Adam. ("Quest" 127).

It is easiest to consider Bowles's fascination with the dance an aesthetic or a psychological response. Certainly Bowles denied any usual Judeo-Christian doctrine and affirms the death of God; nor with his interest in Islam is there evidence that he has accepted Islam, even of an esoteric sort—though his silences are important here. But what may be operating is what Richard Stivers has called "the violations of sacred rules in modern societies as manifested in symbol, myth, and ritual," (2), specifically "the sacred of transgression," modern rituals that celebrate sex, violence, drugs, and revolution (the return to chaos). Such "antimyths" are articulated "not *within* the larger mythical unity (cosmogonic myth) of progress or technological utopianism but *against* it" (134). On a deeper level, Stivers believes, there is "an underlying commonality" to myth and ritual of traditional societies and the antimyth of modern, technological society.

Stivers explains ecstasy in such a socio-cultural context. He combines Marshall McLuhan and Jacques Ellul to describe ecstasy in the modern world as

> a counterirritant to the irritation that technology creates in the central nervous system and psychic self by not permitting human impulses to be released and expressed. Technique is abstract; impulses are concrete. Technique is collective; impulses are individual. Technique denies all emotion and impulse, everything that is not technique. (151)

For the Sufi, dancing is a way to contact baraka, to effect a cure, to reach annihilation, to be one with Allah. Of the Western observers, Isabelle Eberhardt accepted Islam and became a Sufi. The others watched, fascinated. Bowles is the least innocent of the group. Ecstasy involves destruction, and the Bowles who told Daniel Halpern (170–71) that his "grudge" against the world could only be satisfied by "writing words, by attacking in words" also told him that destruction often means "purification." Bowles's fascination with the cultural other, with extreme states of consciousness, with violence—in its most bizarre form, the trance dance—is extreme in its participation and its detachment, in a world in which the sacred of transgression is the only way to speak, when both God and the *civitas* are declared dead. It is also a very American fascination.

Edith Wharton's fascination with and horror of what she considered the irrational and primitive East are most obvious in her observations of the Sufi mystics. Chapter 3 is devoted to those observations in the context of her wider travel in Morocco. The chapter examines a sensitive, highly intelligent guidebook for Western travelers written by a woman who consciously identified with the civilizing mission of the West. Wharton's "high cultural" approach to Morocco is in sharp contrast to the popular early *Desert Song* and also to the anthropologists who were beginning to take an interest in Morocco.

Wharton's *In Morocco* is linked to *The Desert Song* through the figure of the Father, seen in two generals depicted in the two narratives. Between the two works falls the shadow of Freudian depth psychology, which vastly complicated earlier images of the East. From the stage through three film versions, *The Desert Song* provides an index to sometimes small but ultimately important shifts in American images of the East. The four versions help to define, in one register, the three-phase movement outlined in the Introduction.

Chapter Three

Two Fathers General

For Americans in the 1920s Morocco was a story of two French generals, one very real and the other fictional. The first, Louis Hubert Gonzalve Lyautey (1854–1934), was appointed resident general in April 1912, when France inaugurated a protectorate in Morocco. For the American writer who sang his praises, he was, in a way that may have shocked and horrified him, the protector of Western civilization. The second was a fictional construct in a popular stage musical that quickly became a film hit in the early days of the talkies—and lived through two other film versions between 1929 and 1953: *The Desert Song*. The French general in *The Desert Song*, General Birabeau, had already become a stereotypical tyrant-father whose well-meaning but irrational acts would keep a pair of young lovers from marrying. What had intervened between Edith Wharton's *In Morocco* (1920)[1] and the Otto Harbach, Oscar Hammerstein II, and Frank Mandel *The Desert Song* (1927) was popular Freudian psychology. Freud brought with him, in the deep ambivalence toward civilization, an undermining not only of fathers but also of generals.

EDITH WHARTON AND THE GREAT MAN

In the great civilizing mission of the West, Edith Wharton's World War I travel book, *In Morocco*, rests comfortably. Unlike the travelers who are once again capturing the attention of critics and historians—Burton and

Flaubert, Lane, Lawrence of Arabia, Wilfrid Thesiger—Wharton's travel had more modest aims. *In Morocco* does not attempt a new interpretation of the Orient. The product of a visit to Morocco that was as much as anything a much-desired respite from her work in wartime Paris, *In Morocco* is most of all a guidebook in English where none had existed. However, the book is, more than that. It is a measure of the distance between the civilized West, especially the French, and the primitive East. Wharton's admiration for the progress made in Morocco by Resident General Lyautey in only five years of the French Protectorate is evident throughout the work. Ironically, Wharton's measure of the distance is greater than the general's own view, as was suggested in the previous chapter.

Until recently, travel literature could be considered the most innocent of writings. Like scholarly histories and ethnographies, travel books could give the masses a glimpse of worlds the people might never be able to visit themselves. Unlike scientists, though, travel writers since antiquity have been given a free hand to enhance their accounts, like Mandeville, with fantasy and a good share of subjective and often idiosyncratic reflection. The innocence toward travelers in the East has been shattered and may never return. Edward Said, as mentioned earlier, indicted scholars of Orientalism for the way in which Orientalist discourse aided imperialist hegemony. "The major component in European culture," he argued, "is precisely what made that culture hegemonic both in and outside Europe: the idea of European identity as a superior one in comparison with all the non-European peoples and cultures" (7). Rana Kabbani has since indicted the travel writers in *Europe's Myths of Orient* (1986).

Kabbani deals with travel literature from antiquity, but the main thrust is with books written in the nineteenth and twentieth centuries, the time of the emergence of anthropology and, not coincidentally, the expansion of European imperialism (8–11). Americans are almost entirely absent from Kabbani's discussion. Only Mark Twain's *Innocents Abroad* is given a passing mention (139). Just as Edith Wharton (with Henry James) is credited with introducing the international theme into American fiction, her *In Morocco* is noteworthy as an American's entry in a field dominated by the British and the French.

Unlike Isabelle Eberhardt, whom Lyautey had met and admired years before he became resident general of Morocco, Edith Wharton did not travel to the East in search of mystical experience. Lyautey had wanted Eberhardt to help in extending French occupation to areas filled with anti-Christian sentiment. (There is no evidence that she complied with his wish.) During World War I, when Edith Wharton was exhausting herself in the war effort in Paris, Lyautey invited her to Morocco to show off the many changes that had been introduced in the few short years he had governed the country.

It is difficult to assess the work of the astonishing General, later Marshal, Lyautey in Morocco. Jacques Berque is of the opinion that even this most conscientious colonial administrator could not penetrate the interior of Moroccan culture. Berque writes,

> If we consider Egypt in Cromer's time, or Lyautey's Morocco, we observe that the British or French ruler imposed goals which were costly, certainly, and distortive for the national economy and personality but which touched only the outer shell. All the inside and the rest remained as if there were no colonization." (97)

While this may be true, it was not for lack of trying. What Rom Landau called "the Lyautey touch" in the twelve years of his administration as resident general of the Protectorate combined a firm hand with a keen sensitivity to a people who, unlike their neighbors, say, in Algeria, had kept their kingdom independent of the West until the very last. Landau flatly claims that

> the key to his accomplishment was his sincere love of Morocco and the Moors. Because he loved both, he tried to preserve what was best in their civilization, while infusing into it, as gradually as his temperament allowed, constructive elements serving to inculcate a fresh approach, a more modern outlook.[2]

It was Lyautey who insisted that Morocco, though it came under the protection of France, was not to be a French colony.

Lyautey was moved by the long history and cultural achievements of the Moors. "Let us not forget that we are in the country of Ibn Khaldoun, who arrived in Fez at the age of twenty; in the land of Averroes; and of their descendants, who are not unworthy of them." He took the position that the protectorate must maintain what is best in the culture. "Govern with the mandarins, not against them. Do not offend a single tradition, do not change a single habit. Identify the governing class with our own interests."[3]

Lyautey insisted on the improvement of agriculture, the building of harbors, railways, and dams. Certainly he was well aware of the economic benefit the French would derive from Morocco. He resisted, though, the influx of *colons*, settlers from France to run the farms.

France was, for Wharton, clearly the most civilized society, followed by Britain, and somewhat farther down, the United States.[4] Primitive peoples, of course, stand in the sharpest contrast to the world of "culture." The trip to Morocco was Wharton's "only real holiday" (357) from World War I, which she considered a war of civilization against the barbarians. In fact, as Elizabeth Ammons points out,

> During the fighting, Edith Wharton's labor on behalf of France was so remarkable that in 1916 she was made a Chevalier of the French Legion of Honor, an unprecedented distinction for a woman and one sparingly awarded to foreigners. . . . Her contribution to the war-effort was prodigious: she raised funds, organized relief for refugees, founded hospitals and hostels, created jobs for war widows and homeless women, wrote propaganda, took in orphans. (128)

She even set up "Edith Wharton" committees in the United States to gain support for the French cause and for "American Hostels for Refugees" abroad.

An offhanded remark in *A Backward Glance* (1934) connecting Paris to the "more exclusive *salons* of Babylon and Ur" may contain more truth than Wharton intended. Concern for "civilization" is ancient indeed, if "civilized" is considered a quality of city life. The Romans knew the conditions or rights of the *civis*, or citizen: the *civitas*. Quintilian used the term *civilitas* to mean the science of politics (translating the Greek *politike*). It was a term that also meant "politeness" and "civility." But the concept is much older than that—even older than the Greeks, who did much to promote the notion of the 'city.' Bendt Alster discovered that the earliest writers known to history were already worrying about the civilized—the life of those who lived in the Sumerian cities—and the wild, the barbarians. In fact, Alster noted, Mesopotamian society of the late third and early second millennia B.C.E.—in places such as Ur and Babylon—showed an increasing interest in the subject, as is evident in the proverb collections made then.[5] (Whether those city people held sessions in the *salon* is still a matter of some debate.)

Still, as John U. Nef has pointed out, the modern sense of "civilization" is intimately bound up with its opposite, "primitive." Before the primitive had developed its romantic nobility, like "savage" the term was unrelentingly negative, like "atrocity" tinged with evil, especially irrational violence. Such associations reflect an outlook toward violence that was new in the West since the Renaissance. Nef notes that the term *atrocity* seems not to have been used in English before the late eighteenth century. And the word *civilization* itself is not much older. Nef cites the Marquis de Mirabeau, who may have been the first to use the term, in 1757. Mirabeau sometime later (in 1766) offered what is still the root meaning of the modern, Western notion of the civilized:

> The civilization of a people is to be found in the softening of manners, in growing urbanity, in politer relations and in the spreading of knowledge in such ways that decency and seemliness are practiced until they transcend specific and detailed laws. . . . Civilization does nothing for society unless it is able to give form and substance to virtue. The concept of humanity is born in the bosom of societies softened by all these ingredients. (79)

It is easy to see, especially in Wharton's book on Morocco, how General Lyautey could come to embody the civilized world,[6] especially the aristocratic principle that keeps such a world orderly.

> In 1917 I had my only real holiday. General Lyautey, then Resident General in Morocco, had held since 1914 . . . an annual industrial exhibition, destined to impress upon France's subjects the fact that the war she was carrying on in no way affected her normal activities. The idea was admirable, the result wholly successful. To these exhibitions, which were carried out with the greatest taste and intelligence, the Resident annually invited a certain number of guests from allied and neutral countries. (*A Backward Glance* 357)

Her trip was a three weeks' motor tour of the colony. The result was a guidebook that not only described in rich detail a picturesque and exotic place, but included an appendix on "General Lyautey's Work in Morocco." The main sections of the book focus on the great cities of Morocco: Rabat and Salé; Volubilis, Moulay Idriss, and Meknes; Fez; and Marrakech. The appendix details Lyautey's accomplishments: jetties built in Casablanca ("Quays 747 metres long already finished. 16 steamcranes working."); total number of teachers (in 1912, at the beginning of the Protectorate, 61; in 1918, 668); and medical information ("Native patients treated in 1916, 900,000," 171–75).

For the most part, the guidebook describes "these gifted races, per-petually struggling to reach some higher level of culture from which they have always been swept down by a fresh wave of barbarism." The Moroccans, she decided, "are still only a people in the making." When she concluded, "It may be that the political stability which France is helping them to acquire will at last give their higher qualities time for fruition," she would not have expected much opposition from her read-ers (128).

Her prose is studded with the "unknown," the "mystery," the "adventure" of the picturesque and "mystic" land—noble figures, saint's tombs, kif, veils, mosques, the wild land, the light in the "uncitied wilder-ness" (29). In its architecture she found the "secret soul of the land" as well as the most troubling features of the exotic peoples she observed (31). In the Kasbah of the Oudayas in the Arab city of Salé she noticed the "bending of passages, so characteristic a device of the Moroccan builder, . . . like an architectural expression of the tortuous secret soul of the land" (31). She described house plans, towers, Quranic schools, tombs, and bazaars and did not hesitate to assess the significance:

> The whole of civilian Moslem architecture from Persia to Morocco is based on four unchanging conditions: a hot climate, slavery, polygamy, and the segregation of women. The private house in Mohammedan countries is in fact a fortress, a convent, and a temple: a temple of which the god (as in all ancient religions) frequently descends to visit his clois-tered votaresses. For where slavery and polygamy exists every house-master is necessarily a god, and the house he inhabits a shrine built about his divinity. (202)

Fatalism and apathy she also thought were reflected in Moroccan architecture. Discussing the Saadian tombs in Marrakech, she wondered how, "in the heart of a savage Saharan camp," the "fragile loveliness" of the mausoleum could have been conceived. How could it have survived?

In Morocco is filled with accounts of anonymous peoples, crowds, and types: Arabs, Berbers in a land "swarming with hill-people," "Mohammedans," and Jews. She noted blacks, and she took careful note of Moroccan women.

She did not like much of what she saw. The women in Old Rabat were unkind enough to ask Wharton if she had children—childlessness being considered the worst fate in the world for a woman—and she was forced to admit that even in "the western world" childless women were sometimes pitied. She discovered that European fashions were considered ugly by the harem women. For the most part she found, again and again, that the women were vacuous and defeated. Instead of the almost fairy-tale world she seems to have expected, Wharton discovered even in the wealthiest palace "sad expressive" eyes, pale complexions, "remote and passive eyes" (147), a "look of somewhat melancholy respectability" (151).

Slavery, which was still very evident in Wharton's description of Morocco, and the virtual slavery of harem life were, not surprisingly, repugnant to the Western, civilized woman, since the abolition of slavery had been one measure of moral progress in which the West could take comfort.

Clearly, Edith Wharton was not discerning in the Moroccan crowds, in the Moroccan types, or in Moroccan religious practices the softening of manners, the politer relations, the decency and seemliness that Mirabeau found in civilized societies. Much of what Wharton described disgusted her, and much clearly filled her with delight. What makes In Morocco intriguing, though, is not so much the picturesqueness or the (expected) condescension toward a backward people who were being civilized by the French. Rather, it is the barely hidden admiration for certain of the "worst" qualities of the Moroccan people—especially the fascination with the Oriental despot.[7]

When Wharton visited Meknes, she saw the gigantic ruins of Sultan Moulay Ismail's palace, and it prompted her to write a long section (58–70) about the most notorious figure in Moroccan history.[8] One might expect that the immense Imperial City would catch her attention. Its huge walls that stretch for more than a mile, stables for twelve thousand horses, twenty-four pavilions for the five hundred wives of Moulay Ismail, gardens, and room for at least fifty thousand slaves and eunuchs in the compound are staggering now. While he was building the complex—he reigned for fifty-five years, from 1672 to 1727—he impressed Louis XIV, who was busy developing Versailles. Thirty years later, Voltaire, at the same time Mirabeau was defining "civilization," included a satiric portrait of Morocco under Moulay Ismail. Almost every atrocity imaginable could be witnessed there, wanton slaughter and rape especially. A woman, the daughter of Pope Urban X and the princess of Palestrina, tells the story, which involved

Barbary pirates and the dreadful treatment of the woman, her mother, and all the other Italian women who had been captured and enslaved.

> Morocco was swimming in blood when we arrived. There were fifty sons of the Emperor Muley Ismael, each with his own faction; this produced fifty civil wars, of blacks against blacks, blacks against browns, browns against brown, and mulattoes against mulattoes. There was constant slaughter from one end of the empire to the other. (*Candide* 44)

For Voltaire, the sultan was nothing more than another terrible example, more exotic than his European examples and perhaps more extravagant, but in the same vein, of atrocities committed in the name of religion. Wharton's Moulay Ismail was far enough removed in time—as the sultan was not for Voltaire—that he no longer served even for satire. Moulay Ismail is the perfect example of willful Oriental despotism (and the unspoken contempt for the people he victimized, especially if they had adopted the fatalism that is supposed to keep the Muslim peoples passive). What makes her account interesting—and different from Voltaire and the matter-of-fact accounts in modern guidebooks—is Wharton's barely disguised fascination for the man who brought law and order to the land. His was a "barbarous empire" (68), and he engaged in "barbaric warfare . . . palace intrigue, crazy bloodshed" (60). He was a "terrible old monarch, who devastated whole districts, and sacrificed uncounted thousands of lives for his ruthless pleasure" (61). She was intrigued, though, by his (unspecified) "great administrative reforms" and, even more, by the "appearance of prosperity and security" he gave to a land "where all had before been chaos" (69). We have the examples of totalitarian horrors before us in a way that Wharton did not, but readers today cannot but wince at her description of the other side of Moulay Ismail's terrible rule. She cites a chronicler who maintained that, under his administration,

> the country rejoiced in the most complete security. A Jew or a woman might travel alone from Oudjda to the Oued Noun without anyone's asking their business. Abundance reigned throughout the land: grain, food, cattle were to be bought for the lowest prices. Nowhere in the whole of Morocco was a highwayman or a robber to be found. (61)

The extended portrait of this "extraordinary man" (68) is the most conspicuous treatment of the "great man" in the book. Like Lyautey, who flattered the Moroccan caids as a matter of policy, Wharton found some few Moroccan feudal lords commendable, even grand.⁹ Lyautey's policy had a clear goal: to extend the influence of his administration into areas that had never been subdued; and the policy was successful. The caid in Marrakech forgot—either "through Oriental dilatoriness, or a last secret reluctance to admit unbelievers to a holy place" (122)— his appointment to take her through the Saadian tombs; but she had mainly good to say about his household (120). In contrast to the women of his harem, the caid is singled out as a "great man" and a "great fighter," that is to say, "a loyal friend of France." Magnificently "eagle-beaked," "brown, lean and sinewy, with vigilant eyes," the caid is praised for his defense of the French colony. "Enlightened, cultivated, a friend to the arts, a scholar and diplomatist, he seems, unlike many Orientals, to have selected the best in assimilating European influences" (157).

Because of Lyautey and Madame Lyautey, Wharton was admitted to the presence of the Sultan Moulay Youssef and allowed to see the Sacrifice of the Sheep (130–35). Her audience with the sultan she said was "the crowning incident of our visit" (142). Her first glimpse of him was in his public role, the motionless figure around whom more than ten thousand horsemen swirled. He became "through sheer immobility, a symbol, a mystery, a god . . . embodying to the wild factious precipitate horses a long tradition of serene aloofness" (135). In the private audience, "despoiled of sacramental burnouses and turban," the Sultan became "a fat man with a pleasant face, his djellabah stretched over a portly front" (142). While he had less of the sacred about him then, nonetheless he—like the other "great" men of Morocco—came away much more impressive than the women.

The fascination with the great man is not at all disguised or muted when Wharton deals with General Lyautey himself. Madame Lyautey is mentioned here and there, but she evidently, had nothing of the charisma surrounding the resident general. He was the "great Administrator" who made Morocco safe and open; and brought law and order to the land. Wharton devotes, as we have seen above, a section to "General Lyautey's Work in Morocco" (161–76), complete with statistics showing his work on transportation, commerce, justice, medicine, and education. He had been appointed resident general, she claimed, because of a massacre of French officers in Fez, in 1912, when for two weeks "the Oued Fez ran red with the blood of harmless French colonists" (162); and he managed to overcome military adventures to begin "his great task of civilian administration" (162). The "great patriot" and "great general" (165) produced "the Miracle of Morocco" (169).

While Wharton herself had no doubts about the civilizing enterprise of French intervention in Morocco—had no difficulty calling the country a "colony," though Lyautey was careful not to use the term— she did recognize the important role Lyautey's devotion to Moroccan history, arts, and tradition played in his success. "Probably the true explanation of the miracle is that which he himself gives when he says, with the quiet smile that typifies his Moroccan war-policy: 'It was easy to do because I loved the people.'"

THE GENERAL AND HIS SWORD:
THE DESERT SONG, 1927–1953

A second French general, General Birabeau in the first two (of four) versions of *The Desert Song*, retains a general's power but yields it against the Moroccans and against his own son, a hero of the Moroccans in their rebellion against French (and Spanish) overlordship.

If Freud had been able to enjoy a joke at his own expense, he would have found the changes in *The Desert Song* from the 1920s through the 1950s amusing indeed. The musical is a theatrical and film oddity. A "musical play in two acts," *The Desert Song* was originally produced in London in 1927 and was quickly made into a film. Warner Brothers issued three very different versions. The first, in 1929, under the direction of Roy Del Ruth was the first all-talking, all-singing film. Versions of 1943 and 1953 followed.[10] The early version remains popular in the theater. What Freud would have found funny was that the Viennese psychoanalyst, highlighted in the earliest script, virtually dropped out of sight as the piece became more "serious"—and more Americanized. As it became Americanized, *The Desert Song* reflected changes in American attitudes toward the East from a first phase to a second phase, from romanticizing the exotic (and challenging the assumptions of "civilization") to an attitude of skepticism and ambivalence.

Freud, with his discovery of the unconscious and of sexual and aggressive instincts, his skepticism toward religion and his ambivalence toward civilization, offered a discomforting challenge to these notions. Interestingly, though, the early *Desert Song* manages to explore the complexities of the Western man and woman without abandoning the flat stereotypes of the Oriental. (But then again the musical was not meant for an Oriental audience.)

In all four versions, theater and film, a beautiful French woman falls, more or less easily, for the (disguised) Oriental hero, the Red Shadow, and ends up accepting him even when she finds out he is "only" a man. There is always a gap between the Red Shadow and the ordinary fellow playing his heroic role, Pierre Birabeau in the early versions. The lovers always find themselves, and some comment is made about the "Cause" at the end.

Since the names change from version to version, the common elements might be called the Western Man and Hero, the Comedian, the Oriental Man, the Oriental Woman, the Western Woman, and the Cause. Since each version of *The Desert Song* is based on the earlier version or versions, the four provide a unique glimpse of the way techniques, themes, and emphases change from the 1920s through the emergence of the United States as a leading power in the world. Of most importance here is the blocking figure, the General.

All but the Comedian have their counterparts in that much older heroic tale, *The Aeneid*. The mixing of serious and comic elements in a single story would have been a grave lapse in decorum for Virgil, but the medieval and Renaissance stage (at least in England, whose most successful violator of classical convention was, of course, Shakespeare) had made such combinations at least possible, if not always prestigious. Like many American musicals, *The Desert Song* admits a serious interest in sentiment—romantic love—seen against a backdrop of equally serious causes. The comedic elements keep the story from turning, as it might easily have, into tragedy.

First Phase: Versions of 1927 and 1929

The 1920s was filled with talk of the scandalous thinker who found the sex instincts ruling over even the higher "moral," "spiritual," and "civilized" aspects of life. William York Tindall, for example, devoted a chapter in *Forces in Modern British Literature, 1885-1956* to the unconscious, and he included most of the important writers of the 1920s in his survey: critics such as Herbert Read; novelists such as Katherine Mansfield and

D. H. Lawrence, who blamed Freud for missing the point of the unconscious; and poets such as C. Day Lewis—but not Edith Wharton.

The Desert Song is hardly the serious stuff that worried Lawrence
and set intellectuals to writing. Although it deals with an actual place
and an actual event of interest to the newspaper readers of the day—
Morocco and the revolt against French colonial rule there—and though
it raises issues that could, in another genre, lead to grand tragedy, the
musical never lets the audience take it too seriously. That Freud was not
far from *The Desert Song* is shown in the comedians' worry over "It." The
beautiful heroine, Margot, of the story has It. Bennie, a comedian, is
worried that his fiancée, Susan, does not. Or so Bennie thinks until he
kisses Susan, and then he sings of It—that turns out to the Freudian *Es*,
or id.

Elinor Glynn is credited with inventing that most typical of 1920s
frivolity, It. (In *It*, the 1927 silent film with Clara Bow, Elinor Glynn herself has a cameo role and explains the notion for those who might not
have picked it up by then.) Whereas Freud had "employed words we
never had heard of," Glynn defined that complex of infantile sexuality,
dreams, and symbols of the unconscious with a single word. Bennie's
definition of that "indefinable thing" certainly owes little to Freud's
complex discussion in *Das Ich und das Es*, but it is a popular version of the
scandalous *das Es*.[11]

Music, song, and dance enable *The Desert Song* to survive in spite of
an odd and often surprising story line. Those elements speak much
more immediately to the unconscious than the other, conscious discourses that swirl around in the story. *The Desert Song* in that way became
an ideal vehicle for popular Freudianism: scandalous themes and messages packed into a display that would offend no one.

Or almost no one. Already by the 1929 film version Freud was
beginning to disappear from the script of *The Desert Song*. The debate
between Elinor Glynn's It and Freud's id was carried on in the film, and
"Freudian symbols" continued to abound, but Freud's name was deleted
from the script. Perhaps by accident (by self-censoring rather than by
decree), the Freudian elements were reduced in each version as the
story came to be more and more "American."

Like most romances, the basic story line of *The Desert Song* complicates and then finally resolves a few simple problems. The complica-
tions that keep the lovers apart usually make for a plot that is difficult to

summarize—and will not be discussed here. In all versions, the main plot follows the lovers who find themselves (often rather inexplicably) in Morocco.

Setting the story in Morocco is part of an age-old convention in the romance. Morocco is an exotic place, full of mystery, with desert sands, walled cities, palaces, mosques, and minarets. It brings out facets of the personality normally hidden in ordinary places. In one respect, though, *The Desert Song* is different from the usual Barbaresque fantasy: the earliest versions were based on a contemporary event covered by the newspapers.

Americans and the British made a Riffian (a Berber tribesman of northern Morocco) named Muhammad ben Abd el Karim el Khattabi —Abd el Karim for short—a romantic hero in the revolt he led against the French and Spanish overlords in the 1920s. Morocco had been the last North African country to be subdued by the Western powers. Even after 1912 France found the tribes notoriously difficult to subdue. Rom Landau has pointed out that "three Marshals, forty generals, and almost half a million Franco-Spanish troops were required to bring the Riffian warrior to defeat" (Landau 127). Even in defeat—Abd el Karim capitulated in May 1926—he was a striking figure, even to his enemies. Landau recalls an incident that took place while Abd el Karim was riding toward his surrender. He happened to pass a group of French soldiers bathing in a mountain stream. When they recognized the rider, they rushed over to him. "Though naked, they saluted him in correct military fashion, and expressed their great admiration for his qualities as a soldier and leader. Some even assured him of their sympathy in his defeat" (130).

The historical Abd el Karim was no savage, and the Riffians were noteworthy in Morocco for their interest in science and rather severe religious commitment to Islam. For *The Desert Song* based on the Riffian revolt, though, much of that was irrelevant. Abd el Karim was a warrior in the grand style, a horseman and a swordsman who fought for a noble cause, to throw off the colonial yoke. To a society that had seen the nature of war change in World War I, Abd el Karim was a reminder of more chivalrous times, when man-to-man combat and personal honor took precedence over the anonymity of weapons that killed often and at a distance. In *The Desert Song* the enemy is the machine gun.

The major twist *The Desert Song* gives to the story (besides building upon it a love story that comes to overtake the heroic tale itself) is that the hero is not really a Moroccan at all. The leader, though his identity is not known to the French who oppose him, is French. (In the 1943 version, he is an American). He appears in the guise of the Red Shadow, and the story turns on his mysterious identity. In all versions, the identity of the Red Shadow (or El Khobar, as the hero is called in 1943 and 1953) is *the* complication in the piece. That a beautiful French woman, Margot, should fall for such an adventurous *Oriental* is a scandal so basic to the story that elaborate means are taken to account for it.

More even than a story of a revolt of a people against colonial overlords, *The Desert Song* is a story about cultural differences. The Orientals are stereotyped, and it is through the contrast with the Orientals that the Western figures clarify and make explicit what it is that binds Americans, British, and French into a unity. (The Spanish are not entirely ignored in the piece. In 1927 and 1929 they appear as marginally Western, more like the North Africans, seen only as Barcelona courtesans who ridicule "weak, Western man.") One advantage of the 1920s versions is the unfailing confidence in the superiority of the West (Christian/civilized/sensitive to higher moral and spiritual principles) to the East (Muslim/primitive/cruel, and disorganized, prone to follow their baser instincts).

In the early versions (1927 and 1929) Pierre Birabeau is ostensibly the ultimate wimp, and also the Red Shadow. Ordered to raid Riff villages by "the butcher," a French general, Pierre refuses, and is forced to split his identity between a kind of Robin Hood and a sleepy imbecile, who carries bunches of wild flowers, a laughingstock to the European community in Morocco and a disgrace to his father. His father is, ironically, General Birabeau, recently installed as governor, so Pierre is faced with an impossible situation of divided loyalties. (In the film the general often fingers the hilt of a long sword, the most conspicuous Freudian symbol in the story.) He explains what happened between him and the previous governor, the general:

> He sent *me* out to raid villages. I was very young. I realized how unnecessarily cruel he was. I tried to explain to him. He flew into a raging fury. He cried I was a traitor. Then before I knew what he was doing he struck me full in the face. I fell bleeding from the mouth. Oh, how I longed to strike back. (Harbach 11)

Of course he could not strike back, but he disguised himself as a "stupid timid boy," living amongst the French and fighting against them at the same time, holding on to his leadership of the Riffs by a challenge of single combat. He has been in love with Margot, and now that his father has arrived as governor, he is in a double bind.

The hero is also bound by his philosophy of romantic love, while the woman he loves longs for a real man, one who must "take me, shake me/ Break me, make me," one who can "master me" (Harbach 27, 29). She is also bound to one Captain Paul Fontaine, a sophisticated yet rough, tyrannical sort who fills her image of the hero. Of course, the Red Shadow comes to challenge the captain.

In the stage version and first film version, the French represent Western civilization and the Moroccans represent the wild, the natural, the uncivilized. Margot's fascination with the Red Shadow is the purest example of romantic fascination with the exotic other. What is useful about the early versions of *The Desert Song* is the clarity by which two realms—one civilized, the other wild, one Western, the other "Oriental"—are distinguished. While he is disguised before the French, the Red Shadow embodies—and articulates—the passionate, non-white, active, heroic male.

Even greater than the rivalry of Captain Fontaine, the other problem the Red Shadow/Pierre faces is his father—or, one should say, *the* Father. The humiliating blow he receives at the hand of *Paul's* father, the "butcher" (the blow that transformed the idealist boy into the Red Shadow), is matched by one given by his own father, who is disgusted by Pierre. The old man challenges the Red Shadow to single combat. The hero almost responds instinctively, but he cannot bring himself to fight his father. General Birabeau slaps the Red Shadow across the face, but still the hero cannot bring himself to fight. His father calls him a coward.

By the rules of the tribe he leads, the Red Shadow must give up his sword, the symbol of leadership. He is sent into the punishing desert to die, with nothing but a broken sword. General Birabeau sends Paul into the desert to kill the Red Shadow, though the Red Shadow is alone and unarmed.

Tragedy is averted, as it should be in such a dream tale. Pierre is finally reconciled with his father, and he returns to claim Margot—who finally recognizes that Pierre and the Red Shadow are one. Pierre had

Figure 3.1. *The Desert Song* (1929). General Birabeau grasps his sword while he talks with his daughter, Margot Bonvalet. Unknown to General Birabeau his son, Pierre, is the rebel hero, the Red Shadow, with whom Margot has fallen in love.

Figure 3.2. *The Desert Song* (1929). Pierre, as the Red Shadow, and Margot Bonvalet in a passionate embrace, illustrating "Western Love."

symbolically "killed" the Red Shadow when he returned with the "tro-
phies," the garments and the broken sword. But he is again in his Red
Shadow uniform when the story ends.

Second Phase: Versions of 1943 and 1953

In the 1943 film, the story is set, not in the 1920s, but in 1939, and the
enemy of the Red Shadow—now called "El Khobar"—is a vicious
Sheikh Youssef, who is acting in league with the Nazis to build a rail line
through Morocco. When with the help of El Khobar the Riffs win their
fight against Sheikh Youssef, the audience knows that much more is at
stake. Civilization was again at issue, and El Khobar, an American, was
as necessary to the war effort as his tribal brothers were.

If 1943 turned *The Desert Song* into a heroic apocalypse, the postwar
1950s turned it into an adventure tale of the cold war. On the eve of
Moroccan independence from the French—March 2, 1956, is the official date of Independence, a movement said to have begun in 1943[12]—
the 1953 *Desert Song* is, if anything, more distrustful of the "natives" and
less critical of French overlordship than the 1943 version. The French
are not the enemy. In the 1950s version, the Riffs are not even fighting
the French. Rather, one of their own is cruelly mistreating them.

What is most striking about the 1953 film is the way virtue, com-
passion, and empathy are linked with civil order. The hero is now a
French anthropologist from the University of Paris, who quotes
Flaubert and Moorish poetry. When, as El Khobar, he is forced to fight,
the fighting is against one of the Riffs.

To accomplish this switch, the enemy, Sheikh Youssef, is wealthy
and corrupt. He is aided by a traitor within the ranks of the Riffs, the
cruel Mindar. The hero can, then, be at the same time a remarkably
compassionate anthropologist and a fierce warrior. (At one point he
explains to his buddy, "Naturally when you live among people, Benjy,
you get close to them.") There are many good shots of a nomadic tent
village, with sheep, goats, and authentically dressed natives. The hero
knows the Qur'an, Moorish love chants, and native music. He brings
"civilization" to the people in the form of modern science—that is,
medicine.

The love interests are still central to the 1943 and 1953 versions of
The Desert Song, and the love songs and rousing choral pieces are always

Figure 3.3. *The Desert Song* (1943). Paul Hudson (who plays the hero, El Khobar), with the Oriental woman, as John Walsh, the American newspaperman (the comedian in the film) looks on.

Photograph courtesy of Warner Bros. Archives. © 1943 *Turner Entertainment Co. All Rights Reserved.*

preserved. However, what is, missing in these later versions is precisely what gave the story its scandalous Freudian turn: the father. In 1943, no father appears to darken the scene. In the 1953 version, there is a father, but he is not the hero's father, and so is not a rival. He is still the French general, but he is now *Margot's* father, a poor man badgered by a flighty, impetuous daughter. Of course his role is to protect Margot and keep her until the hero proves his worth.

Orientalism is pervasive in every version of *The Desert Song*, though in different ways. In the 1920s, Morocco and the Moroccans are complete Western stereotypes, mostly anonymous and exotic background figures, although the story is sympathetic to the cause of the Riffian rebellion. In later versions, more care is taken to have authentic sets, to give the locals the right "look," with good scenes of "natives" singing, begging in the bazaars, and wandering about towns and villages. In 1953, when Americans, caught up in the cold war, worried that Moroccan independence would deprive the West of Strategic Air Command bases, there is an even greater attempt to get the right look. The hero, as anthropologist, is caring for "his people" and willing to pacify the region to keep order. The enemy of the Moroccans, in the 1950s version, is within. There is no need to show any of the Western power—let alone colonial rule—guilty of anything greater than naivete. When right prevails in this film, it is enough that Mindar is dead and Sheikh Youssef under the guard of the French general.[13]

Both *In Morocco* and *The Desert Song*—in all versions—agree in one respect: that Western women are in a position superior to their Oriental sisters. As the critique of civilization implicit in the Freudian notion of repression recedes in the later versions of *The Desert Song*, the possibility of a cultural critique of the status of women, never strong, was increasingly lost.

In *The Desert Song* one character can be said to embody Western and modern views of the liberated woman, and one character certainly embodied the Western view of the Oriental woman. Both Margot Bonvalet and Azuri, the half-caste "dancing girl," are, ironically, much alike: independent, energetic, and above all attractive to men. Both have "It." Azuri's most obvious reason for appearing on stage or in the film is that as a dancing girl, she can appear throughout the story in as sexy an outfit as the fashions of the pre-*Penthouse* times permitted. Directions merely call for a "native costume" and then "native dancing-costume," once with "shawl." In 1929 that meant a young woman with a beautiful body in a sexy two-piece "native costume" (halter top and tight cut-offs, elaborate headdress, huge earrings, much jewelry). She carries a knife.

It is clear that she is the other side of Woman, in sharp contrast to Margot. (Mothers and mothering are entirely absent from all versions of the story.) In other words, she is the archetypal Eastern Woman, a combination of the cloistered woman of mystery (the harem woman, removed from men's gaze) and the uninhibited sensual woman who does not belong to the repressed, civilized West. Crafty, conniving, extreme in everything, emotional, dangerous, Azuri is celebrated by men East and West, who sing of her, "soft as a pigeon" but "swift as a tiger" (Harbach 40).

Hers is a great part, full of villainy, fascination, seduction—and virtually every stereotype the West has held about the non-Western, non-Christian, "native" (i.e., primitive) world, a world that is ruled by sexual and aggressive instincts that have not been repressed or sublimated. Eli Sagan, a Freudian who is attempting to rid the Freudian tradition of its antifeminist bias, explains Freud's belief, common enough in the 1920s, that noncivilized people were less inhibited than those in the civilized West. Sagan's task was to discover why Freud so insistently associated civilization with the impossibility of sexual satisfaction, incest, feces, sadism, and ugly (female) genitals, and he concluded:

> In Freud's argument against civilization, his indictment indicates that it:
> (1) Represses incest and sexuality (including masturbation), making sexual fulfillment impossible; (2) represses the instinct of aggression, making conflict inevitable; (3) forces us to control our feces, which we don't wish to do; (4) is helpless in the task of separating sexuality from sadism; (5) seems oblivious to our wishes and insists on imposing its demands on us; and (6) makes us unhappy and neurotic. But are not these things precisely those that, unconsciously and sometimes consciously, we blame our mothers for? The manifest content of the theoretical argument is over civilization; the latent content, the hidden quarrel, concerns the inevitable conflicts involved with nurturing and the women who do it. . . .
> (p. 125) People who are less "civilized" will be, rather, sexually free and unconstrained by what the superego demands of us (the audience).
> (Sagan 125)

Figure 3.4. *The Desert Song* (1943). A happy scene with Margot and the American newspaperman before the treachery of Ali Yusef and Colonel Fontaine, above, left, is exposed.

Photograph courtesy of Warner Bros. Archives.. © 1943 Turner Entertainment Co. All Rights Reserved.

Margot Bonvalet, the French woman, is the constant in all versions of *The Desert Song*. She is the object of desire, the object of the male gaze. If Marlene Dietrich's Amy Jolly in Von Sternberg's *Morocco* has become the most notorious example in film history of what Laura Mulvey claims is "the way the unconscious of patriarchal society has structured film form,"[14] Margot Bonvalet may yet be a more seductive image, precisely because she raises no question in and causes no scandal for the audience. Even in her sexiest outfit, she is not likely to offend anyone in a family audience. Naturally, she reflects the American fashions of the era: the 1920s, the 1940s, the 1950s. There is no attempt to give her a "French" look, and no attempt to make her "sound French," though there are others in the different film versions who are made to sound "foreign" in one way or another.[15]

The early versions of *The Desert Song* include a scene that combines not only the "gaze," but also a complex knot of symbols that only Freud could untie. In the Room of the Silken Divans in the Harem of Ali Ben Ali (act 2, scene 3) the sword, so important in the rivalry between General Birabeau and his son, is carefully positioned to center the masculine/feminine, civilized/primitive, and West/East oppositions that operate through the text.

By this time Margot has pulled a pistol on the Red Shadow (but has been unable to shoot him) and has struck him with a whip after he kisses her. In order to prevent her from marrying his rival, the Red Shadow has abducted her (to end act 1). The Oriental men debate "Eastern and Western" love with the hero, and he has regained control of the Riffs when the scene shifts to Margot in the most intimate of settings, the Room of the Silken Divans, which, the film informs us, is Ali Ben Ali's "idea of Paradise." Freud is not far removed from the scene.

The Red Shadow's mask has made him as mysterious and unknowable as the veiled women that have long haunted Orientalist tales and pictures. This "closed" persona is in the sharpest contrast to the openness of his daylight counterpart, Pierre. Neither persona captures the "real" man, who is clearly split between images of the Eastern/Muslim tribal chieftain, with his primitive willpower and enormous energy, attractive to women because of his daring and presence—and the image of the overly sophisticated and sensitive Western/Christian bookish lover of beauty. The counterpart to this split in the Western man is Margot's inability to choose, finally, between her Western upbringing

Figure 3.5. *The Desert Song* (1953). East and West meet as Margot and Captain Fontaine enjoy the hospitality of the cunning Sheikh Youssef. The three watch as the Oriental woman, Azuri, performs her dance.

Figure 3.6. *The Desert Song* (1953). The anthropologist as hero. The hero, El Khobar, in a Riff tent. When not leading the Riffs against Sheikh Youssef, El Khobar is Professor Paul Bernard, French anthropologist.

(which emphasizes independent judgment as well as a commitment to all of the "right" values) and the irresistible outlaw, who represents everything civilization represses.

No longer protected by General Birabeau and the Westerners he commands, Margot is helpless, and the scene plays on the worst rape fantasies. The sword, a conspicuous prop whenever the Red Shadow appears, becomes the central (Freudian) symbol in this, the most complex episode in the story—the episode closest to the world of dreams.

What makes the scene intriguing—especially in the film version, where close shots pick up certain details that are likely to be missed on stage—is the sword, the symbol that reveals what Margot wants desperately to conceal from herself.

Having left the sword on the bed when he leaves the chamber, and before he returns as Pierre, the Red Shadow leaves Margot to herself. She immediately picks up the sword. When she is with the Red Shadow, she claims to appreciate the very life she had denounced in favor of her romantic adventurism. "The quiet life Pierre has planned for me, that's what I want." She finds "the simple life entrancing gentle and calm and kind." She is chided for having changed her mind, but she defends herself by the age-old "To be changing her mind is a woman's way."

The moment she is alone, however, she reveals a tormented spirit. In a scene that harks back in the Western literary tradition to Virgil's *Aeneid*, Margot, like Dido, takes up the sword of the absent Red Shadow and thinks of violence. "Why can't I take his sword here/ And with one quick dart right through his heart/ Stab him as he mocks me?" (The stage directions make it plain even to the obtuse that "the sword represents the RED SHADOW—the man she loves, but doesn't dare yield to.") In her soliloquy she one moment lunges forward with the sword and at another throws it down. She then kneels by the sword and addresses her song to it. (The 1929 film version is even more explicit, as she picks up the sword, caresses it, addresses it, and then puts it down on the bed gently and picks up a mirror). In both cases she sings: "There is his sabre there/ So like the man/In brilliance shining fair,/ So like the man."[16]

Instead of violence against herself (or against the Red Shadow), then, we find the woman discovering something she had tried to hide from herself. The stage directions have her, appropriately enough, dropping the sword, very reluctantly, onto the bed.

The Red Shadow returns to her as the gentle Pierre, with every expectation that Margot is in love with him. She makes it clear that it is not his "sweet self" she has fallen for, and that "deep down" she finds a "terrible fascination" with the Red Shadow. Pierre objects that the man is a "cut-throat" and a "ruffian." She admits to Pierre that she loves him even so. "Oh, Pierre, sometimes I wish *he* were even more of an outlaw and a ruffian. I wish he wouldn't listen to my lies and my excuses. I wish he would make the decision for me." Margot feels free to say this to Pierre because, of course, she thinks of *him* as a "sister." "To a sister you can say anything." Once she is able to say it, there is no turning back for her.

After talking with Pierre, Margot falls on the bed next to the long sword. The Red Shadow picks it up immediately upon returning to the chamber, and he holds the hilt of it while the two sing *The Desert Song* together. He uses the words she had spoken to Pierre: "I have made your decision for you!" She is "afraid" of him, but her fears dissolve in the duet.

As if this were not enough, the sword also figures in the scene that immediately follows, in the same chamber, when General Birabeau himself enters at just the right moment to "take her home." The general and the Red Shadow face each other, and the play of swords brings each to the verge of death.

If the formula, according to Freud, for the resolution of the Oedipus conflict and the emergence of the superego is the father's threat to castrate the son,[17] the drama has never been so obviously played out—in a way that offers offense to no one.

The fear of castration could not be more clearly (and innocently) displayed. General Birabeau challenges the man who has led the Riffian revolt to single combat with swords. When the father calls the son a coward and strikes him full in the face, the son twice tries to unsheathe, but he cannot do it. He accepts the blow, drops his head, and offers the sword in surrender. Ironically Azuri, in her anger, reveals the secret[18] that will eventually reconcile father and son; the Red Shadow and his daylight persona, Pierre; Margot and the man she was fated to marry.

There is no equivalent of the Room of Silken Divans in later versions; no mention of Freud; no conflict between father and son to mystify a pretty straightforward heroic tale. With the disappearance of the father-general, Freudian ambivalence recedes, and with it Freud's critique of civilization. From a story sympathetic to the Riffian rebellion against the Western overlords, *The Desert Song* revalues "civilization" when, in 1943, it was thought to be threatened by Fascist totalitarianism and, in 1953, by a different form of totalitarianism, Soviet communism. "Civilization" is rewritten as a benign, if paternalistic, regard for culturally different peoples—so long as they are in the firm hand of the West.

The Americanization of *The Desert Song* clearly demonstrates two of the three phases in an increasingly complicated imaging of the East by the West in the twentieth century. From World War I until World War II, the romantic fascination with an exotic, fascinating, but unknowable East (and its attendant celebration of the noble savage) easily coexisted with what Edith Wharton's book on Morocco detailed: an acceptance of the civilizing mission of the West to the primitive East. In America as early as the War of 1812 the admiration of Europe's superior "civilization" was moderated by the desire to see America as different from the Old World, especially British society. The American admiration of its own primitive land and the tough men and women who threw off the chains of an oppressive "civilization" can be seen directly in the early version of *The Desert Song*, where such an admiration was aided by the new Freudian ideas of the unconscious and the repression of instinctive drives necessary to have civilized life.

Just as subsequent versions of *The Desert Song* complicated the early image of the East, American travelers to the East increasingly found more of themselves in the East even as their perceptions became more complex. *The Desert Songs* of the 1940s and 1950s projected new American interests in the East, corresponding to the second, skeptical phase discussed in the Introduction. So far no one has attempted a third-phase *Desert Song*, although the musical has been revived on stage. (In the 1980s, nostalgia for an earlier, simpler America seemed to be the major motivation for yet another revival.)

If successive versions of *The Desert Song* complicated American views of Morocco, the ease with which Edith Wharton accepts the fundamental division between us and them—Western and Oriental, civilized and primitive—is no doubt responsible for the irony of her having accepted the French dominance of Morocco even more fully than the resident general himself had accepted it.

Edith Wharton's confidence in the superiority of civilization gives way, in the second phase, to skepticism and ambivalence. The next chapter considers a very different writer, Jane Bowles, an expatriate American who lived in Morocco and was arguably more "mobile" than Wharton—in the sense that Daniel Lerner uses "psychic mobility" as a measure of modernization. Jane Bowles was unable ever to shake the "high art" and "high society" principles of her contemporaries, although she was well aware of Freudian, surrealist, Marxist and structuralist subversions of those principles. Her writings about Morocco are engaged in the other culture in a way Wharton's travel book never is. Bowles's fascination with the ordinary lives of Moroccan women is deeply ambivalent, especially evident when she identifies herself (through her character, Emmy Moore) as a "semi-Oriental" woman, an image Wharton would not have been able to see in the mirror of the other.

Chapter Four

Jane Bowles and the
Semi-Oriental Woman

In the Introduction mention was made that Jane Auer Bowles (1917–1973) could not "stop looking" at the Arab town outside her hotel window. In July 1948 Jane was in her thirties, and she thought that Tangier provided her for the first time in her life a feeling of great joy "as a result of a purely visual experience" (*Out in the World* 81). She was very much the outsider discovering a new world.

She is still very much the outsider when, three months later (writing from another hotel in Tangier), she explains to Paul that she finds herself

> in a constant state of inferiority vis-à-vis these women. Of course they live in wonderful long high rooms (the kind I used to hate and now love). Their beds are massive and covered with printed spreads (very Matisse) and white couches line the blue walls. They have hundreds of white frilly cushions too and they put very beautiful seashells into the water pitchers. The room we sit in when I visit Tetum is always the color of early evening because of the blue walls. I know only that room actually but I imagine it rightly as many rooms—there must be hundreds like it. . . . It is a result of the repetitive note in the Arab life here. (108)

She worries about losing "face," inviting women to their "house in its present condition." (This was actually written before she found a house to rent in the Arab quarter.) The marks of the outsider are everywhere evident in these letters: the inability to speak the language, worry about losing face, a sense of inferiority before the poor women of Tangier. The difficulty she has in placing herself finds expression in the joy of seeing things, in describing the town and the very un-Western rooms she has entered. She cannot "stop looking" and is at the same time profoundly disoriented.

The fragmentation and repetition Millicent Dillon has found in Jane Bowles's fiction, the sudden shifts of plot, the unstable rhythms and uncertain authorial voices that mark her work ("Experiment as Character" 13–14) are also evidence of an even greater disorientation. Like Dillon I do not see these as Bowles herself seemed to consider them, signs of failure. Rather, that "oddity" Bowles accused herself of produced a most compelling experimental fiction. Three of her stories reflect Jane Bowles's experience in the East, in Morocco, by focusing on the cultural construction of gender and sexual relations evident especially in spatial imagery. Those spatial orientations indicate a wide gap between the sense of space and gender in Moroccan and in American cultures.

It is important that Jane Bowles found herself disoriented in another, Eastern culture. That she found herself odd anywhere made it possible to see more than other Western writers have—she could not stop looking, as mentioned above—in the East. In the three stories considered here, "Everything Is Nice," "The Iron Table," and "Emmy Moore's Journal," cultural constructs of gender and sexual relations are deconstructed. Things most obvious and taken for granted turn odd in these stories. That most conspicuous sign of Western presence, the hotel, where an American woman could take a room by herself, if need be, is evident in all three stories, for example.

The hotel, as an image, is the very sign of alienation, since it is by definition not "home." In the first of the stories to be considered, "Everything Is Nice," an American woman is first alone (her husband is away, in the desert), looking out over a Moroccan scene. When she is introduced to a group of Moroccan women, she makes an awkward excuse about the people like her who await her return to the hotel. In the second, "The Iron Table," a woman and her husband talk across a table set outside the hotel in which they are staying. The flimsiest of barriers, a string, separates them from the people who live in the Eastern town. Finally, in "Emmy Moore's Journal," we see the woman alone, in a hotel room. The man (and everything else that might constitute a family and a home) are far away. Only in that story is the hotel described, but its presence as an alienated—and a Western—place is always close to the displaced individual woman at the center of the story.

Linguists such as Edward Hall have tried to characterize social and personal space. Often Hall uses cross-cultural examples to bring the topic into view. Since the Arab-Muslim world presents such a contrast to America in the way people behave in public, in their concepts of privacy, in their perceptions of personal distance and boundaries, in matters of "face" and in involvement with others, Hall devotes a chapter (12) in *The Hidden Dimension* to the Arab world. In *Beyond Culture* he elaborates a general contrast between two kinds of culture, monochronic (characteristic of American society, and related to a certain use of space) and polychronic (whose best representatives he finds in the Middle East and North Africa (18–24). Elsewhere he calls these "low context" and "high context" societies.

Jennifer Coates uses the notion of 'social networks' in a similar way to differentiate male and female language. Where she finds closed networks, with high density and multiplex relations—where, as in British working-class communities, men relate to one another as relatives, neighbors, workmates, and friends—Coates finds a certain kind of (nonstandard) language used as a sign of communal identity. In contrast, where the network is open, low density, and uniplex—where, for example, women are linked in only one way (78–91), Coates notices a very different use of language, tending toward standard usage. William Labov introduced the concept of 'lame' to indicate "isolated individuals on the fringes of vernacular culture." Coates asks if women, then, are lames. In the studies she reported on, Coates noted "that female speakers are less closely integrated into vernacular culture, that female speakers use vernacular norms less consistently than male speakers, and that these two findings are interrelated" (93). (The feature may be related, in the case of Jane Bowles, to her odd, idiosyncratic language, doubly removed from the vernacular norms of male, buddy speech, which would have been seen as low and common, and from Standard English, the mark of educated and socially "better" speakers in the United States of her time.)

Drawing on the work of Hall, Labov, and Coates, Deborah Tannen suggests that women in American society tend to use "rapport-talk" while men typically use "report-talk" (76–77). In some ways these correspond to private speaking and public speaking, and the division accounts, Tannen thinks, for the way women fall silent in public gatherings when both men and women are present. What is somewhat less evident in her recent *You Just Don't Understand* is the use she makes of conversational styles. The "high-involvement" style she notices among eastern Europeans, Italians, some Jewish groups, Africans, and Arabs contrasts sharply with mainstream Anglo "low-involvement" style (207–9).

The advantage here is that even when these sociolinguists cross cultures, they usually begin with an analysis of linguistic performance by white, middle-class, Anglo-American speakers. Hall, for example, makes explicit comparison with non-Indo-European speakers, while Labov examines the speech of minorities in the United States. The contrasts they note are useful in pursuing conversational styles, self-other relationships, and the handling of space as these are represented in Jane Bowles's fiction. Translated into the conceptual framework of the sociolinguists, Jane Bowles's encounter with the cultural other, Arab-Muslim "Orientals," highlights differences: her heterosocial, low-involvement, uniplex/low-density/open Anglo-American social networks with their characteristic monochronic, low-context speakers against the "Oriental" homosocial, high-involvement, multiplex/high-density/closed social networks, characteristically polychronic and high-context. In "Everything Is Nice," an American woman in a strange and fascinating locale is introduced to other women. In "The Iron Table," an American woman speaks with her husband about the East and West, about modern and primitive peoples, about alienation—the conversation is a contest between the two of them. "Emmy Moore's Journal" makes explicit the strange fascination and dread of the cultural other when the middle-aged American writer names herself a "semi-Oriental" woman.

The disorientation that marks the protagonist in these three stories has a historical character to it as well. As Emmy Moore's wandering analysis of the self in relation to a scheme of geocultural types shows, Jane Bowles was aware of what is now called "Orientalism." For the

West as a historical construct, the East provided *the* significant other. It may have been partly by accident that Jane Bowles landed in Tangier, the gateway to the East. (Until air travel changed access to places around the globe, the powerful of Europe and America made their first contacts with the East through Morocco, though the land is, technically, west of every country in Europe except Ireland.) When Bowles arrived, though, she already possessed a cultural map that was centuries old.

It is important to note that in this also Jane Bowles was odd. In the three areas of conversational style, relations to others, and sense of space she was anything but representative of mainstream American society. The stories are eccentric in that the reader is constantly disoriented, like Jane Bowles herself rarely at home.

This is not to say that Jane Bowles would have liked the analytical tools I am bringing to her stories. It is only the fascination with and dread of being away from home that the linguistic and anthropological tools help the reader to see.

Jane Bowles arrived in Morocco after World War II, in 1948, and lived there, with extended leaves in Paris, New York, Ceylon, and Spain, until just before her death in 1973. Much of the time there she lived in hotels, although she and husband Paul Bowles owned a house in Tangier. Her biographer, Millicent Dillon, records a comment made in the mid-1960s about her life there.

> It was only after the end of World War II that I came to Morocco. Paul had come ahead of me and bought a house in Tangier. From the first day, Morocco seemed more dreamlike than real. I felt cut off from what I knew. In the twenty years that I have lived here I have written only two short stories, and nothing else. It's good for Paul, but not for me.[1]

It is not entirely clear which two short stories she is recalling. Dating Jane Bowles's short stories is tricky. She *published* two stories during the time she lived in Morocco. Her notebooks included stories written in the late 1940s and early 1950s, some of which were planned as parts of a novel, *Out in the World*. The novel was never completed, and the stories were published separately in her collected works, *My Sister's Hand in Mine* (1978).

The time was, without question, spent more productively by Paul Bowles, whose novels, essays, and short stories about North Africa continue into the late 1980s, than by his wife. Three pieces she wrote between 1948 and 1951 dealing with Morocco are unusual in many respects, not the least of which is a remarkable handling of cultural differences. The three stories are those discussed here: "Everything Is Nice," "The Iron Table," and "Emmy Moore's Journal."

"EVERYTHING IS NICE"

Edward Hall coined the term *proxemics* in his investigation of what readers of modern, Western "realistic" fiction have long come to appreciate: the human use of space as a specialized elaboration of culture. According to Hall, the human sense of space is intimately related to a "sense of self, which is in an intimate transaction" with the environment. Humans "can be viewed as having visual, kinesthetic, tactile, and thermal aspects of [the] self which may be either inhibited or encouraged to develop by [the] environment" (*The Hidden Dimension* 1). Storytelling that takes into account the kinesthetic, tactile, and even themal aspects of proxemics—in addition to the visual, which is markedly a characteristic of Western "modernity"[2]—can present the problematics of a self in a time when the existence of a stable self is called into question. Sometimes proxemics moves to the foreground of a story and reveals very different cultural constructs of the self.

"Everything Is Nice" is peculiar in two ways. Jane Bowles wrote it, first of all, as a nonfiction essay, and it appeared as "East Side: North Africa," in 1951. Later Paul Bowles transposed it to fiction, mainly by changing a first-person narrator to third-person narration and by removing certain comments about women and society.[3]

Not much appears to happen. Jeanie, a Western woman—a "Nazarene," the catch-all Moroccan term for Western foreigners, as if they were all Christian—in an otherwise unidentified "blue Moslem town" meets a "Moslem woman." The woman who identifies herself as Zodelia takes the Westerner through a narrow alley and into a dark house, where a number of women are gathered with their babies. They talk. An old woman named Tetum puts questions to the Western woman in a brusque manner. Jeanie is offered tea and cakes (which she has purchased herself along the way), but refuses, giving the preposterous excuse that the other Nazarenes at her hotel will be angry if she is late for an appointment there. "They will hit me!" she cries, trying to look "wild and frightened"[4] The ploy does not work, and she is offered food again. She backs out of the room, but not before Zodelia has made her promise that she will return at four o'clock the next day. Jeanie returns to the spot where the story opened.

The short story ends with the effect of the encounter on Jeanie:

> When she reached the place where she had met Zodelia she went over to the wall and leaned on it. Although the sun had sunk behind the houses, the sky was still luminous and the blue of the wall had deepened. She rubbed her fingers along it: the wash was fresh and a little of the powdery stuff came off. And she remembered how once she had reached out to touch the face of a clown because it had awakened some longing. It had happened at a little circus, but not when she was a child. (320)

Millicent Dillon has called attention to the way the original essay ended, with Jane Bowles writing directly to the reader.

> When I reached the place where I had met Zodelia I went over to the wall and leaned on it. Although the sun had sunk behind the houses in back of me, the sky was still luminous and the color of the blue wall had deepened. I rubbed my fingers along it; the wash was fresh and a little of the powdery stuff came off; but no matter how often I walked through these streets reaching out to touch the chalky blue wash on the houses . . . on the walls, I could never satisfy my longing for the town.
>
> I remember that once I reached out to touch the beautiful and powdery face of a clown because his face had awakened some longing; it happened at a little circus but not when I was a child. (Dillon, *Original Sin* 210–11)

Besides the change from "I" to "she," the wording has been changed slightly, mainly for the sake of economy: the sun "behind the houses in back of me" is reduced to "behind the houses"; and "the color of the blue wall had deepened" is shortened to "the blue of the wall had deepened"; "the beautiful and powdery face of a clown" becomes simply "the face of a clown." The changes shift emphasis from the way the woman is situated in reference to the sun; from the blue of the wall, perhaps; from the "powdery" face of the clown, which is both "beautiful" and somehow explicitly like the powder on the walls of the town.

More significant is the decision to drop the comment about the woman's walking often through the streets and her inability to satisfy her "longing for the town." Instead of "longing" then echoing this "longing for the town," the "some longing" at the end stands alone in the revision. Everywhere the changes make for a neater, tighter presentation. The appearance of the strange clown and the little circus, "but not when she was a child" remains as striking as before. What is lost in the transformation is a certain rootedness to place, to the longing for "the town" and not just what would appear as a personal reminiscence. Dillon calls the original ending "one of Jane's most moving closures of her own puzzlement at what the town—the medina of Tangier—and its women actually meant to her" (210).

That the unnamed "blue Moslem town" is Tangier, as Dillon suspects, is shown by the details early in the story. The scene opens on the highest street of the town, with a thick wall at the edge of a steep cliff. The Western woman looks down over the wall at the skinny boys, a dog, a woman washing her legs all far below where the sea meets "flat dirty rocks" while the tide is out. The streets of the town lead down steeply to the place where Zodelia takes the woman. The houses of the medina—the Moroccan native quarter—in the crooked streets are "so close that she could smell the dampness of the walls and feel it on her cheeks like a thicker air" (320). The scene is quite like the area in which Jane Bowles chose to live in Tangier.

The story is about spatial boundaries. It is true that Bowles (or, properly, the Bowleses) preserved in the fictional account names of people Jane knew in Tangier. Jeanie is a thinly enough disguised "Janie" Bowles. Zodelia knows who the Nazarene is because Jeanie is "Betsoul's friend" (314). (Betsoul herself does not figure in the story.) The old woman in the house is named Tetum, and she is described in a peculiar way: "Only a few feet away, in the middle of the carpet, sat an old lady in a dress made of green and purple curtain fabric. Through the many rents in the material she could see the printed cotton dress and the tan sweater underneath" (317). The old woman, in the middle of the carpet (in the deep interior of the house) has "tiny blue crosses" tattooed on her "bony cheeks," and her knuckles are tattooed with the same design.[5] Jane wrote about Tetum to Paul (165) as the "yellow ugly one (!?)" (163), elsewhere as "the Mountain Dyke."[6] In other words, the fictional version retains the real names of Moroccan women, but disguises, if only barely, the protagonist's name.

Moroccan sociologist Fatima Mernissi devoted a chapter in the important *Beyond the Veil: Male-Female Dynamics in Modern Muslim Society* to "The Meaning of Spatial Boundaries" (137–48). Traditionally, the seclusion of women basic to the social system of Morocco, as in other Arab-Muslim societies, meant that women using public spaces were highly restricted: "Traditionally, only necessity could justify a woman's presence outside the home, and no respect was ever attached to poverty and necessity. Respectable women were not seen on the street. . . . Only prostitutes and insane women wandered freely in the streets" (143). From Edward Hall, Mernissi noted two tendencies in her own culture. On the one hand, "it is not possible for an individual to claim a private zone in a public space." On the other hand, "space has a primarily social rather than physical quality" (143). Trespassing, for example, would mean something different in Morocco than it would in, say, the United States. "A friend, for example, never trespasses, while a foe always does," according to Mernissi.

Mernissi has attempted to explain a phenomenon observed by many people inside and outside Arab-Muslim society (among the latter, Jane Bowles) that the spatial boundaries reflect a deep division between men and women in that society.

> A society that opts for sexual segregation, and therefore for impoverishment of heterosexual relations, is a society that fosters "homosocial" relations on the one hand and seduction as a means of communication on the other. Seduction is a conflict strategy, a way of seeming to give of yourself and of procuring great pleasure without actually giving anything. It is the art of abstaining from everything while playing on the promise of giving. (140)

"Everything Is Nice" is about the handling of space in a setting that pits two different kinds of societies against each other. The Moroccan women in the story constitute a homosocial group, and Jane Bowles is carefully attentive to the nuances of cross-cultural misunderstanding. Alice B. Toklas was no admirer of Jane, but she made the shrewd observation that "Jane is strange as an American but not as an Oriental. . . . If accepting this makes her more foreign it at least relieves the strain—that morbidity—she originally seemed at first to be consumed by" (Dillon, *Original Sin* 211).

The great wall along the highest street of the "blue Moslem town," where Jeanie walks freely, alone, is a protective wall, but it cuts the wanderer off from the scene below even as it allows her to see it. The rocks, the dog slipping into the sea, the skinny boys, the woman washing her legs—the people in immediate, if dangerous, contact with the natural world—are observed with a clarity that dissipates once Jeanie crosses over into the life world of Moroccan women. The crossing-over is most obvious when she is taken through a narrow alley and a door is opened to her and Zodelia, a door marked by a "heavy brass knocker in the form of a fist" (316). In the presence of the women sitting in a dark room Jeanie is an intruder, and the conflict in the story rests entirely on the cultural distance between her and the women. The visit to the women's home is framed by Jeanie alone on the high street.

However, he conflict is already a matter of struggling for space and power. Jeanie is drawn into the women's world by Zodelia. The Moslem woman leads her, and Jeanie seems almost helpless to resist. Hall first noticed the conflict between Americans' and Arabs' sense of privacy when, in a hotel in Washington, a man violated "the small sphere of privacy" which balloons around an American in a public place.

> As I waited in the deserted lobby, a stranger walked up to where I was sitting and stood close enough so that not only could I easily touch him but I could even hear him breathing. In addition, the dark mass of his body filled the peripheral field of vision on my left side. If the lobby had been crowded with people, I would have understood his behavior, but in an empty lobby his presence made me exceedingly uncomfortable.[7]

The fellow seemed to want to drive Hall out of his position. An Arab colleague thought Hall's response puzzling. "After all, it's a public space, isn't it?" Hall found that "in Arab thought I had no rights whatsoever by virtue of occupying a given spot; neither my place nor my body was inviolate. For the Arab, there is no such thing as an intrusion in public. Public means public" (156).

While the anthropologist attempts to explain the proxemic phenomenon, the writer of fiction displays it. Tangier was an "international city," really a border town, a refuge for tax dodgers during the years Paul and Jane Bowles were living there (Landau 174–83) which made it a particularly good showplace for the stresses Mernissi found in modernizing Arab-Muslim society, since it preserved a large Moroccan population in a very heterogeneous European community. The women in Jane Bowles's story have only been superficially changed by Westerners in their midst, while many other Moroccans were struggling to become Westernized.

Into the scene with Jeanie on the highest street of the town comes one of the Muslim women who have maintained their traditional ways. The woman stands next to Jeanie, "grazing her hip with the basket she was carrying." Jeanie pretends "not to notice her" and gazes intently, instead, on the scene far below them. "Then the woman jabbed the basket firmly into her ribs," and Jeanie is forced to notice her (313).

It is Zodelia, then, who pushes herself onto Jeanie; Zodelia who introduces herself (and explains who Jeanie is: "Your name is Jeanie and you live in a hotel with other Nazarenes."); Zodelia who asks immediately what Jeanie pays for her hotel room, breaking an American taboo; Zodelia who, unasked, puts on a skit mimicking the people at the hotel; Zodelia who invites Jeanie to attend a wedding, but takes her instead to a shop, where Jeanie buys sweets, and to the house, where Jeanie has the encounter with old Tetum. Indeed, so much is Jeanie drawn along by Zodelia, who pries into matters that Americans are trained to think strictly private, that the American woman has only one free act of will. When the women offer her tea and the cakes she has just bought, Jeanie refuses.

"Eat!" the women called out from their mattress. "Eat the cakes."

The child pushed the glass dish forward.

"The dinner at the hotel is ready," she said, standing up.

"Drink tea," said the old woman scornfully. "Later you will sit with the other Nazarenes and eat their food."

"The Nazarenes will be angry if I'm late." She realized that she was lying stupidly, but she could not stop.

"They will hit me!" She tried to look wild and frightened.

"Drink tea. They will not hit you," the old woman told her. (319)

In this test of wills, Jeanie holds out, although she ends up backing out of the room.

The story is filled with puzzling and odd details that are never clarified. Zodelia carries a basket with a "large dead porcupine" in it with "a pair of new yellow socks folded on top of it" (311). Talk of this porcupine leads the two around. At one point the porcupine seems to be on its way to Zodelia's aunt. But when Jeanie asks about it later, Zodelia tells her, "The porcupine sits here . . . in my own house" (319).

More obviously of cultural importance is the talk about family. Old Tetum wants to know where Jeanie's husband is. Zodelia adds to Jeanie's answer—that her husband is "traveling in the desert"—an explanation that, though false, seems reasonable enough to the group: Jeanie's husband is "selling things." More puzzling to the group is the absence of Jeanie's mother.

"Where is your mother?" the old lady asked.

"My mother is in our country in her own house."

"Why don't you go and sit with your mother in her own house?" she scolded.

"The hotel costs a lot of money." (318)

Whatever this may have meant for Jane Bowles and the relationship she had with her own mother, the dialogue points out one of the major differences between traditional Arab-Muslim society and modern American society. That a woman would be on her own—would *want* to be on her own—when she has a mother in whose home she could be "sitting" is incomprehensible, as a number of Western writers have observed.[8]

There is no ban on Muslims associating with or eating with "Nazarenes," but it is considered a privilege for an outsider to be treated the way Jeanie is treated by the women. The very familiarity the women seem to demand of her and the very direct way they talk to her indicate her acceptance. Hospitality, that ancient and fundamental principle of Arab-Muslim society, is offered her (even though she is offered the cakes "dusty and coated with a thin, ugly-colored icing" [316], she herself had bought). When Jeanie refuses to eat with them, she violates, it appears unwittingly, their hospitality.

Still, the women urge her to return to the room, and Zodelia extracts a promise from Jeanie to return the next day. Jeanie may be led around easily, but she learns quickly. At the door of the house, "opened . . . just enough to let her through" (320), Jeanie tries waffling about her return to the place. The two women change roles momentarily. Jeanie speaks in the language of the Arab-Muslim world. "I shall see you tomorrow, if Allah wills it" (a translation of *ghedda, enshallah*, where "tomorrow" has much the same force as Spanish *manana*, and the pious submission to Allah's will is another way to get out of a promise without appearing to offend). Zodelia is not fooled. She demands an answer in "American time" (or what Hall elsewhere calls "M-time" or "mono-chronic time"), a precise four o'clock, rather than in P-time or poly-chronic time.[9]

As Jeanie is leaving Zodelia's house, Zodelia presses two of the cakes into Jeanie's hand and tells her, "graciously," to eat them "at the hotel with the other Nazarenes" (320). Jeanie returns through the nar-row alley to the place where she met Zodelia. The walls, at first a barrier between Jeanie and the people below, now are seen—or rather felt (with more immediacy, though with less clarity than sight)—from within, and the blue wash of the wall becomes the major symbol of Jeanie's encounter with the cultural other.

The reader is led back by images that connect the powdery blue on the wall to Jeanie's attempt to touch the powdery face of the clown: to images of masks and costumes. Before her name is revealed to Jeanie, Zodelia is a woman "dressed in a haik" (an all-enveloping length of material worn in public), her "white cloth covering the lower half of her face" loose (313–14); her "henna-stained finger" indicates that she has decorated her hands. The woman on the rocks far below them has taken off her haik in order to wash in the sea water.

Tetum reveals layers of garments and is decorated with tiny blue crosses. Zodelia reappears inside the house without her haik—in a "black crepe European dress" that hung down to her ankles. Access to the house, down the steep street, in a narrow alley—far from public gaze—is guarded. A child opens the door and "quickly hid behind it, covering her face" (316). When she leaves, Zodelia opens the door "just enough to let her through" (320).

In contrast to the sunlight on the high street, there is little light inside the house. "Because her eyes had not grown used to the dimness, she had the impression of a figure disappearing down a long corridor. Then she began to see the brass bars of a bed, glowing weakly in the darkness" (316). It is difficult to know these women—difficult to see them—sitting in the darkness, decorated, wearing one garment in pub-lic, another in the privacy of the home. The expression Bowles uses to capture the Moghrebi Arabic, the local dialect, used by the women reinforces this contrast between inside and outside. "Why don't you go and sit with your mother in her own house?" Jeanie is asked. In a society where, on the one hand, interaction with strangers is restricted and where, on the other hand, "sitting" is not disvalued, as it is in the American work ethic, sitting with her mother in her mother's house is the mark of ordered social life.

The American, alone, on the public street or with the "other Nazarenes" (neither kin nor designated as friends) in the hotel becomes, as the story progresses, as odd a figure as the Moroccan women in their private dwelling. Jeanie has more than a little difficulty penetrating their masks. The ending of the story indicates, though, that something deeply moving has occurred in the encounter with the women. The wall between the two cultures is never removed, but Jeanie feels an intimacy, a longing, in touching the wall with its powdery blue decoration.

The language Bowles gives to the Moroccan women reinforces the bind, and Zodelia's "skit"—playful, a play, a representation—gives the best account of it. The skit is successful, "since all the people of the town spoke and gesticulated as though they had studied at the *Comedie Francaise*" (314). As she plays the people in the hotel, though, Zodelia betrays a cultural style very different than Jeanie's. Known as the "wawa" style (after the Arabic *wa* or "and" coordinator used to string phrases and clauses together like beads on a necklace), the style is a marked characteristic of traditional Arabic writing and, as Zodelia's speech shows, ordinary speech.[10] It contrasts sharply with the tendency in Western writings—fiction as well as nonfiction prose—to use subordination and, through it, a hierarchical organization of thought. Zodelia mimics the people at the hotel:

"Good-bye, Jeanie, good-bye. Where are you going?"

"I am going to a Moslem home to visit my Moslem friends, Betsoul and her family. I will sit in a Moslem room and eat Moslem food and sleep on a Moslem bed."

"Jeanie, Jeanie, when will you come back to us in the hotel and sleep in your own room?"

"I will come back to you in three days. I will come back and sit in a Nazarene room and eat Nazarene food and sleep on a Nazarene bed. I will spend half the week with Moslem friends and half with Nazarenes." (314)

Conversation between Jeanie and the Moroccan women quickly becomes futile. Misunderstandings abound, partly because of a language barrier, and partly because certain features of one culture are not understood in the other. Why the porcupine? Is it large or small? Why does Jeanie, when asked about her mother, avoid the question and talk instead about the many automobiles and trucks in the city where she was born? Tetum in particular cannot understand why Jeanie would want to spend half her time with Moslem friends and the other half with Nazarenes. In many cases the exchanges end with an exhaustion of language, with the women using that most empty of American words, "nice."

While the "nice" of the title is, in one sense, a translation of the ubiquitous *mlih* of Moroccan Arabic, Bowles's use of the term betrays the characters' inability to make the kind of subtle distinctions that come from genuine familiarity. Zodelia asks Jeanie if the Spanish cakes are "nice" or "not nice" (316). Jeanie thinks them disgusting, but buys a dozen of them. "They are very nice," Jeanie replies. Later Zodelia asks twice if the "dimly lit room" Jeanie is taken to is "nice." Jeanie does not respond to either question (317). When the women hear that Jeanie spends half her time with Muslims, half with Nazarenes, the women— except for Tetum—say, "That's nice." Trucks are also nice, even "very nice" (318).

By the time the conversation has degenerated to an exchange about trucks, Jeanie seems "lost in meditation" for a moment but then announces, "with a look of triumph," "Everything is nice." The women around her agree, "Everything is nice" (318).

What follows is the offer of food and drink and Jeanie's awkward refusal of the women's hospitality. She does not want to eat the cakes.[11] It is at this moment that Jeanie wants "to go home" (319). The expression marks the rift between the women and the two cultures. Significantly, the term *home* is avoided by the Moroccans when they talk of what Americans mean by the term. Bowles has them using the word *house* instead.[12] Both Jeanie and Tetum speak of Jeanie's mother "in her own house" (318). Zodelia says her aunt is "in her own house" (319), and, more revealing, tells Jeanie, "The porcupine sits here . . . in my own house" (319).

Jeanie, like the expatriate Jane Bowles, who lived much of her life in hotels,[13] wants to go home, but the rhetoric of the story denies her any such place. The displacement of Jeanie is most evident in the split between the public space of the high street, where she is free to look at the scene around her and live in the private bubble Americans create around themselves, and the hotel, where she lives with the other

Nazarenes. Neither place is a home in the sense Americans use the term. Ironically, the Moroccan women live privately in the home the story calls a "house." The self is almost entirely hidden from public view behind haiks, veils, hennaed hands, walls, and doors and is disclosed, if only dimly at first, in a windowless room with women "sitting" together on mattresses, children and babies around them. The final passage of the story, with Jeanie rubbing her fingers along the blue of the wall and awakening some kind of fantasy about the face of a clown in a "little circus," marks the intimacy of barriers.

"THE IRON TABLE"

"The Iron Table," written in 1950, at the same time Bowles had been working on "Everything Is Nice," is a very different kind of story, a brief exchange between a wife and husband, both unnamed.[14] The story contains a very brief setting, a very restrained but intense argument between the two people, and a tiny summary. "The Iron Table" is, in fact, a fragment from Jane Bowles's notebooks that was prepared for publication by Paul Bowles. As with "Everything Is Nice," the two versions differ in a number of subtle ways. The differences between the notebooks and the published story bring the major themes of the work into high relief.

It is a story about moving and not moving. In sharp contrast with "Everything Is Nice," where moving about, walking up and down, even walking backwards, as opposed to sitting at the center, "The Iron Table" includes no movement at all. The unidentified couple sit at a table that has been dragged out for their use.

> They sat in the sun, looking out over a big new boulevard.
> The waiter had dragged an old iron table around from the other side of the hotel and set it down on the cement near a half-empty flower bed. A string stretched between stakes separated the hotel grounds from the sidewalk. Few of the guests staying at the hotel sat in the sun. The town was not a tourist center, and not many Anglo-Saxons came. Most of the guests were Spanish. (465)

The scene immediately suggests torpor and separation. The "old iron" table has been "dragged around." It has been set down in a bleak scene, on cement "near a half-empty flower bed." The string marks off the public domain from one less public but hardly private or personal. The two are odd ones in the town, which receives few of their sort: Anglo-Saxons in a world inhabited mainly by Spanish.

The reader discovers, in small hints, that these are Americans not in Spain but in a Moroccan town from which they are doubly estranged. Millicent Dillon provides a context for the scene (from the notebooks), but the context is never explained in the published piece: a Mr. Copperfield and his wife have been prevented from continuing on a journey that will take them into the desert because of a washout in the mountains. The husband is angry. The trip will cost them more than they had expected; and the villagers are wearing, not traditional garb but a "jumble of Oriental and Western costume" (256).

The ostensible subject of their discussion is the decline of Western civilization and the way in which the West is corrupting North Africa, a favorite topic of Paul Bowles.[15] (In one of his works Paul Bowles cites Claude Levi-Strauss's remark that "what travel discloses to us first of all is our own garbage, flung in the face of humanity," and adds his own, in a collection of essays, "My own belief is that the people of the alien cultures are being ravaged not so much by the by-products of our civilization, as by the irrational longing on the part of members of their own educated minorities to cease being themselves and become Westerners.") What makes "The Iron Table" such an intense piece is that the ostensible subject is not just annulled by a different subtext. There is a subtext—the relationship between the woman and the man—but it stands in a particular tension with the topic they discuss: East/West is to wife/husband as inside/outside is to woman/man.

There is no stable center. An image of loss repeats itself in the short piece. Talk itself is difficult, strained, clipped, elliptical, and the piece ends with the woman's fear of silence:

> She was as bitter as he about the changes, but she felt it would be indelicate for them both to reflect the same sorrow. It would happen some day, surely. A serious grief would silence their argument. They would share it and not be able to look into each other's eyes. But as long as she could she would hold off that moment. (467)

In the time taken up by their conversation, they tear at each other and maintain a kind of relationship. His weapon is anger, hers sorrow. She takes a "sorrowful" tone when she acknowledges to him that "the whole civilization is going to pieces." Her tone is "sepulchral" when she adds that it is going to pieces "so quickly, too." For some reason, the two versions differ when they begin to talk about the desert. For him, the desert is an escape from the disintegrating civilization, a place "where the culture has remained untouched" (466). She wants nothing of it—at least while she is sober. "He was punishing her for her swift agreement with him a moment earlier" (466). Her response is captured in a powerful image.

"Although the sun was beating down on her chest, making it feel on fire, deep inside she could still feel the cold current that seemed to run near the heart" (466). When she says she wants to know if he would really be happy in an oasis—and she thinks perhaps she could be happy for his sake—the conversation breaks down. To speak would invite a tenderhearted sentiment. "The moment when they might have felt tenderness had passed, and secretly they both rejoiced" (467).

He wants desperately to escape, to keep moving. She wants to stop the "ceaseless whining over the piecemeal disintegration of Moslem culture" (Dillon, *Original Sin* 256), as Jane Bowles's notebooks have it, making the ambivalence over civilization all the more explicit. "I'm tired of hearing the word 'civilization.' It has no meaning or I've forgotten what is meant anyway."

The story is seen from the woman's point of view. It may well reflect a long-standing argument between Jane and Paul Bowles. (Dillon thinks it is "the most directly autobiographical rendering of a conversation between herself and Paul that she was ever to write" [256]). Still, it remains a piece about the way things hang together—civilization, a marriage, the cultural construction of gender—and the way they are tested. She gives him the last word.

"I think it's uninteresting. To sit and watch costumes disappear, one by one. It's uninteresting even to mention it."

"They are not costumes," he said distinctly. "They're simply the clothes people wear." (467)

At this she keeps silent, not to indicate that she has been defeated, but to keep the awful game of language alive. In fact, at this moment she agrees with him. She would "hold off that moment" when it must happen that "a serious grief would silence," not one or the other, but "their argument."

Robert Lougy makes the following comment about the way Jane Bowles uses language in her fiction.

Bowles' language, like her world, consists of hard, impenetrable surfaces. Words are flat, disconnected. Trapped within a self that is isolated, apart, and frightened, Bowles' characters try to talk through those barriers that imprison them, only to be reminded by language itself of their separateness. Because her characters are entrapped by a language which is in itself entrapped by its literal and inherited meaning, monologues abound in Bowles' art, but monologues of persons whose solipsism is revealed by a torrent of words that serves only to bury them deeper within their own isolation. (166)

In "The Iron Table," the dialogue reveals, as Dillon puts it, "a searching for what went on between herself and Paul in the spaces between the words" (256). But the agreement about the two cultures, where the woman and the man are closest, cannot be spoken.

"EMMY MOORE'S JOURNAL"

One of the most telling blows in "The Iron Table" is the moment when the woman talks about her "friends": "My friends and I don't feel there's any *way* of escaping [Western civilization]. It's not interesting to sit around talking about industrialization" (467). His retort is to attack, "What friends?" She is forced to think that she has not seen "most of them" in many years, and she "turned on him with a certain violence." Friendship is a code word in "Everything Is Nice" and in "The Iron Table" as well. She adds the comment, preserved in both versions of "The Iron Table," that "He liked her to feel isolated."

The isolation of the woman is most painfully revealed in "Emmy Moore's Journal." Unlike "Everything Is Nice" (set in Morocco and introducing Moroccan characters), and unlike "The Iron Table" (set in Morocco but with no Moroccan characters), "Emmy Moore's Journal" is basically a monologue that is neither set in the East nor concerned with any individuals in the East. But the conflict between East and West figures centrally in this story as well.

"Emmy Moore's Journal" is another fragment, written in 1949 and 1950, a piece that was to be part of a novel called *Out in the World*.[16] Still, like "An Iron Table," the piece possesses a unity that does not depend on a larger context. Emmy Moore constructs a crude theory of cultural types and tries to situate herself in it. Since the types are "American," "Turkish," and "Oriental," the story has a bearing on Jane Bowles's image of Moroccan women—and of herself. In the work she names the "semi-Oriental" woman, located between the extremes of America and the Far East.

In the self-conscious authorship (a journal intended to be published), and in the shifting point of view (from first person to second person to third person), "Emmy Moore's Journal" takes a turn that today would be considered postmodern.

Emmy, 47 and fat, is alone in a place, the Hotel Henry, that is the very figure of isolation. To talk of the place requires a change in point of view. Emmy opens her journal in the first person; includes a letter she has written to her husband (second person); and disappears into a third-person limited narration at the end—when the place is briefly described. The place is an overheated room, with a wicker chair and a bottle of whiskey (449).

In "Everything Is Nice," the hotel where the Nazarenes spend their time is referred to but is not described. In "The Iron Table," the woman is with her husband at the boundary of the hotel and the public space around it. In "Emmy Moore's Journal" the woman is alone, and the description of her room in the Hotel Henry brings the story to its despairing close:

> She could not stand the overheated room a second longer.
>
> With some difficulty she raised the window, and the cold wind blew in. Some loose sheets of paper went skimming off the top of the desk and flattened themselves against the bookcase. She shut the window and they fell to the floor. The cold air had changed her mood. (449)

Only at this moment does the world outside impinge on the space that encloses her. Overheating—the sign of imbalance—brings Emmy to act, and what she does further throws off any chance of balance. She picks up what she has written and, finding it inadequate, abandons herself to her whiskey and her favorite chair. ("I have said nothing," she mutters to herself in alarm. "I have said nothing at all. I have not clarified my reasons for being at the Hotel Henry. I have not justified myself.")

Jane Bowles's notebook includes an additional, short passage that was deleted in the published version. The passage offers something of an authorial gloss on the story. Emmy sees what Dillon interprets as "a representative of power made impotent," "the distant image of a giant steamship lying on its side. She turned her head slightly to the left as she had done in actuality to avoid the sight when the Jewitt Moores had taken her to see the boat dragged up from its ocean bed several years ago" (196). More disturbing is a line Jane Bowles wrote, crossed out, wrote again, then finally canceled: Emmy was "very nearly throwing everything into the fire (mentally)" (197).

"Emmy Moore's Journal" opens with a monologue in the form of a journal that is very personal but "is intended for publication." In order to explain why she is living alone in the Hotel Henry, she copies into the journal a letter to her husband, Paul Moore, a lawyer. Even more than in the other stories, Jane Bowles emphasizes not the statement but the process of thinking and writing. In Emmy's case, the process is slow and difficult, with ironic turns, contradictions, erasures, and spiraling back to the themes of Emmy's obsessions: her attempts at independence and change, her inability to justify herself.[17]

She constructs her theory of three cultural types of gender in order to justify herself. She is not like "Americans"—independent and masculine—though she would like to be. "I am unusually feminine for an American of Anglo stock. (Born in Boston.)" (444). The women of the Far East, she thinks, may be just as independent and masculine as the "Americans," although she is not sure. "I am almost a 'Turkish' type," Emmy writes, what she will come to call the "semi-Oriental."

> But sometimes I feel certain that I exude an atmosphere very similar to theirs (the Turkish women's) and then I despise myself. I find the women in my country so extraordinarily manly and independent, capable of leading regiments, or of fending for themselves on desert islands if necessary. (These are poor examples, but I am getting my point across.) For me it is an experience simply to have come here alone to the Hotel Henry and to eat my dinner and lunch by myself.
>
> If possible before I die, I should like to become a little less Turkish than I am now. (444)

Even in her theory Emmy is uncertain, and she apologizes to the "Turkish" women she wonders about. Have they discarded their veils? An "American" woman would be sure. The "Turkish" women, it should be clear by now, located between America and the Far East in a cultural map, is a generalization of the secluded Muslim women she was getting to know in Morocco, "semi-Oriental."

The three stories are not connected in any obvious way. Jane Bowles worked on them at roughly the same time, after her initial encounter with North African culture. The temptation to read Jane Bowles directly into Jeanie, Mrs. Copperfield, and Emmy Moore is difficult to resist; but the point of this essay is not to pursue that route. Rather, it is to suggest that an encounter with a very different way of drawing gender and sexual boundaries brought Bowles not just to fiction about the other, but as well to a reconsideration of an "American" social identity.

When the protagonist is situated inside her hotel room, she is Emmy, "alone and disconnected," finding it difficult (if necessary) to justify herself, difficult to keep writing. When the protagonist sits at the "iron table," immobile, playing language games with Mr. Copperfield, she has only a temporary place. (Perhaps she will be pressured into following her husband's dream of the desert.) Western civilization is always a matter of importance in these stories. When she leaves the hotel that allows Westerners free travel (Jeanie), the woman is displaced, still, but she senses in Zodelia's house the home lost to the freely moving American.

Jane Bowles died on May 4, 1973. She had been institutionalized in a psychiatric hospital in Malaga years earlier (1967), and her writing career had virtually ended even earlier than that. After 1957, when she suffered a debilitating stroke, she managed to publish her novel, *Two Serious Ladies* (1965), and a collection mainly of short stories, *The Collected Works of Jane Bowles* (1966). Those pieces had been written years before that. The works for which Paul Bowles is best known, "A Distant Episode" (1947), *The Sheltering Sky* (1949), *The Delicate Prey and Other Stories* (1950), *Let It Come Down* (1953), and *The Spider's House* (1955), were written and published during Jane's lifetime. All of them share with Jane Bowles's works the skepticism and ambivalence toward the East that we have called the "second phase." Even in those years Paul Bowles was becoming more seriously involved with nonliterate Moroccan storytellers. In the next chapter, the impact of Paul Bowles's association with the storytellers is discussed. By the early 1960s it was clear that Bowles's stories and essays were entering what we are calling a "third phase" of American responses to the East. After Jane's stroke, and increasingly after her confinement in Malaga, Paul's work became less and less interested in the modernized features of the Morocco he knew and more and more involved in experiments to tap a very different way of thinking, one the storytellers were opening to him.

Chapter Five

Penetrating the Ramparts:

Morocco in the Fiction of Paul Bowles

In the introduction he wrote to *The Hakima: A Tragedy in Fez* (1990), Paul Bowles recalls the pleasure of once living in Fez, "at one moment outside under the olive trees with the sheep, and at the next penetrating the ramparts" (9). Much of his novel set in Fez, *The Spider's House* (1955), is a walking tour of the city Moroccans claim as their intellectual and spiritual center. It is a city that contains, among other things, the world's oldest university (older by decades than Qarowiyin in Cairo, by a century than the oldest university in Europe); a clock built by Moses Maimonides; and a marker where the first anthropologist, Ibn Khaldun, once lived. Bowles mostly recalls it as a walled city and describes it by the gates through which a tourist or resident must pass to enter. He is describing Fez in 1931, but he may well be describing the fascination that has kept the American expatriate in Morocco for five decades.

> Fez is the place where nothing is direct. Going into the Medina is not like entering a city; it is more like becoming a participant in a situation whose meaning is withheld. There is a sense of deviousness and accompanying intrigue in the air, and the inhabitants do little to mitigate this impression. The enclosing ramparts were built high to protect the town-dwellers from the Berber enemy outside, and I remember that in 1931 the

143

gates in the north wall were shut after sunset. The people were convinced that bands of robbers lurked outside, waiting to pounce on anyone who failed to get back inside through the gates before nightfall.
They seemed, however, to be almost equally afraid of each other. I recall
the difficulties involved in trying to walk through the Medina at night.
Between one quarter and the next there were huge doors that were shut
and bolted, to prevent those living on one side from getting into the
neighboring section. It was necessary to find the watchman and persuade
him to let me through. Then somewhat farther along I would come up
against another such barrier. (8)

Paul Bowles (1911-   ) is not the first American writer to take an
interest in Morocco, but his serious preoccupation with Moroccan
thinking in his fiction has been sustained for over five decades, and goes
far beyond the Orientalist fascination with the exotic East. His is by far
the most striking example of cross-cultural influence involving a
Western author and the Middle East and North Africa. Since 1939,
when Bowles took up residence in Tangier and began to publish fiction,
he has written extensively about Moroccan peoples, customs, beliefs,
and stories. A book of essays he titled *Their Heads Are Green and Their Hands
Are Blue* (1963).[1] There, in essays such as "Africa Minor," "A Man Must
Not Be Very Moslem," and "The Rif, to Music," Bowles articulates views
that go well beyond the observations of the casual tourist—and beyond
the Orientalist fascination with the exotic other. "The Rif, to Music" is a
diary of one of Bowles's travels to record Moroccan music for the
Library of Congress ethnomusicology series.[2] It illustrates a continuing
interest for the man who has made his living mainly as a composer. In
the foreward to the 1963 volume Bowles stakes out the following position, for good or ill: "My own belief is that the people of the alien cultures are being ravaged not so much by the by-products of our
civilization, as by the irrational longing on the part of members of their
own educated minorities to cease being themselves and become
Westerners" (viii).

In that statement, written in the late 1950s, Bowles speaks of "our"
civilization and the "alien" peoples he writes about. He appears to be
speaking in the name of the West and writing to a Western audience.
He is very rarely, though, a defender of the West. Bowles is in one sense
the complete outsider, one who felt equally estranged from his own
American traditions—he was born in New York City and returns there

on rare occasions[3]—estranged from his own American traditions and from the Moroccans, whose traditions were so different from his own. What this double alienation has produced, however, is as intense investigation of American ideas and Moroccan Muslim culture has been seen in American letters.

Bowles went to Morocco in the first place largely, it seems, by accident. In 1931 Gertrude Stein and Alice Toklas, who had a habit of sending artists who had sought out the expatriate community in Paris to various parts of the globe, decided on Tangier for the twenty-year-old Bowles (Stewart 11–14). Since it was hardly a well-thought-out decision on his part (if a decision at all), Bowles's appearance in Morocco, and in the international city of Tangier especially, certainly did not suggest any initial sympathy for—or even knowledge of—Morocco. And as late as 1952, when he had lived in Morocco for many years, he was still disconsolate enough to say,

> I don't think we're likely to get to know the Moslems very well, and I suspect that if we should we'd find them less sympathetic than we do at present. And I believe the same applies to their getting to know us. . . . Their culture is essentially barbarous, their mentality that of a purely predatory people. (Stewart 99)

This is hardly the basis of a fruitful exchange. But a decisive turn in his ideas came within two years of that statement. For one thing, he had by then come to know Ahmed Yacoubi, who accompanied Bowles on a trip to Istanbul and provided the American with many insights into Muslim society.[4] He also came to know a number of Moroccan storytellers, and the exchange between Bowles and the storytellers was very fruitful—in both directions.[5] Of the storytellers, Mohammed Mrabet, whom Bowles met in 1965, is probably the best known to the West, largely because of Bowles's translations from tapes of Mrabet's stories.[6]

Many of Bowles's short stories and novels are set in Morocco. The Moroccan characters in the stories often are pushed into conflict with Europeans and Americans. Increasingly they emerge from the background to take the foreground. The more he wrote about Morocco, the more Bowles concentrated on Moroccans and on Moroccan storytelling techniques. Although he may have been discouraged, in the early 1950s, about his ability to come to know the "alien" culture, it is perhaps too much to think of the change that came over him as a decisive conversion. His entry into Morocco may have been more or less an accident, but his fiction shows from the first an intense interest in things Moroccan. When Gore Vidal considered Bowles one of "the three most interesting writers in the United States," he was thinking of astonishing early short stories such as "A Distant Episode" and "The Delicate Prey," which Vidal said "were immediately recognized as being unlike anything else in our literature."[7] Of the thirty-nine short stories published between 1939 and 1976 and reprinted in his *Collected Stories* (1979), twenty-two are set in North Africa. (The others are early stories, in the main. After 1948, the emphasis is almost entirely on North Africa.) A collection of more recent work, *Midnight Mass* (1981),[8] contains thirteen stories, all but two of which are set in Morocco. Even more recently, *Unwelcome Words* (1988) contains seven stories, five of them related to Morocco.

Since "The Delicate Prey" (1948) and "A Distant Episode" (1945) are the best known of Bowles's short stories and have been discussed elsewhere,[9] the treatment here will be very brief. Both are grim and horrific tales. They gain maximum impact from the author's very spare style and his refusal to comment on the horrors he describes. In "The Delicate Prey," intertribal fears and hostilities lead a Moungari to draw a party of three Filala leather merchants traveling in the Sahara into a trap. A young man is brutally mutilated by the Moungari, who is intoxicated on hashish. The Moungari is, in turn, executed in a particularly grim manner by another group of Filali merchants, with the connivance of the French. Apart from the Frenchmen who are mentioned in passing at the end of the story, all of the characters are North Africans, and the story is told in a manner that will become another defining feature of Bowles's narrative technique: insider references to peoples, landscapes, and customs that force the reader (an outsider, of course) to adjust immediately to the alien environment of the story.

"A Distant Episode" also contains irrational brutality and mutilation, and it is also told in Bowles's laconic, deadpan style. A person is betrayed into the hands of a band of the Reguibat in an imaginary town of Ain Tadouirt (somewhere in the south of Morocco).[10] It differs from "The Delicate Prey" in that the victim is from the West, a professor of linguistics, who more or less drops into town to further his study of Moghrebi dialects. For his efforts the professor has his tongue cut out, and he is made to entertain the tribes. When he takes a chance to

escape, the only other Westerner in sight, a French soldier, takes "a pot-
shot at him for good luck" (48).

"TEA ON THE MOUNTAIN"

Even before the publication of those two very celebrated stories, a
decade before he settled in Tangier, Bowles wrote a story that promised
a less violent and more evenhanded study of the great theme that was to
develop in his fiction, the clash of cultures East and West. "Tea on the
Mountain" appeared in 1939.[11] It tells of an encounter of an American
woman, a writer living in the International Zone. She takes up with two
men, university students younger than herself. The men are anxious to
appear modern and Westernized, no longer bound by, for example,
Muslim prohibitions of alcohol and pork. They invite her to a picnic.
Typical of Bowles's main characters, the woman in this story is drawn by
unconscious forces she rarely tries to analyze. She appears to be drawn
into an erotic situation when she is in fact taking the lead. At the
moment when the more skittish and less attractive of the two young
men leaves the "picnic," the sexual encounter she had been yearning for
does not take place. Something had "gone wrong." In a rare moment of
self-analysis the anonymous woman muses,

> "What am I doing here? I have no business here. I said I wouldn't come."
> The idea of such a picnic had so completely coincided with some uncon-
> scious desire she had harbored for many years. To be free, out-of-doors,
> with some young man she did not know—could not know—that was
> probably the important part of the dream. For if she could not know him,
> he could not know her. She swung the little blind shut and hooked it. (22)

There is still some chance of the encounter at least turning sexual
as the other young man, Mijd, begins to talk about himself and his
dreams. He tells her, "Perhaps some day I shall go to America, and then
you can invite me to your house for tea. Each year we'll come back to
Morocco and see our friends and bring back cinema stars and presents
from New York" (24). In this story Bowles offers more authorial com-
mentary than is usual for him in his later works. We know, for example,
how the woman thinks of Mijd's dream (finding it too ridiculous for a
response). We also know how her gestures and actions are related to her
inner thoughts and her outer expression. The session ends abruptly
when the very Islamic faith Mijd had tried to suppress poses an insuper-

able barrier to understanding. The woman hears a muezzin chanting in the distance, and she tells Mijd the call to prayer "always makes me sad." Without hesitation, Mijd explains, "Because you're not of the faith." Notice then the great divide:

> She reflected a minute and said: "I think that's true." She was about to add: "But your faith says women have no souls." Instead she rose from the mattress and smoothed her hair. The muezzin had ceased. She felt quite chilled. "This is over," she said to herself. They stumbled down the dark road into town, saying very little on the way. (24)

There is no resolution in "Tea on the Mountain," no understanding between man and woman, East and West. The two play out a game very much like Jean-Paul Sartre's famous "bad faith" (or "self-deception," *mauvaise foi*) that makes the other unknowable, almost by definition.[12] Indeed, so pervasive is this existentialist alienation in Bowles that even the suggestion that Bowles may have attempted to move beyond it, to certain moments of understanding, seems doomed in advance.

Nevertheless, the major argument here is that Bowles does in fact explore the possibility of overcoming alienation and uses his fiction to demonstrate the possibility. There is little real joy in Bowles's fiction. Individuals clash and violate one another with alarming frequency, and almost never does a story end happily. But there are moments of insight, moments of understanding. What is interesting from our point of view is that the very possibility of understanding is cross-cultural. Bowles succeeds when he adopts the point of view of the other, the Moroccan. His Moroccans may be Arab or Berber, city dweller or not, but they are invariably Muslim in his stories. Bowles's most striking successes come when he takes the view of the Moroccan Muslim.

Sometimes the stories are about cross-cultural misunderstanding, in which case the protagonist or central consciousness is invariably Western, often American. But Bowles came more and more to adopt the techniques of the Moroccan storyteller, and, when he does so, to present a protagonist who is Moroccan. The Moroccan stories are experiments in fictional technique, certainly one of the marks of post-World War II American fiction. We have become used to writers outside the West in the postcolonial period adopting Western postmodern experiments. In Bowles we find the other possibility: a turn to Moroccan storytelling techniques to explore alternatives to mainstream Western modernism.

LET IT COME DOWN

Before turning to examples I think are successful in that vein, I should mention two works written in the Western, modernist style that pursue the East/West theme. The novel *Let It Come Down* (1952), considered briefly in chapter 2 above, contains an acknowledged self-portrait of the author, mildly caricatured in Richard Holland.[13] Not surprisingly, the ironist Richard Holland discusses that mine of Arabic folk literature, *The Thousand and One Nights*, which he admires; and he deadpans by insisting that, appearances to the contrary, Tangier is "in spirit" very like New York City.[14]

As discussed earlier, the novel, follows two deeply alienated men, one, Nelson Dyar, a New Yorker; the other, Thami, a Westernized and disaffected Moroccan who latches onto the American to make money from him. The two prey upon each other until the American, stoned for the first time in his life on kif, murders his Moroccan counterpart by driving a nail into the man's skull. From time to time Bowles experimented with drug-induced surrealist fiction, a kind of automatic writing. In *Let It Come Down*, Bowles explains that the last of four sections of the book was written in "the absolute silence of the mountain nights." "I shut off the controls and let Another Kind of Silence [the title of the section] guide itself, without supplying any conscious direction. It went as far as it could go, then stopped, and that was the end of the book" (8).

The novel would seem just another example of the impossibility of cross-cultural understanding (an understatement indeed in view of the terrible violence of Nelson Dyar), but for the long passage which describes trance dancing (268–71). The dancer mutilates himself with a knife, but in the process liberates his spirit. A related sort of liberation is possible, Bowles suggests, with drugs (which are an important part of the trance dancing as well). The West is dominated by alcohol, Muslim lands by a very different kind of intoxicant.

> Alcohol blurs the personality by loosening inhibitions. The drinker feels, temporarily at least, a sense of participation. Kif abolishes no inhibitions; on the contrary it reinforces them, pushes the individual further back into the recesses of his own isolated personality, pledging him to con-

templation and inaction.It is to be expected that there should be a close relationship between the culture of a given society and the means used by its members to achieve release and euphoria. For Judaism and Christianity the means has always been alcohol; for Islam it has been hashish.[15]

Let It Come Down was written just at the time when Bowles's despair at understanding the people he had been living with for years was giving way to a confidence that he could indeed appropriate something of "their" world. The stories in which that appropriation becomes apparent were published through the 1960s, 1970s, and 1980s—at the time when Bowles came to know Moroccan storytellers personally and taped, edited, and translated their stories into English.

FICTION SINCE THE 1960s

Beginning with "The Hyena" (1960), a very brief beast fable in which a hyena lures a stork into his cave,[16] Bowles published a whole series of stories that tried to represent the experience of the Muslim from an insider's point of view. (In "The Hyena," the holy one, the saintly stork, is taken in by the cunning hyena, who praises Allah for giving him a brain to outwit the stork and for the eyes and nose to survive in a pitiless landscape).

Several of these stories are worth mentioning briefly here. In "The Garden" (1963),[17] a man's great delight in his garden leads his wife to poison his food. She thinks the man must have a treasure hidden in the garden, and the *tseuheur* she gives him will prompt him to reveal the secret. The man becomes so ill and confused that he can no longer remember the name *Allah*. That alarms the villagers, who end up killing the man. "Little by little the trees died, and very soon the garden was gone. Only the desert was there" (365).

"He of the Assembly" (1961) is another story from the same period.[18] Unlike "The Hyena" and "The Garden," which are written in the manner of folktales, "He of the Assembly" is an extremely complicated narrative filled, perhaps, with personal jokes, for it was inspired by Bowles's friendship with Boujemaa, a Moroccan from Marrakech— hence the title (Stewart 129). The narrative is difficult to follow, since it attempts to take the reader inside the head of a man intoxicated with kif. It is almost impossible to distinguish fantasy from reality in the story. Fragments, wildly accidental turns to the story, and an ironic ending make this story of two men, one racing around the streets *m'hashish* and in terror, almost impossible to describe. But it is well crafted for all that, perhaps Bowles's most brilliant attempt at the stream-of-consciousness technique.[19] Bowles himself suggested that the story is

> built on four levels. It's in seven paragraphs, the story. Level 1 is the same as level 7; 2 is the same as 6, 3 is the same as 5, and 4 is a kind of interior monologue which is told in the first person, which is the crucial part, which is the center—or the top, if you like—of the pyramid. (Stewart 130)

Bowles was busy at the time recording the oral narratives of storytellers such as Boujemaa and Larbi Layachi (considered, with Ahmed Yacoubi, in chapter 8), and he was much impressed by the way their stories worked in Moghrebi. "He of the Assembly" aims at some of the same effects in English. "I've discovered," Bowles said of the story, "that it makes sense when I read it aloud. To me it makes more sense, even. When I read it on the paper I can see that it lacks a certain dimension that it needs. . . . Actually, it has to be read aloud" (Stewart 129–30).

The period also produced what is very likely Bowles's most sensitive stories about Muslim life, "The Time of Friendship" (1962).[20] Longer than most of his short stories and written entirely in the traditional Western mode of realistic fiction, "The Time of Friendship" follows a Swiss schoolteacher, Fraulein Windling, through an encounter with a young man, Slimane, who is twelve when they meet, a boy who uses her to join the military. Fraulein Windling is a Westerner who has developed a deep sympathy for the way of life she experiences deep in the desert. A teacher, she wants to impart something of Western history to the young Slimane. The young man is polite and balks only when he hears her talk of religion. In spite of her numerous attempts to understand the boy, she continues to make well-meaning errors of judgment. In one particularly moving episode, she sets up a Christmas scene decorated with candies, and the hungry Slimane virtually attacks the scene to get at the food. Fraulein Windling is quite shaken by what, she comes to realize, was her own mistake in judgment. She had thought the boy "like herself," and had miscalculated the cultural differences. The "time of friendship" ends; a new era begins. The story is a powerful anticolonial parable. Like all Bowles's stories, it is laced with irony. Unlike the others, though, the irony does not undercut the compassionate treatment of two very different persons from different cultures who manage, at some moments at least, to overcome their mutual otherness.

Bowles has continued to produce, in the 1970s and 1980s, stories that attempt to get into the minds of ordinary Moroccans, stories that are marked by an intense seriousness. The technique, as in "The Fqih" (1974), is one of paring away everything but the essentials (*Collected Stories* 377–79). "The Fqih" is built on a very simple plan; the diction is simple and uncluttered; the story is apparently artless. It pursues a favorite Bowles theme, one suggested by his understanding of Islam, the theme of fate. A boy is bitten by a dog. The advice of the village *fqih* is that the boy should be locked up. After more than a month of incarceration, during which the boy and his brother become terrible enemies, the boy's mother returns to the *fqih* and is startled to learn that the *fqih* assumed the boy was dead, that it had been fated. When the family again consults the *fqih*, they receive what looks like double talk. The story ends with one of the boys taking off for Casablanca, never to be heard of again in the village.

MOROCCAN STORYTELLERS: MOHAMMED MRABET

It should be clear by now that Paul Bowles is rarely interested, in his fiction, in the more modernized, Westernized features of Morocco he sees around him. The Western and Westernized characters are nearly always deeply divided and alienated, and they prey upon one another. He is far more interested in portraying the ordinary, often nonliterate, villager whose understanding of Islam is profound and unreflective. He also uses magic, spirits, and ancient figures such as Aisha Qandisha.[21] In order to portray these characters from the inside, Bowles experiments with quite a variety of narrative techniques. The most effective of the techniques are those Bowles picked up, not from the tradition of modern Western realism, but from the Moroccan storytellers he befriended.

Mary Martin Rountree (who concentrates almost exclusively on Mohammed Mrabet [born ca. 1940], by far the storyteller best known to Western readers) traced Bowles's interest in the storytellers and concludes,

> Taken as a whole Bowles's translations from the Moghrebi represent an enormous labor. The accumulation of volumes over the years shows the extent to which he was willing to divert his creative energies from his

own work. If, as Mohammed Mrabet suggests, Jane Bowles did indeed resent her husband's working as a translator at the expense of his fiction, she would surely have been alarmed by his absorption in the Moghrebi translations after her death in 1973. (399–400)

The nonliteracy of these cafe storytellers is part of their power. Bowles says, "I'm inclined to believe that illteracy is a prerequisite. The readers and writers I've tested have lost the necessary immediacy of contact with the material. They seem less in touch with both their memory and their imagination than the illiterates" (Stewart 112). They are also less burdened with the sort of "depth" that is celebrated in the characters of modern realistic fiction, a psychological complexity that derives from the Judeo-Christian confidence in the individual soul. The storytellers, like many of Bowles's characters (Western and Eastern), seem to lack the "center" that the Western literary tradition assigns to persons. Rather, they appear like the contextualized persons Geertz and Dwyer found in Morocco. When Daniel Halpern asked Bowles about the "unconscious drive for self-destruction" in characters like the Americans Kit and Port in *The Sheltering Sky*, Bowles responded by denying any such depth:

> But it seems to me that the motivation of characters in fiction like mine should be a secondary consideration. I think of characters as if they were props in the general scene of any given work. The characters, the land-scape, the climatic conditions, the human situation, the formal structure of the story or novel, all these elements are one—the characters are made of the same material as the rest of the work. Since they are acti-vated by the other elements of the synthetic cosmos, their own motiva-tions are relatively unimportant. (165)

Mohammed Mrabet's stories are full of magic, poisons, kif, and violence. On occasion, his stories develop in the manner of modern realism. *Love with a Few Hairs* (1968) is an example, as Rountree demon-strates (392–94). Not surprisingly, this appears when the Moroccan character is influenced by the West. The main character in that novel meets the West in the figure of a certain Mr. David. "Besides being an intensive look at the psychology of obsessive love and marriage, *Love with a Few Hairs* offers in its protagonist Mohammed an example of a young Moroccan stranded between two cultures: his native Islamic traditions and values and the European manners of Mr. David's expatriate world" (393).

A more recent series of stories translated by Bowles, though, shows a different Mrabet, a storyteller much more securely situated in the traditions and values of Islam. *The Chest* (1983) contains the same themes as Bowles's stories—bizarre turns to stories that emphasize a Muslim sense of Allah's will in a situation that does not make sense in ordinary Western terms. A Muslim boy in "El Fellah," for example, goes away to work for a Christian couple in France, takes up with the couple's daughter, and influences her so deeply she converts to Islam. She falls ill (without explanation) and dies. When El Fellah uncovers her grave, he sees, instead of the girl, "the body of an old man with a long white beard" and with ancient amber beads around his neck. When El Fellah returns to Morocco and tries to sell the beads, he is promptly arrested for having stolen them. People think El Fellah is insane, but the qadi investigates and finds the body of El Fellah's girlfriend in the grave of a long-dead old man. The qadi orders the amber beads returned to El Fellah.

In "The Chest," Cheikh, a poor man, is miraculously given the use of a rich man's wealth after he makes a long journey to see Allah and on the way encounters a compassionate wild man of the forest and a greedy hermit. Finally, all alone in the forest, Cheikh meets Allah, who tells Cheikh the fate of the two men Cheikh met along the way. When Cheikh returns to find that a magical switch has given him the wealth of a greedy rich man of the village, Cheikh is generous to the rich man, who has lost everything in the switch. The story ends when the rich man tries to repay Cheikh for his generosity.[22]

> I won't take it, said Cheikh. If you force it one me, I'll burn it. He understood that Allah had taken the chest from Haddad and transported it to his house, but he could not tell Haddad about it.
>
> Time went by. The seven daughters married seven of Cheikh's workmen, and had many children, and these grew up and had their own children. Many called Cheikh Father, and many called him Grandfather, and still more called him Great-Grandfather. And when Cheikh died he left everything behind him in perfect order. (79)

"The Chest" comes at the end of *The Chest* and thus may (though it is not necessarily the case) be considered a conclusion. Like a number of other stories in the collection, it contains a miraculous transformation. Cheikh counts his wealth only in his seven little daughters (ironically).

The household is so poor that Cheikh's wife keeps a boiling big caul-
dron filled with water and stones, which she stirs until the hungry children go to sleep. Cheikh is an honorable man, as is clear from the
incident in which Haddad's wealth falls into Cheikh's hands, and
Cheikh returns it.

The story, which line is clear, precise, and straightforward,
strongly recalls, along with the characterization, folktales and parables
that anthropologists and biblical scholars in particular have studied. We
have certain tools for the investigation of such stories. In other stories in
The Chest Mrabet seems to be dealing with Islamic concepts and practices that are remote from the Christian West, but have been studied by
Western scholars.

In most of them, the miracles of Allah are not explained away at
all. The stories seem to have an edge—the inadequacy of the Nazarenes
(the Christians) to understand the profound truths of existence. What is
tantalizing about the collection is the possibility that it is directed
against the West. Of all the stories, "The Chest" is the most generous in
its vision of existence. Quite possibly the informing principle is a brand
of Sufism, still widely practiced in Morocco.

For all its surface clarity, "The Chest" is enigmatic. It is a story that
demands, not so much a knowledge of Morocco, Islam, Sufism, and the
like but a commitment to an alien culture. Mrabet is a storyteller who
delights in funny tales of rascals and scoundrels. Bowles has said of the
"smooth-rolling" Mrabet, clearly his favorite among the Moroccans he
has championed, that he "has no thesis to propound, no grievances to
air, and no fear of redundant punctuation. He is a showman; his princi-
pal interest is in his own performance as virtuoso story-teller" (*Five Eyes*
8). Reading "The Chest" is a profoundly disturbing experience because
it seems to challenge the reader not to understand it but to do something else—a response that leads away from our now-familiar way of
responding (coolly) to literature. In "The Chest" we are faced with the
other in a way that separates us even as we are invited in.

"New York 1965" (1988)

John Stenham, a character in *The Spider's House*, like Bowles an American
writer living in Morocco, has a problem explaining to his American
companion, Lee, "how living among a less evolved people enabled him
to see his own culture from the outside, and thus to understand it better"

(251). A very recent story, from *Unwelcome Words* (1988) presents a rather different American writer, one who not only sees American culture from the outside but goes native.

"New York 1965" (15–26) is a rather unusual short story for Bowles, a monologue in the form of a lengthy, incomplete sentence. The speaker is an American woman, unnamed, who travels for a weekend to Tangier in order to see her Sarah Lawrence classmate, Kathleen Andrews, who is living there. The peevish tone of the speaker is announced at the start, when she appears to be reading from a review of Kathleen Andrews's poetry:

> a dazzling accomplishment Kathleen Andrews has succeeded in forging a language capable of bearing her to the highest reaches of lyrical expressivity the poems soar above the stratosphere what idiotic reviews they write you know her mother has a certain amount of influence she's also very rich so I wouldn't be surprised if there'd been a bit of quid pro quo under the table publishers and critics are human too (15)

The speaker spent her life conforming to upscale American values, and her friend Kathleen Andrews has taken a far turn in her life. In 1965 Kathleen's decision to have a child on her own made her a "sort of freak," and her ideas about child care—such as reading the *Analects* of Confucius to the child in the womb (18)—mark her as a dangerous radical, from the speaker's point of view, probably crazy. That she calls the child "Alaric," a name that has not been used "for the past fifteen hundred years" is odd, but Kathleen's shocking behavior in Tangier is enough for her Sarah Lawrence friend to write her off.

The speaker responds to a letter she has received from Kathleen and flies down from Europe "for a weekend," "intrigued American girl living alone in the native quarter" (22). When after hours of searching she finds the house, the details upset her: Kathleen is dressed "in some sort of flashy native costume"; the house has no furniture, only mats and cushions on the floor; and there is a huge pile of marijuana on the only other bit of furniture, a large table. Alaric she finds running wild with the neighbor kids. Alaric's hair has not been cut in a year, and he is as filthy as the native children. Even more shocking is Kathleen's lover, "about six foot three and jet black" (23). The final trial of this delicate sensibility is the gurgling animal in the next room, a sheep they have been feeding in anticipation of the feast.

The feast is the important *eid* in which a sheep is sacrificed. The speaker thinks it is a pet and tells Alaric, "it's nice you have the sheep he can be your friend and follow you around wherever you go" (24). But the boy responds in an entirely different—culturally unexpected way: "and that kid looked straight at me and said oh no we're going to cut his throat next Tuesday" (24).

The speaker leaves the house immediately and does not look back. "She says, what a waste I have no patience with people who refuse to abide by the rules of the game." The fact that Kathleen has been "writing lots of poetry"—and received glowing reviews of her work—means nothing. The peevish monologue breaks off with the idea that Kathleen will never know "how much harm she's caused it'll never cross her mind that her life has been one great mistake from the beginning pretty ridiculous isn't it" (25).

Kathleen Andrews has, of course, "gone native" in a way that even the meticulous Jane Bowles was unable to do. In a way, though, her decision to bring up her child the way the poor Moroccans do, to live the way they do, and, presumably, to follow Islam is the logical extension of the kind of expatriate experience that fascinated Paul Bowles himself—but an extreme he could not reach. If we recognize in Kathleen Andrews many of the essential characteristics of the 1960s American rebel, the American-ness of hers and the Bowles's attack on Western values comes clear.

"The Eye" (1983)

One last example will have to suffice to show that Bowles is pursuing his favorite themes and interests. The second edition of *Midnight Mass*, which appeared in 1983, is a collection of thirteen stories, all but two of which are Moroccan. "The Eye" (1983) is the last of the Moroccan stories in the collection.[23] It is a mystery story, reminding the reader of one of Bowles's favorite authors, Edgar Allan Poe. It is a story of Duncan Marsh, a Canadian, who had come to live in Tangier and was thought to have died, "one more victim of slow poisoning by native employees" (152). The mystery is, in a sense, solved. The reader does find out the circumstances of the death. Duncan Marsh, it turns out, died in an attempt, sanctioned by the *fqihs*, to counteract a spell that Duncan Marsh had put on a little girl—"the eye." The little girl's mother had slipped soporifics into the man's food, and four men of the child's family had helped the *fqih* hold a ceremony that ended with Marsh's death.

What is extraordinary about this tale, which manages to touch upon nearly all the main Bowles themes, is not the story of the death itself, but the first-person narrator, whose probing into the story is, finally, bizarre and disturbing. "The Eye" is really a story about story-telling, about myth making. It is a postmodern story about the relation of story to life. We discover that the narrator is a Westerner who has spent five decades of his life in Tangier. His attitude toward the people involved in the story he has chosen, rather arbitrarily, to investigate, is so dispassionate and nonjudgmental that as the story goes along, the narrator becomes himself the most unusual character in this tale of clashing cultures.

It turns out that the victim was himself a rather odd figure. The eye that is the center of the story is the I/eye of the narrator, another Westerner trying to grasp (in quite a violent way) the cultural other. Notice how the eye is ironically reflected in the actions of Duncan Marsh, the actions that end up causing Marsh's death. He had hired a cook named Meriam:

> The woman was hired. Two or three days a week she came accompanied by the child, who would play in the patio where she could watch her. From the beginning Marsh complained that she was noisy. Repeatedly he sent messages down to Meriam, asking her to make the child be still. And one day he went quietly around the outside of the house and down to the patio. He got on all fours, put his face close to the little girl's face, and frowned at her so fiercely that she began to scream. When Meriam rushed out of the kitchen he stood up smiling and walked off.

Our clear-eyed (?) narrator eventually dismisses the mother's actions against Duncan Marsh with an obviously patronizing gesture. He was, finally, disappointed that he had not found out someone "on whom guilt might be fixed": "What constitutes a crime? There was no criminal intent—only a mother moving in the darkness of ignorance. I thought about it on my way home in the taxi" (162). Such is, perhaps, the most cunning of Paul Bowles's parables of alienation.

While Paul Bowles's essays, stories, and translations of Moroccan storytellers represent a shift from phase two to phase three in the movement of American images of the East, Elizabeth Fernea's works, from her earliest writings on the Middle East, already locate her in the third phase. Her writings show none of the ambivalence toward "civilization" one sees tearing at Jane and Paul Bowles. Rather, there is a genuine sense of cultural difference and an awareness of the difficulty in knowing the other that take her beyond the exotic East of the Orientalist tradition. When she decided to take on the veil and learn colloquial Arabic to enter the lives of the Iraqi women in the village she was visiting in the 1950s, the account she wrote of her years there, *Guests of the Sheik* (1965), was difficult to categorize in earlier genres. It was not exactly travel literature. Certainly it was not a guidebook, as Edith Wharton's *In Morocco* had been. Fernea's penetration into the privacy of Iraqi women was deep enough that *Guests of the Sheik* came to carry a subtitle: *An Ethnography of an Iraqi Village.* Since then her works have continued to combine memoir, journalistic reportage, and anthropological fieldwork. Fernea's observations of Moroccan Sufi practices were discussed in chapter 2. The following chapter takes up *A Street in Marrakech* (1980) as pilgrimage of the American, who without emptying herself of American culture, nevertheless consciously seeks the other at a level of shared concern.

Chapter Six

Elizabeth Fernea's Moroccan Pilgrimage

Elizabeth Fernea, whom we have discussed briefly in earlier chapters (2 and 4), is a well-known journalist and teacher/scholar at the University of Texas. Her contributions to the new scholarship on women (as president of the Middle Eastern Studies Association in 1986 she inaugurated the Association for Middle East Women's Studies—AMEWS) are gaining a large audience in the United States and in the Middle East/North Africa as well. She represents a very different generation than Edith Wharton's, and that of Jane Bowles and the "early" Paul Bowles, for that matter. Fernea, as was suggested before, writes in the third phase of American attitudes toward the East. Since Wharton and she write directly of their visits to Morocco, rather than through the mediation of fiction, their respective works, *In Morocco* (1920) and *A Street in Marrakech* (1980) provide a sharp contrast between early twentieth-century attitudes that were already quite traditional and more recent attitudes.

Traveling in Morocco long after it reached its independence in 1956, Fernea carried none of the Wharton's imperialist rhetoric to her stay there. Fernea's and Wharton's books are both very much the products of what one might call the "translocation of ethnicity:" whatever

161

ethnic heritage the traveler may recognize at home is transposed into another ethnic character in the presence of the cultural other. Without referring directly to their ethnic backgrounds, and certainly without advertising any nationalism they might have held privately, their ethnicity is transferred to "American" in a cultural sense.

The transfer is rather like the shifts from one linguistic style to another, usually imperceptible, such as sociolinguist Martin Joos described in the way Americans shift from "casual" to "consultative" speech or from "consultative" to "formal" speech as an example of homeostasis. Without necessarily being conscious of the shift, the cultural outsider finds comfort in another mode of ethnicity which the other "American"—whatever differences the two may have when both are "home" and insiders—can share: "To a social animal, the question of first importance always is 'What group am I in?' The second question is 'How do I stand within the group?' Only third are the message transactions." (*The Five Clocks* 9).

Like the tourist who is suddenly delighted to see a familiar American in a mass of other bodies, the traveler finds an identity that may never have been recognized before. However much Wharton wanted to be a "Western" (i.e., "civilized") person, more at home in Paris perhaps than anywhere in the United States, her World War I narrative of a brief trip from Paris to Morocco is filled with Americanisms. Fernea, to the contrary, went with her family to live in the traditional area of an old Moroccan city, and she made it a point to get to know her neighbors, especially the women, since they remain the least known of Middle Eastern/North African peoples.

It would not be wrong to consider Fernea's visit a pilgrimage. While the "path" is very common—almost inevitable—in narratives about encountering the other, the pilgrimage is a very special kind of path. It, too, is common and has its own history. The path can be a walk into familiar or unfamiliar territory, but it invites the possibility of meandering and odd encounters along the way, with no particular destination clearly sought beforehand. The pilgrimage may allow diversions and often involves uncertainties, but it is structured by a destination. In his travels Aeneas is not always certain where he shall settle, but the goal is always in mind, and he only needs to be reminded of his "destiny" to see that his sojourn in Carthage, for example, is an erroneous side trip that threatens his main task (and has serious consequences for the Romans later on). The narrative of Aeneas is in that sense a pilgrimage.

The lengthy account of Fernea's stay in Marrakech is organized, as Wharton's briefer visit was not, I shall hope to show here, by the concept of pilgrimage.

Far from holding herself superior to the people of Morocco, and far unlike Edith Wharton in that regard, Elizabeth Fernea reveals a decidedly post–World War II American concern with the cultural other, one that falls short of "going native," certainly, but one that approaches the other in anything but the Orientalist mode criticized by Edward Said and Rana Kabbani.

Pilgrimages have been around for so long, as forms of behavior—people actually taking the road in search of a holy site—and as a "primordial image" (the notion that led Carl Jung and, after him, Maud Bodkin and Northrop Frye to posit archetypal patterns in art and literature) that it is difficult to know if any culture can lay claim to having recognized the pattern first. Pilgrimage is at least as early as literature. The earliest cuneiform texts that have been deciphered, written in the third millennium B.C.E. in the ancient Middle East, contain references to journeys of the gods and heroes to the places that were already considered sacred, great temple cities such as Eridu and Uruk.

Whole works were shaped by the pattern. In a Sumerian poem, "Inanna and Enki," the great goddess of Uruk, Inanna, makes a journey along a canal to Eridu, where she manages to wrest the "divine decrees" from the god Enki and to take them back with her to Inanna's own city of Uruk (Kramer and Maier 87–117). Better known from the same early period of literature is the double quest of the hero Gilgamesh, who, having lost his friend to death, travels the world in search of an answer to the great questions of life (Gardner and Maier VII.v–XI.vi). While quests, often taking the form of pilgrimages, are well known to the Judeo-Christian tradition (Augustine, Bonaventure, Dante and Chaucer, not to mention *Heart of Darkness* and Billy Pilgrim's dark visions), the pilgrimage is much more ancient than even that long tradition.

Elizabeth Fernea's straightforward narrative of her life in the southern Moroccan city of Marrakech is, of course, a much different work than, say, *Gilgamesh*. Hers is a story of a cultural outsider who seeks the center of a culture that is normally hidden to the West—the life of

women in an Arab-Muslim society. Fernea knew going in that the society she was entering was publicly dominated by men. Except for the
Westernized, modern women of Morocco (who do not appear in
Fernea's account), the Islamic women are in a profound way secluded, as
Moroccan sociologist Fatima Mernissi has repeatedly demonstrated, in
such works as *Beyond the Veil; Male-Female Dynamics in Modern Muslim Society*
(137-147) and *Doing Daily Battle; Interviews with Moroccan Women.* Access to
the lives of Moroccan women is virtually impossible for even the most
sympathetic male anthropologist. Quite unlike Edith Wharton,
Elizabeth Fernea knew that the assumptions of Western superiority over
the East have certainly been called into question. The easy assurance
that "civilization"—to be equated with Western styles of life—will
gradually replace "primitive" thought is nowhere held by Fernea.

The pilgrimage is perhaps one of those "antiquated metaphors and
archaic concepts to which the Western traveller is . . . inescapably subservient," in Kabbani's phrase, but in Elizabeth Fernea's account of her
days in Marrakech, pilgrimages to holy places take on a particular
importance in the religious life of Moroccan women. And her visit to
Morocco comes to be seen as a pilgrimage.

In the long tradition of Western pilgrimage literature, the pilgrim
achieves a coming of age, psychologically, morally, and spiritually.
Except in one area—the possibility of gaining authentic friendship with
a woman from a different culture—Fernea's autobiographical account of
her journey to Morocco does not claim to be a life-changing experience. Her earlier work, *Guests of the Sheik* (1965), contained much of that.
In Iraq she was younger, more impressionable, and vulnerable (since she
knew almost no Arabic before she went to live in a tiny, remote village),
far more subject to culture shock than she would be later. But she learns
so much about the women of her Moroccan neighborhood, the old and
the young, and she observes her own three children growing up in an
alien culture that Fernea certainly grows in understanding, certainly in
empathy, in her encounter with Moroccan women.

Although she does not claim a transformation in herself of the
type explored, say, in *Pilgrim's Progress*, there is a moment of fundamental
change for her in the story: the moment when, suddenly, the woman
she has come to know, Aisha, opens up to her as a friend.

Fernea's pilgrimage pursues the limits of friendship for women
across cultural barriers. She experiences the translocation of ethnicity.

Her leave taking is emotionally charged, when she must depart Marrakech for America. But the real leave taking had occurred before that, when the friendship between Elizabeth and Aisha founders on a barrier that simply could not be crossed: religion. Fernea's crisis reveals the deep division between West and East, Christian and Muslim. It is all the more difficult for her because Fernea had attempted so thoroughly to understand Islam. The last of the pilgrimage narratives in *A Street in Marrakech* turns, as so many modern literary quests have turned, ironic.

Islamic practices in Morocco, especially when they involve women, are often condemned today by Islamic reformers, who see trance dancing, fortune telling, and healing rituals—not to mention visits to the tombs of saints—as un-Islamic borrowings and as vestiges of ancient pagan practices. Pilgrimage—the hajj—may be one of the pillars of Islam, but pilgrimages to the tombs of saints do not have the sanction of orthodoxy, according to some Muslim scholars. But the rich spiritual life of Islam for women in Morocco is mainly revealed in precisely those unorthodox practices. Of those suspect activities, though, pilgrimage has the greatest claim not only to Islamic tradition but also to the much longer tradition of Semitic cultures, including biblical Hebrew but also the much earlier Akkadian culture of Mesopotamia.

Most Islamic holy places in Morocco are strictly off limits to non-Muslims. To gain the confidence of her Moroccan neighbors, who of course knew she was not a Muslim, in such a way that they would invite her to visit the holy places, was to gain an intimacy few Westerners can claim. The cultural differences are simply too great.

Sometimes the distinction between fiction and nonfiction, so dear both to humanists and to social scientists, is not terribly useful. Often in attempting to cross cultures and describe customs that separate writer and reader from the cultural other, the best writers turn to narrative. "Fiction" may mean very strange fantasies—ogres and aliens—but in the modern West, the first meaning is, ironically, "realism." Concepts of what is real—and with it, concepts of realism—change over time and differ from culture to culture. But mainstream Western fiction since the eighteenth century has been a construct of Western "modernity," one that denied the supernatural and increasingly located itself in ordinary reality, with ordinary people and their everydayness.

Elizabeth Warnock Fernea's books are carefully crafted, and they use the techniques of modern realistic fiction to great advantage, even when they attempt, as the subtitle to *Guests of the Sheik* suggests, a nonfiction purpose, *An Ethnography of an Iraqi Village*. *A Street in Marrakech* (1975), on which this chapter concentrates, carries a very different kind of subtitle: *A Personal Encounter with the Lives of Moroccan Women*. Such a label takes the work out of the realms both of "scientific" ethnography and of "artistic" fiction. Personal encounters cannot take place without the social constructions, culture, that enable them to happen; and authoring a narrative that negotiates between the intimate and the momentary and a public form of discourse, is another kind of social construct. What deserves to be recognized in *A Street in Marrakech* is the artistry Fernea takes to the account of her stay in that southern Moroccan city. The pilgrimage is a narrative pattern that is even more important than that in *Guests of the Sheik*. Through the figure of the pilgrimage, Fernea manages to capture the extent—and limitations, of course—of the West's understanding of the East.

Her two trips through the city provide a frame for the many episodes that make up the book. The first occurs near the opening of the work (pt. 1, ch. 2, 49–59), and it mainly serves to indicate the terrible sense of alienation that gripped the family at their first contact with the city. The small neighborhood to which the Ferneas had moved is typical of the *medina* of Moroccan cities, preserved by the policy of Resident General Lyautey: from the outside an odd jumble of houses, stores, blind alleyways, hotel, and bathhouse crowded together in no particular order, as if none of it had been planned. Outsiders are often baffled by what appears to them a hopeless confusion, and are sometimes led astray by the locals who resent the penetration of others into their neighborhoods.

From their own neighborhood, where B. J.—the name she usually goes by in the book—is bothered by the stares from the *drari* and the people within their usually shuttered windows high above them, the family works its way to the most famous public square in Marrakech, the Djemaa el Fna. Along the way they—B. J., husband, Bob, children, David, Laura Ann, and Laila—pass by a group of Americans, "with their multicolored locks, patched jeans, backpacks, and boots . . . all stoned together in the postsiesta heat" (51), the most conspicuous sign that Americans were present in Morocco. (Later a small group of drug-taking Americans create problems when they move into Fernea's neighborhood.)

What first strikes them about the famous square, which all European tourists visit in Marrakech, is a begger boy asking for baksheesh. Daughter Laila recoils from the boy, whose "twisted arm . . . extended from a ragged piece of sleeve," and wonders why B. J. drops a coin in the boy's dirty palm. Fernea takes the occasion to point out a difference between East and West in the handling of poverty, disease, and deformity. The middle class in America have (in 1971, at least) no need and few occasions to see such problems, since "Western cities manage very neatly to bundle up all of those troublesome sights and put them into institutions called old people's homes and prisons, orphanages and correctional centers, or into sections of town and country not frequented by our middle classes" (51). In that Moroccan city, the poor and rich, sick and healthy were not so neatly divided.

They do get to see what people travel to Marrakech to see, the grand medieval fair in the square, with its "marvelous fairy-tale quality" about it. Jesters, acrobats, snake charmers, magicians, and storytellers vie for the attention of the crowds in the shadow of the magnificent tower, the Koutoubia. Fernea explains the history of the place, including the legend that the square was saved from destruction when Eleanor Roosevelt persuaded King Mohammed V to keep it the way she remembered it from her youth, one of the most wonderful places in the world. Like so many Western visitors before her, B. J.'s description of the square is replete with the "medieval" and "dreamlike haze" of a fairy-tale world, an enchanted palace of delight like Disneyworld.

The Fernea family had not been there long before the enchantment wore thin. The "gnarled, misshapen dwarf" of the fairy tale is a blind man standing with his fellows, "a little band of misshapen and maimed men like himself" (55). "The jesters and acrobats are pale children, and the cheap, shiny silk of their costumes clings to their bony bodies." The Fernea children beg for a buggy ride through the city, another favorite of the tourists. To their credit, they insist on riding through the old city rather than spending their time in the usual tourist haunts, the palaces of Marrakech. The tour is, at first, interesting and informative. They learn from the driver, for example, that King Hassan is "afraid to come to Marrakech," the first sign of political unrest that will affect the Ferneas as it does most of the city later in the story (57). They pass shops of ironmongers and charcoal merchants, as well as sidewalk restaurants, and then they head into an old residential section of the city.

There, in the streets so close that the houses on either side could be touched from the buggy, the mood changes abruptly. Street children, *drari*, shout insults and begin pelting the carriage with clods of dirt and then stones. The driver manages to bring the Ferneas out safely. When the family returns to the neighborhood, though, two boys accost them, one shouting, "Baksheesh!" and tweaking one of the daughters' blond hair. Bob, normally temperate, raises his hand in defiance and threatens the boys. When they finally retreat to the safety of their home, the Ferneas discuss the episode rationally. After all, they are foreigners, and foreigners have treated the Moroccans badly in the past. Still, the tour of Marrakech has not gone well for the Americans, and B. J. concludes the episode on a melancholy note: "The tiles gleamed brightly, the pond glimmered in the artificial light, the door was shut on the narrow, forbidding street. This was no fairy tale, I told myself. We were alone, strange and alien, in a strange and alien world" (59).

Gradually the family settles in, and the city becomes less strange to them. For B. J., the transformation involves a great many minor incidents. The narrative focuses on two initially unrelated aspects of Moroccan life: the way ordinary women live in a society that demands a separation of the sexes most Westerners find difficult to comprehend; and the meaning of the Islamic concept of 'baraka.' The two aspects come together in B. J.'s increasing involvement in the lives of the women in her neighborhood. Slowly she learns what Islam means, not just to the theologians but to the women of Rue Tresor. The climax of the narrative comes when the two aspects converge in the rich symbolism of a pilgrimage to the shrine of Sidi Bel Abbas (pt. 4, ch. 21, 370–76).

Fernea is good enough to provide the reader with a map of the *zanka* in which the family lived—Rue Tresor, off Rue Bab Agnaou—and a lengthy cast of characters. The dramatis personae is useful, but a distortion of the narrative, in much the same way that the list of characters in a Shakespearean play is a distortion. From the list, in which virtually everyone mentioned in the book is placed in the context of a family, and each family is dominated by the man of the household—the man mentioned first, his wife and children following—except where a widow has taken charge of the family, one might gather that Moroccans live in households divided between the sexes and arranged hierarchically the way most English families were, say, in Shakespeare's day. Certainly there is a good bit of truth to that way of looking at Moroccan society, as social anthropologist Fatima Mernissi has made clear, for example, in *Beyond the Veil*, (20–24). In *A Street in Marrakech*, however, the women dominate the narratives and men are mentioned for the most part only as they have an association with women. The stories tell of a rather complicated social order in which women are hardly the passive and dull creatures Orientalist fantasy has made them out to be.

Getting to know the women of Rue Tresor was not an easy task for Fernea. Although the family rented a house from Hajja Kenza, a widow, and retained the services of Aisha—and Fernea was by now fluent in Arabic—B. J. found herself on the outside of a small group of women who knew one another well. The main thread of narrative follows B. J.'s relationship with Aisha, and it is through Aisha that she learns about baraka.

The Ferneas moved to Marrakech in August 1971, and it was not until December that Aisha opened up to B. J. The story is told in the chapter that ends part 1, "Rooftops and *Zankas*." The chapter opens with as bleak an impression of Moroccan life as Fernea paints. She happens to pass a man, smeared with blood, lying in his ragged clothes and muddy, broken shoes, perhaps alive, perhaps dead, but unattended by the passersby. A man behind her suggests that she leave the scene: "It is not your business" (103). The sense of her helplessness—as a woman and as a foreigner—leads her to lament,

> The man with the bloody face stayed in my mind, and a host of other pictures came, unbidden: the vagabond children who slept in doorways around Djemaa el Fna; the babies, crying unnoticed in the slings in which their mothers carried them on their backs; the fighting in the streets, the teasing and the insults that seemed to be general, for Bob and I had both realized that the Moroccans were as hard on each other as they were on us, the foreigners! What kind of people were these? (104)

The ease with which Fernea moves from incident to incident obscures the patterning that gives the book a tight narrative structure. From this wintry, depressing note, Fernea comes suddenly upon a very different scene, one that changed her life in the community in a very profound way. She learns that rooftops are the preserve of women, who work without their veils and talk to one another across the roofs. Aisha begins to identify the women B. J. has never seen in their public garb, and she talks briefly about her own life in the *darb*, or neighborhood: "We stood together on the roof in the sunshine, while Aisha began to talk about 'her' darb. From that day, her manner toward me changed. Why? I will never know. Perhaps she enjoyed talking about her darb, her family, her neighbors, even to me, a stranger" (108).

The change in her relationship with Aisha is reflected in the discussion between them that follows: the changes taking place in the larger world, in Morocco since independence. Part 1 is mainly exposition, as one might expect. By centering the explanations of Moroccan history and culture in ordinary human events, Fernea once again demonstrates a deft command of her material. The reader comes to know about Arab-Muslim culture in a way that seems almost accidental to the episodes that occur. The possibility of a friendship between an American *nasrani* and a nonliterate Muslim working mother makes it possible for the reader to understand a very different culture.

Time and again the relationship with Aisha offers B. J. an opening to a life world. The difficulty of such an opening is illustrated by two anecdotes. Just as Fernea is learning about her neighbors on the roofs, Aisha tells her the women do not visit one another informally, unless they are relatives. "How can you know about people," Aisha tells her, "if they are strangers and not of your family?" (113). Later, one of Bob Fernea's Moroccan friends tells her that the way Moroccans kept the French from capturing their souls was by not inviting the French into their homes. The man, Abdul Aziz, a French teacher, recalls an incident in his life when a Frenchman, with whom he was close, asked Abdul Aziz to recommend a servant from among his entourage. The Ferneas protest that Abdul Aziz had misunderstood the French term, which means, not "family," but "people around you." Abdul Aziz is not persuaded, however. He answers with his understanding of the term *entourage*: "And who would they be, Madame, except the members of your family?" (321)

Largely through Aisha, Fernea is invited to a wedding, learns of the Islamic festivals, discovers the way elaborate designs are made with henna to decorate women's hands, has her daughter's fortune told, and generally comes to know the customs of the land. Only in spring, when she can walk through Djemaa el Fna without having the locals badger her—and she feels herself a Marrakechi—does it become clear to her that religion is important in the lives of the women she has gotten to know. Since women do not participate in the mosque to the degree that men participate in much of the Islamic world, it is particularly difficult to grasp a Muslim woman's understanding of Islam. Traditionally, education—literacy—in the Muslim world has meant instruction in reading the Qur'an. Since women have been excluded from much of that training, an untrained woman like Aisha could not read as much as the Arabic street sign in her *darb*. When Fernea tries to enter this part of the life world, she is allowed to see what few outsiders see, but her curiosity pushes her friendship with Aisha to its limits.

The first hint that religion is indeed important to the women of the zanka comes at the beginning of part 3, when, as mentioned earlier, Fernea learns that one of the women, Fatima Henna, is joining a *zawiya*, a religious sisterhood, equivalent of the Sufi brotherhoods that visitors to Morocco have written about so frequently. (According to Clifford Geertz, Morocco had some twenty-three brotherhoods at the outset of World War II, and nearly one-fifth of the male population belonged to one of the brotherhoods [51–52]). Fernea did not know *zawiyas* for women existed (233). Aisha did not join one, but she did visit the *murabits*, the tombs of *sidis*, or saints. Since the *murabit*, in Morocco, is forbidden to non-Muslims, Aisha is faced with a problem when Fernea indicates a desire to visit one.

At first Aisha tries a socially acceptable solution, and Fernea is disappointed when she is taken to the Saadian tombs, one of the chief tourist attractions in Marrakech (238). ("Few people were visiting on this cold day of our false spring; the vines, leafless in winter, hung down bare tendrils over the walled passage.") Her disappointment lifts when Aisha then agrees to take her to a small *murabit*, the tomb of Allala Arkiya (239–42). Clearly foreign and Christian—Fernea is dressed, not in djellaba and veil, but in a red scarf, plaid coat, black stockings and shoes—she is introduced by Aisha as "my friend, she is Christian but she wants baraka from Allala Arkiya, believe me, she is in need of baraka, and who knows, she may need it more than we do, since she is a Christian" (239).

The visit to Allala Arkiya is successful in prompting an understanding of the *murabits*, but one of Bob's friends, Abdul Lateef, irritates Fernea when he patronizingly dismisses her understanding of baraka (243–45), something like the early Christian concept of 'grace.' Even more infuriating is that Fernea's husband smiles in recognition of her apparent naivete. If she was curious before, her treatment at the hands of the superior males only strengthens her determination to know what the term means—how it functions in the lives of Moroccan women.

Her complex motives in pursuing this very serious interest in Islam are beautifully captured in the description of Fernea's preparation for visiting the shrine of Mul el Ksour (discussed in chapter 2). She is embarrassed when Aisha's son laughed at her when he saw her wearing a djellaba and head scarf. The sky that day is strangely colored, a detail that seems ominous. She notes a drummer with wild and matted black hair drumming near the saint's tomb. And she has to jump aside to avoid being hit by a tourist carriage "full of fashionably dressed English ladies" (284). Although B. J. is unwilling to join the dance itself, the girl inside the shrine who led the group by dancing herself into a trance state impresses the American observer.

The mystical trance dancing (*derdaba*) has had an impact on many observers, as we have seen in chapter 2. Since it is sometimes accompanied by slashing and self-mutilation, the effect is often one of fascinated horror. Recall that after Fernea watched it, her patronizing acquaintance, Abdul Lateef, proceeds to explain her experience to her. He can not appreciate her response—that it was "fun" (294)—when he sees in the activity a very serious attempt to find baraka.

So often did Fernea hear about baraka that she devoted a whole chapter of *A Street in Marrakech* (pt. 3, ch. 14) to the elusive concept. She learns from Aisha that it is like *na'ama*, a "gift of God to the people in this world, food, water, things like that" (248). From Abdul Lateef she learns that baraka is "like an investment . . . you give something and get back something more" (248), but he cautions that without the proper *niya* or intention, it is of no use. Abdul Lateef suggests she attend a *moussem*, a religious festival, if she wants to understand baraka. She does just that, making a pilgrimage to the village of saint Moulay Ibrahim (ch. 15).

At Moulay Ibrahim, Aisha guides Fernea, in djellaba and head scarf, through the shrine. Fernea panics momentarily when she loses Aisha's grip. In the tomb she prays but does not throw herself across the tomb the way another woman does, nor does she kiss the tomb the way Aisha does (266–67), but it is clearly a moment of intense devotion for her. The sacrifice of a camel (and subsequent dragging it about the dusty streets of the village) fascinates her. But she does not follow Aisha when her friend dips a handkerchief in the blood of the sacrificed camel. Aisha explains that the handkerchief is for her daughter, in hopes that it will cure her of the terrible headaches she has been experiencing (275).

One or the other of Fernea's episodes involving baraka touches upon virtually the entire complex Geertz describes. Potentially, the greatest opportunity to come in contact with baraka presents itself in the pilgrimage to the most important holy place in Marrakech, the shrine of Sidi Bel Abbas. Aisha, whose friendship with B. J. has become more and more open, is once again the agent. With her help Fernea embarks on the pilgrimage, the climax of the narrative line, which comes just before the end of the book (pt. 4, ch. 21, 370–76). Once again the pattern repeats itself. The pilgrimage to Sidi Bel Abbas exhibits the finest in Christian-Muslim cooperation; it also pushes the friendship of individuals from two cultures to its limits.

Just before the Ferneas leave the city, B. J. discovers she has come between Aisha and Hajja Kenza. Without meaning any harm, B. J. had placed a burden on the old friendship of the two women; unwittingly she "had given more" to Aisha than to Kenza. Helping Aisha obtain a work permit was, Fernea, thought, a simple enough gesture for a friend. She had not foreseen that it would generate problems for the women in the neighborhood (350).

Their friendship is further complicated when B. J. makes her final, and most important, pilgrimage, to Sidi Bel Abbas. With all the expectation, she finds herself put off the pilgrimage again and again (368). Something keeps her from being drawn fully into the rituals. Although it is a hot day when they begin the pilgrimage, Aisha tells B. J. she will not need her djellaba, so Fernea appears in Western garb, a yellow summer dress and sandals, and Aisha wears her old djellaba.

They make their way along Rue Bab Agnaou, past the shops, schools, cinemas, and peddlars—the life of the city—and finally arrive at the shrine. Many beggars sit in the courtyard of the mosque. B. J. is increasingly nervous, wondering if she should enter the shrine or not. In the courtyard, Aisha makes the decision for her: "I'll go in and light the candle and say a prayer for your daughter Laila. You wait here" (373). Fernea is "startled" by the decision. Left alone outside, she has a particularly disconcerting experience, which she offers as a metaphor for the complex of motives surrounding the event. A beggar in a wheelchair, "a strange figure with his leather-patched legs, his bald head," stares at her and pushes toward her. She recognizes that he is "almost as strange as me" (373). Closer and closer he pushes toward her, close enough that she "could see clearly the sparse black hairs on his chin," and she becomes more and more uncertain of his motivation.

At the last moment the beggar, apparently warned away by a veiled woman, swerves away from Fernea, and Aisha arrives to relieve the tension. The experience is enough to convince her that, however close she has gotten to Aisha and to the Muslim women of her *zanka* in that year, she is still the outsider: "I moved backward again, realizing suddenly what an incongruous figure I was in this setting, far more incongruous than the beggar, bald, broken, and patched as he was—for the beggar had a place in his shrine, he belonged here, this was his territory. I was a stranger, and alone" (374).

The pilgrimage does not end with that. For a final time B. J. winds her way, this time the reverse of her early tour of the city, "through the labyrinth of the medina" (374). Through the confusion of crowded lanes she makes her way back to the Djemaa el Fna, where she recognizes again the man walking on broken glass, the acrobats, the pigeon man: "My education had just begun, and I was already leaving." As she leaves the square an African boy selling cowrie shells whispers to her, "in heavy, strangely accented Oxford England, "If you don't know the way, Madame, there is no other, you see" (375).

Anthropologist Paul Rabinow conducted his fieldwork in Morocco just a few years before Fernea arrived there. He wrote a now classical treatise, following philosopher Paul Ricoeur, on the nature of the hermeneutical journey, "the comprehension of self by the detour of the comprehension of the other," in *Reflections on Fieldwork in Morocco* (1977). He marked the stages of a kind of cultural pilgrimage in which he moved, typical of "his" American culture, by degrees, through a series of Moroccan informants, toward an understanding of the other culture. Like Fernea he observed a wedding, attended a *moussem*, watched the ritual dancing, and finally made contact with an informant who became a friend. Each stage of the journey was marked by disruption. For the most part he learned the same truths about Islam that Fernea did, though his informants were exclusively male—the importance of *niya*, the intention (144), for example.

Rabinow also encountered the limits of friendship. Just before he knew it was time for him to return to America, Rabinow asked his friend Driss ben Mohammed one final question. Are we all equal? The friend could not refuse to answer, and the answer confirmed what Aisha's leaving B. J. in the courtyard of Sidi Bel Abbas meant to her:

> The answer was no, we are not equal. All Muslims, even the most unworthy and reprehensible, and we named a few we both knew, are superior to all non-Muslims. That was Allah's will. The division of the world into Muslim and non-Muslim was *the* fundamental cultural distinction, the Archimedean point from which all else turned. This was ultimately what separated us. (147).

The confrontation produced the vivid awareness of a gap that in retrospect can be seen to govern the rhetorical situation of *A Street in Marrakech*. The book is as much a pilgrimage in the "making of an American" as it is a description of Moroccan Muslim women. Written by an American, who is situated in a certain historical and cultural milieu, for Americans, in American English, Fernea's account is a pilgrimage into the cultural self, a transfer this author has called a "translocation of ethnicity."

Elizabeth Warnock Fernea discovered that ordinary Muslim women in Morocco have a deep sense of religion that is not easily seen by the outsider. The closer she was drawn into the lives of the women around her, the more she saw just how pervasive Islamic concepts and rituals were for them. The women in Morocco have access—beyond the many private and home-based practices—to the holy places, to ritual dancing, to participation in rituals, to encounters with baraka in much the same way as men—though, of course, separately. There are, of course, reformers who wish to strip Islamic practice of what they consider un-Islamic magic and saint worship. B. J.'s pilgrimage revealed to her, though, a rich and complex, if seldom observed, religious life of women. In the process she encountered the limits of cross-cultural understanding.

To this point, the voices have been Western, even though Jane Bowles, Paul Bowles, and Elizabeth Fernea strove to hear the other. The five Moroccan stories that are discussed in the next chapter do not entirely escape the distortions of the Orientalist mirror. Four of the stories were written in Standard Arabic by Moroccan writers; the fifth was written in English by a Moroccan whose first language is Arabic. Translation of the first four, however well accomplished, only brings the problem of *cultural* translation to the foreground. The fifth story was conceived in English does not escape the problem any more than the others. Even the fairly straightforward discussion of the stories that is carried on here is burdened with it. How can even the simplest plot outline of a story avoid the Orientalist trap?

The studies of five stories do not pretend to be exhaustive, nor do they claim to escape the central problem this book has been written to explore. However, they do offer a step in a certain direction, an invitation to the other to retranslate what is written here—a Rogerian strategy that is considered in the final chapter.

The five stories, by five Moroccan writers, date from the end of World War II to the early 1990s. Since the term *postmodern* was first used by a historian (Toynbee) to describe a world profoundly changed by World War II, it is fitting that the earliest of these stories dates from just after the war and before Moroccan independence, when anticolonialist protest was particularly strong. None of the works discussed here avoids the struggle for independence; all of them reflect the burden of confusion and disillusionment when it became clear that the modern West would not go away, that Morocco itself would continue to struggle with its identity long into the postcolonial era.

Chapter Seven

Insider Views:

Five Moroccan Writers

ORIENTALISM AND OCCIDENTALISM

The stereotypes of Orientalism are studiously avoided by Elizabeth Fernea, who described the women in her Marrakech neighborhood in the most ordinary circumstances of their daily lives. Fernea's narrative is ostensibly a matter-of-fact record of events as they happened, though the previous chapter studied the careful orchestration of those facts. In particular, the American woman went with her family to Morocco in order to understand the reality of Moroccan life, to experience it from the inside. The journey that shaped her narrative was no random wandering but a quest, a pilgrimage, as many stories about entering a territory from the outside tend to be. In this third phase, the Western traveler enters with a very conscious awareness of Orientalist stereotypes and tries to avoid them herself. If at some level Fernea considers Western civilization superior to Eastern, she nowhere hints at it. Rather, she finds a way to let the cultural other speak to her. She pushes relationships beyond the dispassionate public concern of cultural anthropologists—at least of the earlier anthropologists—careful not to "participate" too fully in the participant observation they conducted in the fieldwork. Fernea comes close to an authentic friendship with a

177

Moroccan woman, only to discover a barrier separating them despite the good will the two had developed between them.

The chapters that follow also try to listen to the many different voices of the East—by considering Moroccan writers, storytellers, and persons who may or may not be representative of a larger reality but who in any case have been interviewed by Americans and Moroccans in the Moroccans' own locations and in their own language. The short stories, folktales, and life stories are never free of mediation by translators and others who have "interests" in the East. The Moroccan writers and informants, it will become clear, are never free of the West. A question to be kept open in the following chapters is whether an Occidentalism has emerged that is the reverse of Orientalism. To the extent that the West has deeply penetrated and disturbed the East, and not vice versa, the West as it appears in the thinking of the East can never exactly be the reverse of Orientalism. But the Moroccans discussed here are ever aware of the outsider. Their images of the West again and again reflect deep ambivalence about modernity, modernization, and Westernization.

THE MIRROR AND THE PATH

Orientalism is a mirror by which the West constructs itself in images. We are used to thinking of mirrors as reflecting an undistorted (and unmediated) self: we look into a mirror and see ourselves. But, as the previous chapters have tried to show, photography, especially moving pictures, sociology (much of it derived from Marxist thought), and depth psychology (especially of the Lacanian sort) have challenged that naive view. The dismantling of onto-theology has further subverted our earlier confidence in the existence of a self. The Orient is mainly a projection of our fears and desires, but it constructs a cultural self for us.

A key principle is that the questions we ask, the genres we give to the East, and our own discourse of modernity and modernization cannot simply be brushed aside. They are part of us, and if others borrow, for example, realistic fiction, they are not simply borrowing a technology of storytelling. To those in the East who are learning to describe themselves (in the last hundred years), the tools of the West are irresistible, like the automobile. The borrowing of modern literary realism changes the shape of lives and the shape of narratives. The psychological and sociological understanding of existence, supplanting earlier onto-theological understandings, is written into the simplest of stories. What Daniel Lerner called the "psychic mobility" of the modern cannot simply be canceled by the one who has borrowed modern technology.

The question remains: How dependent upon an equally distorting (but equally productive) Occidentalist mirror are these Eastern images? A second concern arises with the figure of the path. Visitors entering an unknown, but exotic, territory "without a guidebook," to use Edith Wharton's phrase, are often troubled and fall back upon old patterns of behavior—the way Commodore Trunnion did. Wharton knew guidebooks to Morocco, but they were in French and all but inaccessible to most of her readers. The writings that have been discussed thus far quite often portray journeys to the outside. In the case of *The Aeneid*, the journey that takes Aeneas to Carthage and to Dido is a misstep, a swerving from the hero's destiny to find a home for his people. The stereotypes that still describe Arab-Muslim peoples as overly emotional and irrational, primitive, savage, and backward—or as veiled but secretly erotic—derive from a long tradition that defines the Oriental man and the Oriental woman as significantly unlike the ones who visited their lands.

Eastern writers, storytellers, and informants also use the journey as a way to describe encounters with the West. In all but one of the short stories discussed in this chapter, characters are engaged in journeys that end in disaster. The outside is the danger, and the outside largely is seen under the sign of the West. Home, family, and the safe haven are under threat of ruin or are already ruined. (The exception is the first story, which proves the rule. In that story the West, in the form of French *colons*, invade the home territory and seize it. There is no journey out, but the village is destroyed by the strangers.) Even the women victimized at home, some of whom are forced to make painful journeys into the wilderness outside, are safe inside. The struggle for Moroccan independence and the complexities (especially for women) after independence are implicated in these journeys. At stake is always the search for identity amidst the alienating forces of modernization.

As in Western literature, the Eastern stories develop through contrasts between individual and family, the atomistic self and *homo contextus*, between (uniplex, low-density) society and true community. (According to Ernest Gellner [29–30], the first to have pointed out the last distinction was, perhaps ironically, Ibn Khaldun, whose home is still marked in the Old City of Fez.) Skepticism and agnosticism in the West are contrasted with a religious understanding of the world that has penetrated into everyday Arabic speech.

The Western forms of exploration and the descriptions of people's lives found in the next chapters—the short story and the life story—are so well known to the West that they often pass unnoticed before us. Because the forms are still connected with Western interests, they speak to us; but they certainly do not exhaust the forms available to the East. (Poetry, with its great prestige in the Arab-Muslim world, is not considered here, for example.) The stories do not comprise "Moroccan literature," and the claim cannot be made that they are "representative" of Moroccan experience. But because the stories are told in such a way that we can hear them, they allow us a glimpse of the other from the inside.

MODERNISMS AND POSTMODERNISMS

The influence of the West is a burden on all Arabic writers who opt to write in narrative forms invented by and for the West. For Arabic fiction writers in the twentieth century, realism and high modernism are not so much opposed to each other (as they are for many Western authors) as they are different facets of modernism. Postmodern experimental fiction that subverts traditional forms has had a major influence since 1967 (as it has in America), but it has offered more recent authors the opportunity to combine Western forms with traditional Arabic storytelling and thus to confront the hegemony of the West. Anton Shammas's *Arabesques* (1986), begun in Arabic and then written in Hebrew, is a striking case in point of a novel that continually subverts the narrative forms in which it is written, retelling stories from different points of view and allowing conflicting versions to stand.

In his survey of recent "cultural studies" (mainly Anglo-American, but involving, as in the case of Said's *Orientalism*, the problem of cultural diversity), David Bathrick ends with a series of questions about stories and national identity: "What forms of narrative express the ideology of the modern nation? How do questions of race and gender, class and colonialism change the boundaries of national identity? How is

national identity itself the construction of a particular historical imaginary?" (337).[1]

The five narratives discussed in this chapter present very diverse
answers to Bathrick's questions. The diversity is the most noticable
aspect of the stories. The five writers are Moroccans who have begun to
gain international attention.[2] With the exception of Jilalai El Koudia,
they have chosen to write in Arabic, when they might well have chosen
French. (El Koudia is the only Moroccan writer to have had a short
story written in English accepted for publication in an Arabic journal—
but only when the editor had the story translated into Arabic!) As
Moroccans, they have insider views of their own culture that are never
completely available to Western observers. But the choices facing them
in writing short stories involve a complex interaction with, on the one
hand, Western modern and postmodern fiction and, on the other hand,
centuries of Arabic oral and written storytelling.

Daniel Lerner rightly notices the importance of "modern" fiction
(by which he means both literary realism and high modernist fiction) to
the "psychic mobility" or "empathy" he sees as the most important
Western quality that transforms traditional societies whenever they
"modernize." In *The Passing of Traditional Society: Modernizing the Middle East*,
Lerner claims, "The typical literary form of the modern epoch, the
novel, is a conveyance of disciplined empathy. Where the poet once
specialized in self-expression, the modern novel reports his sustained
imagination of the lives of others" (52). His understanding of the "modern" is not shared by literary critics who prefer to contrast modernism
with realism, but it explains the way realism *and* high modernism could
alike influence the East as Western forms of the modern (i.e., modernizing vs. traditional society).

Leila Abouzeid, who was a young girl when Morocco gained its
independence and is a product of the Arabization of the Moroccan
schools, is the most determined of the five in her choice of Arabic,
rather than French. She is also the one most aware of the double bind in
which Moroccan women writers find themselves. The heroine of her
novella, "Year of the Elephant," is a nonliterate woman who learned to
read and write in order to help her husband resist the French protectorate. The not-unexpected outcome of her efforts is the terrible helplessness the woman feels when her husband repudiates her once
Morocco gained its independence. The angry protest against a particu-

larly conspicuous form of "phallocentric order" is reflected in her short story, "Divorce."

It is probably not surprising that Leila Abouzeid's fiction is the most conventionally realistic of the five writers considered here.[3] Ben Jallūn's "A Stranger" is more obviously a call for political action than is Abouzeid's story, and it derives more than hers does from the romantic tradition of heroic narrative, a tradition that often looked to Oriental stories for much of its inspiration. (Ben Jallūn's story, of course, was written decades before Abouzeid's, and it is important to remember that his "A Stranger" was published during the Protectorate, rather than after independence.) The other writers are, in different ways, postmodernists.

The term *postmodern* seems to have been used first by Arnold Toynbee to describe the world emerging from the devastation of World War II. For Western writers and artists, the apparent collapse of a world order after World War I, which heavily influenced high modernism, was exaggerated by certain events of World War II: Nazi and Communist totalitarianism; mass extermination; the possibility of mass destruction in atomic warfare; overpopulation; and the degrading of the human and natural environment. As M. H. Abrams has observed, "An undertaking in some postmodernist writings is to subvert the foundations of our accepted modes of thought and experience so as to reveal the 'meaninglessness' of existence and the underlying 'abyss,' or 'void,' or 'nothingness' on which any supposed security is conceived to be precariously suspended" (120). The way "both modernism and postmodernism have been interpreted according to Western intellectual, ideological and aesthetic models" has been raised recently (Brooker xii).

One of the many critics who have attempted to explain postmodernism is Ihab Hassan. His version of a postmodern "culture," dubbed "star fleet postmodernism," highlights the gap between modernism and postmodernism. A chart of contrasts, which begins with romanticism vs. pataphysics and form vs. antiform, purpose vs. play, and design vs. chance, includes over thirty contrastive features. The genital/phallic is opposed by the polymorphous and androgynous. Origin/cause is challenged by difference-differance/trace. The chart ends with irony in opposition to metaphysics, determinacy undermined by indeterminacy, and transcendence subverted by immanence (Brooker 11–12). For Hassan, according to Peter Brooker, postmodernism is nothing less than "a new *episteme* and way of criticism" (11). At this point, star fleet postmodernism, at least, is a challenge, not just to high modernism, but to the foundations of modernity—and an extension of the challenge to onto-theology in which literary realism was conspicuously participant.[4]

As a movement that has challenged modernism in virtually all of the arts, postmodernism gained momentum in the late 1960s, when so many political, educational, and artistic traditions were called into question. What has been labeled a "third phase" here indicates a turn that many artists, fiction writers, and anthropologists have taken. With so much of the traditional West called into question, the cultural other may offer at once a critique of the West and an opportunity to see alternative realities.

In the Arab-Muslim world, the 1967 war was certainly a triggering event, and postmodern experimentation is at least partly the result of a general questioning of "identity" (personal, national, and cultural). The highly conscious play of narrative forms, one derived from modern Western realism and the other from the Arabic tradition of the oral storyteller, such as one sees in the Syrian fictionalist, Walid Ikhlassy (Maier, "Postmodern" 73–76), has been taken up elsewhere in the Arab-Muslim world. Moroccans Mohammed Barrada and Mohammed Chukri, whose backgrounds could not have been more different, find themselves writing strikingly unusual fictions that are certainly postmodern. (Chukri, who learned to read and write at age twenty-one, was the only one of Paul Bowles's *Five Eyes* storytellers to work from a written text, while Barrada is a very highly educated critic, well aware of the latest European theories.) Jilali El Koudia's stories, unusual in that he prefers to write in English rather than in Arabic, are postmodern in the other sense, in that they allow traditional Arabic to enter in very unexpected hybrid phrases, in a kind of postcolonial or "new" English.

Until very recently, when Moroccan scholars such as Lahcen El Yazghi Ezzaher have begun to see a reason to translate Moroccan writers, the very idea of a "Moroccan literature" would have seemed very odd, rather like a New York State literature or a California literature. The use of Modern Standard Arabic by writers throughout the Arabic-speaking world has maintained a sense of identity that transcended modern nation-states. (Only Egypt has dominated the center to such an extent that it seems reasonable to produce volumes of Egyptian short

stories.) The five writers here are Moroccans, but they do not constitute
a Moroccan literature.

'ABD AL-MAJĪD BEN JALLŪN, "A STRANGER" (1947)

However realism, modernism, and postmodernism are defined, there is
little doubt that Arab writers have often felt the uncomfortable bind in
having appropriated Western literary forms in their search for an Arab
identity. It may be, as Syrian author George Salim argued, that the
Western novel reads and performs trivially and that Arabic fiction has
escaped the "captivation" of the Western novel and has grown into its
own proper identity (7). But the influence of Western fiction, a form of
writing whose prestige is one of the defining characteristics of modernity, on Arab writers is uncontested (Roger Allen, *The Arabic Novel*
163–65).

That influence is probably most easily seen in a work that is direct
in its attack on the West—and yet appropriates a literary form not from
traditional Arabic storytelling and poetry but from Western realism,
'Abd al-Majīd Ben Jallūn's "A Stranger" ("Gharīb").[5] Salih J. Altoma's survey of Arabic fiction showed that one important tendency among
Arabic writers of fiction has been an anti-Western and pro-Islamic position. Faced with the conflict between Islamic and Western values, some
writers underscored the corruption of the materialist and atheist West
and stressed Islam as the foundation of modern society (Altoma 81).
Ben Jallūn's "A Stranger" does not explicitly stress Islamic values, but it
certainly portrays the West in a most negative light.

The story, published almost a decade before Moroccan independence, is simplicity itself, and it is more a call to action than a study of
the characters involved. Set in the early days of the French
Protectorate, it follows the destruction caused in a rural Moroccan village by a poor Frenchman from the south of France. The "stranger"
(rajul gharīb) is called André, though the narrator, who speaks for the
village, thinks the name may be just another of the many deceptions the
stranger carried out to take control over the village. The "trickster"
André insinuates himself into the village, appears to accept the village
ways, and eventually becomes the "dictator" over the families that had
taken him in. The story focuses on one of those families.

André's rise to power involves a manipulation of the most basic relationships in traditional Moroccan life. He seeks refuge on an "intensely dark winter's night" in a violent storm. The hospitality of a landowner, Uncle 'Abd al-Salam, opens the farm to the man, "the like of whom they had not seen before." André learns Arabic, dresses and eats like the villagers, attends the mosque, and works hard on the farm. At first the villagers do not notice that he has a plan. They like him for his "energy and intelligence." He begins to offer advice on "modern (*hadith*) agricultural methods" (269).

Once he dupes the old landowner André introduces change that will destroy the traditional relationship of people to the land (*al-ard*) and to the patriarch, called by Ben Jallūn "a sort of socialism (*ishtirakiya*) which was common among Moroccan tribes (*qaba'il*)." Where he had once become a different person in taking on the customs of the community, he changes again when he takes over for Uncle 'Abd al-Salam. The change in André is exactly the change caused by French overlordship.

The remote village hears news of "the war and the occupation," but the events are too far away to disturb them. But their new "chief" (*ra's*) begins to slip away for meetings with his "masters in Rabat" (271). As he gains control and begins to act rather arbitrarily, favoring some at the expense of others, he changes back to the old André, wearing "strange shoes" and avoiding the mosque. He brings in advisers, a group of Frenchmen, with plans to improve farming. At that point the villagers raise their first protest, against the intruders who had already destroyed the cities and were bent on changing the farms as well.

Their protest leads to the first outbreak of violence: "André lost his temper, and his hot French blood rushed to his head. He attacked the man, seized him by the chest, shaking him, saying, 'Don't you ever talk like that again, or I'll break your head in, you filthy fellow'" (271). The villagers, who could not "conceive of chiefdom without friendship," become agitated, and André calls in a detachment of fully armed soldiers to quell the uprising. With now dictatorial powers, André drains the beauty out of the life of the farm. "That beautiful fertile land also was no more, that land which used to feed their bodies and souls at one and the same time" (270). Finally it sinks in that the villagers have become slaves.

The climax of "A Stranger" comes when André, having secured for himself a life of wealth and power, decides to satisfy the one remaining natural urge. Uncle 'Abd al-Salam has two sons, Muhammad and Ahmad, and a daughter, Fatima. André arrests the sons on an arbitrary charge and sets his sights on the young virgin. When she goes to the "palace" in which André has installed himself, he tries to seduce and then force himself upon her. She becomes a true heroine when she acts for her family and the village by destroying the dictator.

The virgin liberates the village by, ironically, turning that symbol of Western control upon the stranger. In a highly charged scene, André pulls out a revolver (*musaddas*) to threaten her, then tosses it unwisely on the desk when he rushes at Fatima. Given her chance, she snatches the pistol from the desk, gives an impassioned address, and shoots him.

At the beginning of the story, when the stranger first enters, he drops a book (*kitab*) unnoticed on the floor. The narrator hints darkly, "The wind was shouting: 'Read that book! Read that book!' But nobody heard." If the book is the Bible, taken as a symbol of the hated Protectorate, the story takes on a religious subtext. One would expect the opening to be matched in the virgin's heroic speech at the end of the story, but any explicitly Islamic message is muted, perhaps because it is already implicit in the traditions of the villagers.

The rhetorical force of the virgin's speech is hardly a reflection of a highly individualized character, for nothing is known of Fatima apart from her age (fourteen or so) and her virginity. She is obviously Morocco, her innocence (*tahara*) all but violated (*khadasha*) by the stranger. (The phrase it is translated as "rape" in the final words Fatima speaks in the story.) Her brothers try to keep her from shooting André, but she will not have it. The speech, with much of the rhetorical flourish of traditional Arabic poetry, is worth noting for its control of the story's major symbols.

> Vengeance for the cultivators and the shepherds! Do you remember how you first came to us, a mere nobody, shabbily clothed, covered in mud, trembling in the storm from weakness and exhaustion? Today, we see you in your true light, a dastardly devil! You hold power over this farm and others around it, near and far. But you can never have power over our hearts. And so long as you are powerless to take away the contempt I feel, you are still as you were when you arrived, weak and exhausted! You are now in my hands—I, the simple farm-girl. And you are trembling with terror and fear, despite your knowledge and your authority— because it is I who hold the weapon today. I have snatched it from you,

you coward, to reveal you as a weak man cringing before a weak girl. Because the weak girl has a piece of steel in her hand.

Her final words are brief, but they illustrate the power of the paratactic style so much favored in Arabic prose. The brothers ask her not to kill the dictator, and she answers, "What? Not kill him? He snatched from us our land and liberty, our cattle and contentment. He seized this land which our forefathers owned for thousands of years. And only a moment ago, he came at me, with the intention of raping me!" To preserve a prose style favored in English, the translation departs slightly from the repetition in the original, as in "our land and our liberty and our cattle and our contentment" (*arḍna wa ḥurritna wa mashitna wa raḥatna*). But the translation certainly captures the force of this appeal to throw off the "protectors" who would rape the land of Morocco.

MOHAMMED BARRADA, "LIFE BY INSTALLMENTS" (1979)

Dr. Mohammed Barrada—Arabic books are careful to include authors' titles on the cover—is in many ways the most sophisticated and cosmopolitan of the new Moroccan writers. Born in 1938, he earned degrees in Arabic at Cairo University and in modern literary criticism at the Sorbonne. A translator and critic as well as a writer of postmodern fiction, Barrada is professor of Arabic at the University of Rabat, and he has served as president of the Union of Moroccan Writers. His story best known to the West, "Life by Installments" (1979),[6] is a learned, highly self-conscious blending of Eastern and Western traditions.

It is a bitter, despairing piece. If the Moroccan tradition appears inadequate to the alienation pervading "Life by Installments," the West is no help either, and is, indeed, the enemy. Not directly, or simply, as in Ben Jallūn's romantic-heroic "A Stranger," but more insidiously, since in "Life by Installments" the West has penetrated to the very cortex of Moroccan consciousness and jarred it into a kind of diplopia. The story is virtually plotless, decentered, a series of quick cuts, shots that only with some forcing constitute a scene.

The diplopia is evident immediately, in the opening words of the story. In good Moroccan Arabic, the first-person narrator is multiplied into a plural. "We woke (*qamna*) late, yawning as we lay on the bed, our bones feeling as though they'd fall apart" (128). What unity is given to the story is simply the time, a day that begins in this unpromising way,

staggers through a series of apparently unrelated and often generalized events, to its dispirited end: "In the evening we were conscious of
the same feeling of disintegration in our bones, also an even gloomier
melancholy (*ka'aba*)" (133). The day is unusual only in that it is a holiday and "we" do not have to work, but the release from work offers no
relief. In the evening, after having awakened and taken pills, tried
unsuccessfully to read, had a guest for lunch, wandered about looking
for love, "we" ends up with no gain. The melancholy persists. "The
cars fly past, the buses are slow, jam-packed, the cinemas advertise
their heroes. It appeared to us that everyone around us was running
away (133)."

Hamid Eddijli, whose theoretical position derives from Lucien
Goldman's *Towards a Sociology of the Novel* (1964), struggles with this
unusual point of view. Clearly the subject is the center of the story, a
suffering subject quite clearly. But for this Moroccan critic it was not all
that obvious what the "we" represents. The we in some way stands in for
the author, but not as an individual. What, though, is the group? Since
the Marxist theory depends on a class structure that may not account
for Moroccan society, Eddijli finally decides that the we represents a
group of low- and middle-class "small bourgeoisie," not really a class,
since it has no coherence or shared ideology, but a "class of cultured
men" (19).

The we is not exactly a generation, although the story exactly distinguishes three generations: we between an older, believing generation
and a younger generation represented by a mindless boy of seventeen:

> The boy eats greedily; perhaps he's not thinking about anything. He is
> drawn to what is taking place around him, be it only in a mechanical
> manner. He has discovered the pleasure of smoking, chasing after the
> neighbours' daughters, also the football craze. After some thought he
> announces his desire to travel to Europe during the summer vacation,
> even if he has to walk (which would multiply the cost of his pilgrimage).
> (132)

One thing is certain about this group of cultured men: it is
markedly male. In the homosocial society reflected in the story, we
might possibly be either masculine or feminine through some of the
early shots, but is revealed when we think of sex, love, and marriage.
"Enthusiasm will vanish when we see the extent of our impotence. We'll
set off anew into the street. We'll feel lust renewing itself through the

vibrations of the rounded and curved portions of women's bodies"
(132).

Love is a most important topic of "our" discussion and longing.
Usually it is seen as a traditional ideal of married love, now impossible
in our world. The seventeen year old has no connection at all with that
ideal. We do, but only as a measure of the loss that, for the most part, is
laid to Western influence. When married friends are asked if they are
satisfied with one sexual partner, they admit that though they "love"
their wives, no one desires other women more than they do. "No doubt
it's due to the mixing of the sexes, to provocative advertising, to make-
up, to high heels and . . . what else?" (132).

Barrada pursues this theme beyond the obvious Western influences to something more basic, more corrosive, and prototypically
Western. We hear a familiar love story, told to illustrate that love can
prevail over the infatuation of sex. That banal, traditional tale is precisely what is now almost unheard of in the West. "Of course his story is
run-of-the-mill: they wanted to marry her off to an old man, so she
threatened to commit suicide and the two of them pledged themselves
to love each other until death etc." This traditional Eastern tale is not
rejected because the social order has changed to make it unlikely.
Rather, Barrada makes a surprising turn. What makes love no longer
possible is the insight of that preeminent modernist, Freud: "He won't
understand us then; no point in repeating to him what Freud said: 'I am
accustoming myself to the idea of regarding every sexual act as a
process in which four persons are involved'" (133).

Like much that is recounted in Barrada's story, the point is made,
and then not explicitly linked to the rest of the narrative. Sexual frustration itself is not destructive of the community. Certain other features of
this society are destructive, however, and they are linked to the West.
Barrada presents a list of those features: suicide, drink, and revolt, perhaps writing itself. Barrada only suggests as much: "And writing?" These
"destroy the familiar" and have created a generation dependent upon
foreign needs.

The modern West is readily apparent in the sights noticed by the
narrator on a gloomy walk through the city: the mixing of the sexes and
provocative advertising, in the bottles of beer, the cars, the buses and
the cinemas that have changed the public face of Morocco. The West is
somewhat less obvious in its symbolic capital. Freudian depth psychol-

ogy is one such Western borrowing. Once the unconscious is admitted into the discussion of human relations, the traditional religious understanding of humanity and fate can no longer offer useful explanations. The healing presupposed in Freudian analysis seems not to matter here. There is no healing. The depth—complexity itself—leaves no way out.

The West also appears in an odd little anecdote related near the beginning of Barrada's story. A woman described only as a neighbor (*al-jara*), a foreigner (*al-ajnabiya*), and a car owner, has a nasty habit of playing a trick on taxi drivers. Having been taken to her door by the cabbie, the foreign woman claims she has forgotten her money and then disappears into the building, leaving the cabbie hooting away in frustration (128). The point of this ironic tale is that the woman's mad laughter at the sadistic joke makes the narrator laugh enough to leave the despairing bed and begin a day of aimless wandering.

Although the episodes in "Life by Installments" do not add up to a coherent narrative, the beginning and the end of the story are marked by the presence of two other less obvious Western imports: modern medicine and a foreign concept of 'time' itself, the "life by installments" of the title (*hayah b-al-taqsit*). Hamid Eddijli has pointed to the three representations of time in "Life by Installments": the time of the short story, the time of the Marrakech journey forty years earlier, and the time of the book alluded to in the story, the tenth century (11). The latter times are meaningful, constituting a tradition that has been lost by the "class of cultured men" who narrate the story. One might describe what replaced the tradition, the life by installments—glimpsed in the meaningless wandering of the we at night that closes the narrative—by what Edward T. Hall termed "monochronic time." Monochronic time, characteristic of certain kinds of societies, most notably northern European industrialized societies, "is characteristic of low-involvement peoples, who compartmentalize time; they schedule one thing at a time and become disoriented if they have to deal with too many things at once."[7] In contrast to monochronic or M-time Hall posits polychronic or P-time. "Polychronic people, possibly because they are so much involved with each other, tend to keep several operations going at once, like jugglers" (173).

Clearly the we of the story is dislocated and disoriented. From the beginning this is a condition that requires a doctor. "Our sight was cleared and no doubt a dark yellowness overspread our face. Having previously visited the doctor, we had submitted our state of health to him and he had shaken his head knowingly" (128). The doctor has no real cure, but he offers pills that will help the patient. At the end of the story the doctor is mentioned again, and the connection between modern medicine and time is made explicit. The narrator is still suffering the "disintegration in our bones," and the melancholy has deepened. "We thought of ridding ourselves of it through the same famous medical prescription, but we hesitated because the doctor was precise about determining the time it should be taken: in the morning, not the evening. We shall wander round the streets" (133).

Eddijli located the center of the story in the suffering subject, and he located what he considered the key sentence in Barrada's story, a sentence uttered, no doubt ironically, by the doctor. Faced with the disordered state of health, we are told: "You're not alone—all those who think and dream and aren't content with reality are afflicted with your condition" (128). The opening and closing of the story show that the disaffected condition of the subject has no cure. We are condemned to wander the streets in the dark. Still, the largely plotless narrative has a kind of center, though it is one that ironically measures the gap separating the we from the tradition. The most traditional part of the story comes at a time that best illustrates polychronic time, which Hall sees still characterizing the Arab world. We have a guest at lunch, a relative, a member of the older generation ("getting on for sixty").

At lunch the three generations are, for the moment, together, and the historical depth of the tradition is elaborated. The preparation for this is a casual wandering in the "well-stocked library," where we happen to notice a book written "forty years ago" (i.e., during the colonial period, before independence). Barrada patches in a long passage from Mohammed ibn Mohammed ibn Abdullah al-Mu'aqqat's *The Marrakesh Journey or the Temporal Mirror of Vile Deeds*, also titled *The Sword Unsheathed against Him Who Renounces the Prophet's Sunna*. For one thing, the passage is written in a prose style at great variance from the postmodern blending of discourses—"polyphonic," according to Eddijli (19), following Mikhail Bakhtine.[8] Al-Mu'aqqat's book refers to an even earlier period, the tenth century, when the leaders through tyranny "have eaten flesh and drunk blood: they have sucked the marrow from the bone and have swallowed up the brains, leaving people neither the world nor yet religion" (129). How much more, the author asks, is this true of "this time of ours which has become like the unbelieving night?" The response by the "class of cultured men" is already predictable: boredom.

The narrative cuts quickly to lunch, where we are introduced to the sixtyish relative and the seventeen-year-old boy. The older man is himself deeply rooted in the Arab-Islamic tradition. He had memorized the Qur'an as a boy, become a *muezzin*, and, after his wife's death, opted to go on the hajj rather than marry another woman. Barrada adds an explanation: it is not permissible for a *muezzin* to go unmarried. By doing his sacred duty and pursuing the pilgrimage, the man lost his chance at marrying a relative of his choice; but he is still searching for another wife.

The Hajj takes the opportunity at lunch to tell yet another story, one designed to inspire the teenager. It does not. Nor does it sway the we who only adds an empty admonition to the boy but cannot believe as the Hajj believes. The Hajj tells them of an Uncle Abdurrahman, a "martyr," who died of drowning. It appears that Uncle Abdurrahman had secured an "amulet of the sea" to protect him from drowning, but left it in his *kaftan* when he stripped to go swimming—and promptly drowned. The Hajj sums up the tale with a vigorous acceptance of the will of Allah. "His skill in swimming helped him not and the sea has kept him swallowed up until now. Thus did Abdurrahman die and, where the sciences of this world and the next are concerned, it is we who are the losers" (131). The seventeen year old does not see the point, and neither does the representative of the middle generation.

The older man tries again with some remarks about the time of Moulay Abdul Aziz up to the time of the entry of the French into Morocco. "However, finding that this would be tedious, we thought instead to ask him about his private life." That turns out to be tedious as well, and the middle generation can draw neither comfort nor cure from the relative's wisdom. The seventeen year old has his own version of the hajj, a summer vacation in Europe where he can indulge his desires. For the we of the story, there is not even that refuge. The rest of the story is a wandering about and the discussion about the impossibility of true love (seen in traditional Eastern terms).

Eddijli cites a 1987 remark by Mohamed Barrada that underscores the melancholy of his earlier "Life by Installments." Of his generation of "writers and cultured men," Barrada insisted that

> we are not writers in the European way. We belong to a generation whose experience developed in the milieu of independence, sometime

before and sometime after. We started to spread a certain concept of modern literature at the same time we were devoted to political and cultural activities, and this gave our writings the aspect of committed writing. Those years were the years of independence, "boiling." We were doing our best at whatever cost to change society. We had such an illusion, we carried such a dream inside us, we were fighting to embody the concept of a committed literature . . . and this went along with the larger tendency toward change that characterized the national movement and the progressivist movement in their beginnings. (20)

"Life by Installments" follows the disillusionment that comes from the recognition that the West had penetrated far more deeply into the consciousness of the Moroccan than had been suspected. That generation had become so alienated from the religious and cultural traditions that in their diplopia, "We asked ourselves: Is there anything that endures? Then we returned home to write the story of this life we live by instalments" (134).

MOHAMMED CHUKRI, "FLOWER CRAZY" (1978)

In Mohammed Barrada's "Life by Installments," only one detail locates the story in space. The story within the story, about Uncle Abdurrahman, includes a reference to the Moroccan cities on either side of the river, Abu Raqraq. Other than that reference, the story might well have been set in any of a number of Moroccan locations. The city in which the narrator wanders is simply *the* city, an urban complex marked by Western technology.

Similarly, Mohammed Chukri includes but a single detail to locate "Flower Crazy" in Tangier: the Grand Socco, where a woman peddlar calls the green goods she has for sale. The story distinguishes sharply between the Europeanized city center (once the heart of the International Zone) and the slum area that has grown up around it. But it, too, is simply the city, where alienation reigns.[9]

The story focuses on the desperate poor in their quarter of the city. There are a few glimpses, though, of the other side. In Madame Porte's tea salon the waitress is "beautiful" and customers read illustrated women's magazines and smoke gold-tipped cigarettes. Women are welcome there, as they are in the bank. Only one of the characters in "Flower Crazy" moves freely in that world, the nameless prostitute who crosses daily from her home among the poor to the Westernized sector where she works.

The prostitute is, of course, the very figure of malaise in an Arab-Muslim society. The woman's family cannot protect her in the home. She dishonors the family, but in a world turned chaotic, she also supports them. Hers is a familiar world of money and its ability to buy fascinating goods, to buy people, to destroy the traditions that are barely alive in the quarter. (Contrast the woman peddlar in the Grand Socco, "her eyes on the security guard who chases away" people like her.)

In contrast with Mohammed Barrada, well-educated in Egypt and France, Chukri (of the same generation, born in 1935) is the voice of the poor and the alienated. A street kid independent at eleven, Chukri could neither read nor write until age twenty-one. Now he writes Standard Arabic, has taught and served as a cultural adviser to an international radio station. In 1990 he was unemployed and, in spite of a certain success (and a good bit of notoriety), not much changed from the man whose autobiography, *For Bread Alone* shocked the Moroccans with its sexual frankness. His writings are still forbidden in Morocco.

In a 1990 interview with a young Moroccan woman, Chukri demonstrates the values of a cultural rebel.[10] The interview is interesting in that, after a first question that might be asked of a writer anywhere, "Who is Mohammed Chukri?" the interviewer follows with one that makes perfectly good sense from a Moroccan point of view: "Since it's clear you are old enough, why haven't you thought of marriage, of founding a small family?"

To the first question Chukri answers, "I am an ordinary man, for the moment living a spoiled laziness. I'm enjoying unemployment." To the second he responds that, much as he has thought of it over the years, marriage holds no interest for him. He has no regrets and no inclination to meet with his own family. "I'm used to living alone, since the age of 11, so what is family to me?" He has many friends and spends much of his time in cafes and bars, so he has no time to spend at home. As a child-vagabond, he learned to live without the traditional supports. He admits that he consorts with prostitutes and considers his own society hypocritical for objecting to his candid speech. Not surprisingly he has little taste for politics. Had he not gained a bit of success from his writings, he would have been a smuggler. He weeps little: "I am accustomed to failure, to pain. So, why weep? Even when my mother died, I did not cry. I had not had a notice of her death until two years after the fact. I have no nostalgia to see my sisters and brothers. I live alone and am content with my way of living."

One suspects that in "Flower Crazy" the character closest to Chukri is the writer, known only as the "crippled poet of the quarter" (*shabir al-bayy al-kasib*). But in at least one respect he is close to the flower crazy (*majnūn al-ward*) of the title: according to his interviewer, Chukri enjoys eating flowers.

The narrative cuts, often abruptly, from an anonymous prostitute to the crippled poet of the quarter to the character known as "Flower Crazy" to children playing in the streets. A mood of miserable poverty is established early and never lifts, even when the prostitute takes her daily walk from home through the streets to the western section of the city. The degradation of the woman is evident at once, as she awakens:

> Rising unsteadily, a hand over her mouth, she goes to the lavatory. Its loathsome smell helps her to be violently sick: viscid, yellow vomit. The sound of her vomiting is choked like that of an animal being slaughtered. Her elder brother brings her a plastic bucket containing some water. She drops back exhausted on the bed. She is sobbing. The younger brother goes out, the other is sitting silently in front of her. She sits up and they exchange glances sadly. Her lustreless eyes water with tears. She smiles. (143)

What is immediately noticeable in this dreadful scene is the woman's relationship to the children. Children in the Tangier neighborhood are glimpsed often in the story, yelling, drawing water, excreting, insulting one another. The story closes with "a child with a dying sparrow in his hand deliberately pees on the shoes" the woman had left in the hedge (148) when she changed into the Western shoes for the new city. The children are not romanticized, but there is, within the family, a certain affection for them. The prostitute is hardened to her situation, but the family, two brothers and her mother, the wary peddlar in the Grand Socco, manages to survive at least for the time. The story is a series of brief takes and ends without resolution.

Flower Crazy is another representative of this hostile environment. An adult who follows his mother, a beggar, to the new city every day, Flower Crazy is too distracted for anything but flowers, which he distributes to beautiful women and girls. One woman, out of sympathy, responded to his gesture, and that incident now dominates his life:

Once, out of sympathy for his madness for flowers, she threw him her handkerchief. That night he dreamed of gardens of flowers that he would pick with mad joy and of handkerchiefs that fell upon him from the window of the handkerchief woman. The day of the handkerchief is better than a thousand days. Peace she is, the woman, after the day of the handkerchief. So did he start talking to those he knew. He began to date his life as from the day of the handkerchief. (145)

At the center of this chaotic place is the Crippled Poet of the Quarter, otherwise anonymous, what Hamid Eddijli calls (after Lukacs) a "problematic hero" (23). That he is crippled is a sign of the poet's marginality, both deeply part of his world and yet fundamentally ineffectual, a "lame." As Eddijli points out, the Crippled Poet of the Quarter operates both as "eye" and as memory to the community. Where others have, mainly through coercion, succumbed to the demands of a money economy, the poet is problematic in that he keeps up "qualitative" values where the others have merely "quantitative" values, best symbolized in the prostitute herself.

The poet is the voice of the quarter "ever since all the people of this lane were living in shacks." In the original Arabic, his activities are set off as verse: "He teaches the young and the old, for a fee or for thanks; he reads and writes lovers' letters; he gives support to the ailing by reciting the Qur'an, to love through poetry; he plays with the children and sits of an evening with the old men" (143). Flower Crazy's devotion to flowers approximates the devotion the poet seeks. But the poet is also reflective. The others are described by their activities; the poet tries to keep them together, writing not only about what he has seen in the land but "also about things in the town, things he hasn't lived through or seen but has heard of from those who have seen them or related them" (146).

Eddijli remarks that the language of "Flower Crazy" is polyphonic and includes a number of phrases that oddly recall the Qur'an, as in the "day of the handkerchief" cited above. The Crippled Poet of the Quarter fills his memoirs with the despair of those around him, but he maintains a steady religious faith:

> What befalls you from the right is from Allah and what befalls you from the left is from yourself. Allah divides and you multiply but you do not act equitably and Allah is best at acting equitably in computation. To destroy all idols—that is what you know. But Allah does not plot against you if you should do away with what you built for yourselves. (146)

The loss of faith that pervaded "Life by Installments" is absent here, though there are few signs that the desperate people of the lane are conventionally religious. "Sex! Sex! Sex! This is your misfortune," the poet writes. The poet himself is not immune. "Under compulsion I circumambulated the Kaaba, trailing a woman for three whole days, and after her I no longer circumambulated for more than a day of its sun or its moon" (147). Eddijli senses a kind of optimism in the face of painful reality, and the poet is the one whose agonized reflections provide a certain tough optimism. The situation is ugly and vicious, but, like the prostitute in the family, it is the poet's identification with the other that rescues the story from blank despair.

> Like me the bachelors of this town have become addicted to the night and to the glass of wine, or to merit in the Hereafter or to emigrating before reaching thirty, fleeing from madness, ignorance and death. Today I am alone with my glass, like those who escape to the bars or the brothels in the hope of retrieving some of their bachelorhood. They glorify drink in the evening, curse it in the morning. Every soul will taste of its sweetness and splendour and of its curse. But in all the brothels I have found my sisters and my friends' sisters. I have seen the delirium of night melting away their make-up and ripping off their masks, while, in the prime of youth, their teeth are being eaten away with decay. (147)

The trappings of the modern West are particularly evident in the final shots of the story: references to romantic novels and films; the prostitute in the new city at the bank, buying women's magazines and ordering a continental breakfast at Madame Porte's salon. Her activities place the woman at some remove from the rest of her family who are glimpsed at the end of the story: mother selling onions, brother playing soccer in the street, another brother playing with a kitten. The ironies of such an alienated life are everywhere noted, but the surprising note, finally, is one of gritty survival.

LEILA ABOUZEID, "DIVORCE" (1983)

"Divorce" is a brief but unrelentingly bitter story, in the style of Western (and by now comfortably Arabic) realistic fiction. The story deals with a topic that is popular in the West, as the title suggests: divorce and its terrible effects on a family. The main characters, husband and wife, are never named. The focus is on the man, who might, with few exceptions, have appeared in "Bartleby the Scrivener" or Kafka: the archetypal bureaucrat. If the setting were not the Arab-Muslim world, it might have been any modern Western-style city, anonymous and indifferent to the nameless inhabitants.[11]

From the start, the "emaciated young man" (*ash-sha:bb an-nahi:l,* a fixed epithet) is suffering in an otherwise unidentified office among the familiar signs of Westernized Morocco: pen, desk, watch. Crushed by the news that his promotion (from what? to what?) has been rejected, the young man leaves the building and seizes his motorcycle like a weapon. The public way might be anywhere, with its traffic signs, cars, buses. "Moving like an expert roller skater, he attempted to pass a bus from the left" (84) but is thrown from his cycle when the bus turns unexpectedly. Humiliated and distressed, the young man pushes his motorcycle to the sidewalk and weeps.

Until this point there is nothing to indicate an Eastern setting. The scene shifts to the interior of the young man's home. An anonymous wife uses iodine on cotton to clean his skinned hand and knee, while anonymous children "clung together, motionless, as they did every time their father came home in a bad mood" (84). Only when the man "lay on a mattress on the bare floor," a common enough sight in Morocco but unusual—and with an entirely different, stigmatized association attached to it—in the West, does the local culture begin to emerge.

Soon the reader sees more of it. The man's brother walks in unannounced. The call to evening prayer (85) is heard by the two men, and the bitter man's anger dissipates immediately: "As soon as the prayer call was over, he spoke more calmly and even affectionately to his brother." They talk about an incident in the past, before the religious festival Eid al-adha, when the father of a family is expected to bring home a sheep for sacrifice. Later, the man puts on a djellaba, the familiar overgarment worn in Morocco, and rushes out to the office of the *'adil,* a legal officer, and pays the man a fifty-dirham note (87). The details situate the story first in the Arab-Muslim world and then in a Moroccan city that has been at least superficially Westernized.

There is nothing particularly subtle about the presentation of the problem, of divorce. The young man whose sense of failure is growing with every check to his career storms off to the *'adil* to file for a divorce, which only the Moroccan male is able to do alone. (A woman needs a *wali:y* or guardian to initiate the process; and every phase of the process is made difficult for the wife.) The author portrays the man in about as unpleasant a light as can be imagined, and she makes explicit what might have been left implicit, that easy divorce for the man destroys families over several generations. In one of the more moving scenes, the young man repeats to his brother the old story of an encounter with his father, whose marriages the brothers cannot even count. By accident the boy kicks a ball and hits his father in the nose: "I vividly remember him looking me in the eye and saying, 'Take me to see your father, you evil omen. I am not letting go of him until I see the filthy dog who fathered him" (86).

The husband himself laments that men like his own father, "who produce delinquents, are a curse on our society. They should be banned" (85). The brevity of the story makes the irony only too visible when the son ends up repeating the father's mistake, perpetuating an immoral—but not illegal—tradition. To reinforce the point, Abouzeid has the young man, in a less bitter mood, remind his brother that his dear mother sacrificed to buy him a bicycle! "Children's happiness is so essential, isn't it? And it can be destroyed by a number of things, one of which is divorce. I know that. It marks children with psychological scars that never fade" (86). The next day he heads for the 'adil's office.

Clearly it was important to make the obvious explicit when the story crosses cultures, for what is obvious, unremarkable, is precisely what has to be marked for the outsider to understand the story. What gives the story its force is the intense exchange between husband and wife. All the talk before the climax of the story is between the emaciated young man and other men—fellow workers, bystanders at his motorcycle accident, his brother. Men talk with men, and talk is the domain of men.

The transition between past and present is marked by the "shirt collar" the man's father had grabbed when he yelled at the son he had not recognized, and the "shirt collar" (ya:qa) the husband throws into his wife's face when the man awakens the morning after his accident. "What a mess this shirt collar is!" The children draw close to the woman for protection. Abouzeid puts the more formal Modern Standard Arabic in the mouth of the educated husband, instead of the ordinary vernacular words (atfa:l for children vs. local, Moghrebi tfal, and Modern Standard qami:s vs. Moghrebi qamezza, the shirt he then throws in the wife's face). The educated language aims at humiliating the wife.

The wife—in the text, not even that, but "their mother"—does the unexpected and precipitates a crisis. Instead of remaining silent, she speaks up.

> "Her voice climbed over his, and she shouted back. "Don't you dare assault us anymore with your frustrations over your own failure! Don't make things any worse than they are! Don't add your behavior to every-thing else—depriving us of food and clothing! . . . Do you suppose I've not spoken up for so long because I worry about your own well-being? Of course not! My forbearance has been strictly for the children's sake. Otherwise, I'd be happier being somebody's maid!" (86)

For this outburst, the husband decides to divorce her. "He was flabbergasted by her boldness." He is humiliated by her speech and resolves to discipline her. For her part, she makes it worse again. "Encouraged by her own rebelliousness," the wife speaks up again: "'You'd rather throw these children into the street , wouldn't you?' she yelled. 'Exactly like your father did to you. A family tradition you want to keep, huh?'" (87). It is interesting that Abouzeid now has the wife respond to him in Modern Standard (*sha:ri'* for street vs. Moghrebi *zenqa* or *triq*). Even the word for the most conspicuous feature of Moroccan clothing, the outer garment or robe, *djellaba*, is given in Modern Standard, *djilba:ba*. The net effect of these formal terms is, finally, to intensify the ironic reversals in the story.

The end of the story is grim not only because the woman is pun-ished for speaking up to her husband, but also because the scene returns to the stifling air of bureaucracy such as was glimpsed at the beginning. Only this time the law officer, who asks for details blandly enough and reminds the emaciated young man of the fee he will be charged for the service, represents the perfect union of Western legal bureaucracy and Islamic tradition. Even the emaciated young man is taken aback by the *'adil's* attitude to his work: the "image of a gravedigger flashed through his mind. He was suddenly amazed by the fact that some people live on the calamities of others" (87).

One of the ironies in modern Moroccan life is, as Fatima Mernissi puts it, that traditional family life is breaking up because, "for the first time in the history of modern Morocco, the husband is facing his wife directly" (170–71). The man's ability to repudiate his wife is still legally sanctioned, but the sexual segregation that held traditionally (and the increasing absence of mediating figures like the mother-in-law, who usually had the major conflicts with the wife) is giving way to marriages in which husband and wife are together in a way they had not been before. Leila Abouzeid's "Divorce" is a protest against an old system that, even when the man seems to have grasped the problem of divorce, so favors the man that even the partially Westernized clerk makes use of the law at the first sign of marital difficulty.

To write in Arabic is to compose in a dialect derived from Classical Arabic. Writing in Modern Standard Arabic (*al-'Arabiyya al-fuṣha*) rather than in one of the regional dialects of Arabic such as Moroccan Arabic (Moghrebi) has an important advantage: the writing is intelligible throughout the Arab world. It does not reveal the writer's local origin, and it is the mark of education. Grammatical features and vocabulary (often just phonological variants) differ between Modern Standard and colloquial Arabic (Bakalla 79–94). In "Divorce," the connection between "bicycle" and "motorcycle" is reflected in MSA, since the first is *darra:ja*, and the second a special kind of *darra:ja* (*darra:ja na:ri:ya*, Wehr 277). Moghrebi Arabic uses the same term for motorcycle, but is likely to favor *beshklita*, obviously a variant of French *bicyclette* (Sobelman 21), terms that do not maintain the phonological association of the standard terms.

Quite ordinary vocabulary items, as we have seen above, appear in "Divorce" in their standard variants. Wife (*zaujta* vs. *zewza*), woman (*imra'a* vs. *mra*), even father (*abu* vs. *bu*). "Collar" (*ya:qa* vs. *reggabiya*) presents a more obvious contrast. When "delinquent" (*musharrad*) or "outlaw" (*qutta:' at-turuq*, a highway robber) appear in Modern Standard, they could be understood anywhere in the Arab world. Still, the accumulation of verbal forms and grammatical elements that are not used in ordinary conversation is disconcerting in a story such as "Divorce," that depends upon ordinary people in typical situations, the marks of realistic fiction. However, Modern Standard is particularly appropriate to the "emaciated man" who finds himself caught in a world that has been changed by contact with the West and appears to be undermining traditional values.

JILALI EL KOUDIA, "ROLLING RUBBER" (1990)

To date, the most successful product of the West in the world at large has been the promotion of the English language. Even in those areas where colonial rule is still bitterly resented after almost half a century of independence, the English language survives when other Western languages have stopped spreading and in many cases receded. It is not always seen as an imperial language. In 1976, for example, the black township of Soweto near Johannesburg erupted into protest when authorities tried to introduce Afrikaans into the school curriculum instead of English. English had become the language of opposition to apartheid and the Afrikaans authority.

According to *The Story of English* (1987) 750 million people use the English language, but barely half of those people speak it as a mother tongue (20). A chapter in that book, "The New Englishes," suggests that the 400 million who use English as a second or as a foreign language are already transforming the language. Already English, either in British or in American versions, has slipped from the control of the people who introduced it to the non-English world. English is well established in Jamaica, West Africa, India, Singapore, and Hong Kong—but in the Maghreb? While it is easy to find Maghrebi writers of French, and while Moroccans in particular have gotten used to professional writing in English, the writing of fiction in English is still quite unusual. Certainly the teaching of English is spreading in Morocco, though it has no official status in the kingdom. More and more Moroccans are studying in Britain and the Unites States, and it was in a sense only a matter of time before Moroccans began to speak with an English voice. The famous polymath Mohammed Abu-Talib has published poetry, still the favored literary genre in the Arabic-speaking world. Writing fiction in English rather than in Arabic or in French still means taking a considerable risk.

Moroccan fiction in English does already exist, though, in the short stories of Jilali El Koudia. "Rolling Rubber," which appeared in the American journal *Collages & Bricolages* in 1990,[12] provides some hint at the direction an Arabic-English fiction could take. Deeply rooted in its place and culture, El Koudia's fiction is written in fluent English, but English that is somehow bent to carry its cultural load. The setting is entirely symbolic, the contrasts elemental. Two anonymous characters, one male, one female, meet after they walk by accident along a country road. Their movement is measured by the direction toward or away from the center of an unnamed city. Time, too, is measured by shadows cast by a rising or setting sun. A car accident leaves the man dead and the woman despondent.

Almost nothing is used to identify the two main characters. He becomes identified with his "old pale brown jacket"; she, at the crisis of the story when she puts on a "new rosy dress" and then becomes the "dazzling rosy figure." El Koudia shifts from one to the other, outside and inside (by soliloquies). The technique of simplifying contrasts underscores the movement as "inevitable." Their talk as they walk through the deserted country, at first difficult, as well it might in a culture that keeps the sexes separated, becomes more fluid, but still elemental. Their relationship takes an inevitable romantic turn. (Perhaps the emphasis on inevitability in the story is conditioned by Islamic "fate," but there are no explicit Islamic references in the story.) From fascination to a union that is not yet sanctioned by society, the couple moves to a new and infinitely more dangerous stage.

The early, shy scenes of romantic infatuation are idyllic, as the two decide against walking toward the "City Centre" and walk instead through a deserted landscape toward the Atlantic Ocean. The danger comes when they decide—through her urgings—to turn toward the city. Suddenly the accident destroys everything, and not surprisingly the "rolling rubber" of the title, the insane traffic at rush hour, kills the man on the main avenue of the city he despises. The last glimpse of him occurs as the sleeve of his old jacket "flapped up and down towards her in a mock farewell gesture" (75). A blind man's cane is kicked away from him in a mindless gesture by a crowd hoping to see what happened. An ambulance removes the body, nothing more than an "obstacle that blocked the traffic." "Rolling black rubbers" soon obliterate the last sign of his presence, a "small scratch in the middle of the road" (76).

This gloomy tale of anonymity and inevitable loss participates in a Western romantic tradition in which the countryside represents freedom and individuality and the city a hostile and dehumanizing sameness. Indeed, El Koudia uses the now-familiar reversal, where the civilized place becomes a jungle. The woman meditates,

> that's where they go to meet and mate with each other like beasts in a jungle. The City Centre! They contrived it thus to meet with their dark desires. . . . The excitement that the distinct individual arouses is extinct. Nothing but a fast moving mass of humanity. Uniformity has killed individuality. Dear me! In the crowd, what am I? Any woman. And he is any man. It's only by bumping into each other that two meet. Well, I'm different and wish to be regarded as such. (72)

However, the simplified contrasts lead, to a series of ironic reversals. The lonely road that leads the couple to their idyllic moments is precisely "westward" toward the Atlantic Ocean. When they turn toward the city Center, they are headed east. The contrast is not accidental. East and West are mixed in a more complicated way than in the earlier Moroccan stories. The single detail that identifies the man, his jacket, already marks him by his dress as having been influenced by the West. His need for free space and individuality, his hatred of the crowd, are greater than the woman's, and those may be considered romantic or existentialist values. However, the city is defined almost entirely by the trappings of modernism: signposts, roads, an ambulance, twinkling lights in shop windows, cameras, televisions, films—and especially the traffic at rush hour. The man muses, "I'm used to wide, open and empty space. I've developed the habit of walking miles and miles absent-minded, the imagination unhampered and the sense grow like the grass that surrounds them. Traffic could be fatal" (72).

Of course it is fatal in his case. But what gives the story a depth it would otherwise lack is that the city also stands for the collective and its values, the roles they impose on the individual, in this case very traditional Arab-Muslim roles. The man is perfectly content to meet his lover along the lonely roads. It is only when she draws him into the city with her need for legitimacy that the tragedy exists.

After about a month of dates, she proposes that he meet her mother "to validate, so to speak, their relationship." He agrees readily, but shrinks back "at her mention of the place and time of the meeting," the main street at rush hour. As he approaches the city, he feels nausea: "He felt like a blind man losing grip of his cane, his only guide, support and armour in the face of a metallic-hearted world" (73). The meeting with the mother brings the story quickly to a crisis:

> The mother was standing at the edge of the main avenue, contemplating the big spectacle of the hour, when the daughter tapped her on her shoulder. The interview between mother and future son-in-law took place against the general uproar. She was smiling, talking and gesticulating at the same time. His ears were not accustomed to the new atmosphere. The mother's words and gesticulations were indistinguishable from the general chorus. (74)

He is rewarded for his responsibility with his "first valid kiss" from the bride-to-be. She appears in her new rosy dress, and they promptly have their first disagreement. She wants him to walk her down the main avenue, to acknowledge her publicly. This public identity is difficult for him. In a small detail that says a great deal about this troubled individualist, he touches his familiar old jacket and notes that he never stuffed its pockets with papers—especially the ubiquitous (and required) "sharp-edged identity card" Moroccans carry with them at all times. "Documents of that kind were indeed unnecessary in quiet and safe places" (74).

Now the woman is in a rush to buy a ring, and he follows just behind her. The fatal accident takes place when she rushes across to the middle of the busy roadway and stops. He is hit trying to reach her.

The climax of the story is heavy with the specifically Western malaise in which reality and fantasy become indistinguishable, when the crowd gathers to view the scene of the accident as if it were a television show.

> The spectators were looking at the scene with uniform expressions—of curiosity more than terror. The spectacle was giving them a sensational moment, which was no less exciting than what they were used to on television or at the movies. The present scene had simply slipped from the screen into the avenue; or perhaps some company or other was shooting a film there. Such spectacles framed their imaginations. How many they were consuming while comfortably sitting—smoking or drinking! Even the new reports had become part of the Show. (75)

The depiction of a world "where sensitivity and sensibility had long since perished" was foreshadowed in the musings of the man just before the accident. He thought about the possibility of a camera that would "register inner visions and dreams in speech and image," and the secrets about "man and the universe" such a camera would reveal. The image of the universe that summarizes his view derives from the same source: "The present scene before his eyes was like a horror film where metal creatures were invading the world" (75).

The way these images of the West have to be drawn, with such explicitness, is the gap between the Moroccan writer's and the Western writer's now-familiar cinematic analogies, a source that has been exploited at least since John Dos Passos.

However, El Koudia does not stop with this dehumanized mass of anomic spectators. The final shot returns to the mother of the woman and the mother's companion. The companion sees, with no little envy, that the daughter has become the center of attention. She wishes she were the daughter's age, to have her many admirers: "How lucky you are to belong to this generation." The story ends with the daughter, whose loss has reduced thought to nothingness. "To her, life had become nothing but an endless, desolate road to travel with a heavy load" (76).

In literary studies we are accustomed to thinking of modernism (high modernism, from 1910) as opposed to realism, basically a nineteenth-century movement. As was suggested earlier (in the Introduction) such modernism is only one of several waves of modernism—modernisms, properly, constituting modernity—that are intimately tied to a Western self-identity. After noting that modernity rarely means simply "to be new" (as it is used in advertising), Stephen Toulmin asked about the origin of modernity: 1436? 1520? 1648? 1776? 1789? or even 1895 (with the publication of Freud's *Interpretation of Dreams*)? Even *postmodern*, as a term that challenged the notion of the modern nation state, used soon after World War II (5–17), can be considered another wave of modernity. To the student of literature it may seem almost perverse of a social scientist such as Daniel Lerner to link literary realism with modernism (*modernization*, a term now supplanted largely by *Westernization*). However, the collapse of an otherwise useful distinction between modernism and realism can be justified in the rather unusual context it is done here. Following upon Lerner's understanding of modernization, the claim here is that high modernism is itself a particular moment in a much larger movement, one characterized by a fundamental challenge to a "traditional," earlier Western cultural construct. Literary critics since Jacques Derrida's "Structure, Sign, and Play in the Discourse of the Human Sciences" (English translation, 1978) are increasingly fond of Martin Heidegger's "onto-theological" destruction of metaphysics (395). When we are speaking within the discourse developed in the West practically from its first appearance in Plato, that is, onto-theologically, it makes good sense to mark a clear division between the end of the old order, in the nineteenth century, and its more recent challenger, high modernism.

For the purpose of crossing over to a new discourse between West and East, the distinction loses some moment. The East in this book has not entirely been constructed by the West. There are Eastern writers, speakers, and thinkers whose words are important to the West. But it can hardly be denied that modern Western literature has had a profound influence on the Arab-Muslim world, especially in the last century. More useful than the distinction between modernism and realism is the recognition that the two together appeared to liberate the East from its own onto-theological (and certainly "traditional") discourse.

Realism, as a movement, subverted onto-theology (West and East) by redescribing human activity in psychological and sociological terms. Where, earlier, acts had been understood in terms of an ethical system derived from metaphysics or theology, as one would find in, say, Dante, related to final causes, fate, or the will of God, realism claimed only to interest itself in individuals and in the relationships of individuals. The supernatural was banished, to be allowed in as psychological states. Ghosts, afreets, deities, devils became the irrational fears of primitive minds. Consider, for example, the changes in words such as *ecstasy* and *inspiration*. Or consider the uncanny voice of Rochester in *Jane Eyre*. The "modern" reader need not even deny the existence of a larger world order impressing itself on an individual's actions. When she heard her lover's voice at a distance, Jane Eyre might have been having a hallucination, but no reader takes seriously that the will of God is exhibited in that character's hearing the voice.

A complete discussion of this question would require another volume. Suffice it here to say that the appeal of realism was as liberating to the East as it was to the West, and it is always seen in the East as a modern, that is, Western innovation.

For the Arab-Muslim world, perhaps, the combination of modernity and realism that is captured in the phrase *modern literary realism* is more useful than modernism, as opposed to realism; but it may turn out to be more important still to distinguish modern and postmodern sharply. That has been attempted many times and will be again in the following chapter. For the moment, if postmodern is specifically associated in the Arab-Muslim world with the art, literature, and attitudes formed in response to the events of 1967, postmodernity in the East is marked, in storytelling at least, by a conscious return to traditional forms and themes, by an attempt to remove the conspicuous dependence of the East upon modern, Western forms.

One of the advantages of specializing in the study of literature is directly related to high modernism: the separation of literature (and the arts generally) as works of art from other forms of writing, especially scientific discourse. The chapters that follow will have to challenge that comfortable separation. The five stories in this chapter share the high modernist principle of artistic autonomy (whatever the political ideology that might be involved). The following chapters will qualify that principle in two ways. First, the texts are products, initially, of orality, not literacy, and they will bring to the fore the problematics of what Walter J. Ong considers the "technologizing of the word" caused by literacy. The Moroccan storytellers, to the extent that they are nonliterate and incapable of writing in Modern Standard Arabic, exist in an entirely different world from the writers. The next chapter will explore the implications of that division.

A second qualification, though, leads in a different direction. *Modern realism*, as the term is used here, embraces both literary and scientific discourse. If realistic fiction invites the reader to understand action in psychological and sociological terms, modern scientific discourse, especially in the social sciences, also challenges the traditional onto-theological construct of reality, and these discourses allow us to view the objects of their study in their ordinariness—that is, without reference to teleological and theological discourse. What follows in the next three chapters is not only different forms of storytelling, but also stories produced when anthropologists prompt their informants to talk about themselves. The way the informants are prompted tells us as much about the social-scientific aims of the anthropologists as it does about the informants themselves. Or, rather, the storytelling that results when one who does not have a ready pattern from the tradition to tell a life story is a hybrid text. The shape of the story is subtly altered by the fieldworker's questions. Since many of the nonliterate informants have had no education in Western thought forms, they often reveal a traditional or premodern (and onto-theological) frame that gives the story a very different feel from the literary texts that have just been considered. The frank appeals to magic and the occult, to supernatural agencies, to the will of God, and to fate can, of course, be *interpreted* in modern/realistic/scientific terms, but the informants do not usually interpret them in those terms.

Eventually, in chapter 10, when the anthropologist is herself a Moroccan and the informant is a powerful traditional woman who takes control of the story, the Orientalist mirror reveals itself in an unexpected way. The discussion between Fatima Mernissi and her informant, Habiba, the psychic, subverts Western Orientalist discourse even as it presents a woman who might earlier have been dismissed as an ignorant, superstitious primitive. Before that, chapter 8 looks at two storytellers translated by Paul Bowles and chapter 9 considers the unlikely power of women in a traditional patriarchal order.

Chapter Eight

Two Moroccan Storytellers in Paul Bowles's *Five Eyes*:

Larbi Layachi and Ahmed Yacoubi

I f, as Michel Foucault claims, "Western man" has become a "confessing animal" with a narrative literature appropriate to that role, does the Western author/confessor elicit from the cultural other a story that makes sense either to the priest or to the patient? The Western listener in this case is American expatriate Paul Bowles. The other culture is Moroccan, on the margins of the complex Arab-Muslim culture of the Middle East and North Africa. As the country in that Arab-Muslim complex with the easiest access for Europeans, a country that has argued within itself whether it ought to belong more to the Arab League or to the European community, Morocco is also on the margins of the West. Indeed, its very name means, in Arabic, the "farthest West."

We ask the others ("primitives," nomads, third world peoples, traditional societies) to speak to us—and listen well. We take photographs of them and analyze the photographs. The professionals in this enterprise are anthropologists and sociologists such as the Moroccan Fatima Mernissi, who studied in her own country and then went to Paris and to Brandeis to complete Western-style Ph.D. work and who now interviews nonliterate Moroccan women. The women tell her their life stories, and she lets them talk without imposing much of the Western auto-biographical styles we have been developing since St. Augustine.

As we have seen in the Introduction, American anthropologists have had ready access to Morocco. Many of them—Clifford Geertz, Paul Rabinow, and Vincent Crapanzano especially—have come, like their counterparts in literary studies, to question the fundamental assumptions of their profession. Each has found a different way to have Moroccans speak: for Geertz, through symbols like stories told of seventeenth-century Sufi saints; for Rabinow, through the hermeneutics of fieldwork (following Paul Ricoeur to the "comprehension of the self through the detour of the comprehension of the other"); and for Crapanzano, through the stories and esoteric lore of a Meknes tile maker who is convinced he is married to the seductive she-demon Aisha Qandisha. All entered Morocco and found ways to have Moroccans speak to them.

These anthropologists are witnesses, among many others, to what Richard E. Palmer has called the "end of the modern era," and to what Palmer claims is a "major change in worldview" to "postmodernity" ("Postmodernity" 363–64). The postmodern turn is evident immediately in the short stories and novels of Paul Bowles discussed above (chapter 5). (A possible exception is *The Spider's House*.) While there has been some experimenting with point of view, for example, "The Eye" in *Midnight Mass* and "New York 1965" in *Unwelcome Words*, a key element is probably Bowles's refusal to accept the assumptions of modern Western realistic fiction about character. How much theorizing about literature this has involved is moot. My guess is that Bowles's refusal of the modern notion of character, derived from an image of the self that had developed during the period of modern philosophy (i.e., since Descartes), comes from his reading of eccentric fiction—from a lifelong interest in Edgar Allan Poe and an adult interest in surrealism.

Bowles's fiction seems at first to be straightforward realistic fiction, one of the defining characteristics of modernism. But the modernist readings nearly always fail. Characters have little "depth." They rarely "develop." Instead of closure, there is most often irony: "relationships" collapse, dialogue falls apart. There is no "self" such as has been assumed in the modern West. In the non-Western storytelling of nonliterate Moroccans Bowles found a very different sense of self.

One way to detect this postmodern turn in Bowles's work is to look at Bowles's translations of Moroccan storytellers. By the mid-1960s he had almost abandoned his own fiction writing for the strange bicultural hybrids that were produced by Bowles, such as Mohammed Mrabet's *The Chest* and especially *Five Eyes* (1979). To see what is happening in these texts—literature in English (for an English-reading audience, of course) whose origin is oral performance in Moroccan Arabic—consider a distinction that has arisen in the "modern" world and fundamentally constitutes the West's image of itself as modern, namely a distinction frequently encountered in the social sciences: "traditional" vs. modern. Although it is especially evident in anthropology, the distinction is the latest in the West's powerful "gaze" upon the cultural other: traditional replacing to a great extent the earlier "primitive," modern replacing the earlier image (still sometimes found in advertizing) of "civilized" society.

In *The Passing of Traditional Society: Modernizing the Middle East* (1958), Daniel Lerner collapsed the elements of a modern society—a certain type of economic development, urbanism, literacy, media exposure, and political participation—into a simple, telling comment. In the modern or "participant" society, "most people go through school, read newspapers, receive cash payments in jobs they are legally free to change, buy goods for cash in an open market, vote in elections which actually decide among competing candidates, and express opinions on many matters which are not their personal business" (50–51). As was noticed earlier, the psychological mechanism he isolated in the change from a traditional to a modern society Lerner called "psychic mobility" or "empathy":

> The mobile person is distinguished by a high capacity for identification with new aspects of his environment; he comes equipped with the mechanisms needed to incorporate new demands upon himself that arise outside of his habitual experience. These mechanisms for enlarging a man's identity operate in two ways. *Projection* facilitates identification by assigning to the object certain preferred attributes of the self—others are "incorporated" because they are like me. (Distantiation or negative identification, in the Freudian sense, results when one projects onto others certain disliked attributes of the self.) *Introjection* enlarges identity by attributing to the self certain desirable attributes of the object—others

are "incorporated" because I am like them or want to be like them. We shall use the word *empathy* as shorthand for both these mechanisms. (49)

From this point of view, Lerner, a sociologist, considered the novel "the typical literary form of the modern epoch" and "a conveyance of disciplined empathy" (52).

Concepts like 'modern literary realism,' thought to support the novel as Lerner conceives of it, derive in part from a literary tradition, from texts that form a tradition. We increase our psychic mobility by reading literary works. But we also draw in our reading upon socially constructed concepts of the self. When such concepts of the self, maintained by a culture other than our own, clash with our own, we find it difficult to accept the other's self-disclosure.

Narratives coming to us from the margins of the Arab-Muslim world can be particularly trying. Arabic literature is old enough and prestigious enough—no matter how small the percentage of readers literate enough to read Standard Arabic might be—to exert influences that are not easily detected by the Western observer. Edward Said, for example, has noticed that "Arabic literature before the twentieth century has a rich assortment of narrative forms—qissa, sīra, hadīth, khurāfa, ustūra, khabar, nādira, maqāma—of which no one seems to have become, as the European novel did, the major narrative type" (Roger Allen 17). John A. Haywood (126–37) and more recently Roger Allen (9–19) have struggled with the problem of distinguishing Western influences on Arabic narratives, novels, and short stories, from the influences of the Arabic literary tradition.[1]

Bowles, who has never claimed to have mastered Modern Standard Arabic, the dialect used for writing throughout the Arab world, deliberately sought out nonliterate storytellers. His preference for the oral performance is an indicator of much that has changed in the Western view of the non-Western world. (Bowles remains, though, one of the great examples of Lerner's "mobile personality," a modernist feature that would be impossible for Bowles to suppress.[2])

In 1958, Lerner could confidently oppose "illiterate" with "enlightenment," so obvious was it to him that literacy was valuable without question. Since then much research into the distinctive changes introduced by literacy has qualified that easy confidence. When Walter J. Ong distinguishes the psychodynamics of orality from the thought and expression of literacy, he does not devalue the former:

Additive rather than subordinative;
Aggregative rather than analytic;
Redundant or "copious" vs. spare and economical;
Traditionalist vs. experimental;
Close to the human lifeworld vs. knowledge at a distance;
Agonistically toned vs. abstractions that disengage;
Empathetic and participatory rather than objectively distanced;
Homeostatic vs. novelty; and
Situational rather than abstract (37–49).

(Note that Ong considers the oral culture "empathetic and participatory" in a much different way from Daniel Lerner, who sees the empathy not in the known and the traditional, but for the other.) In the case of Bowles's translations, the non-literate Ahmed Yacoubi and Larbi Layachi are certainly traditional, according to Lerner's model, and marked by the orality of Ong's. The one who elicits their stories, Bowles himself, remains a modern in Lerner's sense, since he cannot avoid the empathy that is so much a part of modern society.

At least one reason for Bowles's incessant travel outside the United States and his settling into Tangier in the late 1940s was a dislike of most everything Western and "civilized." As pointed out above, Bowles was disgusted by the dumping of the West's "garbage" on the the rest of the world and by the longing on the part of the educated minorities of non-Western societies to become Westerners, in effect canceling themselves (*Their Heads Are Green* vii). The stories he translated, not from written sources but from his recordings of oral performances, are successful to the extent that Bowles lets the other speak, in writing, in the best American English: he lets them be themselves.

Daisy Hilse Dwyer, another of the American anthropologists who have had access to Morocco, based her study of "male and female in Morocco," *Images and Self-Images* (1978), on Moroccan folktales she recorded there. She followed Geertz in seeing a different concept of 'personhood' operating in Morocco and evident in the folktales—a self socially embedded, relational, interactional: "personality or character varies rather flexibly from relationship to relationship" (182). This is in contrast to the Western stress on the person as "isolate."

If the sense of self, personhood, character contrasts strongly with the West's self-concept, then stories, whether they are consciously fictions or self-disclosures, are not likely to have the same shape as mod-

ern Western fiction. Fatima Mernissi defended her practice in interview-
ing nonliterate Moroccan women, in which she violated "Rule No. 1
that I learned at the Sorbonne and at the American university where I was
trained in 'research technique': to maintain objectivity toward the person
being interviewed" (*Doing Daily Battle* 18). And she violated rule number 2
in the way she developed "as much as possible an attitude of self-criti-
cism" and testing of subjectivity as she edited the interviews. She let the
storytellers, who had never been given the opportunity/task to tell of
themselves in such a (Western) fashion, speak in as comfortable a manner
as she could allow. The results were life stories that are "relaxed, often
confusing" in the way time sequences and events are narrated. "An illiterate woman who has virtually no control over her life, subject to the
whims and will of others, has a much more fluid sense of time than an
educated Western reader, who is used to analysing time in an attempt to
control it" (20). A non-Western sense of time operates in the stories
Bowles translates as well. Whatever one makes of the "reality" in literary
"realism," so important to the modern West, it is rather differently shaped
in the Moroccans' accounts.[3] (One of Mernissi's subjects, Habiba, "the
psychic," is discussed in chapter 10.)

Bowles has provided English-speaking readers with stories that
challenge their ability to translate a culture very different from their own.
Among the tales collected in *Five Eyes* (1979) are two that play on the
Western reader's expectations. One seems bizarre indeed, and the other
only too easily read. "The Night before Thinking," by Ahmed Yacoubi
(1931–), and "The Half-Brothers" by Larbi Layachi (1940–),
Moroccan storytellers, illustrate an unusual hermeneutical bind.

Both Ahmed Yacoubi and Larbi Layachi are nonliterate storytellers
the expatriate Bowles met in Morocco. In "Notes on the Work of the
Translator," Bowles indicated his admiration for oral storytelling such as
he had heard in the cafes of Tangier. Once the tape recorder had arrived
in Morocco, in 1956, he began recording oral tales. Like all the spoken
texts in *Five Eyes*, "The Night before Thinking" and "The Half-Brothers"
were performed without stopping, at a single sitting. Yacoubi's story
derives from traditional Moroccan materials and is full of imagination;
Larbi's story, is more of a realistic piece, like an oral history rather than a
traditional North African tale.

As popular as storytellers are in Morocco, the stories have no
appreciable value there "as literature." Virtually every traveler has com-

mented on the storytellers in public places, such as the square known as "Djemaa el Fna" in Marrakech, where performances daily take place before enthusiastic audiences made up not of Western tourists but of the people who know the traditions and the languages, Arabic and Berber. Elias Cannetti, who visited the square in the 1960s, was struck by the contrast between the quiet scribes who made themselves available to the many who are not literate in the society (and with whom, as a writer, he felt a kind of kinship), and the flamboyant storytellers:

> The largest crowds are drawn by the storytellers. It is around them that people throng most densely and stay longest. Their performances are lengthy; an inner ring of listeners squat on the ground and it is some time before they get up again. Others, standing, form an outer ring; they, too, hardly move, spellbound by the storyteller's words and gestures. . . . Having seldom felt at ease among the people of our zones whose life is literature—despising them because I despise something about myself, and I think that something is paper—I suddenly found myself here among authors I could look up to since there was not a line of theirs to be *read*. (77, 79)

Thanks in large measure to Milman Parry, Albert Lord, Walter J. Ong, and now a journal devoted to *Oral Tradition*, the debate over orality and literacy has become respectable in the academy and the value of oral narratives is gradually coming clear to those whose teaching and scholarship have been almost entirely preoccupied with the written word. Before such a revaluation can take place in Morocco, however, an almost insurmountable obstacle has to be overcome. The gap between Modern Standard Arabic, the dialect of Arabic used in writing, and the regional dialects of Arabic is much greater than, say, between Appalachian English and British Received Pronunciation or American Broadcast Standard. Any literate Arab speaker can understand Modern Standard, whether it is written in Iraq, Egypt, or the Maghrib; but the local dialects are often mutually unintelligible. Because of that gap, Arabic provided the classical case of what linguists call "diglossia."[4] The rich nuances of an oral tale may delight the Arab speaker but will not be enough to raise the tale to the prestige of writing.

Ahmed Yacoubi[5] and Larbi Layachi are in a peculiar situation, then. Their oral tales are not available to Moroccan literature, and the English translations are the only texts available to any audience. The original situation of the oral performance, the *Sitz im Leben*, is not accessible; recordings in the Moghrebi Arabic dialect have not been made available to the public. The written text, in American English, is the product of a collaboration between Bowles and the storytellers; it is all that remains of what was first of all an oral performance in a culture and language strikingly different from the English-speaking readers. The "authors" of the tales find themselves unable to read the texts.

AHMED YACOUBI, "THE NIGHT BEFORE THINKING"

Ahmed Yacoubi's "The Night before Thinking" is a tale in a vein familiar to Middle East and North African storytellers, a tale of magic and the supernatural.[6] For that reason it is both familiar to the Western reader—after all, Western literature is filled with magic (*Dr. Faustus*, the romance tradition)—and inaccessible to us. "Magic moonshine" is appropriate to the romance writer, as Hawthorne pointed out long ago, so that "the floor of our familiar room [becomes] a neutral territory, somewhere between the real world and fairy-land, where the Actual and the Imaginary may meet, and each imbue itself with the nature of the other" (38). But serious treatment of magic is reserved for special genres—children's literature, where it is supposedly appropriate to the "magical phase" of human development (to be cast off in normal development), or science fiction and fantasy, where it is part of the game.[7]

"The Night before Thinking" begins in one generation and ends in another. In revenge for the killing of her brother Difdaf, "Raqassa" (whose real name turns out to be Aaklaa bent Aaklaa) lures an unsuspecting Hakim into her power. Instead of killing him, she ends up marrying him, and a strange boy is born of their union. Raqassa possesses very powerful magic, inherited from her father and supported by Satan. Thus it is not entirely unexpected that the strange child finds a way to kill both parents. With their death, their daughter, whose growth had been stunted for twenty-five years, begins to grow.

Yacoubi's bizarre tale includes a reversal that might go almost unnoticed by the Western reader but would have fit into the familiar pattern of traditional narratives. The terrible seductress and mother, Raqassa, explains that she gained "the power" because of an accident of birth. When her mother, Lalla Halalla, was carrying twins in her womb, she slipped while running, and the girl was born five minutes before the boy. "The one who came out first had to be given the power," and so she, not Difdaf, gained the power that is exhibited, for example, in throwing "a darkness" over the face of Hakim, spreading his lips all over his cheeks, and seizing the man with the force of "sixty thousand kilos" (24), capturing him. The story is filled with oddments of magic, burning "bakhour," an "egg of Rokh el Bali," humans turning to smoke.

Later, when Raqassa and Hakim produce a most unusual child—a boy with eyes all over his body—they try to explain how they had been able to produce a child with such strange powers. The child himself only laughs at them:

> What a lot of lies you both tell! he said to them. One of you says the eye in the top of my head comes from one thing. The other says the eye in the middle of my forehead comes from something else. You are saying that your eyes are in my eyes. I already existed before you ever met each other. I was hidden and neither one of you knew me. Only God knew I was going to be like this. You didn't know. Now you think you understand all about it. You don't know anything. How can anyone know what's hidden inside the belly of a woman? It's God who decided I should be like this. He cut out my pattern. And neither of you knew how I was going to look. It was written in the books that I was going to be born like this. It was already known. (33)

The second child they produce is a girl, strangely deformed and very weak. Twenty-five years later, she remains as tiny as she was at the time of her birth. When the son manages to kill the parents, the girl begins immediately to grow. Instead of the live parents, the children keep only two three-colored cloths, one representing the father, the other representing the mother. The son asks his sister which of the cloths she wants. "The girl laughed. She said: I take my mother. Because I'm a virgin. And the boy always goes with his father" (35). The power is returned to the proper relationship between male and female. In spite of the supposed gap of twenty-five years, the offspring of Hakim and Raqassa were magically constrained as pre-adolescent children. Now they are prepared to grow into their "normal" roles.

Magic and the supernatural in the story are far from imaginative decorations or self-conscious inventions of the author, as they are in the "magic realism" of Western postmodern writers. Rather, the supernatural reinforces a traditional, religious understanding of reality, an important part of the onto-theological "metaphysics of presence" that has come under such strong attack in the West. Ultimately, reality is the expression of the will of God, or fate. Much is unknowned by humans; much is unknowable by humans, including human motivation. Such an attitude does not make traditional storytelling any less inventive or "creative" than modern storytelling. Since motivation in the West is understood in psychological and sociological terms even in science fiction, fantasy, and magic realism, characters in such traditional stories seem to the Western reader remarkably unconstrained and unmotivated. Postmodern writers often directly challenge modern assumptions about the self and therefore question modern views of character and motivation, but Yacoubi's story is not of that sort.

The way the story returns to "normal" at the end is the best example of that distinction. However colorful, bizarre, and unexpected the narrative turns are, however many eyes a boy might have all over his body, the explanation is finally traditional: "It's God who decided I should be like this. He cut out my pattern." The boy's fate was "already known," "written in the books," certainly not a product of genes or of early childhood development. "It was already known," but not by humans. It may come as some surprise, then, that the concept of 'social roles' turns out to be quite traditional as well. Male and female are fundamental divisions, and the entire social order—of the type known today as "homosocial"—is implied in that division.

"Normal" social roles are not necessarily the same in different cultures, of course. In an often-cited essay on "Family Structure and Feminine Personality," Nancy Chodorow, after discussing the "family" and "personality" exclusively from a Western standpoint, expresses considerable interest in the Moroccan Muslim family as one that, even in a patrilineal, patrilocal society, maintains the self-esteem of women— largely because daughters see themselves, in a way strikingly different from daughters in the West, as "allies against oppression," able to develop strong attachment to and identification with other women (65). Obviously, the family in "The Night before Thinking" is a perversion of Moroccan norms, due to the peculiar situation of Raqassa. The story ends with a return to normal psycho-social roles, understood in traditional terms.

Chodorow's view of Moroccan Muslim mother/daughter relationships derives from the work of Moroccan sociologist Fatima Mernissi, whose work is highlighted in chapter 10. Mernissi's *Beyond the Veil: Male-Female Dynamics in Modern Muslim Society*, as has been mentioned earlier, explores the family in Arab-Muslim tradition and in emerging new models (165–77).

LARBI LAYACHI, "THE HALF-BROTHERS"

In reading Larbi Layachi's "The Half-Brothers,"[8] as in tracking down political chicanery, it is useful to follow the money. The ten-year-old Larbi works with fishermen, pulling nets, for wages that rarely seem to have connection with the work expended: five rials and a basketful of fish one day, three rials another, one rial on yet another occasion. The boy seems not to expect more (or less), and he does not complain. One day when he is ill and barely able to pull the nets, the other fishermen notice and suggest that he take the day off, but Larbi insists on working (62). He gets three rials and is paid twelve pesetas for a basket filled with metal he dug out of a garbage dump (71). He pays a rial for half a loaf of bread, a can of tuna fish, and two oranges (72). He pays two bily-oun for the cinema (68). He finds in the garbage a five-rial note, which he first thought was only a peseta (74). Usually he gets three gordas for a kilo of bones he sells to "a Jew who lived near the bull-ring" (70–71).

Bowles offers no dollar equivalence for these exotic monies.[9] In one sense it does not matter: the amounts are so small relative to the wealth of an American reader that the meaningless currency is a powerful sign of poverty. From the point of view of a ten year old, money is simply "there," a fact in a world that does not require explanation or expectations. But the arbitrary payment of wages, the caprice in finding money on the streets, the crude exploitation of the boy's step-father, who regularly takes everything the boy makes at his job (while the other son attends school and is forbidden to work) are part of a world that seems to lack cause and effect. The boy is industrious and clever enough to survive. He does not try to put the experience in a "larger context," and neither does the storyteller, Larbi, who offers almost nothing in the way of comment on incidents in his past. The money is a gift, *baraka*, the will of Allah. Paul Rabinow, who did his fieldwork in Morocco, noted that

> poverty does not carry the stigma in Morocco which it does in America. It indicates only a lack of material goods at the present time, nothing more. Although regrettable, it does not reflect unfavorably on one's character. It simply means that Allah has not smiled on one, for reasons

beyond normal understanding, but that things are bound to change soon. (116)

What is most surprising to the American reader is the apparent lack of causal connectedness between events narrated in "The Half-Brothers." True, the story leads to the moment when the ten year old decides that he will no longer return to the home in which he is exploited and beaten by his step-father. The step-father, Si Abdullah, pockets the five rial note Larbi found in the garbage and forces the boy out of the house to work, though Larbi is not feeling well. Henceforth, Larbi will live on the beach: "I went out. I was thinking: I'll work. But the money I earn I'll spend for food, and I won't go back home at all. I can eat here on the beach. And I was thinking that it would be better for me to sleep in one of the boats than live there in the house" (74). Larbi works that day, dizzy and with a headache, and takes the two and a half rials the chief gives him to a cafe. After dark he finds a boat and sleeps warmly under the fish netting in the boat. When, in the morning, he is asked, "Why didn't you go home to bed?" the boy answers simply, "I didn't go . . . . That's all. After that I lived on the beach" (75).

The story thus presents a string of episodes, a linear development, a clear structure with episodes leading to the decision of the boy to live on the beach, but with little of the sense common to Western realistic fiction that all details fit into a larger, causally related whole. The problem emerges early, in the very different treatment given the boy and his half-brother by the mother's second husband, Si Abdullah. The episodes are strung together without moving toward a climax of intensity. Sometimes the father is awful, occasionally generous; he is always seen from the outside, and there is no interest in (and no comment on) the father or the mother. They act; that is all. However, the boys are somewhat rounded, but they move about unconsciously, accepting social norms that are often puzzling to the outsider, the Western reader.

In "Africa Minor," Bowles describes a "culture where there is a minimum of discrepancy between dogma and natural behavior": "In Tunisia, Algeria, and Morocco there are still people whose lives proceed according to the ancient pattern of concord between God and man, agreement between theory and practice, identity of word and flesh" (*Their Heads Are Green* 22). The unselfconsciousness of "The Half-Brothers" is a narrative correlate of that ancient pattern. The story retains some features common to oral tales. A formula, "Let us say . . . ," is repeated throughout the piece. The boy makes his money pulling the nets of the fishermen, and the activity is repeated a number of times in virtually the same language. In almost no way does it resemble the storytelling traits of "The Night before Thinking," traits that go back at least as far as *The Thousand and One Nights*.

Cultures mix and appear to clash as "naturally"—unreflectively— as a rainstorm floods the shed where the boy and the family donkey are housed together. The West is present, not remarked upon, not remarkable: the Spanish (simply identified with "the Nazarenes," 60–61); canned food; the telephone; an ambulance; needles in the hospital. The cinema is remarked upon, since it was the first time the boy had seen a movie: "I bought a ticket at the window and went in. That was the first time I had been inside a cinema. Now I see why people like to live in the city. This theatre is very fine, I thought. There were pictures of war, and there were airplanes flying" (69). As is usual in Bowles's own fiction, even the remarkable is presented with no indication of changes in intensity, in intonation, rarely an indication of enthusiasm. This, too, is part of the cultural code: all facts are equal and equally valued.[10]

The voice of "The Half-Brothers" may be Larbi's, but the questions that prompt it—the questions raised by the hidden author/audience— are Western, American. Larbi is prompted to talk in a way that is not a traditionally Moroccan way of speaking. Rather it is a confessional manner that, as Michel Foucault has insisted, increasingly characterizes Western discourse. The result is a story that is closer to oral history— the purest example of this new authorship in the West—than to fictional modes—the portraits of the artist, for example—that help to organize the narratives.

Foucault, in volume 1 of *The History of Sexuality* (1976), points out that in the West, since the Middle Ages "at least," confession has been a major ritual in the production of "truth." "We have since become a singularly confessing society" (59). There is a certain irony in Paul Bowles's prompting the words of Larbi, since he is notoriously reticent about revealing himself directly, even in his autobiography. *Without Stopping* (1972) records that Bowles learned early that he would always be kept from doing what he enjoyed and forced to do that which he did not by his family, particularly by his father. Bowles says, "Thus I became an expert in the practice of deceit, at least insofar as general mien and facial expressions were concerned." He could not, however, bring himself to lie, "inasmuch as for me the word and its literal meaning had supreme importance" (17). Except for the hostility toward his family, Bowles's autobiography is striking in the way it avoids self-disclosure and analysis of the many people, famous and not, who crowd the pages of *Without Stopping*.[11]

Foucault noted the change in the West that was first religious and legal but came to have great significance for literature. He rightly emphasized the power of the one eliciting the confession:

> For a long time, the individual was vouched for by the reference of others and the demonstration of his ties to the commonweal (family, allegiance, protection); then he was authenticated by the discourse of truth he was able or obliged to pronounce concerning himself. The truthful confession was inscribed at the heart of the procedures of individualization by power (58–59).

As "Western man" became a "confessing animal," according to Foucault, there was correspondingly a massive change in literature:

> We have passed from a pleasure to be recounted and heard, centering on the heroic or marvelous narration of "trials" of bravery or sainthood, to a literature ordered according to the infinite task of extracting from the depths of oneself, in between the words, a truth which the very form of the confession holds out like a shimmering image (59).

In "The Half-Brothers," Larbi is brought to a point where he can and must abandon his family to live on the beach. It is important that Larbi does not become a writer, as Bowles did, or others, such as Joyce, who inscribed their lives in "portraits." Larbi was not educated and remained nonliterate, while Bowles recorded, translated, and wrote down the storyteller's words. There is nothing in the story (or in Bowles's comments on his nonliterate storytellers) to indicate that there is anything wrong in that. (The one storyteller in *Five Eyes* who presented difficulties for Bowles was Mohammed Chukri, discussed in the previous chapter, the only one to become literate and the one who insisted that Bowles follow the Arabic text word for word, comma by comma, when the two worked together to translate the stories [8].)

Bowles is the partner to Larbi's confession, but it is not clear where the power lies. Success as an "author" had given Larbi enough money so that he could look for a bride (*Without Stopping* 350); but the anxiety over official objection to his book, *A Life Full of Holes* forced Larbi to leave

Morocco, never to return (355). The story of a ten year old who leaves his family, mainly owing to oppression at the hands of his step-father is not in the traditional repertory of the Moroccan storyteller. (Larbi's mother is sometimes sympathetic to her son's needs; she tries to moderate her husband's attacks on the boy. She also gives him food, but she, like the rest of the family, merely ignores the boy while he is in the hospital.) It is also a scandalous tale in that it does not fit into the curve of development expected of men in the Arab-Muslim world.

Larbi is "about ten" when he leaves home for the beach. It is significant, that he is not yet an adolescent, not yet bothered by sexual urges. If a certain degree of wild behavior is allowed the *drari*—even encouraged by cultural norms of child rearing—there is a larger pattern captured by the proverb,

> The boy of ten is like a peeled cucumber.
> The man of twenty makes friendships with fools.
> The man of thirty (is like the) flower of the garden.
> The man of forty is in his prime. (Dwyer 87)

From the child's earliest days, according to Daisy Hilse Dwyer, the Moroccan boy's "egotistical spontaneity" is encouraged (91). Even in the womb "the male is believed to be a bundle of energy that is predisposed to movement. The male fetus is believed to flit from side to side in the abdomen, nervously covering his ground." Still, this exaggerated freedom of the boys running wild in the streets is but one phase in a "developmental pathway" (166) in which a male eventually achieves the potential of his *'aqel* (intelligence, responsibility, rationality 152), wisdom, and spiritual insight, usually in middle age.

Anthropologist Paul Rabinow found his way literally blocked by the *drari*, when he first entered the village of Sidi Lahcen Lyussi, where he was supposed to conduct his research:

> The car was greeted . . . by what seemed like hundreds of *drari*—which is inadequately translated as children. These fearless little monsters surrounded the car, much to the annoyance of their elders. Screaming, yelling, and pushing they proceeded to examine all of my possessions. One of the villagers' main fears, it turns out, was that these *drari* would do some irreparable damages either to me or to my belongings. Their fathers threatened them with beatings, curses, and exclamations, to little or no avail. (84)

Fortunately, the Fernea family came to be accepted in the neigh-borhood. A young boy even alerted them to a key they had left in the door, an invitation to robbery in most cities. And Rabinow, similarly, found little to complain about later in his stay, regarding the boys. Daisy Hilse Dwyer, though, notes the anxieties of Moroccan families over the unruly behavior of sons even much later in the sons' lives, before the wisdom of age enters them. And the beatings Rabinow found the fathers threatening their sons with are very much a part of the fathers' prerogatives.[12] The expectation that men normally improve with age (and women do not) is a common pattern in Moroccan folk-tales (Dwyer 52–57).

Precisely because it is not difficult to "follow" such a story, what is revealed is our way (tradition) of reading, the genres and expectations with which we are familiar. Larbi's theme, Bowles tells us, is always "injustice and the suffering it causes," and his purpose is "to 'tell them outside' what it is like to be shut inside" (*Five Eyes* 8). Presumably, the outsiders are the readers. But the very familiarity with realistic fiction which makes the story accessible may obscure the concept of 'character' that informs the piece.

Both Daisy Hilse Dwyer, who studied Moroccan stories for the light they shed on Moroccan ideas of male and female and their sepa-rate pathways of development (166), and Clifford Geertz, upon whose work she drew, distinguish between a Western and a Moroccan view of the person, such as was sketched above in the Introduction. Recall that in "On the Nature of Anthropological Understanding," Geertz describes Morocco as a "wild-west sort of place" filled with "rugged individuals" of many types. Yet he cautions that "no society consists of anonymous eccentrics bouncing off one another like billiard balls" (51). He emphasizes the connectedness of individuals, the *nisba* that binds persons to families, occupations, religious sects, and even spiritual sta-tus. The outsider might see them as individuals of the Western sort, but insiders always know the *nisba* of the person. "They are contextualized persons," Geertz maintains.

> Behind this is a very different concept of the person from what has devel-oped in the West since the Renaissance: The Western conception of the person as a bounded, unique, more or less integrated motivational and cognitive universe, a dynamic center of awareness, emotional judgment, and action organized into a distinctive whole and seen contrastively

both against other such wholes and against a social and natural background is, however incorrigible it may seem to us, a rather peculiar idea within the context of the world's cultures. (48)

By prompting a decidedly Western style of story from Layachi, Bowles decontextualizes the ten year old. In particular, the developmental pathway (which, as Dwyer points out, has a moral curve quite different from "the predominant Euro-American sort" [166]) is obscured in the manner of closing the story—with Larbi as the triumphant individual who has thrown off the constraints of his family and society.

In contrast, Yacoubi's "The Night before Thinking" returns the reader—after any number of magical turns and imaginary leaps that are by definition unexpected—to the familiar context of the Arab-Islamic family. Yacoubi includes one jest at the expense of the Western reader, who is routinely inscribed as the Nazarene in these stories: when he tells the story of the accident that brought Ragussa to birth before her brother, Yacoubi's character says, "And she was born five minutes before I was. Five minutes for the Christians is a long time. For us it's not such a big thing. But this time it was like a thousand years" (25), since the power fell to the woman's lot and not the man's.

In a more innocent age these stories might have been enjoyed and dismissed as products of a "primitive" mind. The dangers of an attempt only slightly less suspect are still common: to read in the "Oriental" mind a strange, unfathomable otherness, and to see these others as what Edith Wharton called "unknown and unknowable people" (whom she nevertheless was able to describe; 113). Said has alerted us to the dangers of such Orientalist thinking. Paul Bowles himself, attracted by surrealist ideas, felt that in the part of the East in which he settled he was finding the unconscious that civilization, the West, had repressed.[13]

Listening to nonliterate Moroccan storytellers, recording their voices, translating their culture into a form of printed text, into a tradition that developed a certain kind of "realistic fiction," Paul Bowles has formed a curious kind of hybrid text. Authorship of "The Night before Thinking" and "The Half-Brothers" is not the simple process—an individual drawing on individual experience to produce a work—that the West has considered somehow fundamental to the very notion of literature. Now that an anthropologist, Clifford Geertz, is drawing on Roland Barthes and Michel Foucault to understand the anthropologist "as author" (*Works and Lives* 18–20), and Geertz himself is being drawn into a newer, more complex understanding of the authorship of literary works (Hernadi 757), it is becoming increasingly useful to look at texts produced by unusual "authors."[14]

It would, in one sense, be helpful to have the tapes of Ahmed Yacoubi's and Larbi Layachi's stories in Moghrebi Arabic. One could then trace the changes from speech to writing, from a local dialect of Arabic to a regional dialect of English, in a more detailed way than is now possible. However, when a nonliterate Moroccan friend thought one of Bowles's translations was "shameful" *because* he had "written about people just as they are" (in the friend's view making them seem "like animals"), the friend dismissed the "objective truth" of the representation: "That is statistical truth. We are interested in that, yes, but only as a means of getting to the real truth underneath" ("Africa Minor" 32). On one point the American reader can be certain, however. Paul Bowles may have sought the primitive, the unconscious, in Morocco; but the longer he remained there and the better he came to know the people and the local dialects, the more he was able to appreciate the different sense of "reality" he found there.

Larbi Layachi and Ahmed Yacoubi are, ironically, more likely to be considered "authors" in the English-speaking world than in the Arab-Muslim world, since they have not mastered Modern Standard Arabic. They could become known in Morocco, though, as storytellers, since their inventive tales can be told in public. The anonymous teller of the story in the next chapter, though, retreats behind the story itself, a story of a woman's heroism most likely told in private by one woman to other women, or by a woman to her family. The division between public and private space, marked on the individual by the traditional veil, is reproduced in the organization of the family compound, its high (often unpainted and undecorated) walls shielding the beauty and the activity within the walls from public gaze. For those who do not live within walls, the tent provides that absolute separation and keeps matters private. The chapter considers first the heroic tale in a traditional storytelling mode and then turns to the patience and power of a rural Moroccan woman, who tells her story to an anthropologist.

Chapter Nine

Tented Visions:

Woman as Hero/as Victim

The hidden woman of the Arab-Muslim world gives rise to more fantasies than perhaps any other feature of the East. Whatever led to the veiling of women, the traditional seclusion of high-status women provided the Western visitor, mainly men, with few occasions to see them, let alone come to know them except through the mediation of men. The odalisques who populate nineteenth-century Orientalist paintings look beautiful, languid, erotic, and bored.[1] Flaubert's Salammbô is perhaps the best treatment of the femme fatale in Western literature, but there are many rivals. Hidden away where she can only intensify her erotic and mystical longings, the Oriental woman is seductive to the extent that she is unknowable. (Flaubert's Salammbô was inspired by a prostitute the writer knew briefly in upper Egypt.) Paul Bowles's protagonist in *The Sheltering Sky* is drawn first to a prostitute with whom he cannot speak and then, deep in the desert, to another one who is blind as well.

The alternate image is not much better. To a society that had written universal education into the very idea of intelligence, the nonliterate woman of the East is the very image of the enslaved primitive. Even today feminists and anthropologists argue whether a woman can be uneducated, controlled by men, and kept apart from the public and maintain any kind of power. Edith Wharton certainly found nothing to envy in the women she met. The rather sketchy portraits Jane Bowles presents in "Everything Is Nice" are a refreshing change in the Western image. And Elizabeth Warnock Fernea's far more detailed portraits continually provide new insights because virtually everything she sees requires interpretation. Though Arab-Muslim writers, mainly men, have written of women for centuries, there are still few insider views of the not-yet Westernized woman. Two very different views are provided by a traditional folktale and a life story.

INEA BUSHNAQ, "WUDEI'A, WHO SENT AWAY SUBEI'A"

Inea Bushnaq includes a good number of Moroccan stories in her collection of *Arab Folktales*. In all but one of the categories—didactic tales—Moroccan stories appear, and there is no reason to believe memorable tales of that sort are not common in Morocco. Bushnaq's intent was to collect interesting and representative stories from wherever she found them in the Middle East and North Africa. That so many happen to have come from Morocco may reflect the continued interest in traditional storytelling there. After all, the public storyteller in, say, the famous Djemaa al-Fna in Marrakech, is still a popular entertainer. That linguists, interested primarily in recording local dialects, preserved stories in Morocco is also a factor.

For whatever reason, the Bushnaq's categories are well represented by Moroccan tales. Among Bedouin tales ("Tales Told in Houses Made of Hair") she includes two; in "Tales of Magic and the Supernatural" two more; one, "The Boy Magician," appears in stories of "Magical Marriages and Mismatches"; five animal fables, two stories of fools and rascals (about the notorious Djuha and Bablul), and one of the tales concerned with "Wily Women and Clever Men" can be found in the collection.

Especially interesting are the tales told by women. Public storytellers in Morocco are male. As in other situations where the traditional separation of men and women in the Arab-Muslim world holds, it would be improper for women to perform in cafes and public squares. Women tell stories within the household, though; and they tell stories to one another. According to Bushnaq, the stories of ghouls and afreets are particularly popular with women. They are "the household tales proper" (65). Often the teller is a grandmother or an aged servant.

Bushnaq emphasizes that the spoken word contains magic, "strong enough to attract unknown forces of evil" (66). Even "in ordinary conversation there is no mention of death, sickness, or accident" without calling upon Allah's protection. The supernatural creatures who form so much a part of these stories have a basis in the Qur'an, where a sura is devoted to the Djinn, for example:

> Indeed, just as God created man from potter's clay, so he formed the Djinn from a smokeless fire. He sent the prophets to enlighten both worlds of sentient beings, that of the Ins, or humans, and that of the Djinn, or spirits. Much of the excitement in the tales of magic lies in the removal of the boundary between the two worlds. (67)

Djinn, ghouls, she-ghouls, and afreets—those figures banished in the West from the domain of mainstream realistic fiction (but which return in fantasies, children's stories, and popular films) are the defining features of these genres.

"The Girl Who Banished Seven Youths" (119–24) is a Moroccan story Bushnaq includes as one of the household tales. The title contains a pun. The girl's name, Wudei'a, is a play on Subei'a, the seven, whom she sends away (wada'a). Two elements of the story, closely related, stand out, as much as anything because they are unexpected: the woman as an active force in bringing good fortune on the family; and the woman as "father."

Folktales often have a complicated surface, because the characters and the episodes are unusual. Sometimes they reflect reality rather than stereotypes. Reading across cultures is difficult precisely because the emphases in the stories are seldom clear; assumptions often remain obscure for the outsider trying to peer into traditions that are perfectly clear to the insider. This story begins with what seems like an unfortunate incident at the birth of a daughter; it ends with the triumph of the daughter. A woman had seven sons and wanted a daughter. When the daughter is finally born, the father's sister trecherously switches the signals set out to tell the sons whether a daughter or son was born. (A spindle over the door is to mark the birth of a girl; the sister hangs a sickle over the door instead.) The sons, who had gone out to hunt, disappear into the desert when the sickle is displayed. Although their motives are never explained in the tale, the sons had agreed to return home if the child is a girl; if the child is a boy, they will simply "cut loose and go" (119). Note that from the start the "normal" preference of family members for (yet another) son is skewed.

The neighborhood children taunt the daughter because her brothers have disappeared, and Wudei'a begins a series of adventures in search of her lost brothers. Misfortune sets in almost immediately. A crafty manservant forces the girl to walk while a servant girl rides the camel. (Wudei'a's mother can help only as long as the camel and the girl are within earshot; then Wudei'a is on her own.) The manservant rubs Wudei'a's skin with pitch so that she will look like the servant when the group arrives at the brothers' castle. The trick works at first, but when Wudei'a weeps, the white flesh appears; she is cleaned "until her skin was white again." The brothers cut the heads off the manservant and the maid for the deception they had attempted. Wudei'a is installed in the house of her brothers.

Wudei'a is warned to give half of anything she eats to a certain cat. When she forgets to give the cat half of a bean she found among the sweepings, the cat urinates on Wudei'a's cooking fire. The girl must go searching again, this time for fire, and she finds a ghoul. Bushnaq points out that in Arabic folklore the ghoul is the "wildest and most repulsive-looking of the spirits" (68). Ghouls love to eat human flesh, but when they are humored, "they often prove surprisingly sentimental and good natured."

Wudei'a addresses the spirit as "father Ghoul," and the greeting saves her. Had she not greeted him, the ghoul would have torn her to pieces. He gives her advice on securing fire but demands of her a strip of her skin. Wounded, she walks back to the castle. A raven covers up the blood that drops onto the ground, but the raven startles Wudei'a and she scolds it. So the raven uncovers the bloody path—showing the way for the ghoul to find her.

The circumstances arising from her second mistake (the first one was not sharing the bean with the cat; the second was scolding the raven) prove to be too difficult for her to handle alone. Her brothers finally return and find a scheme to destroy the ghoul. Before the ghoul is destroyed in a pit of embers, ironically, he visits the girl, hidden away behind seven doors in her brothers' castle. The ghoul refers to her by name and asks, "What was your old father doing when you came?" At the answer, the ghoul laughs and begins breaking down the doors.

Wudei'a sends a dove with a message: "O dove, whom my brothers love . . . carry my words to them through the air above" (122). The boys come immediately. When the ghoul returns—he had been checked by the seventh door, made of iron, he again asks her about her "old father." This time she does not try to soothe him, and her answer reveals that she knows who he really is:

> He was flaying mules and donkeys,
> Drinking blood and sucking entrails.
> Matted hair so wild and long
> It was his bed to lie upon. (123)

The ghoul is completely destroyed except for the nail of his little finger, which wounds her when she tries to clean the room. She lies on the ground, apparently dead, and the brothers sorrowfully prepare her for the journey back home. Their father's camel takes her back. On the way, men try to rob her body of a ring, and the robber unwittingly dislodges the nail. Immediately, Wudei'a awakens and cries out, "Long life to him who brought me back from death" (124). She returns to her brothers' castle. The brothers and Wudei'a return together to their parents' home, they on seven horses, she on a camel. The father asks the boys, "O sons, what made you leave the world I live in?" For three days—a Bedouin custom—they do not answer, but then they are completely reconciled with their father and mother. The tale ends happily with the family together again. Until the end, when Wudei'a remains "inside," doing the work she is expected to as a women, she puts herself in danger—her blood leads the "old father" ghoul to her, and he attempts to break into the innermost room of the compound. When she is "outside," she makes mistakes, but she is remarkably resourceful (for a woman in a sexually segregated society). Even though she needs the help of her brothers to destroy the ghoul, the story focuses on her adventures. Her initiatives are, finally, rewarded when she becomes the instrument to bring the "dead" sons back to life, even as she is brought back to life. The wilderness in which the brothers have lived is assimilated to the place where the ghoul resides.

The ghoul as the "old father" who is first humored and then grows perverse, as a ghoul is supposed to do, wants to break in, kill, and devour her. He is balanced, in a sense, by the good father—the true father—who has been saddened by the loss of his seven sons. What is most intriguing about the story, though, is the language used by the brothers when Wudei'a, thought dead, returns to them. They see her as their savior. The brothers say to her, "You have been a father to us," and "your word" has been "like a father's" (124).

Like a hero, Wudei'a has risked slavery, torture, and finally death in a quest that takes the hero out of the ordinary, the known world, into the wilderness where the ghoul is father. Such a story would be less startling if the hero were male or if the woman had succeeded by doing what women are supposed to do.

In *Images and Self-Images: Male and Female in Morocco* Daisy Hilse Dwyer examines Moroccan folktales for the way in which the stories reflect assumptions about male and female roles. What she finds for men and women is a certain "developmental directionality" reflected in the stories. The developmental path for women, though, is strikingly different from the path for men:

> As an ideology of becoming, Moroccan sexual ideology focuses upon how individual character changes or can change with respect to the incidence of these moral qualities. Its message concerns relative morality more than absolute goodness, and so expresses itself as a vector relation. Women—perhaps virtuous, perhaps wavering, perhaps evil—fall into greater disrepute as they act our their innermost tendencies. At their best, they might avoid the fall, but in few cases do they show evidence of enlightenment. Men—perhaps sinful, perhaps wavering, perhaps virtuous—become more respectable with time. If they do not exhibit improvement, still their morality does not diminish. (53)

The stories Dwyer presents show just such a different developmental pathway. While a majority of stories about men and women show no particular (positive/negative) development of the character, of those that do, the direction is very clear: the male characters improve far more often than not, and the women deteriorate far more often than not (54). Moreover, character change is seen as irreversible (57). Male and female are complementary in another way. While men "move toward goodness and virtue through striving and effort, seldom achieving it, women are more nearly endowed with a degree of moral fiber which only certain of Morocco's assiduous men are believed able to match" (59). Wudei'a would seem to be a case of this. But Dwyer also points out that "women are born with it to a degree, unknowingly cultivate it, and then, when men are most apt to attain it, women find that it is lacking" (59).

Dwyer noted that even when a woman had achieved the goals she is traditionally prepared for—marriage without dishonoring the family before it, and bearing children, especially sons—maternity is not the guardian of virtue. The woman still must struggle against her sexual passions. Only when she is too old to be concerned with such matters does she achieve a different status—but then is likely to be feared as the possessor of powerful magic.

It may be that Wudei'a is unusual in that she achieves something like sainthood before she leaves the family—before men, sex, and children enter her life. Perhaps the success of Wudei'a does not guarantee success later. The way she moves in and out of situations, even returning from the dead to be praised as "father" (with the ghoul on one side, as a kind of father, and the real father on the other, who is remarkably passive in this story) suggests that this household tale is quite subversive in the message it carries about women.

SUSAN SCHAEFER DAVIS, "ZAHRAH MUHAMMAD: A RURAL WOMAN OF MOROCCO"

This story is almost too good to be true. A girl who begins life in a prosperous home falls into the hands of a wicked step-sister when her father dies. A man tries to take from her the one thing she must guard, her honor, symbolized, as in Ben Jallūn's "A Stranger," by her virginity. Though she is young, she is powerful enough to resist him. Having made it, finally, to a mature age, she dreams of faraway places, cities she might visit.

Fortunately, the story is not marred by the formulas of Bowdlerized fairy tales. The farm girl does not turn into a princess. The wicked step-sister does not disappear like the ghoul in "Wudei'a Who Banished Seven Youths." And there is assuredly no prince to take her away. It is the story of Zahrah Muhammad, a Moroccan woman, which has been told with the help of anthropologist Susan Schaefer Davis. A large piece of the story was published in a volume devoted to letting Middle Eastern Muslim Women speak.[2]

Elizabeth Warnock Fernea, a co-editor of *Middle Eastern Muslim Women Speak* (1977), provides a context for the oral history of Zahrah Muhammad in a story told by her husband's informant, Abdul Aziz. Abdul Aziz shocked Fernea with the claim that "the liberation of the Maghreb began the moment the French first set foot on our soil" (320). Realizing that the French were really after their souls, Abdul Aziz went on to say, the Moroccans did not invite the French into their houses, and that saved them from the damage done to the Algerians, and perhaps the Syrians. He concluded, "It is not possible to be friends with a Frenchman." As noted earlier, Abdul Aziz underscored his point with the story of a friendship with a French teacher gone sour. Recall that the teacher had asked Abdul Aziz to suggest a servant from Abdul Aziz's "entourage." Abdul Aziz was deeply offended because the entourage could be none other than his family.

Entering in any important way into the homes of Moroccans is no less easy for Americans than for the French. Even anthropologists who are professionally committed to an investigation of the culture of an other are not always convinced real contact can be made. For men, trying to gain an insight into the lives of women in the Muslim world is difficult even if the man is an insider, one raised in the culture, for the separation of the sexes is still profound. Hence an oral history like "Zahrah Muhammad" is particularly useful to those who will always be on the outside of Moroccan life.

The beauty of such a story is that it has no "author," in the usual, Western sense of the term. It corresponds to no genre of the literary tradition (though it does have a deep root in the socio-literary tradition that produced literary realism in the West) or of the storyteller tradition that is still strong in Morocco. What presents itself—a printed text, part of a volume on Middle Eastern Muslim women speaking, in English—is somewhat removed from the performance of the story, a taped conversation between Zahrah Muhammad (whose name was changed in the tradition of Western social science) and an American woman, Susan Schaefer Davis. Between the conversation, in Moghrebi Arabic, and the printed text stand two intermediate, unpublished texts, one a transcript, in Arabic and English translation, done by a friend of Susan Schaefer Davis; the other, an edited typescript, is like the final piece written without indication that the story is really a dialogue, and a fuller account of the original conversation than finally appeared in print.

(Only a limitation on the length of the printed text kept the whole typescript from being published.)

The intermediate stages are, fortunately, available. More important, "Zahrah Muhammad" was not polished in the way many oral histories are. The sense of the person speaking is clear throughout the piece because Davis declined to change the voice of Zahrah Muhammad. There is editing, to be sure, as will be noted below, but what remains by not removing the slips and apparently quirks of thought and speech is a most powerful story.

The story is not exactly unstructured. The women knew each other well before the conversation, so the usual problems with interviews in the field, especially at the beginning when excessive formality and fear of the tape recorder intimidate the informant, were avoided. What is not clear from the printed translation is that the opening was prompted, not by a question, but by an announcement, "Well, I am going to tell you about when my father, May God have mercy on his soul. . . ." Davis intervenes to complete the sentence, "When you were very small." When Zahrah agrees, but says she will go back to when she was about ten years old, Davis prompts her to begin earlier, and she obliges by recalling the first things she remembers: "I remember when my father—may God have mercy on his soul—existed, when I was seven years old" (AE 1–7). From the start the story is a negotiation between speaker and listener, who is always active in the conversation. And Davis is remarkably restrained. In the typescript Davis writes,

> Although I asked occasional questions (which are not included), Zahrah basically told the story herself, so that the selection and order of topics are in themselves interesting. . . . She presents interesting background material on rural life and customs in her youth, and her emphases on weddings, birth and interpersonal relationships show the main areas of concern to many Moroccan women. (T 1)

Davis cannot claim that Zahrah Muhammad is a "typical Moroccan woman," but she is typical to some extent of "an older (40–55) village woman who is neither poverty stricken nor wealthy and who is quite assertive and outgoing—as women her age are apt to be, when they become mothers-in-law after their long apprenticeship as daughters-in-law" (P 202). Zahrah's story spans the years between about 1930 and 1972.

Zahrah's father dominates the early pages, and he clearly stands for the society and its Arab-Muslim values, few of which are challenged by Zahrah—even though her discourse is marked by contrasts between then and now. The father owned a house and a lot of land: "He had farm land, he had sheep, he had cattle and he had hired workers. There were people who washed clothes, people who milked cows, people for everything. The land was ours alone" (203). This is clearly not the desert land of Orientalist imaginings; rather, a fertile area in the foothills of the Middle Atlas Mountains, near the city of Meknes. From this idyllic scene Zahrah is displaced, and she talks about several places where she was compelled to live.

Indeed, it is not difficult to see the spatial dimensions of social relations in Morocco, especially involving the family and the separation of the sexes, operating as the main unifying element of the narrative. The center of the story is marked by Zahrah's first decision to stay in a certain place, to remain with her in-laws (P 208). The end of the story is marked, in turn, by the possibility of movement. Her sister's children live all over Morocco—and some abroad, in Mecca and in Europe. Having found her place, Zahrah thinks about visiting them:

> And we . . . I *could* go to visit them . . . it's just my idea, now I'm used to it here and I can't leave my son and I can't leave the house, and that's that. But if I *were* to go to visit them, they wouldn't let me go back. After this week passes, I'll go, God willing. After the feast is over, we'll see. . . . I'll probably go now. (P 217)

The last passage could—probably must—be read in a number of different ways, that is, without resolving the problems the story has touched upon and yet without a sense, simply, of despair. She cannot go; she will not go; she is able to go; she will go; next week, after the feast, maybe. By itself, the passage certainly suggests failure and imprisonment; but the story as it leads up to this point suggests otherwise. True, she can barely contain her hatred for the (now deceased) step-sister who made her early life miserable. The sister's children are not simply the objects of affection she makes them out to be, when one by one she catalogues their locations and activities. But that she has found her place and is unwilling to move from it is more a stubborn assertion that she has found herself than (as it might seem) a timid refusal of the larger world.

It should be noted that the end of the printed story is not actually the end of the interview, which trails off in questions about a number of relatives who have had brushes with the law. The concern with travel is prompted by Davis, and in one sense the prompting is as typical of a modern, Western woman's sense of freedom—to travel anywhere, for one thing—as the assertion of place is typical of a traditional Arab-Muslim woman. In a segment not prepared for publication, Davis seems to suggest that Zahrah could travel with the Davis family, who are about to depart. Davis jokes with Zahrah about kidnapping her and taking her with them "to India" (AE 485–89).

From the prosperous farm through several stages of difficulties to a place of her own, Zahrah's story is a most compelling narrative. One of the curious rhetorical patterns that develops—curious because it is coming to be seen more and more in ancient literature and in oral compositions—is chiasmus, and as usual, it creates some difficulty for the modern reader, who is more accustomed to linear developments of a story.

Chiasm, or ring composition, may happen when a conversation strays and then is brought back to an earlier topic. "Zahrah Muhammad" is intriguing because the selection of topics is only rarely made by the anthropologist (who, nevertheless, actively encourages a topic of interest to her by insertions, questions, and repetitions along the way). Davis did ask that Zahrah talk about her first marriage, which intrigued Davis "as an example of how 'subservient' Muslim females *can* defend their own interests" (T 1). However, the conversation moves mainly in the way Zahrah links one topic with another, and when the topic returns to an earlier point, what is enveloped is intricately embedded in the larger pattern.

For example, the following sequence occurs in the story line:

1. Zahrah's mother goes to court for custody of her children.
2. Zahrah's life with her half-sister; she is married off (to Muhammad);
3. Zahrah's brief first marriage and her escape from her first husband;
2'. Zahrah with husband Muhammad, moves to a village;
1'. Zahrah's mother's custody fight. (AE 33–93)

Chiastic patterns emphasize the center, often even more than beginnings and endings. When the pattern is not noticed, the reader of originally oral narratives are often confused by repetitions and apparently unrelated episodes. Chiasm allows the large concerns to be highlighted in the middle, and reinforced as the story winds down, often without the sense of climax and denouement so prized in modern literary realism. Zahrah's first marriage and her escape, the central episode, is thus not just one more bead on a string. The center keeps some measure of control over the otherwise meandering story.

But the time consciousness so much discussed by modern literary criticism seems distorted because the time sense is so different from Western time, what Edward Hall calls "M-time" (monochronic time). Instead, the narrative contains many twists and turns. Digressions on weddings and other customs (of great interest to the anthropologist) freely enter and are pursued as long as there is time to pursue them.

The major episodes are the following:
father selling the farm to a Christian
life on the farm
mother marries again after father dies
half-sister takes Z to Meknes
Z's mother to court for custody
Z married to Muhammad
Z's first marriage
Muhammad takes her to his village
Z's mother to court for custody
about brothers Mustafa and Ali
Z's life in a village, living in a tent
pregnancy and birth
Z's decision to remain with the family
loss of her first child, birth of other children
child ill, helped by foreigner and doctor
life in tent
wedding customs
women unable to shop in the *suq*
attending weddings with husband
"embellishing" the bride in the wilderness
giving birth in the wilderness
problem visiting people

other restrictions on women
move to another village; wedding customs
marriage contracts
contract with the first husband
her sister's children

For someone who grew up on a prosperous farm, and whose life was jolted by the death of her father, displacement became the major theme of the narrative. Prosperity, suffering, and later something like prosperity is a pattern that leads Zahrah to compare things then and things now, although there is curiously no sense that Zahrah herself developed over time. The many restrictions on the movement of a woman obviously bothered Zahrah from an early age, and self-assertion emerges early.

First there is the idyllic youth on the farm. Her father was prosperous enough to own land for farming and for the raising of sheep and cattle (P 203). In the days of her youth, according to Zahrah, there was more food, but more restrictions on women. The women could not visit one another freely. To visit the suq was shameful for a young woman. At an early age the women were married off, without a hint of choice in the matter. Zahrah's Muhammad beat her, and his brother threatened to beat her and there was no recourse. The best food went, without question, to the men; women ate what was left. A woman could not even make tea for herself. She had to wait until the men asked for it. "For the woman, her boundary is the edge of her tent" (P 214).

When she was young, the old people were naive and very strict. Now there is more freedom, as Zahrah can at least envision traveling around Morocco to visit her sister's children. Probably because her status has changed and the times have changed, too, a woman well established with her grown children, Zahrah appears to have more power and greater freedom of movement. In her study of Moroccan women, *Patience and Power* [1983] Davis claims that the image popular in the West of a woman merely submissive and passive is mistaken; rather, the Moroccan woman is "patient," holding her power in check "until the right moment to act." In adulthood, the Moroccan woman has others to do much of her work, is able to visit the suq, and when she achieves maturity in her "life cycle," she gains a great deal of freedom of speech and action (39–45).

The stages in the woman's life cycle are not marked by Zahrah Muhammad, although they are implicit in her increasing freedom to act. To a certain extent she sees the changes in her life as coming from the outside, in particular through the emergence of a market economy based on money. (Earlier everyone would have the proper animal for sacrifice and the proper food for a festival; now one needs money to have these things.) The chief outsiders are the *nasara*, the foreigners, French, Christians. "But, really, now when the Christians have come and there are machines and there are tractors, and there's all this . . . it's not like at that time" (P 211). (Now, at least, there is more fabric, and the women have far more clothes than they used to have.)

There is surprisingly little rancor in the Muslim woman's talk about the *nasara*, especially since she claims that her father lost his land when a Christian cheated him out of it. Her father turned over the wrong deed to the Christian in a deal for another piece of land (P 203). What is most remarkable about the oral history of Zahrah Muhammad is the way her language about the other reflects her treatment of space. Just as the woman's boundary is "the edge of her tent," the larger world outside is conceptually restricted, divided between those near and those far removed from her life world.

The world of relatives and in-laws is close, and the complexity of reference is difficult for the Western reader to follow. Hildred Geertz appended a lengthy list of Moroccan kinship terms to her article, "The Meanings of Family Ties" (380–85). Easily handled with great precision are relationships that require awkward qualifications in English (*bent 'amm-i* for "my father's brother's daughter"; *nsib-i*, "my wife's brother son's son"; *rbibt-i*, "my husband's daughter by another wife" and the like). Zahrah's brother-in-law tells her to slaughter a rooster (T 11), and her mother-in-law orders her to get water. Her husband, Muhammad's aunt, sister of Uncle Abbas (her father-in-law) brings her couscous. The wife of her father-in-law, one of two co-wives, gets into a row with the mother-in-law over wood to be used for fuel:

> I brought in some wood for fuel and she came, my mother-in-law, and picked it up and took it. The wife of my father-in-law came (he had two wives) and said, "Why did she take the wood?" I told her, "My mother-in-law took them," and they up and started fighting. One beat the other with the iron shovel until the blood was running. They went to court, they tried everything. One bit the other right here, so hard her teeth met

through the skin. The co-wives were fighting, my mother-in-law and the wife of my father-in-law. My mother-in-law left and the wife of my father-in-law stayed with us. She had left before my father-in-law went to jail. (T 12)

The translation is awkward precisely because the kinship terminology is obvious to the insider and bewildering to the cultural outsider. Zahrah's story is filled with problems with her relatives. Her brothers, Mustafa and Ali fight about Ali's stealing merchandise from Mustafa—to give to their mother. Mustafa, the brother who simply disappears (Zahrah seems to think he may have drowned), has been wronged by Ali, but Zahrah seems to shift the blame to him: "Meanwhile, the other had begun to bring home women or to get drunk or to smoke cigarettes and everything . . . and he went broke and his shop was seized" (T 7). Ali, for his part, decides "to disappear and wander," and his story becomes one of almost constant moving about: to the Sahara, to Tangier, finally to Europe. Zahrah, who had been spending her time in a tent, seems puzzled about this brother, who wanders the countryside and has not even phoned these many years (T 9).

Kinship terms are not the only problem in translating between cultures. One of the most interesting wedding customs Zahrah explains involves the *wzara*, the "best men," a term used otherwise for ministers of state (Standard Arabic *wazi:r*). The best men play roles in two strange rites: "embellishing" the bride in the wilderness and "tenting" the bride during a seclusion that resembles a rite of passage. The customs are much like those surveyed by Edward Westermarck early in this century. What Zahrah adds is the perspective of one who has not only observed the customs but has participated in them as well. Her voice adds a dimension lacking in ethnographic summaries.

"Shame" (*hshuma*, Standard *hishma*) is clearly the notion that drives Zahrah. (What is usually translated inadequately as "sin" [*denb, haram*] is not much in evidence in Zahrah's account.) Zahrah is aware that the custom of deflowering ("embellishing," *ziyyen*, a word related always to adornment, decoration) the bride in the "wilderness" (*xla*) is now coming to be considered shameful. It is certainly an ancient and widespread custom. A Sumerian poem, from the third millennium B.C. about Inanna and Dumuzi may treat the custom in a mythological way (*Inanna* 40). (Westermarck noted the custom in *Marriage Ceremonies* 238.)

How many brides I've seen with my own eyes! Now, for example here, the best man comes and he carries the bride on his back, and another best man carries two pillows and he carries a rug. Well, they go and take her far away and they take the groom there and he embellishes her there in the wilderness and they bring her back. (T 22)

The "best men" she likens to the bride's brothers. While the ceremony is organized around the sign of the "sultan," the groom as sultan with his court of *wzara*, Zahrah does not register, or chooses to ignore the sign: the attendants are *wzara*, but the groom is only *razel*, not the sultan. The men wait "until she's embellished" and the groom calls them back. They lift her, take her back to the tent, cook breakfast for her, and feed her—"the men who feed her with their hands" (T 22). There is a ritual fight for her. One of the "best men" threatens that, if he does not get to see the bride and receive "fruit" from her, he will "drag her along the ground or tie her up or put irons on her." Another steps up to redeem her. He offers to pay for her.

(Zahrah also reports on the custom of ceremonial fighting. Bride and groom beat each other with a cane until one breaks. "Whoever wins, they say that . . . if the man's broke, they say, 'That's it; he'll be henpecked.' And if the woman's breaks, they say, 'That's it; he will dominate her' " [T 26]. Slippers are important, as Westermarck noticed, as a symbol of domestic rule [*Marriage Customs* 257]; and Zahrah observed the groom ritually beating the bride with a slipper [T 27]. However, the groom is treated like a woman. After the ritual beating, he is decorated with henna.)

The custom of displaying the blood of a deflowered bride is widespread in the Arab-Muslim world. In Zahrah's account three garments are stained, pantaloons, dress, and robe, and all three function symbolically in the ritual. The best men are important in bringing the blood-stained pantaloons to the community to show that the bride is a virgin. (Zahrah tells of the symbols used when the family is shamed by a bride who turns out not to be a virgin—her wearing a sack and the filling of a large straw dish with flour, as if a death had occurred [T 27], but she does not indicate that the woman is beaten or killed; she returns to her parents' home.) When the blood-stained robe is displayed, another woman covers herself with it and dances, then they tie it to the wall of the tent. For seven days the bride is secluded, stuffed in a little tent within the family tent (T 28). Zahrah emphasizes how uncomfortable it is to be stuffed into the tent and forced to sit there for a week in the dirty dress (*shamir*) in which she had been embellished. Throughout the interview, Zahrah emphasizes clothing, and the marriage ceremony turns joyous for the bride once the dirty clothes are removed, the bride is cleansed, and she receives very pretty clothes. The best men then participate in an elaborate ceremony of girdling the bride with a belt (T 29; see Westermarck, *Marriage Customs* 293).

Men are important in Zahrah's life, but they represent an alien, remote presence. Her father is a master signifier in a patriarchal code; his role—he is never assigned a personal name by Zahrah—is always blessed in the traditional way, "May God have mercy on his soul." His presence guarantees order and security; his mistake in losing the farm is not considered shameful, and his absence breaks up the family. Zahrah's mother, for her part, remains shadowy and unblessed: "At the time when my father died, he left my mother to farm the land. My mother remained, farming the land; she farms today and she farms tomorrow, and she shares with some people and she gets into arguments" (P 203).

When she remarried, Zahrah fell into the hands of her half-sister. Even when she sues in court to gain custody of the children, Zahrah repeats the words of the qadi (judge) to the mother: "'Why did you go and get married and leave them?' She went and married that pagan and left us all alone in the house. When she got married, she didn't take even one child with her" (P 204). Clearly it is important that the unnamed "new husband" is a "pagan" (*kafer*). In the strongest language she calls him an unbeliever when she thinks of him as a good-for-nothing. Even the term translated as "husband" is a condemnation of him: the *rumi* (AE 46). Although the word usually means "foreigner," she uses it in the sense of a city person, modernized but not necessarily what the West means by foreigner, that is, one from outside the nation-state.

The males who are named are her second husband, Muhammad ("Husband" is more accurate. The "first husband" was the one who "signed the paper"—more like a fiance. The one she actually married—to whom she gave up her virginity—is only in a technical sense a "second" husband), and her brothers, Mustafa and Ali. The rest are designated by the social roles they play. Even her first husband remains nameless, simply "that man" (*hadak razel*). Her second husband, with whom she presumably has had a fairly prosperous marriage, is himself barely mentioned. Once he beats her, taking the side of his family against her. At one point he plows land for his father, with whom he had had a dispute about a donkey (T 12) because the father had been sent to jail. Her father-in-law was obviously important, ruling the family, deciding if she could visit someone or not (T 23). A brother-in-law takes upon himself the duty of punishing Zahrah and an unmarried woman with her for singing. ("Do I have dancing girls [prostitutes], that you're singing in the house? They're singing and people are passing next to the tent! Goddamn your father!" [T 25]) The incident is recalled mainly to show that the old ways have gone and now everything is "topsy-turvy" (P 215).

An exception to the anonymity of even the males close to her remain is a short list of people from the village where she lived in the tent who have, like her, moved to the larger village: Dhan, Si Mohammed Zituni, Driss, Tall Ahmed, Lame Ahmed (T 25). They are little more than names; and it is intriguing that none of the women associated with those males are mentioned in the story. However, the women in her family, and especially in her husband's family, are often mentioned both by name and by role (e.g., the always-dreaded mother-in-law).

Other males, those outside the family, are designated by social role: farmer, qadi, "police" (really, a "government man," *mxezni*), electrician, mason, peddlar. (The only woman who has such a designation is the midwife.) Zahrah Muhammad's life is one that stretched from the nomadic past through the settled agriculture (in many ways organized and certainly encouraged by the French, who urged *colons*, like the Christian who took the father's land, to settle in that area of Morocco and develop its agricultural resources). To the extent that Zahrah's life, once she was married to Muhammad, was life in a tent, her world is structured by that tented vision. The Westernizing of Morocco is clear, if at all, mainly in its effects, changes brought about by the *nasrani* and their machines and tractors.

France, Europe, for Zahrah, is a place to which her brother, Ali, for unclear reasons, escaped. America is mentioned in a rather telling incident. Zahrah became pregnant one year when there was no harvest. America gave them wheat. When Davis tries to determine the approximate date, before or during World War II, Zahrah is puzzled. "The war of what?" The attempt to clarify details turns into a muddle (AE 207–18). The cities of Morocco have some associations for her, since her family has people in a number of them, Casablanca, Rabat, Tangier; but she has no interest in them beyond that. Meknes, where Zahrah lived for a time, and where her mother lived, is mentioned several times. The court is important, for the mother's custody fight and for the marriage contracts. Otherwise, there is no curiosity about the place.

As the other impinges on her life, Zahrah marks its presence. A *nasrani* appears to swindle her father, yet he allows the family to remain on the land. The Christians have brought tractors and machines and an economy based on money. The changes are sometimes good (more fabrics) and sometimes not so good (less food). Her mother marries a scoundrel ("pagan," *kafer*) and a city slicker (foreigner, *rumi*). Her first husband, actually her fiance, is "that man," or the "other man," assimilated almost to "the others" (*axrin*, AE 234). And "strange people" (*an-nas berranyin*, 336) from the outside or from her own village might attend a wedding and make it uncomfortable for the women, who would then have to separate themselves from the group and not stand with the men.

There is no question that Zahrah Muhammad is comfortable in her Islamic faith and in the customs of her people, even though they are changing. The cultural others are the *nasara*, and they appear frequently in Zahrah's story. Besides the Christian who let the family remain on the land, a foreigner and Christian helps Zahrah when her second daughter seems in danger of dying from the illness that claimed her firstborn. (Zahrah believed the children nursed when she was asleep and pregnant with another P 208.) The foreigner gives her "a paper" to present to the Christian doctor. The doctor gives the child "a really good shot" and tells her to return, which she does not do, but the child recovers (P 209).

A Christian figures in yet another important episode in Zahrah's life. For all the difficulties she mentions, Zahrah comes across as anything but the passive female of Orientalist fantasy. Although her vision is shaped by an extraordinarily confined life world, she is assertive from the start. She refused to tell her in-laws that she was pregnant, for example, and had her baby when the women in the family were away from the tent, even though the ability to have children was what settled her into the life of the community (and let her make the decision to stay with her husband). Susan Schaefer Davis was, as we have seen, much interested in the first marriage that had been forced on Zahrah. She discovered that a Christian played a large role in Zahrah's release from "that man." It is important that the first man did not take her honor—

and her sense of self-worth—from her. He was unable to take her virginity. *That* she was powerful enough to resist.

The incident epitomizes the different stands of this report on the rhetoric of the other in this most remarkable oral history: Zahrah's discursive style, her awareness of forces operating in her life, the relationship between male and female, and the cultural other:

> The man I married before that—I didn't stay with him. My mother gave me to that man when I was still small; my mother hadn't remarried yet. My father died, God bless his soul, and my mother gave me while I was still small. And that man would bring one big basket of grapes and he brings henna and he brings things . . . I take it and I dump it all out and I let the chicken eat that stuff; he ate it all up! And if he brought meat, I didn't want to eat it. When he had the wedding, I ran away and went to this woman's house and stayed with her; it was in the same village.
>
> They came and caught me; they brought me back. I ran away again, and they slapped me into irons, on my legs they put a chain—on my legs they put iron rings like those for animals. A girl friend helped me and we took them off one leg and I hung it around my neck and I had the iron ring in my hand and I ran away from the village until I got to the farm. It was the farm on which that Christian lived; the Christian who took my father's land. When that Christian saw that iron on my leg, he took it off. And he telephones Meknes and took me away from that man . . .that's that. From that time, I never went near that man; that was it. That man didn't take *anything* from me. (P 205)

Traditional Arab-Muslim storytelling freely recognizes that a divine will, even if inscrutable, guides reality, shapes it, and gives meaning to it. Magic and the demonic are frequent and largely unquestioned elements of such storytelling, as the heroic tale of Wudei'a makes clear. Such elements have not been reduced to anything like Western literary realism. As prompted by the fieldworker, though, Zahrah maintains her traditional beliefs in her life story and gives explanations that make sense in the West—that is, they do not require the Eastern belief system to understand Zahrah's predicament and her actions.

The cases presented in the next chapter are rather more difficult to follow. Much of the motivation comes from a figure known in Morocco as Aisha Qandisha. Even Moroccans who are familiar with stories of this powerful figure have trouble explaining her. She is the Evil Eye. She is a demoness in a world view that does not admit the possibility of a goddess. Why she would share a sacred space with two of the most powerful saints in Morocco is not easily explained. American anthropologist Vincent Crapanzano offers explanations from a Western perspective. Moroccan anthropologist Fatima Mernissi, bound with Crapanzano to a scientific explanation of reality, intervenes less than Crapanzano in the story. Elements of ancient Western Orientalism abound in the stories, but earlier explanations (primitive superstition) no longer have the force they once had.

Tikva Frymer-Kensky has argued that the marginalization of the powerful goddesses of antiquity had begun by the early second millennium B.C. (70–82). As the goddesses were increasingly marginalized, the roles of women in the public sphere diminished as well. It has been suggested—though proof is difficult to establish—that Aisha Qandisha is a remnant of those very ancient goddesses, perhaps a Canaanite goddess known to the Carthaginians. Should that prove to be the case, the circle would be complete: having begun with the goddesses and the women who were associated with them—Juno and Dido, Isis and Cleopatra, the stories close with a demoness who manages to disempower men and empower women.

Chapter Ten

In the Service of
Aisha Qandisha

Had German theologian Rudolf Otto not undertaken his journey to the East in 1910, when he visited North Africa, Egypt, and Palestine for the first time, there is a good chance this book would not be ending where it does: with the life stories of two nonliterate, unschooled Moroccans. The two, Tuhami and Habiba, have made no contribution to Arab-Islamic history. Their names are probably known to few Moroccans. Without Otto these chapters on Orientalist and Occidentalist images would not have moved from Dido and Cleopatra through a drunken Azuri to a demoness who shares a sanctuary with two important Sufi saints. They would not have come to combine the work of a disaffected American anthropologist and a Moroccan feminist whose paths cross only at the grotto of Aisha Qandisha near the old imperial city of Meknes.

Otto's journey is in its own way as important as Napoleon's 1798 invasion of Egypt. The author of conventional treatises in Christian theology, Otto is now known to the West almost entirely for the book that changed his views in light of the Sufis he encountered along the way.[1] He took the first step in the philosophical investigation of *mana*, much like the baraka discussed by the Americans in this volume. Otto's

The Idea of the Holy (1923) carries the illuminating subtitle, *Inquiry into the Non-Rational Factor in the Idea of the Divine and Its Relation to the Rational.* From antiquity rational control over the passions has been coded male and female. The East, once feminized, was thought to need control. At least the superior, rational civilized West could see the East as inferior. The more the East was imaged as primitive, savage, mystical, occult, and superstitious—in a word, irrational—the more Oriental men as well as women, rulers ("cruel tyrants") as well as subjects, groups as well as individuals (if individuals could be said to exist in the mass-minded East), could be seen as "fanatics." Medieval images of Islam carry some of that burden, issuing from the Crusades. But it was the modern world, particularly in the Enlightenment, when the rhetoric of reason brought all of those images into sharp focus. The twentieth century, with its interest in myth and the unconscious, with a loss of confidence in reason, is even allowing the East that *does* resemble ancient stereotypes to provide positive counterimages for a too-modernized West. Otto's journey to the East was just one instance of the turn. More than anyone else, Otto made the mystical and irrational East respectable again.

Aisha Qandisha is at once the heart of the irrational East and, like the ancient pre-Homeric and prebiblical goddesses she most resembles, the greatest challenge to phallocentric thinking.

Whether the demoness Aisha Qandisha actually derives from the Phoenician goddess Anath is not the issue. The presence of this projection of men's deepest fears in the midst of strict Muslim monotheism—recalling that the Holy Prophet of Islam himself banished the goddesses from the Kaaba—is important in two respects. First, she is the castrating female, the most dangerous of the femme fatales since the ancient world recognized her in their Great Goddess: Inanna, Ereshkigal, Ishtar, Astarte, Anath, Aphrodite, Artemis of Ephesus, the Syrian Goddess. Virgil saw her in the passionate Dido and in Cleopatra. She is the basis of the Orientalist fears of (and fascination with) the East itself.

Second, Aisha Qandisha is important here because the *interpretation* of such a figure (her meaning to the community) of irrationality is conditioned by certain movements in Western thought that have undermined early "modern" confidence in reason. Depth psychology, ritual, the history of religion, the analyses of phallocentrism and such would have been impossible when the Orient was merely exotic. Before Freud's *Moses and Monotheism,* Jung's *Man and His Symbols,* De Beauvoir's

The Second Sex, Neumann's *The Great Mother*, Eliade's *Shamanism*, Kramer's *The Sacred Marriage Rite*, Pagels's *The Gnostic Gospels*, Eisler's *The Chalice and the Blade*, Exum and Bos's *Reasoning with the Foxes: Female Wit in a World of Male Power*, Stivers's *Evil in Modern Myth and Ritual*, Frymer-Kensky's *In the Wake of the Goddesses* and Kristeva's "Stabat Mater"—to name just a few—this focus on Aisha Qandisha would have been empty, would have been able to see in her only the worst sort of "superstition."

Without Otto this chapter would be merely an embarrassment to Western thinkers and certainly to the Moroccans, since it deals with the voiceless and in some ways the lowest of Moroccan society. To the Muslim fundamentalist the material here may yet be irritating, since it involves the very un-Islamic folk beliefs the fundamentalists are striving to eradicate. Only in this historical time and in this cultural situation could a Moroccan intellectual turn to a Moroccan *shuwafa* to learn something about power.

VINCENT CRAPANZANO, *TUHAMI, PORTRAIT OF A MOROCCAN*

In a 1975 story that is really a collection of brief observations on Moroccan folk beliefs, "Things Gone and Things Still Here," Paul Bowles drew attention to the curious custom of burying pocket knives, all of them clasped shut on a scrap of paper. The knives are buried by women in order to make certain men impotent. Opening the knife can release the curse on the man. Particularly dangerous, then, are knives buried deep in the water at the bottom of cliffs. The likelihood that the knife will be found in such a place is remote. Even if the water dissolves the paper, the curse continues (408).

Reading the symbol of manhood that has persisted in the West since the Bronze Age[2] into a non-Western culture is certainly dangerous, but there is some evidence that the knife bears the same psychological heft for the Moroccan that it does in the West. (However, the gun—whether handgun, rifle, or machine gun—as we have seen, is a sign of the modern West, notwithstanding the symbolic associations it clearly has had for many years among tribal peoples, such as the Berber horsemen who fire simultaneously while riding at full gallop in the Moroccan *fantasias*.) Vincent Crapanzano's analysis of the dreams and fantasies of the Moroccan tile maker he calls "Tuhami" is much conditioned by Crapanzano's Freudian-psychoanalytic assumptions. To Crapanzano, the fiftyish Meknes bachelor is deeply troubled and sexually dysfunctional. Tuhami attributes his problems to the most powerful of the demons who control his life, the demoness Lalla Aisha Qandisha. He claims to be one of the men "married" to the demoness, who jealously restricts Tuhami's relationships with women.

Tuhami is a mine of Aisha Qandisha lore because he is not only a devotee but a man sought out for his knowledge of the supernatural. He tells Crapanzano at one point that Lalla Aisha can be controlled by the clever man. She appears as a beautiful woman, but she can be detected if the man looks at her feet. (Aisha has the feet of a camel or a goat.)

> There are men who are married to her. You see a beautiful woman. You talk to her about marriage without looking at her feet. If you are clever, the moment you see her, you thrust a steel knife into the ground. Then Lalla 'A'isha disappears. She then says, "Excuse me. Let me go." The man says, "I won't let you go until you promise to give me everything I want." He can ask her not to strike his children, not to take possession of them. He can ask for beautiful clothes. He can ask for a car. He can ask to enter a government minister's office without being seen. Then 'A'isha tells the man what she wants. (101)

Sometimes Aisha appears to help him. In a dream he reports to Crapanzano, Tuhami is fighting with people and always wins because Lalla Aisha is on his side. The "people" in the dreams, though, turn out to be demons, jnun, "some with horns and others without horns. There were some with slippers and others without slippers. There were some with hair and others without hair. All of the jnun were men. The women were on my side" (69). Women protect him, but he is unable, as a spouse of Aisha Qandisha, to do what is strongly enjoined in the Arab-Muslim tradition, to marry and produce offspring. Tuhami finally discloses to Crapanzano the seduction by the prototypical female, Aisha Qandisha. By that time Crapanzano had put together Tuhami's bitterness toward his father, who had abandoned him; his mother, who had danced with the Sufis; and the woman who had deeply influenced his youth, a French woman, Mme Jolan, who hired Tuhami to work for her. On the road home from Mme Jolan's, Tuhami meets a woman and invites her home. The woman wants to sleep with Tuhami. At first he hesitates, but then he makes love to her. She leaves him twice, first for a month, then for two years. At one point he is suspicious of her and demands to know who she is. "I'm a woman like all women," she answers (165).

Only after two years, Tuhami tells Crapanzano, did he notice that she kept her slippers on in the house and he looked at her feet. Her camel's feet revealed that he had been tricked. Aisha Qandisha quickly made her will known. "'If you want to marry,' she said, 'I'll choose the woman. She'll be my choice. It is I who command now. If you don't accept, you'll remain a bachelor for the rest of your life'" (166).

Crapanzano inquires about his feelings when Tuhami saw the woman's feet.

> My head changed. My head was swollen. My mind ['aqel] told me to put a knife in the woman. But I had no steel knife. If I had had a steel knife, I would have killed her. I would have plunged the knife in the earth, and then it would have been I who commanded. She would have had to agree with me always. She would remain there as though in a bottle. I could have done anything. I could have slapped her. I could have beat her. She would have had to run errands for me. Since then . . . (*Tuhami's excitement drained away. But the emotion that had been missing in his initial recitation was still there.*) Since then my affairs have not been very good. If she came now—now that I am well trained—I would win. (166)

This violent language is mirrored in the ordinary Moroccan metaphors Tuhami employs. When women are taken to his room for an assignation, the room becomes a "slaughterhouse," intercourse a "sacrifice" of the woman as "victim." In such an event the penis is a "knife" (108).

Crapanzano, an American anthropologist, listened long enough to Tuhami that he felt a deep kinship with the Moroccan. But he was the outsider, in Morocco to carry out his fieldwork, and the time came when he had to leave. The farewell comes at a good time, for Tuhami feels strong. He awakened to see Mme Jolan in his room—and recognized that it was really Aisha Qandisha. "Today I feel like a bird. Last night was a miracle" (172). In this optimistic mood, Crapanzano offers the informant/friend a most useful parting gift: "a large steel hunting knife" (172).

Having discovered the symbolic importance of the knife, Crapanzano adds that he hopes the knife will "give him strength and be the key to his liberation." The anthropologist passes quickly over Tuhami's response. What made Tuhami, otherwise such an eccentric, a useful person in his community was his ability to talk, to use the great lore he had accumulated to help others around him. (Tuhami was the object of a certain good-natured joking by the men, but was not shunned by them.) Given the knife, Tuhami "was at a loss for words and put the gift quickly away" (172).

The exchange of knives, one an actual knife, the other stories and language about knives, is not the only important feature of Crapanzano's study. Clifford Geertz, the most imposing of anthropologists engaged in symbolic or interpretive cultural anthropology, is more than a little skeptical of the "I-Witnessing" style of contemporary anthropology that calls into question the very assumptions of the professional study of the other. The "highly 'authored-saturated,' supersaturated even, anthropological texts in which the self the text creates and the self that creates the text are represented as being very near to identical" are disquieting because Geertz finds "little confidence here and a fair amount of outright malaise" (*Works and Lives* 97). But Crapanzano's almost tortured self-questioning and self-examining leads to a moment that lays claim to a more authentic and a deeper understanding of the other than is claimed even by his fellows in the interpretive school.[3]

After Sartre, Crapanzano calls the moment of understanding the "fatal instant" (129). Tuhami tells him a story and, suddenly, reveals "*the* event that was central to Tuhami, the subject of his persistent metaphorizations, the root of his emptiness, his impotence, his being as dead"; the story also became symbolic of Crapanzano's own "transformation." With his understanding of Tuhami Crapanzano overcame of his own "cultural bias" (130).

Tuhami's "fatal instant" is a memory prompted when Crapanzano has him talk about the grotto of Aisha Qandisha near Meknes, part of the complex that includes the sanctuaries of the important saints, Sidi 'Ali and Sidi Ahmed, the founders of the Hamadsha brotherhood of Sufis. Lalla Aisha's grotto is below a giant fig tree. Tuhami goes there to dream, especially when he is sick, and he receives advice there. In this case, he goes with a friend, Mohammed. What begins as a straightforward description of the grotto turns out, in Crapanzano's analysis, to be much more.

> Tuhami went on to describe an argument with Mohammed over the exact location of 'A'isha's grotto. The grotto itself is divided into two chambers.

I then asked Tuhami if he was afraid of heights, dogs, closed-in spaces, or wide-open spaces. He said he was not. I then asked him if he was afraid of water.

—No. I've been afraid of rivers ever since I was little. I was a shepherd. My friend fell into the river and was carried away. Since then I've always been afraid of rivers. I was with my friend. He said that, if he ever saw Lalla 'A'isha, he would hit her or throw a rock at her. There was thunder, and suddenly the river swelled and carried him away. We were trying to climb on a mule at the moment, and the mule fell into the river. My friend let go, but I held onto the mule. I didn't know how to swim. I couldn't help him. My parents always said that they would throw me into the river if I ever cried. I was afraid of nothing else.

—What did you do?

—I took the sheep back to the village, all alone, and told my father what had happened. My father gave a *sadaqa* [a feast], with scribes who read from the Koran. I came to Meknes right after that.

—How did you feel when all this happened?

—My head was dry, like a rock. I was mute for two days. Ever since then I have found myself in misery on the road. Some say I'll never marry. All my friends are married except for me.

—Did you ever think that you could have saved him?

—We were both carried away. Neither of us knew how to swim. I could have helped him if the mule had been closer. I couldn't let go. If I had touched my friend, he would have pulled me off and down. If I had been carried away by the river, then all the flock would have been lost. (128–29)

Crapanzano took the story as "real, just as Freud took as real the seductions of his female patients by their fathers" (129). The story certainly has some familiar features—that is, expected given Crapanzano's lengthy transcripts of his interviews with Tuhami and given already extensive analyses at that point. The ambivalence toward friends, the sense of loss, and of course the centrality of the demoness Aisha had been familiar themes. The association of Aisha with water is worth noting, since it is one of the most frequent images attached to her and her grotto. The incessant walking Tuhami does is glimpsed in the way he leaves the village immediately after the feast and the "misery on the road" so evident in Tuhami's many journeys, especially to Aisha's grotto. If this story is one of a boy entering puberty, the sexual symbolism is clear enough. The friend's boast that he would hit or "throw a rock" at

Lalla Aisha, were she to appear, is immediately—"fatally"—followed by thunder and the flooding waters. (Afterwards Tuhami's head was "dry, like a rock.") The fear of being "carried away" begins the long recital of the man's loss of control.

Some features are surprising. Tuhami does not otherwise talk of his being a shepherd, and the care of the sheep is a metaphor that hardly requires Christianity to account for it in this cultural milieu. What is most surprising is the reaction of the villagers, especially of his father, upon the boy's return with the sheep. The father is said to have given a feast, significant enough, since Tuhami would be the center of attention, but the *sadaqa* also brings in scribes who read the Qur'an. (Tuhami, at about fifty, was still nonliterate.) The image of a boy, surrounded by the generosity of the father and in the company of the prestigious males of the community, is the closest we read of Tuhami being successful and comfortable with other men.

FATIMA MERNISSI, "HABIBA THE PSYCHIC"

If Aisha Qandisha is at the center of a very divided Tuhami, who needs her and seeks her out, she is the figure who brings wholeness and success to a very different Moroccan individual. Fatima Mernissi calls her "Habiba the psychic" (*Doing Daily Battle* 126–44). Mernissi, born and raised in Fez, trained as a sociologist in Morocco, France, and the United States. In the interviews of Moroccan women she published in *Doing Daily Battle* (1988; originally written in French in 1984), she was not troubled with the problem of the cultural outsider, like Crapanzano, who made an "empathic leap" toward an understanding of the Moroccan. Nor is she troubled, like the American by a certain American self-image, an ideology he describes as "self-reflective, involuted, inevitably circular, ironic, and not without a certain iconoclasm" (x). Mernissi, rather, is concerned that the Western scientific sociology she has learned can present barriers to a cultural understanding.

As was briefly noted in chapter 8, Mernissi was cited in an important article by Nancy Chodorow on women in cross-cultural perspective, "Family Structure and Feminine Personality." Chodorow argued that daughters in a Western middle-class families have problems with self-esteem that grow out of a too-close identification with mothers seen as "devalued" and "passive," whose own self-esteem is low.

Chodorow's single counter-example comes from Mernissi, who was already arguing that Arab-Muslim society was in many ways healthier than that of the West (64–66). Mernissi, in *Beyond the Veil*, claims that, in spite of the difficulties of women in the homosocial Eastern societies, those women are more likely than Western women to change their status in a revolutionary way (176–77).

> Even in patrilineal, patrilocal societies in which women's status is very low, women do not necessarily translate this cultural devaluation into low self-esteem, nor do girls have to develop difficult boundary problems with their mother. In the Moslem Moroccan family, for example, a large amount of sex segregation and sex antagonism gives women a separate (domestic) sphere in which they have a real productive role and control, and also a life situation in which any young mother is in the company of other women. Women do not need to invest all their psychic energy in their children, and their self-esteem is not dependent on their relationship to their children. In this and other patrilineal, patrilocal societies, what resentment women do have at their oppressive situation is more often expressed toward their sons, whereas daughters are seen as allies against oppression. (65)

The sexual antagonisms and sex segregation Mernissi details in *Beyond the Veil*, where she comments that the socioeconomic needs of the poorer Moroccans are beginning to show the emergence of a new relationship between men and women, the marital couple. In such a relationship women demand and receive fidelity and love. In some cases women refuse their parents' choice of marital partner. *Doing Daily Battle* provides a remarkable example in Habiba (8).

Mernissi has clearly had to fight to be heard in Morocco. Born into a middle-class family in Fez, her interests in reading were encouraged by an adoring father, who nonetheless bought her a djellaba and tried to force the veil upon her at the age of eight. Once educated, she has had to struggle against the "terrorist tactics that men, who monopolise the symbolic values of our society, use to stop [her] from expressing [her]self" (14). One of the terrorist arguments is that she is breaking with tradition, importing ideas about men and women from the West. A second is that her work is not "representative" in a way demanded by the science in which she has been trained. She has thus had to justify her use of the interview rather than a quantitative approach to sociology based on the questionnaire. In order to "break" the "ancestral silence" of women (1), she turned to a qualitative approach that she considers scientific, though not quantitative, "since one of the criteria of 'scientificalness' is capturing reality" (16).

To interview the women she violated certain basic rules of her training. She did not attempt to maintain "objectivity," since she maintains a special affective relationship to the Moroccan woman: "I identify with her" (18). She also gave up the technique of control, letting the women talk, even at the risk of wasting time and "looking ridiculous." "I have learned that an illiterate woman has her own narrative pace," and she wanted the women to speak in a way proper to their lives.

Eight interviews are included in *Doing Daily Battle*. The women are very different, from two who were young girls in a harem, to a nonliterate woman who has gone from being a peasant to being a "citizen of the world," and who worked in Germany, Spain, France, and Iraq. Most of the transcriptions required a certain amount of editing, since they were fragmentary and repetitive. For our purpose it is worth noting the relationship between narration and causality in a situation where there is no cultural tradition of self-disclosure as there has been in the West since Augustine.

> Another aspect of the interviews that I wanted to preserve is the relaxed, often confusing, way in which many of the interviewees relate time sequences and events. An illiterate woman who has virtually no control over her life, subject to the whims and will of others, has a much more fluid sense of time than an educated Western reader, who is used to analyzing time in an attempt to control it. One of the charms of the interviews is to confront such readers with these inconsistencies, which give a taste of how confusing a lifetime of powerlessness is. (20)

Clearly the best of the interviews is Habiba's. It prompted Mernissi to explore further the religious life of women, much the way Elizabeth Fernea had, but with an idea to understanding the therapeutic value of women's visits to sanctuaries and addresses to saints and jnun.[4] It was also the only interview that did not require editing. The interview contains all the dark mystery that intrigued Paul Bowles—and the Western Orientalist tradition generally—but is a world away from the Orientalist stereotypes. Habiba suffered from such a complex of socioeconomic and psychological problems that it would have been remarkable had she simply survived. Quite unlike the confusion and loss detailed in many of the other interviews, Habiba's life story is one that leads from disorientation to success. It is as close to the American dream of rags to, if not riches, comfort and status as one is likely to hear from a nonliterate Moroccan woman.

Habiba's story is organized simply, in chronological fashion from birth to 1977, when Habiba was about fifty. (The organization was imposed by Mernissi, who prompted Habiba to begin in that way.) There is a brief account at the end of Habiba's life as an increasingly successful *shuwafa*, a quasi-mystical female seer. Habiba tells of the spirits who visit her, including a "black man," the "Master of the *ladun*," a chunk of lead used in seances, who tells her to increase the fees she charges her customers. She has even built a shrine to Lalla Aisha Qandisha in her home.

Most remarkable is the confident, powerful voice of the woman who had such a problem-filled life until she found her vocation. In the interview she speaks frankly about her problems, but there is no trepidation—certainly no fear that she might be found out by men in the family. In fact, the interview took place with the whole family present: her second husband, her son, and two of her son's teenage friends.

For the most part the story, is Habiba's quest, begun when she was almost fifty. From the time she was young she suffered from seizures, which her mastery of the supernatural enabled her finally to control. The Western reader is likely to be shocked at the experiences in her early life. A sister, for example, was married at seven, though the marriage was not to be consummated until she was ten. (However, the husband did not, keep his promise.) Habiba herself was married at fourteen, but the marriage did not last. She had two children, but her husband mistreated her, and she left. As might be expected, Habiba still sees herself as a dutiful servant of Allah: "Allah did not let that marriage succeed" (128). She remained a divorcee for four years, after which "Allah arranged for me to meet this man," her second husband, a legless cripple. Habiba expresses no resentment at all at the second husband, who it turns out is particularly helpful—the example mentioned above of the new "marital couple" in Morocco. But Allah had not given her children by her second husband.

Because of her seizures, Habiba was thought to be crazy. Her first husband was ashamed of her and locked her up. The second, though, throws himself on top of her to protect her during a seizure, has her car-

ried to a safe place, cleans her up, and comforts her—even though she
was unable to give him sons.

Her call to become a *shuwafa* came in the form of visions, the most
persistent of which was Aisha Qandisha as a woman with the feet of a
sheep (130). She had a compulsion, not unusual in shamanic literature,
to eat raw meat. (Several times in the interview she relates tales of the
trance dancers in procession falling upon animals and eating them raw,
much in the manner of the women in Euripides' *The Bacchae*.) Her
prophetic powers were revealed on one such occasion when she ate her
fill, the spirits took possession of her, and she predicted the destiny of
her brother-in-law. She was not a psychic, though, before making a pilgrimage to the sanctuary of Sidi Ali.

The tale of this journey is most interesting because it is the
account of a Moroccan woman who sets out, alone, without knowing
where she should go and with no certainty that she will find the solution to her problems. "Was I perhaps going to be doomed to wander
from one saint to another? I would follow the decisions of Allah, whatever they might be. So I left" (132). She takes this bus and that. (Once
she is cheated by the driver who demands that the passengers pay double for the trip.) She wanders from person to person. This one tells her
not to wear black. That one invites her home on a very dark night. "I
said to myself, 'He is going to lead me somewhere and cut my throat.'
But, on the other hand, I was deeply convinced that I was following a
preordained path and that no harm could come to me" (133). The man
turns out to be a *sherif*, descended from the Prophet, who has no ill
designs upon her, but whose wife bitterly rails against him bringing
Habiba home.

Anonymous people appear to guide her on her pilgrimage, and
she finally makes it to the grotto of Lalla Aisha and the sanctuaries of
the Hamadsha saints, Sidi Ali ibn Hamdush and Sidi Ahmad Dughughi
(135). She joins the dance, once she discovers the rhythm peculiar to
herself, and dances until she goes into a trance. Men and women
together fall into trance. As in the scene witnessed by Edith Wharton,
who had viewed this same *zawiya*, "Some crack their heads with a
hatchet, others break earthen pots on their skulls. You see blood spurt-
ing and running down their faces. . . . Others devour mud, and still others swallow spiny cactus—all according to their own rhythms" (136).

Her vocation is confirmed in Lalla Aisha's shrine when she is told to
take bread when it is offered her. A "holy fool" (*buhali*) is moved to choose

her rather than the woman next to her, who is also searching: "I was with another woman to whom he said: 'It is not you that I want to speak to.' And, pointing to me, he said, 'It is to her that I have things to reveal'" (137). As the man leads her about, she gains confidence in herself.

Once back in Rabat, Habiba performs a "blood sacrifice" and is initiated by the *muqaddam*.

As a *shuwafa*, Habiba represents all that the skeptical West used to find backward and ignorant in un-Enlightened and uncivilized societies. Paul Bowles's narrator in the "The Eye " takes that position. It is not surprising, then, that the Western-educated Moroccan often expresses contempt for such traditional "superstitious" practice or that Islamic reformers would like to purge the society of what they consider un-Islamic practices. The West has, to an extent, come around from an attitude similar to that of Edith Wharton. As Elizabeth Fernea discovered, the religious life of Moroccan women is deeply rooted and very important for the life of the community. The psychic, like the sanctuaries to which the women resort, provides much-needed therapy, particularly in a sexually segregated community. Even if the traditional mystical claims of the Sufi brotherhoods—that trance dancing, for example, may lead to union with God—are no longer part of the practice (and, as we have seen, are sometimes denied as incompatible with Islamic monotheism), the practice appears to be not only widespread but useful. (Certainly Bowles's response is more complex than his narrator in "The Eye," for example.)

The problems in Habiba's life did not suddenly disappear once she became a *shuwafa*. In one sense, dealing with the sheer complexity of a spirit world raises additional difficulties. One measure of this, which is evident in ancient spirit lore as well as in contemporary figures like Tuhami, is the need to master the many names of the spirits and the multiple ways in which they are served. Each person, as Habiba says, must dance for his or her own master spirit, or *malik*, and the manifestations of this particularly are quite varied. "Each one of us, the possessed, dances their own dance: one handles fire, another pours water on the head to feel well, and still another must tear their clothes to find relief. Another, seeing a person they don't like, runs after him and hits him. That's the way it is in our world" (138). Such diversity would seem to allow each adept to cultivate a small part of a vast lore, but the evidence suggests rather that the initiate takes on the burden of almost the whole lore.

As a *shuwafa* Habiba is still plagued with her own problems. She tells Mernissi that she suffered from a foot wound for over a year, and that she has already lost a finger "in this business." The spirits make demands on her and threaten injury if she does not follow them. One threatened to burn her, and Mernissi was shown the still-visible evidence that Habiba's legs were burned in three places. To the Muslim's submission to the will of Allah is added further burdens from the spirit world for the believer. One might expect a life of passivity and uncontrol, a life crushed by "fate."

What is remarkable, then, is the great confidence that is evident, not simply in Habiba's control over the lore of the *shuwafa* but in the manner of her speaking about her life. Habiba is no cringing, terrified, or—more important—confused and irrational informant. Where Mernissi had to edit the interviews of women who were clearly not used to organizing their life stories, she had no need to edit Habiba's narratives. The best illustration of Habiba's confident voice is an example she gives that is, actually, an admission of failure.

The story is prompted, as most are, by Mernissi's questions. Habiba uses the term *hajba*, which involves a tray loaded with watermelon seeds, figs, and the like, isolated in a room where people are not supposed to enter. The *hajba* reminds Habiba of a niece who, at seventeen, was "touched" one night and brought involuntarily into a life dominated by the spirits. One aspect of the *hajba* involves placing a scarf on the horns of a cow as it is being sacrificed. This is the way Habiba tells the story.

> When she saw the cow with the scarves, she let out a crazy laugh. Then "they" struck her. Now she dances more than I do. I stopped after a certain time; she, the poor thing, continues. I have really tried to intervene with "them" to free her, but in vain. One time a participant at the Hamdushi ceremony that I had organised got up to dance. In twelve years Lalla Aisha had never made an appearance to her. That night Lalla Aisha came. I begged her to free my niece: "Why has my niece been chosen? She is only a child. It is right for you to choose me, who is beginning to age, who has lived a long time and has accepted life's hard knocks. But she is a girl; she still knows nothing of life." She replied to me: "We want our family to grow. You don't want to be our only kin, do you? That's why we are going to keep her among us." So my niece was obliged to pay all the expenses necessary for the ceremonies; she had to finance all the activities for healing, and today she is still possessed. She "sees" everything. She sees everything just as I see everything. (139)

There is nothing in this narrative to suggest that the "wa-wa" rhetorical style sometimes thought to characterize Arab-Muslim thought. According to Robert B. Kaplan, "certain languages, like English, seem to favor the use of subordination over coordination, a form favored more in certain other languages, like Arabic."[5] The preference for, say, more or less explicit use of logical connectors is sometimes taken as a measure of a society's ability to think logically (a point Kaplan does not make, by the way). A style that uses careful subordination is, of course, prestigious in the West, where it is preferred in scholarly, scientific, and, of course, philosophical writings. Less prestigious is taking a series of parallel points in a kind of zigzag fashion instead of attacking a topic head-on in a linear demonstration. There is no good reason to think one kind of organization is inherently superior to another, as there is no reason why one dialect of a language should be perceived as superior to another.

There is also no reason to expect that a traditional rhetorical style—particularly a style of *writing*—is a simple map of logical thinking. As Habiba's story shows, Habiba has good control of the opening and the closing, a seventeen year old who is "touched" one night and comes to "see" everything. The center of the story is clearly marked: Habiba's plea to Lalla Aisha to free the niece. The only feature that needs to be explained is that Lalla Aisha Qandisha is thought to appear to the trance dancers, especially among the Hamdushi Sufis, since the great demoness is so often associated with the two saints of the Hamadsha. Habiba used the appearance of Lalla Aisha as an opportunity to plead her case.

The *shuwafa* does not present herself as cringing in fear even before the most powerful of the demons. She gets her chance, speaks to Lalla Aisha, presents her reasons, and listens to the demoness's response. Since Lalla Aisha explains the "touching" of unbelievers in terms that make the most sense to Habiba (and her culture)—family and kinship—the argument stands. (With more prompting by Mernissi, we discover that the niece has not been able to turn her psychic ability to good use. She "sees" everything, and often sees Lalla Aisha, but she laughs in the demoness's face. "She has never recovered, the poor thing.") Throughout the story, Habiba carefully subordinates detail and argument to organize a narrative that says a great deal about the psychic's freedom and power—even when the result (not being able to persuade Lalla Aisha) is not what she had wants.

One reason for Habiba's confidence is her knowledge of her audience. The story of the niece leads, by way of her insistence that trance dancing is not just "acting," to a story that contrasts with it. Another young woman scoffs at the spirit world, "laughing at us," and suddenly falls down across from Habiba's house, spraining her ankle and twisting her toes. When Habiba demands the woman's obedience, she pulls the toes and heals the young woman. "Afterwards she became a *habitue;* she came and brought everything that was necessary. She is a wonderful young woman" (140). In the latter part of the interview, Habiba appears to be subtly inviting Mernissi to believe in the spirits and become a client—and Mernissi explains, in a note, that she did in fact participate in a seance and was diagnosed by the psychic, the first step in what can be an expensive procedure for the client. (Mernissi does not admit to any follow-up therapy.)

Habiba explains how the spirits demanded she increase her fees, though she was reluctant to do so. She also describes the process by which she turned part of her house into a shrine for Lalla Aisha. She tells Mernissi about the charms she "writes" for her clients, a process of automatic writing and engaging the services of a local *fqih* (since Habiba herself is still not literate). From what Mernissi presents, Habiba is clearly a success as a psychic. She has prospered, and her way of speaking reflects that prosperity.

It is not surprising, then, that Habiba is one of the few women Mernissi interviewed who speaks well not only of herself, but also of what "Morocco" means, that is, the image the country has for others. She tells Mernissi, "I was embarrassed to announce this rise in my fee to my visitors. I could already hear what they would say: 'You know our Morocco'" (141). The other women in the interviews, of whatever status in society, were so deeply involved in their own local, usually family, matters that they rarely speak of the outside. Habiba, in contrast, has regular dealings with outsiders, male and female, has traveled, at least in Morocco, and has begun to show something of the mobility Daniel Lerner finds so important in the West.

Conclusion

PATHS AND MIRRORS

For Virgil the Oriental woman is already visible when Dido, obsessed with love for Aeneas, cannot concentrate on her queenly duty. She ignores the building of Carthage and allows the great construction projects to stand idle. Cleopatra, seen as Virgil's contemporary version of Dido, is condemned already when her unruly governance is seen in the gods she worships and embodies: the gods in monstrous animal forms.[1] There was another Cleopatra in the ancient world, though. The alchemical *Book of Commarius: Philosopher and High Priest Who Was Teaching Cleopatra the Divine the Sacred Art of the Philosopher's Stone*[2] addresses her as the "wise woman," who reveals the mysteries of "blessed waters" to a group of philosophers. The waters of creation, of birth and resurrection are explained by the "divine" Cleopatra in this mystical and magical text.

There would seem to be an insuperable gulf between the esoteric Cleopatra, goddess/queen from antiquity, and the nonliterate Habiba Fatima Mernissi has enabled us to hear. Habiba's discourse is full of the very mysteries dismissed by Western modernism: demons and other supernatural agents intervening in the lives of humans, ecstatic dreams, and miraculous cures. The Western-educated reader dismisses such superstition by denying its reality, explaining it instead by reducing the mysteries to the psychological and sociological explanations productive of "realism." It would not be difficult to explain Habiba's odyssey and her commerce with the spirit world by, say, the twenty-two "major" and twenty-six "minor" ego defenses outlined in a standard textbook on "mental mechanisms."[3] 'Compensation,' 'fantasy,' 'identification,' 'introjection and projection,' 'repression,' and 'symbolization' are some of the many concepts used regularly to understand the ancient mysteries.

To her credit, Fatima Mernissi, whose Western education provided her with the tools to analyze Habiba in this way, resists the impulse and lets Habiba speak. Habiba, poor, uneducated, only dimly aware of the world Fatima Mernissi represents, is the figure furthest removed from complex social construction we are calling the "West;" the most easily "explained" in psychological and social terms; the most difficult to hear. Yet given the chance to speak, Habiba comes across to even the most skeptical reader as a strong, intelligent, resourceful individual. Quite unlike that ancient Oriental woman, Dido in *The Aeneid*, who built a city but could not live without her Aeneas, Habiba does not destroy herself in a room she arranged as an emblem of her weakness; rather, she builds a sanctuary for Aisha Qandisha inside her own home.

In lieu of a theory, the cultural studies[4] tied together in this volume precipitate tropes. It may be useful to keep Habiba in mind, for her story vividly illustrates the two main tropes: the path, or pilgrimage, and the mirror. Habiba reconstructs for Mernissi a journey that, initially, had no clear purpose but led, through Aisha Qandisha, to the home she now inhabits with her husband and children, a home that is also her place of business. In the story she describes, largely through the dream vision of the divine/demonic other, Aisha Qandisha, the strengthening of the self. One might describe Habiba's middle-age rebirth as a kind of belated "mirror stage," to use Jacques Lacan's famous phrase, about which more will be said later.

THE JOURNEY TO THE OTHER

The path and the mirror organize many of the images in the title of this book. "East/West" and "America/Morocco" describe two complex symbolic formations. The slashes in each case indicate necessary implicature. These tropes seem so natural that it is important to note that they are not inevitable, nor are they necessary. Classicist Walter Burkert has shown, for example, that there was much contact between Greece and the Semitic East long *before* the Greeks came to see themselves as a special people culturally other than the peoples to their east. Burkert concentrates on the archaic period (ca. 750–650 B.C.E.), when with Assyrian conquests and Phoenician commerce the Greeks borrowed freely skills, technology, stories, poetry, magic, and medicine from the East[5] without coming to the recognition Aeschylus has in *The Persians* (472 B.C.E.), that is, the recognition of two incompatible social systems, a special identity that designates the other as the Oriental.

Once established that the East is not simply "something else," but a culture that can only be known in the *difference* between the newly recognized "us" and "them" (neither known previously), contacts then become a series of approximations, a sort of calculus of the other. Possibly the mirror has to precede the path, but once the recognition is made, the journey to the other becomes the first trope in the approach to the other.

The path suggests movement, dynamism, process. Is the destination ever reached? The mirror suggests the instant of recognition, insight, definition. Is the image always a distortion? Orientational metaphors[6] such as paths and mirrors suggest that one can be more or less proximate to an object, "close" or "distant," perhaps "intimate" as the object is seen to have an inside that can be reached—a "deep" understanding of another. While it is difficult to tell if the other is reached or seen, it is important that one making the journey or looking into the mirror locate the self historically and culturally.

In the case of these studies, I am—as a "cultural self"—closest to the most ancient, chronologically remote *Aeneid*, that male "master" narrative that has been reinforced through centuries of reading, that is, of use. To write this book has meant to situate myself, not using my "native" speech (what linguists call "Appalachian" speech, a dialect of American English), but rather Standard English, with many Americanisms. In much the same way, Moroccan writers use Modern Standard Arabic, with some hints of the vernacular ("Moroccan Arabic"). In both situations, the more we use Standard English and Modern Standard Arabic, the more we approach one another through what Jaroslav Stetkevych called a "cultural linguistic community."[7] The West had achieved such a cultural linguistic community "through centuries of internal cultural commerce" (118), and Stetkevych thinks that Arabic too has "entered into cultural linguistic affinity with the broad supragenealogical family of modern Western languages" (119) through a new lexicon and cross-borrowings. This book could not be written in

Appalachian speech. Habiba the psychic, for her part, could not write it in Moroccan Arabic. Were she to learn to read Modern Standard Arabic, however, she would not find this book difficult to translate.

The reader will have noticed a direction to the previous chapters, from what is most familiar, most comfortable *to the author* and, by extension to the interpretive community who can read it without translating from Standard American English, to what is most remote. Habiba might make a very different collection of stories. Certainly the direction would be different, if she began with the stories familiar to nonliterate Moroccan women who constitute her cultural linguistic community.

From the odd maneuverings of Commodore Trunnion, tacking across open fields to find the place where he will be married, through Habiba's journey to the grotto of Aisha Qandisha, the studies have from time to time suggested that cultural studies is rather like a pilgrimage whose destination is a place to be "approached." Edith Wharton makes her way through a mysterious landscape in the company of French soldiers. Paul Bowles's fictional protagonists in *The Spider's House* and *Let It Come Down* restlessly wander through North Africa when it is clear they can no longer settle in the West. Jane Bowles's semi-fictional Jeannie in "Everything Is Nice" is as rootless as her Moroccan companions are rooted, and she remains condemned to the labyrinth that fascinates her so much. Paul Rabinow tries to explicate the journey that constitutes anthroplogical fieldwork. Elizabeth Warnock Fernea frames her life in a Marrakech neighborhood with journies that are explicitly pilgrimages.

For their part, the Moroccans tell of similar restless wanderings. Leila Abouzeid, in "The Stranger," tells of a Muslim who converted to Christianity and became a priest, who later tries to go back home, to the old city of Fez, and is rebuffed at the door. Storytellers recount the quest of a heroine, Subei'a, who rescues her brothers. Mohammed Chukri organizes a story of a poor prostitute who travels from one part of the city to another, from one culture to the next. And even the unusual "we" narrator in Mohammed Barrada's "Life by Installments" narrates the fragmented life as a series of movements through the town.

The path is a familiar narrative strategy for nonfiction as well as fiction, particularly as a way of figuring a "self" that is moving—changing, defining, and redefining itself in interaction with others, even questioning the foundation of the self. From at least as deep in antiquity as the Mesopotamian *Gilgamesh* the path takes the explicit form of the

quest. The very notion of the 'journey as an odyssey' derives from the
name of the Greek hero whose story is still one of the most prestigious
in Western literature. (Aeneas, his resolve sorely tested by the side trip
to Carthage, may not appear to change through his experiences; nevertheless, he follows his destiny in a clearly mapped out journey.) The
path also provides a frame for seeking out, listening to, and discussing
the other as if that process were a movement to and from a destination.
The two senses of path are joined from the start of this book, as a persistent theme in the narratives and as an approach to—a series of steps
toward—the understanding of the cultural other.

THE QUEST AND THE POSTMODERN CONDITION

Ihab Hassan thinks that "the historic experience of America proved singularly congenial to the spirit of quest. That experience conjoined
energy and wonder, violence and sacrament, alienation and reverence,
in unique measure" (123). Autobiography, adventure, and quest "coalesce," Hassan suggests, "in a contemporary genre that conveys both the
perplexities of the postmodern condition and the ancient, visionary
powers of myth" (125). The contemporary resurgence of travel literature is one bit of evidence. That interest has retrieved older travel
pieces, such as Edith Wharton's *In Morocco*. Moreover, for Hassan, it is
the adventure of the West that gains access and promotes, willed or not,
change.

> The adventurer/seeker, then, is a Westerner. Quest is the motive of his
> history and its deep wound. But it is the wound from which history flows,
> sometimes suppurates. His flight from modernity can not avail. His
> yearnings for desolations of sand or snow, in Arabia or Antarctica, lead
> him to an abandoned Coke can which rules that desolation more than
> Stevens's jar ever did the hills of Tennessee. Yet his will, malaise, disequi-
> librium, some radical asymmetry in his being, has made our world know-
> able, made the world we know. (129)

Hassan might have included (but did not) contemporary American cultural anthropologists in his study of the quest. Of course,
anthropology is a professional investigation of the cultural other. Since
the mid-1960s, though, the field has become as questioning of its
assumptions as has literary study. In an important 1975 statement, "On
the Nature of Anthropological Understanding," Clifford Geertz

described the Western concept of 'personhood' as a kind of atomistic individual. The West sees the person as "a bounded, unique, more or less integrated motivational and cognitive universe, a dynamic center of awareness, emotion, judgment, and action organized into a distinctive whole and set contrastively both against other such wholes and against its social and natural background" (59). In contrast, he found the Moroccan concept of the person radically different, as socially embedded, contextualized selves. Morocco itself he thought "extrovert, fluid, activist, masculine, informal to a fault, a Wild West sort of place without the barrooms and the cattle drives" (64). Yet he did not think of the Moroccan as a free-swinging individual. Rather, he used the Arabic term, *nisba* ("relationship," "affinity," "connection," "kinship," and so on), to show that Moroccans are defined by contexts, such as regions, tribes, religious sects. The contexts themselves are relative and provide something like a "vacant sketch" to be filled in by interactions with others: "relativism squared," as Geertz put it.

Daisy Hilse Dwyer, another of the American anthropologists who have had access to Morocco, based her study of "male and female in Morocco" on Moroccan folktales she recorded there. She followed Geertz in seeing a different concept of personhood operating in Morocco and evident in the folktales—a self socially embedded, relational, interactional: "personality or character varies rather flexibly from relationship to relationship" (182). This is in contrast to the Western stress on the person as "isolate." Ettibari Bouasla has recently called this great range of arrangements by which the Moroccan negotiates his life "homo contextus" (223–44).

Prominent in the "Heideggerian destruction of metaphysics, of onto-theology," as Jacques Derrida acknowledges in the essay that has profoundly influenced contemporary literary theory, "Structure, Sign, and Play in the Discourse of the Human Sciences" (395), is the calling into question of the Western definition of self as an isolate. So relentlessly has the traditional concept of the self been subverted that it is worth noticing how important it had become to the West's self-representation in literature. The *confidence*, if not the philosophical underpinnings of the self thus understood for many centuries in the West, as the West was becoming increasingly self-conscious, derives from Christianity.

Ernst Cassirer traced the philosophical impasse in the Renaissance that led to the emphasis on such an atomistic concept of the self (125–30). The *mythological language* Plato used of the soul in the *Timaeus* and the myth of Er at the end of *The Republic*—the soul captive in the prison-house of the body—may not have been adequate to Plato's concept of the 'soul,' but it certainly influenced the Platonic tradition and, hence, most thinkers into the Renaissance. The logical development of Platonic thought on the soul, articulated in Arabic philosophy by Averroes, ran into conflict with Christian faith, and the conflict took Western thought into the celebration of the individual. Cassirer explains that, "by letting the soul re-enter completely into the sphere of objective-metaphysical forces, Averroism abandons not only the principle of subjectivity but the principle of individuality as well. . . . The true subject of thought is not the individual, the 'self.' Rather, it is a non-personal, substantial being common to all thinking beings; one whose connection with the individual Ego is external and accidental" (127). By the thirteenth century, Thomas Aquinas was arguing for a thinking self. "The *Christian* faith, at least, cannot abandon the principle of 'subjectivism,' the principle of the independence and *personal value* of the individual soul, without, at the same time, being unfaithful to its own basic religious assumptions" (127). The well-known assertion of individuality one sees in Petrarch flows from this conflict, according to Cassirer. In Petrarch, "The lyrical genius of individuality takes fire at the religious genius of individuality" (129). The later shift from a religious-cosmological notion of the self to the psychological individual is already prepared for in Petrarch, even in his mysticism.

With the twentieth century, and the self as experienced in psychoanalysis (among other factors), the challenge to the self as isolate is almost as frequently met as is the now traditionally Western view, found in different ways in Descartes and, later, among the early phenomenologists. It is not surprising that Jacques Lacan's famous short essay "The Mirror Stage as Formative of the Function of the I" (1949) charges that the psychoanalytic experience "leads us to oppose any philosophy directly issuing from the *Cogito*" (1). Lacan's essay is useful for our purpose not only because it has received so much attention and has been so influential on literary theory in recent years, but also because "The Mirror Stage" provides the best account of the second figure that directs these studies. In Lacan the "specular I" is deflected into the "social I" in the mirror stage (5).

A MIRROR STAGE OF CULTURE(S)

Jane Gallop takes an interesting tack in her discussion of Lacan's mirror stage. The essay itself seems to have taken some form in 1936, but it was not until the end of World War II that the essay itself appeared. Gallop sees the gap in time as much like the mirror stage itself, like Catherine Clement, who is quoted as saying that the mirror stage is "the germ containing everything" for Lacan. "When the war comes along, Lacan's thought is formed" (77). Suddenly, the essay is there. In a similar fashion, one finds hints of an attitude in the West before World War II that the West is not the simple protector of civilization that had been assumed—what we have called the "classical phase." The war itself seems almost immediately and necessarily to question that assumption. The war acts like a mirror stage for the West, suddenly revealing a specular image of itself in relation to a newly seen East and introducing a new discourse about the East. The skeptical phase, which might be said to focus on the imaginary, appears fully formed in the works of Paul and, to a lesser extent, Jane Bowles. The symbolic, again in Lacanian terms, is made possible then but appears later, in what we have called the "postmodern phase."

Gallop devotes a full chapter to the question, "Where to Begin?" a study of Lacan—or of the mirror stage itself. From the age of six months, the human infant acts in a way that goes beyond the actions of other mammals, who at that stage are far more developed and powerful than the human.

> Unable as yet to walk, or even to stand up, and held tightly as he is by some support, human or artificial . . . he nevertheless overcomes, in a flutter of jubilant activity, the obstructions of his support and, fixing his attitude in a slightly leaning-forward position, in order to hold it in his gaze, brings back an instantaneous aspect of the image. (*Écrits* 2)

The event will be repeated until about eighteen months, when the infant is transformed into the "symbolic" order, alienated, as Lacan might have it, *into* language, when in an instant the human will see itself as "always mediated through a totalizing image that has come from outside" (Gallop 79). According to Gallop, in the instant of rebirth (from "nature" into "culture"), the human retroactively imagines itself as a body torn into pieces. Gallop is reminded of a story that transformed the West, the biblical story of Adam and Eve, which Gallop sees as a tragic rebirth of the human into history. In the mirror stage, paradise is always lost the moment it is glimpsed.

An even better Eastern story, earlier than the biblical story of paradise, might be the humanization of the wild creature Enkidu, in the Mesopotamian story of *Gilgamesh*. The people of the city-state Uruk cry out to the gods because their king, Gilgamesh, is oppressing them. The gods, father-god Anu and mother-goddess Aruru, respond by forming Gilgamesh's savage double, Enkidu, and tossing him into the wilderness.

> When Aruru heard this, she formed an image of Anu in her heart.
>   Aruru washed her hands, pinched off clay and threw it
>   into the wilderness:
> In the wilderness she made Enkidu the fighter; she gave birth
> in darkness and silence to one like the war god Ninurta.
> His whole body was covered thickly with hair,
>   his head covered with hair like a woman's;
> the locks of his hair grew abundantly, like those of the
>   grain god Nisaba.
> He knew neither people nor homeland;
>   he was clothed in the clothing of Sumuqan the cattle god.
> He fed with the gazelles on grass;
> with the wild animals he drank at waterholes;
> with hurrying animals his heart grew light in the waters.
>   (Gardner and Maier 68)

When Enkidu frees the animals from the traps humans have laid for them and terrifies a hunter, Gilgamesh sends a temple woman in the service of the goddess of love and war, Ishtar, to trap Enkidu. She reveals her nakedness to Enkidu at the watering hole, seducing him into sex for "six days and seven nights." When he is finally sated, Enkidu yearns for the beasts of the wilderness but cannot return to them. The animals flee from him and his legs are too weak to follow them.

At this point, the temple priestess/prostitute turns motherly, teaching Enkidu how to eat and drink as humans do and instructing him in the ways of shepherding. Through the woman Enkidu is brought into

the city, where he fights Gilgamesh and immediately becomes friends
with his urban rival.

Between the week of sex and the training in human culture, what
Lacan calls the "mirror stage" is captured in a very few, succinct lines of
Akkadian poetry.

> Enkidu grew weak; he could not gallop as before.
> Yet he had knowledge, wider mind.

> Turned around, Enkidu knelt at the knees of the prostitute.
> He looked up at her face,
> and as the woman spoke, his ears heard.

> The woman said to him, to Enkidu:

> "You have become wise, like a god, Enkidu.
> Why did you range the wilderness with animals?
> Come, let me lead you to the heart of Uruk of the Sheepfold,
> to the stainless house, holy place of Anu and Ishtar,
> where Gilgamesh lives, completely powerful,
> and like a wild bull stands supreme, mounted above his people."

> She speaks to him, and they look at one another.
> With his heart's knowledge, he longs for a deeply loving friend.
> (Gardner and Maier 78)

Weak and alienated, longing for the double that will complete him,
Enkidu, having heard his first words, speaks to the woman. The first
words of the wild man repeat, with little change, the woman's words.
But the speech (and the episode) ends with something completely new,
the I. To call attention to the new mode, the Akkadian text employs the
emphatic pronoun, anāku: "I, I will call to him; I'll shout with great
force."[8]

The mirror stage organizes and orients the self, Gallop points out,
but the "self" is totalized and unified. Before then there is no self. Gallop
emphasizes what Lacan observed, the infant "jubilantly" assuming the
posture when the image appears in the mirror, anticipating what the
infant will become. The mirror stage already anticipates and retroactively images what was.

Literary critics have tended to emphasize the anxiety accompanying the mirror stage, the paradise lost the moment it is recognized (and

misconstrued, Lacan's *méconnaissance*).[9] Our recovery of Orientalist distortions in the Western images of the East, a postwar phenomenon, for the most part, has been filled with similar anxiety. When even the most dedicated scholars, those most careful to take a scientific detachment to the study of the Middle East, Islam, and the ancient Near East are—as Edward Said charges—guilty of a scopophilic gaze, then it becomes increasingly easy for us to see how the East was misconstrued at the instant it appeared in the mirror. In that image was the projection of Western desire and the motive to dominate the East—at the moment a Western cultural self appeared, even in its infancy. The East of Aeschylus's *The Persians* is already the not-Greek of the hardy warriors such as Aeschylus who found themselves in resisting the much greater but corrupt enemy.

At the instant the West discovered itself as the not-East, the discourse about an East became possible. Said, Martin Bernal, and now many others have been decoding that discourse, particularly in recent days. When one sees, after all, the crude Orientalism of American Barbaresques, of *In Morocco*, or of *The Desert Song* (in spite of its initial romantic identification with the suffering Riffs), its justification can only be the simple presumption that the primitive may hold much fascination for "us," but "we" are, like it or not, civilized in a way that the East can never be. The audience, of course, is always assumed to be the West.

Anxiety in the discovery of our Orientalist distortions is almost enough to end with the distorted image, to announce that the East is *entirely* the fabrication of the West, and to rest the case in the Lacanian imaginary realm. That the cultural studies in this book attempt to go beyond that point admits that an East has been formed through the discourse of Orientalism. Mohammed Barrada, Leila Abouzeid, and Jilali El Koudia *do* write short stories that borrow from Western traditions. Tuhami, Zahrah Mohammed, and Habiba the psychic do speak, though we must depend on a series of Western and Westernized mediations to hear them.

Listening to the Eastern speakers is a process much like that in which the Orient becomes Westernized. We no longer think, like Daniel Lerner, that Westernization is necessarily a good thing, but it is difficult to deny that the process has taken place. Leila Abouzeid's Moroccan Muslim-turned-priest in "The Stranger" literally cannot go home again, but it would be futile to argue that he has not gone somewhere. The trap for literary studies is to rest confident once a meaning of the story is discovered, even if it is not *the* meaning. I will suggest in the remaining pages that contemporary literary theory provides us with ways of dealing with the "meaning" of a text (even in the denial of meaning). What I finally want to suggest is that *use* is more important than *meaning*. My hope is that the strategy called earlier a "Rogerian" strategy opens discourse that enables East and West to speak freely with one another.

To make sense of that strategy I will turn to an earlier phase of Western modernism, one that is so taken for granted in Western narratives, that we often fail to recognize its formative influences on colonial and postcolonial literature. That phase is modern literary "realism." Even though it has been declared dead many times, and contemporary literary theory has pointed up the hidden agendas of realism, its influence persists, and postcolonial literature is all but unreadable without seeing it.

One way of looking at realism historically is in opposition to the onto-theological definition of reality that dominated official discourse in the West from its Greco-Roman and Judeo-Christian beginnings. Jacques Derrida provides a convenient list of "names related to fundamentals, to principles, or to the center" that "have always designated an invariable presence—*eidos, archē, telos, energeia, ousia* (essence, existence, substance, subject), *alētheia*, transcendentality, consciousness, God, man, and so forth" (394).

To put it rather crudely, to a writer in a tradition that defined human in terms of *telos*, or end—the purpose of being human—as something not immediately evident in the actual thinking, walking, playing, and speaking of humans interacting with other humans, a kind of storytelling that brackets, if it does not outright deny, the supernatural and world-historical purposes of humanity, the agencies of "fate" and/or the will of God, the celestial and demonic influences, and God's immanence in the world, is as liberating as it came to be thought "natural." We reduce this for convenience to the formula that human behavior is explicable in psychological and sociological terms. Considering "conversion," "absolution," "atonement," and "penance" as "ego defenses" is one example. Dialectical materialism is another.

One feature of early realism that is getting increased attention as the psychdynamics of orality and literacy has come to be debated[10] has been noticed by Ruth El Saffar.

ABORDERING NEW QUESTIONS

In "The Making of the Novel and the Evolution of Consciousness," El Saffar argues that literacy led to a shift in consciousness that became evident in the West at the very moment when the novel emerged.

> No longer one with earth, the mother, the mother tongue, the collective (un)consciousness, the new genre separates and problematizes teller, audience, literary convention, the "hero," the word itself. With separation come doubt, conflict, desire. The hero becomes thief or madman; the teller, a liar. The close look we are about to take at the early novel shows clearly the pain, conflict, and guilt that surrounded the rejection of the oral culture, and, more basically, the rejection of the realm of the mother that was our collective Western European experience in the 1600s. (232-33)

It is well to remember that with the domestication of the novel in the West—the realistic novel having become the signature of the modern West—it has never fully escaped the trauma of separation from the oral. In Morocco, where oral storytellers are still seen in the marketplaces and the cafes as well as in the home, where the Qur'an is still learned by rote, and where centuries-old poetry is kept alive in oral recitation among nonliterate and literate alike, the pain of separation is still very near.

An insight into that anxiety can be glimpsed in Western resistance to realistic fiction.[11] When the new literature was considered feminine (and therefore close to "nature") rather than masculine (in the domain of reason, law, and transcendent order that is captured in Lacan's name-of-the-father), the new was considered dangerous and subversive. The case of a mid-nineteenth-century divine is instructive.

In a letter written in April 1853, by F. W. Robertson, M.A., incumbent of Trinity Chapel, Brighton, 1847–1853, Robertson, a great lover of books and art, nonetheless took the modern novel to task. He had just finished several of Sir Walter Scott's romances and had been stirred by those stories of the "outer life" of men, stories that elicited "a vigorous, healthy tone of feeling" (Brooke 301). Contrast that healthy-mindedness with the "sense of exhaustion and a weakness which comes from feeling stirred up to end in nothing" he found in the French and English novels of his day. Robertson offered an explanation (beyond the "horrible materialism" of the times and the French, writing "with the full licence of a nation to whom Duty has no meaning") that blamed women. The contrast between Sir Walter Scott and the modern novel is accounted for

> by the fact that in his stirring times life was an outer thing, and men were not forced into those mysterious problems which are pressing for solution now; and partly by another fact, that women have since then taken the lead in the world of literature, and imparted to fiction a new character. They are trying to *aborder* questions which men had looked upon as settled; and this might have been expected, from their being less able to understand or recognise the authority of statute law and conventional moralities than men, and much less disposed to acknowledge their eternal obligation, and also much more quick to feel the stirring laws of nature—mysterious, dim, but yet, in their way, even more sacred. The result of this has been, that questions which men would rather have left unexamined, or else approached with coarseness, are now the staple subjects of our modern fiction. (Brooke 301)

Jane Eyre (1847) is the first example Robertson provides. Margaret Waller has more recently reminded us that

> by the 1830s, the novel was no longer a woman's genre. The advent of realism, for example, made the novel a serious form with pretensions to social commentary, and the serialization of novels in newspapers made writing novels a commercial enterprise and a workaday job for men. (23)

The Rev. F. W. Robertson may simply not have gotten the message two decades later, in England, but his judgments must have been shared by many, at least among those who were not professional writers and critics. What I have called in an earlier chapter the "domestication" of the novel is really a complex process that invented realism—the circumstances of actual life rather than the epic events of an "outer life," and the exploration of psychological and sociological principles of ordinary persons rather than the metaphysical and religious explanations that had provided the ground of earlier "serious" narrative.

To the extent that realistic fiction depicted the inner life, it could be decried as "women's" literature—but only to a point. It gained pres-

tige[12] in the West when it became a vehicle for social analysis and was
defeminized in the process. By the 1870s, when Arabic narratives had
changed under the influence of Western novels and short stories
(Haywood 126–32), the association felt between women and the novel
was apparently not a factor. John A. Haywood pointed out that some
thirteen novelists were active in Arabic between 1865 and 1914, most
of them Christians who had traveled in the West and who knew
Western languages (132). By World War I the prestige of realistic fiction was secure. For the Western forms to be accepted in Arabic, there
needed to be changes in language and style, mainly simplification of the
elaborate rhetorical devices that had been traditional in Arabic literature and oral performance, and a focus on "incident, atmosphere and
characterization" (126).

In the West, realism challenged what is now considered the "phallic" self and the "master" narratives such as *The Aeneid* and the many
heroic romances that, if anything, simplified the transcendent values of
the tradition. Realism rejected the immanence of the divine in history,
rejected miracles, spirits, and the supernatural. By late in the nineteenth
century, intellectuals such as William Dean Howells were finding it
necessary to challenge the archaic assumptions of popular romances. In
The Rise of Silas Lapham (1885), Howells's protagonist paint manufacturer
Silas Lapham, listens intently to a dinner table conversation in which
the last vestiges of the medieval romance tradition, with its "old-fash-
ioned hero and heroine" and its self-sacrifices, are ridiculed. Another
minister, Mr. Sewell, reverses F. W. Robertson's view. Mr. Sewell opines,
"The novelists might be the greatest possible help to us if they painted
life as it is, and human feelings in their true proportion and relation, but
for the most part they have been and are altogether noxious" (183).

Mr. Sewell, and perhaps Howells with him, now wanted "life as it
is, and human feelings in their true proportion and relation" represented
in fiction. Ironically, though, the minister argues on psychological
grounds that a vestige of heroic literature, still prevalent in popular literature, is unhealthy. Self-sacrifice, so much a part of the romantic novels of the day, is, for Sewell, "nothing but psychical suicide, and is as
wholly immoral as the spectacle of a man falling upon his sword." (Note
that the tradition of "noble suicide" is now seen as masculine, though
immoral, rather than a tragic mistake made by the Didos and the
Cleopatras of antiquity.)

Realism is as much a part of modernity as the automobile and the industrial refiguring of society needed to produce it. Daniel Lerner's *The Passing of Traditional Society, Modernization in the Middle East* (1958) has been justly criticized because it assumed that the values he associated with modernization were, without question, positive and that modernization was necessary for the third world. When a traditional society is transformed by the modernized in its midst, the consumer, the reader, the moviegoer, the citizen of a democracy that is expected to have opinions about things beyond the local and the family, the new person gains "psychic mobility" or "empathy." It is quite in keeping, of course, with the most fundamental shift in Western thought, from a religious (or, better, onto-theological) explanation of human events to a social-psychological explanation, that Lerner would see the psychological mechanisms of projection and introjection behind this "psychic mobility."[13] If we are less confident in modernization/Americanization for the world than we were in the 1950s, there is still much to be said for Lerner's analysis.

What needs to be considered along with the psychic mobility of the modern is the separation—alienation, disorientation, transgression, sometimes madness—that Ruth El Saffar argues affects the one who leaves home. Her chief examples, sixteenth- and seventeenth-century texts, *Lazarillo des Tormes* and *Don Quixote*, "reflect upon the pain experienced by the young boy and the guilt of the old man whose life experience was to grow up separated from the world of mother, home, and the oral culture" (245).

The trauma of separation problematizes, as El Saffar put it, "teller, audience, literary convention, the 'hero,' the word itself." The five Moroccan writers we saw in chapter 7 reflect that in various ways. 'Abd Al-Majīd Ben Jallūn's "The Stranger" is, of the five, closest to the romantic novels of self-sacrifice Mr. Sewell decried. It is also closest to traditional Arabic storytelling in its rhetorical flourishes and its evocation of heroic resistance, a staple of even pre-Islamic poetry. Yet "A Stranger" has clearly drawn upon Western models of literary realism in the telling of, especially, the circumstances of ordinary village life.

Western realism in its early, now "classical," form is still useful in the Arab world. Leila Abouzeid is an ardent nationalist who belongs to the generation who saw independence for Morocco at a young age, a woman who takes Arabization seriously and chooses to write in Arabic rather than in the language of the colonizer, French. "Year of the Elephant" is a novel that angrily protests the treatment of those Moroccans who worked hard for independence, only to find themselves hurt by it—women, whose rights are trampled. To tell the story she borrows from Western realism far more obviously than Ben Jallūn.

The Moroccan who buys a Fiat assembled in Casablanca need not think of the car as a Western invention. Attempting to build and manufacture a Moroccan automobile, though, requires more than imitation, it requires a rethinking of the automobile. Much the same is the ubiquitous modern Western fiction, with its assumption of a certain kind of psychological and socio-historical "reality." That reality rules out the supernatural, miracles, and metaphysical purpose for ordinary human reality. Texts that resemble Western literature, such as those of Abouzeid and the others in chapter 7, are more accessible to the Western reader than the texts that follow them—Moroccan folktales and life stories elicited by Western (and Westernized) anthropologists.

One reason for having concentrated so much on Jane and Paul Bowles in this book is that their fiction, which looks so much like realistic fiction, calls into question the comfortable assumptions about modern realism. Without recourse to the literary theorizing that is so important today, Jane and Paul Bowles subverted the domesticated novel. Paul Bowles, especially, is not just an observer of an exotic culture from the safety of his own sense of cultural personhood. By calling into question the concept of 'self' that had developed in the West—the concept that allowed for the domestication of the novel after the pain of separation El Saffar discusses—Paul Bowles's works explore alternative concepts. Those derived from an understanding or misunderstanding of Moroccans are particularly significant. If he does not actually accept the notion of a negotiated, contextualized self, Paul Bowles certainly plays with the teller/audience/literary convention/"hero"/word in a way that depends upon his empathic leap to an understanding of the cultural other.

It is, no accident that Jane and Paul Bowles, considered very eccentric in the 1940s and 1950s, are now being revived in the postmodern era. The other Moroccans considered in chapter 7, Mohammed Barrada, Mohammed Chukri, and Jilali El Koudia, in very different ways are part of the postmodern turn. While they may not refer to political events explicitly in the fiction discussed here, they are in their own ways responding to what Abdullah Al-Udhari has called the "Huzairan" (June) Experience, the effects of the stunning Israeli victory over the Arab armies in 1967. Disillusionment and disorientation—much as one finds in Western postmodern literature that began to appear massively by 1968—are the marks of Al-Adab al-Huzairani (the June literature) as well as what Al-Udhari calls the "flood of political frustration and anger" throughout the Arab world (23). In the apparent collapse of Western models of socialism, nationalism, and modernism generally, Arab writers turned to new literary models—especially Western postmodernism. They could do this at the same time they called upon traditional Arab storytelling as a model for postmodern fiction (Maier, "Postmodern Syrian Fictionalist" 73–75).

The readings presented here, especially in chapters 7 through 11, are not exhaustive, and they are less sure as subject and form become less accessible to me. However, the reader who knows the subtleties of the Arabic originals will see the misrecognition in this author's readings. The Arab-Muslim reader will be the first to see that these are "outsider" readings and may well object that they are simply wrong. At this point then, this chapter will take another Trunnion tack.

READERS MAKING MEANING AND USING TEXTS

In his 1982 article, "How Readers Make Meaning," critic Robert Crosman reported on a literary-critical experiment he had used in his college class. He wondered what constraints and impulses, what conventions and strategies determine meaning. He had his students write in their journals as they read certain literary works and after they had completed the works. Crosman then examined their responses. At the same time, Crosman himself was writing his "feelings, thoughts, and fantasies" about the works. His experiment is instructive for our purpose here.

He asked students to read a well-known short story by William Faulkner, "A Rose for Emily." The much-anthologized and much-discussed story follows Miss Emily through her adult life. A Southern woman bound by the strict conventions of a patriarchal and patrician society, Miss Emily was carefully guarded by her father, who dismissed the one promising (if socially inappropriate) suitor, and Emily remained unmarried even after her father's death. As the story is conventionally read, Miss Emily provides a shock for the nosy community—and for the reader. At her death, the community discovers that Emily had apparently poisoned the suitor and kept the decaying corpse in the bed where she had slept for many years. Most read the story as an example of American Southern Gothic literature, in the tradition of Edgar Allan Poe.

Crosman was startled to discover that at least one of his students had missed the horror at the end of the story. Stacy, Crosman's student, was so taken by the portrait of Miss Emily depicted by a very ambivalent narrator—the ambivalence, too, was missed by Stacy—that she could only read "A Rose for Emily" through a reverie about Stacy's grandmother, who bore some resemblance to the aging Emily. Crosman did not entirely reject Stacy's reading of the story, though it differed markedly from his own (and that of others in the class). Rather, he found himself discovering features of "A Rose for Emily" that Stacy's odd reading had brought to light. Crosman then advances a theory of reading that is both solitary and communal (365), psychological and sociological. Faced with the codes by which readers negotiate oppositions in the text, Crosman abandons a single "right" reading in favor of readings that construct a critical community.

> The reader's freedom is limited both by the elements in the story, and by the codes he has learned from his culture, but since he is free to select which codes he applies, which elements he constitutes, he is in practice no more constrained by them than putting on a pair of sneakers compells me to run. What he *is* forced to do is to apply *some* strategy, look at *some* elements of the text (since that, after all, is what reading is) and in so doing he joins a community of which all other readers, and the author himself, are members—he enters, that is, a dialogue, all of whose voices speak within him, all of whose roles he plays. (365)

For reading across cultures, it is important to specify an element of what has been called a "Rogerian" strategy, after psychologist Carl Rogers, the noted mediator. Just as in a conflict between, say, labor leaders and management, progress in negotiation demands not just hostile threats and claims that one side is alone in the right, the reading of a text involves negotiating positions. One of Rogers's most important suggestions is that one side needs to state the opponent's position—in a way that is satisfactory to the opponent. That is not an easy task, but it is necessary to make explicit certain assumptions about the cultural other in order to give the other a chance to speak (even in rebuttal).

Crosman's own reading of "A Rose for Emily" reveals a different dimension of the problem of reading. He admits that he came to Faulkner's story, not innocently (as, in many ways, Stacy had), but as one he had known by reputation for many years. His expectations included the ways others had read the story, of course. He read the story, fully expecting an ironic and horrifying denouement. In these readings of a variety of *Desert Songs*, this author approached most of them much like Stacy approached "A Rose for Emily." A specialist in any of the areas—Arabists, film critics, anthropologists, classicists—would not blunder into these texts in the same way. Only by deconstructing Orientalism, with the help of Edward Said and the others who have followed his lead, could certain assumptions and expectations have been made explicit. Only if the readings themselves are of use to the other will a critical community form to continue the readings.

TRUNNION TACKINGS STILL

In one sense it would have been preferable to end this book with the previous chapter, with the voices of Moroccan women. The *process* or path this book traverses was largely complete at that point. Readers have been invited to play through a series of texts, from the highest of high culture in the West (*The Aeneid*) through literary fictions and travel literature to popular stories such as *The Desert Song* in order to draw attention to the Civilizing Mission, and challenges to it. In those texts the West speaks for an East that is assumed to be barbaric—and seductive. At worst, the Orient of the Orientalist was too obviously a project of the West's desire to dominate an inferior other. At best, the Orient presented a distorting mirror that revealed problems in the West.

However, much of *Desert Songs* attempts, to move beyond this deconstructive practice. Paul Bowles and Jane Bowles—and the Moroccans they described and let speak—are hardly innocent witnesses, but their fascination with the East is a quantum leap beyond the stereotypes that fill not only James Bond and Indiana Jones stories set in exotic locations, but quite serious fiction as well. Even such a brilliant fictionalist as Lawrence Durrell rarely escapes the tradition of odaliques and cruel despots. Few other writers of fiction have bothered to steep themselves, as Paul Bowles and Jane Bowles did, in the ordinary language and activities of the Arab-Muslim peoples they describe. Elizabeth Fernea,too, turned away, while in Marrakech, from the French-inspired New City to a neighborhood almost without a Western presence, but she did not do it to "go native." The Moroccan women she encountered were not invited—let alone required—to change their ways in light of Enlightenment, modernist thinking. Nor were they expected to act like noble savages.

One might still argue that the texts presented in chapters 7 through 10 do not escape the hegemonic discourse of the West, either. However rich the oral and literary storytelling traditions in Arabic might be, the stories by Ben Jallūn, Barrada, Chukri, Abouzeid, and El Koudia derive, in form, from expectations developed in modern and postmodern Western fiction. Moroccan tales such as "The Night before Thinking" and "Wudei'a, Who Sent Away Subei'a" are mediated by their English-speaking translators. Certainly the life stories elicited by anthropologists Susan Schaefer Davis and Vincent Crapanzano are not (and do not really pretend to be) "author-evacuated texts," to use Clifford Geertz's telling phrase (*Works and Lives* 141). Where earlier anthropologists may have been comfortable describing primitive peoples without the self-conscious attention to their own rhetoric, anthropologists can hardly avoid their role in shaping the narratives they elicit. Prompts by Susan Schaefer Davis in the form of questions put to Zahrah Mohammed may be edited out when once the interview is published, but the questions surely express the anthropologist's—and her culture's—interests.

Fatima Mernissi is the major Moroccan anthropologist represented in *Desert Songs*. In her interview with Habiba the psychic, Mernissi speaks as one native speaker to another, one woman to another, a member of one history and culture to another. Mernissi does not disguise her questions, and she does not disguise her feminist desire to empower Moroccan women, which motivates her interviews in *Doing Daily Battle*. (Mernissi also makes her discomfort explicit, when Habiba turns the tables and tries to become a therapist to the anthropologist.) Surely in this text we can sense the unmediated presence of the other. But the feminist and scientific enterprises of a Mernissi are grounded in Western thought—the very Enlightenment thinking that is now subject to frequent attack. Mernissi can no more erase the education that she received than she can erase her Fassi upbringing.

Commodore Trunnion's zigging and zagging did carry him to his destination. Of the two figures informing this search for and description of the cultural other, one would like to know if the search has been successful—or if it has misrecognized the signs—and if the Western images of Morocco and the Moroccan images of the West are accurate or simply distorted in a different way. It would be infelicitous, without hearing the response of the other, to answer.

Notes

INTRODUCTION

1. Lakoff and Johnson, chs. 24–30, on the myths of objectivism and subjectivism in Western philosophy; also Lakoff and Turner 195–213.

2. For a sketch of Moroccan history as it relates to the United States, see Damis 30.

3. For a sketch of the early history of Morocco, see Laroui, "Colonizer Follows Colonizer," *The History of the Maghrib* 27–89, and Terrasse 39–48.

4. The word appears a number of times in the Qur'an, usually in hendiadys with East. Allah is addressed as "Lord of the East and West" (e.g., 26:28), that is, of the whole world, a formula that is at least as old as the Sumerians. In the Qur'anic references there is no preference given to East or West. See Kassis 471–72.

5. Bouasla 223–44.

CHAPTER 1. ASIA UNDER THE SIGN OF WOMAN

An earlier version of this chapter appeared in *Works and Days* 18 (1991): 89–116.

1. De Beauvoir 70. Moi considers de Beauvoir "surely the greatest feminist theorist of our time" in spite of de Beauvoir's rather late acknowledgment of her feminist, as opposed to her socialist, viewpoint. See Moi's essay, "From Simone de Beavoir to Jacques Lacan" 91–101.

2. Kramer and Maier 202–4.

3. Eisler 64–66.

4. Knight 118. Quinn prefers "pitifully," which can yet be related to the Greek tradition of tragedy, with its "pity and fear" the proper response of the audience. Quinn considers "The Contribution of Tragedy" 323–49.

5. The Latin text follows Hirtzel, with the punctuation suggested in Fairclough 1:442.

6. Bono 83. For the Eastern influences on Virgil, Bono follows Johnson 135–54. The transformations of the Antony and Cleopatra story form the basis for Bono's main thesis—the self-conscious "transvaluation" of values found in Virgil (1–2). In a review of Bono's book, Newman argues that Virgil's Dido may be less mired in the Homeric past than she is "too 'modern,' too Alexandrian," that is, Apollonian, 166.

7. Michael Grant 294. For Clausen, Dido is Epicurean while Aeneas is Stoic (49).

8. Knight, *Aeneid* 358. Thornton argues that, in the Augustan revival of religion, *The Aeneid* is a "cosmic poem" and the story of Aeneas the working out of god's purpose in history. Jupiter is the hero of the story; Aeneas but Jupiter's agent, even in the episode in which the forces of the Cruel Goddess are operating in Aeneas to kill Turnus (148). However, Spence finds a more subversive subtext in Virgil, one skeptical of the very rhetoric that has guided interpreters of *The Aeneid* through the centuries; instead Spence sees in Virgil "a rethinking of the assumptions of the rhetorical tradition" (21) and with it sympathy for Juno, Dido, Cleopatra, and Turnus.

9. Putnam, who carefully examines the poetic devices that unify the text, notes the many references in Book XII that associate Turnus with Dido. His reading of the end of the work goes beyond, say, Clausen, who finds Aeneas's killing of Turnus "disturbing to the reader," since there is "no sense of a high moral purpose attained . . . only the grim reality" (100). For Putnam, Aeneas's loss of control means that Aeneas has lost, ironically to Turnus; in the "madness" of Aeneas Juno appears to win, subverting the cosmic order (193, 200–201). Turnus would now be considered a throwback to a primitive heroic way of fighting quite out of step with "modern," "rational" warfare in which the survivability of weapons systems is of greater importance than "collat-

eral damage" done to humans. For an account of the new way of speaking and thinking about warfare in light of nuclear weaponry, see Cohn, "Sex and Death in the Rational World of Defense Intellectuals," 687–718.

10. Knight, *Aeneid* 110–111. The Latin reads: *Talibus orabat, talisque miserrima fletus/fertque refertque soror. sed nullis ille movetur/fletibus, aut voces ullas tractabilis audit;/fata obstant, placidasque viri deus obstruit auris./ac velut annoso validam cum robore quercum/Alpini Boreae nunc hinc nunc flatibus illinc/eruere inter se certant; it stridor, et altae/consternunt terram concusso stipite frondes;/ipsa haeret scopulis et, quantum vertice ad auras/aetherias, tantum radice in Tartara tendit:/haud secus adsiduis hinc atque hinc vocibus heros/tunditur, et magno persentit pectore curas;/mens immota manet, lacrimae volvuntur inanes.* (IV.437–49)

11. Robert M. Grant 29–42. Among the figures he notices are the Baal of Sarepta, Asclepius, the Great Mother of the Gods, Isis, Sarapis, Dionysus, and Mithras. Of course, Judaism and, not long after Virgil, Christianity became in some ways the most important of the Eastern religions to move westward to Rome. Even the Olympian figures are tied to the East, most conspicuously in the cases of Diana (the mother goddess of Ephesus) and Venus (in a line from Sumerian Inanna and Akkadian Ishtar). Cleopatra's attempt to manipulate the symbols of earlier Egyptian religion, to have herself seen as Isis, is discussed in Hughes-Hallett, esp. 45–62. Augustus tried to portray a very different image of Cleopatra. Hughes-Hallett notes that Virgil's contemporaries were surprised to discover that his epic concentrated not on Augustus and Cleopatra but on Aeneas and Dido. Hughes-Hallett follows the many different images of Cleopatra through the ages.

12. See Warwick 81, for Asia and the great number of references in *The Aeneid* to things East, see for example, Tyre and Tyrian, 896–97; Phrygia, 655; and Phoenicians, 654.

13. Bono sees Carthage as displaying "a gorgeous, potentially decadent and effeminating luxury that the duty-pressed Trojans must repudiate" (28). She includes the description of the banquet (I.631–34), Aeneas's dress and Numanus's later taunts (IV.259–67, IX.614–16). The Eastern skill in the arts is opposed to "the uniquely Roman virtues of peace, law, and justice"—Rome's relationship to Hellenistic culture, including Virgil's relationship as a Latin writer to "the highly sophisticated, precious, Hellenistic literature" he, like the Trojans in Italy, grafts onto "a more vigorous primitive stock."

14. The mantle of "Tyrian purple" Aeneas wears is a gift from Dido, not so much "foreign dress," as Clausen considers it (45), as it is a mark of Aeneas carrying Dido—and the East, to which he already belongs—with him. It is that which must be stripped from him (and may not be done with complete success, if the grim ending of the work is an indication). On the speech which is taken away from the Trojans—their language and the culture it bears—there may be symbolic expression in the great distinction Highet examined in *The Speeches in Vergil's "Aeneid"* between the way the heroic male speaks (or does not speak, since Aeneas "lacks the sort of characterization that can only be conveyed through speech. . . . Aeneas makes one big speech, and one only: his narrative of the destruction of Troy and wanderings" (40), and the "most eloquent" character by far, Dido, whose speech shows a wide variety of emotions and is more suited to tragic discourse than heroic (45). Hughes-Hallett notes that the Romans considered the Egyptians effeminate for, among other reasons, being ruled by a woman, for Cleopatra's supposed sexual promiscuity (associated with animality), for luxury, and for wearing "foreign" (non-Roman) clothes (48–56).

15. To the extent that Virgil symbolically links Juno and Allecto to the demonic order—to civil and foreign war, to the soul as passion, and to death and destruction of nature, as Pöschl suggested (18)—Juno lines up with Dido, Turnus and Antony as figures conquered by the demonic and thus not as positive as may at first appear. Pöschl took Juno to be "the divine symbol of the demonic forces of violence and destruction" and saw in the victory of Jupiter order subduing the demonic. More recently Thornton has emphasized that Juno's anger is "evil and the instigator of strife" (155). Against her will Juno fulfills the divinely ordained founding of Rome. Even Highet thinks that the poet "always paints Juno in the darkest colors" (265).

16. According to Robert Grant, the Great Mother of the Gods, who entered Rome from Asia Minor, was at first resisted but then accepted. Augustus restored a temple to the goddess; but the orgiastic rites were forbidden to Roman citizens. Only much later, with Julian, was the Mother taken as the source of "intellectual and creative gods" (33).

17. Knight, *Aeneid* 103–104; *Virgil* 408–10. For Jerome's comment on Iarbus, see Hughes-Hallett 381.

18. Dionysus, another figure from Asia Minor, best known to the literary tradition from Euripides' *The Bacchae*, was not accepted in Rome, according to Robert Grant, "before the end of the Roman republic." The "secret and dangerous" rites, practiced by slaves and women, were not authorized by the state. Later it became acceptable when the cult was held under greater social control (40).

19. Pöschl, who gave particular attention to the Allecto scenes (28–33), emphasized her hellish nature, giving symbolic expression to Virgil's concept of war "as a creation of Hell, a godless crime and sinful mania" (30). The more Virgil's story is seen as a power struggle between forces of good and evil, light and dark, heaven and hell, as Hardie thinks it is (268), the more important becomes the bargain between Jupiter and Juno and Jupiter's handling of her threat to cosmic order. If the victory of order requires the subduing of the demonic—and Juno is "the divine symbol of the demonic forces of nature and destruction," as Pöschl believed (18), the forces line up as he claimed they did: on the one side Jupiter, Aeneas, and Augustus; opposing these on the cosmic and historical planes, Juno, Dido, Turnus, and Antony (18)—the latter two males who had been overcome by passion. Thornton saw in the reconciliation of Jupiter and Juno the decision to send the cruel goddess against Turnus, a judgment executed by Aeneas in killing Turnus" (148).

20. The classic study of the high and low styles in antiquity and the constraints upon representation is Erich Auerbach, *Mimesis: The Representation of Reality in Western Literature*, esp. 20–42.

21. Knight, "The Holy City of the East" 292–93.

22. "Confessions" I:692. On Book IV, the shortest book but Virgil's "masterpiece," much appreciated in antiquity, see Quinn 135–49.

23. Highet treats the speeches of Dido exhaustively, with the many resonances from earlier literature, especially Euripides' Medea, the Medea of the *Argonautica*, and the Ariadne episode in Catullus (218–20).

24. Clausen 47. The tradition of heroic poetry constrained the expression of the hero's passions, but Virgil's hero is less apt than Homer's to speak at all, as Highet noted (22). Aeneas is "aloof," "alone," and has "no one with whom he talks freely," according to Highet (41), who interprets this as Virgil's image of the godlike monarch. While Aeneas has far more lines than any other character in the poem, and is

given an eloquent formal speech "of refutation and self-defense" when he rejects Dido (72–79), he is given only three monologues, and those early in the epic (39). In his refutation speech, Aeneas is concerned about his duty, his love for Dido, and, perhaps especially, his fear of Dido's passion.

25. Although the tendency among Virgil scholars has long been to compare and contrast Virgil with Homer, Clausen emphasizes the influence of Hellenistic poetry on Virgil. In particular, the love story is in the Hellenistic style ("there being no other" 40). Dido's speech to Aeneas is, for Clausen, "almost incoherent" (though Virgil, of course, is not incoherent), 49. Of the Hellenistic poets influential in Virgil's works, Clausen ranks Callimachus first, then Apollonius and Theocritus. He concludes that the *Aeneid* is "not an abandonment but an extension of Callimachean poetics" (14).

26. Clausen traces the metaphor of love's burning wound to Apollonius (41).

27. Knight, *Aeneid* 102. The last phrase translates *coniugium vocat; hoc praetexit nomine culpam* (IV.172).

28. Quinn points out that even in antiquity there was some doubt about whose sword it is, e.g., for Ovid and Silius (148).

29. David K. Shipler discovered a passage in a textbook for Jordanian high-school juniors that drew upon the heroic tradition to denigrate Israeli (modern and Western) superiority in warfare.

> They fight only when they stand behind fortified villages or behind walls, according to their inherent behavior in all times and at the present time as well. Even now, when they use warplanes in fighting, these in themselves serve them as a shield to protect them. Similarly the tank, and any implement of modern warfare, all put in their hearts the audacity to fight us. These implements used by the Jews do not indicate that they have courage and have nothing to do with the objective situation. (201)

30. Carol Cohn, "Sex and Death in the Rational World of Defense Intellectuals," examines the sanitized abstractions and acronyms, the sexual, patriarchal and (unexpected) domestic imagery in the way defense planners speak about the unspeakable —nuclear warfare (705).

CHAPTER 2. SILENCE AND ECSTASY

An earlier version of this chapter appears in *Journal of Ritual Studies* 4 (1990): 41–64.

1. Consider Donne's quatrains:

> This Ecstasy doth unperplex,
>   We said, and tell us what we love;
> We see by this it was not sex;
>   We see we saw not what did move:
> But as all several souls contain
>   Mixture of things, they know not what,
> Love these mixed souls doth mix again,
>   And makes both one, each this and that. (30)

In *Tuhami* Crapanzano touches on the extent to which the modern West has extended psychological categories into realms other cultures explain very differently. Among the religious brotherhoods in Morocco, for example, conditions we would explain as hysterical or schizophrenic are seen as possession by demons, which "function at times like extrapolated superegos, externalized consciences" (18).

2. Ritual dancing is, of course, very old, attested in the ancient Near East at a very early period among the Sumerians and Akkadian-speaking inhabitants of Mesopotamia. Mutilation of, for example, the *gala* or *kalû* priests of the great goddess has been described in antiquity, from Ishtar to the Syrian goddess. Among the Sufi orders in Morocco, the Hamadsha (variously transliterated as Hamatcha, or Hamadcha) reserve a particular importance to the female Aisha Qandisha ('A'isha Qandisha, or Aisha Qandicha), thought by some, e.g., Westermarck, *Ritual and Belief in Morocco* (I.395–96) to derive from the great goddess of Carthage, Tanit, herself a form of the Canaanite goddess Anat. Crapanzano suggests that belief in Aisha Qandisha may derive from sub-Saharan Africa (331). The Hamadsha dancers, in the frenzy (*jidba*) of the ecstatic trance sometimes see Aisha Qandisha (341). Crapanzano presents an excellent generalized description of the rites, organization, and social variation among the Hamadsha. See Chapter 11 in this volume. Bowles follows Westermarck in his opinion of Aisha Qandisha; see Bailey (94) and Pounds (*Paul Bowles: The Inner Geography* 117).

3. In one sense the interest in Sufism shown in the West since the 1960s has obscured both its esoteric character and its intimate connection with Islam. Robert Graves's introduction to Shah's *The Sufis* is a good example of the tendency. Others, like Seyyed Hossein Nasr, have come to emphasize the Islamic origin of Sufism (11) and "the unbreakable link connecting Sufism to Islam" (12). There are three types of

writings these days on Sufism, including those "which often contain many genuine teachings of the founder of the movement but which have become intermingled with all kinds of extraneous matters" (15). Still, Sufism could have an impact on the situation Bowles takes as characterizing the doomed modern West. In his essay on Islam and the Modern World, Nasr comments:

> The daily Muslim rites also bestow the great advantage upon man of being able to carry his centre with him. The great malady of modern man can be reduced to his loss of centre, a loss which is so clearly depicted in the chaotic so-called literature and art of modern times. Islam offers the direct remedy to this illness. (167)

4. For an account of the "classical style" of Moroccan Islamic practice, Sufi mysticism that includes veneration of the tombs of dead saints, religious brotherhoods, and the importance of the Sultan, see Clifford Geertz, *Islam Observed*, esp. 48–54. The "classical style" of Islam has been challenged by reformers of the "scripturalist" movement, which aims at purifying Islam from the accumulation of non-Qur'anic practices, much in the way Western Puritans attempted to strip "pagan" practices from Christianity. The scripturalists and others who feel the practices of the brotherhoods are not properly Islamic do not provide the only objections to the practices. Among the Hamadsha, Crapanzano points out, many of the participants have little knowledge of saints' lives and litanies, and they consider the idea of mystical union with Allah "extremely blasphemous" (1972:346). The *hadra* or "presence" (used by Sufi mystics as the presence of Allah) is more often than not interpreted by the Hamadsha as the presence, not of Allah, but of 'A'isha Qandisha (344).

5. Wharton perceptively noted (the "more naive interpretation") that the ritual split practices across two classes, the free men who devoted themselves to the saint, and the slaves who devoted themselves to the slave of Hamadcha (57). Crapanzano, "The Hamadsha" 331, agrees that earlier observers had made that distinction, but today members of both Hamadsha brotherhoods mutilate themselves. Crapanzano points out that the Hamadsha are in fact two separate brotherhoods: the 'Allaliyyin, followers of the saint Sidi 'Ali ben Hamdush, and the Dghughiyyin, followers of the saint Sidi Ahmad Dghughi, the servant of Sidi 'Ali Hamdush (329). The two groups have separate *zawiyas*,

where they meet, in, for example, the city of Meknes. Crapanzano draws a more important distinction between the Hamadsha of the shantytowns that have built up as countrypeople have left the land for the cities and the Hamadsha of the medinas, the old cities in Morocco (334). The leader Wharton found so sinister is the *moqaddam*, whose role in the brotherhood and in the rituals is particularly important.

6. Hassan ("Pilgrim as Prey") was one of the first to notice that Bowles's "pilgrims" "move in a world from which choice and regeneration are absent" (24) in a quest as "vague as it is obsessive." Hassan notes that Bowles's style—"hard, crystalline vividness of imagery," "stark rhythm," a semblance of externality, distance, and objectivity—is rather unlike Hemingway's: "Unlike Hemingway's style, which conveys a constant shimmer of emotions restrained, radiating from a sensitive core, Bowles' communicates a sense of rigidity, a bludgeoning of sensibility, a determination not to feel, or escape, or claim pity, a determination which is itself the final source of terror" (35).

7. For André Breton, the Dadaists, Auden, and Kafka, the major twentieth century influences on Bowles, see Tindall 234–45.

8. Pounds was the first to detail correspondences between Bowles and Poe, perhaps the most important literary influence Bowles has admitted, *Paul Bowles: The Inner Geography* 3–4. Pounds sees the quest for self-destruction, a major theme in Bowles, as a direct inheritance from the earlier American author. *Let It Come Down* is treated at length in Pounds's chapter on the schizoid personality of Dyer and is particularly persuasive in his treatment of the looming figure—the sky mother, for example (43–56)—and the Jilali dancer (54). The poor light in which the "strong-minded woman" in Bowles is seen—Eunice Goode, for example, Dyer's mother, even Daisy de Valverde—owes less to misogyny, according to Pounds, than "the plight of woman, traditionally the carrier of civilization, the first agent of socialization" (79).

9. Pounds has described the way the sky functions for Port Moresby in *The Sheltering Sky* as the "geographical correlative of the refuge Port attempts to build for himself" (*Paul Bowles: The Inner Geography* 28), and Dyer's return to infant dependency on the sky-mother is just as striking; for the moment the sky provides shelter. But the sky mother is also the "looming figure" Pounds finds such a threatening presence in the novel, the formidable mother figure (59–62); Pounds, too, connects the passage with the trance dance Dyer witnesses (53–54). The loom-

ing figure is probably to be associated in Bowles with Aisha Qandisha (see Pounds 117; Bailey 94). The almost irresistible tendency of critics to see Bowles's own conflict with his parents as the motive behind his fiction obscures the point in *Let It Come Down* that the threat to the American Dyer is his powerful mother, while the threat to the Moroccan is rather the father (see LD 257–60). For the very different kinds of socialization of children in the two cultures, see, for example, Chodorow's use of Fatima Mernissi on Morocco (65) and Mernissi's major study of male-female dynamics in Muslim society, especially the contrast between Freud's (Western) and Al-Ghazali's (Eastern) view of instincts and sexuality (*Beyond the Veil* 27–45).

10. Crapanzano, "The Hamadsha" 341, also emphasizes the dangers to the dancers if the music should stop or if a dancer were interrupted. Among the Hamadsha, a dancer has his or her special tune (*rih*), which is used to bring the dancer out of the frenzy.

11. The ceremony Bowles witnessed "took place in the open, with several hundred people participating and several thousand spectators outside the circle. The time was about two in the morning."

12. Shah notes, "The unification which the Sufi attains is termed *fana'* (annihilation)" (341). Nasr notes that the "appropriate forms of meditation or *fikr*" directs the Sufi to "an integrated soul, pure and whole like gold, and then in the *dhikr* he offers this soul to God in the supreme form of sacrifice. Finally in annihilation (*fana'*) and subsistence (*baqa'*) he realizes that he never was separated from God even from the outset" (49–50). Shah is quick to point out that *fana'* does not require mortification of the flesh. Indeed, "self-mortification is not permitted, and the proper physical upkeep of the body is essential" (341). Clearly, both guides to Sufism are keen to separate authentic Sufi mysticism from what they consider excessive and extraneous admixtures of the kind found in popular Islamic practice and in some versions of Westernized Sufism.

13. Sufism almost always has an esoteric component. The followers possess a "secret" wisdom and enjoin silence toward those outsiders who might distort the message. The use of erotic language to describe mystical experience is a good example of simultaneously revealing and concealing the mysteries. The *Rubaiyat of Omar Khayyam* provides the most obvious example of a Sufi work that has gained the interest of the West, though its esoteric character has often been ignored.

14. The postmodern turn is to be found not only in Western authors like Bowles, but in contemporary Arabic literature, e.g., in the Syrian Walid Ikhlassy (Maier), mainly since 1967. While Moroccan storytellers have influenced Bowles, he has not claimed any influence of Arabic literature on his own writing (except, perhaps for the *Thousand and One Nights*), since he denies knowing how to read Arabic script.

CHAPTER 3. TWO FATHERS GENERAL

1. For an overview of the work, see Funston; she notes the dances of the Hamadshas, witnessed by Wharton (3).

2. Landau 90. Landau underscores Lyautey's insistence that Morocco not become a colony. "A protectorate, and not direct administration" was his motto.

3. Landau 95, 93. That this was by no means a judgment shared universally by the French is clear from, for example, the lengthy diatribe against all things Muslim that constitutes André Servier's *Islam and the Psychology of the Musulman*, written in the early 1920s and translated into English in 1924 by A. S. Moss-Blundell. A glance at the table of contents is enough to see why Servier urged France to take a stern approach to North Africa. "There is no such thing," he declares, "as Arab civilization."

4. Gargano (48), for example, concludes his analysis of the novel *The Reef* with what he takes to be Wharton's vision of the possibility that "civilization as it has existed in the West" will collapse, a vision much like Eliot's in *The Waste Land*. As an indication that the values sustaining this view of "civilization" are not just the trappings of "high culture," see the suggestive comparison between a Wharton character, Lily Bart, and Drieser's Carrie Meeber, who represent different social classes yet are "cultural sisters," in Price 238–45.

5. Alster 86. The tendency is clear in the proverbs of the old Babylonian period (early second millennium). The Mesopotamian story of the hero/king Gilgamesh and his friend Enkidu, who was brought up in the wilderness, develops this theme. See Gardner and Maier, *Gilgamesh*, esp. Tablet I of the Akkadian text.

6. Landau (96) points out a result that Lyautey might not have foreseen that by removing the French to their "new cities," there would be relatively little mingling with the Moroccans. "Thus, by 1954, it was

only on the rarest occasions that French people would receive Moroccans in their homes" (97). Elizabeth Fernea noted the other side of the coin. One of her friends, Abdul Aziz, claimed that "the liberation of the Maghreb began the moment the French first set foot on our soil!" Puzzled, Fernea asked how that was so. "We realized immediately they wanted our souls," the man said. "The French always do. But they did not get them. Algerians, maybe, Syrians, yes, but not the Moroccans. That is because we never invited them into our houses" (*A Street in Marrakech* 321).

    7. Wharton, like many of her contemporaries, tended to equate Islam with fanaticism. *In Morocco* is studded with references to the "Moslem fanaticism" of "ferocious old Salé" (35), the "old religious fanaticism of Salé" (37), "Oriental philosophy" that kept Moulay Idriss holding out "fanatically" against the French (51), and the Moorish "fanatical antagonism against the foreigner" (124).

    8. It might be useful to compare Wharton's enthusiastic account with the factual but subdued account of Moulay Ismail in *Fodor's Guide* 46, 126.

    9. Landau points out that Lyautey's policy operated against middle-class interests, usually those involved in "modernizing" a country. Of Lyautey he writes,

> Small wonder that Lyautey enjoyed nothing more than to spend an evening in the house of a great caid in his mountain lair or in the ancestral palace of a distinguished Makhzen member, hidden in one of the winding lanes of old Fez. He would set out for his host's dwelling on horseback, preceded and followed by mounted soldiers in flowing robes and by running torchbearers to light the way. He knew that, upon arrival, he would find his host with all the senior members of his family, dressed in their riches djellabas and burnouses. (95)

    10. For the script of the 1927 Drury Lane production, see Harbach, *The Desert Song*. The three film versions are

> 1929. Director Roy Del Ruth. Screenplay by Harvey Gates. Stars John Boles as the Red Shadow, Carlotta King as Margot. Louise Fazenda and Johnny Arthur were the comedians, with John Miljan, Edward Martindel, Jack Pratt, Otto Hoffmann, and Myrna Loy (as Azuri). Library of Congress Motion Picture Collection FCA 5143–45.
>
> 1943. Director Robert Florey. Screenplay by Robert Buckner. Stars Dennis Morgan, Irene Manning, Bruce Cabot, Gene Lockhart,

Lynne Overman, Faye Emerson, Victor Francen, Curt Bois, and Jack La Rue. Additional lyrics and music by Romberg and Jack Scholl. Library of Congress Magnetic Recording Laboratory LWO No. 23111.

1953. Director Bruce Humberstone. Screenplay by Roland Kibbee. Stars Gordon MacRae, Kathryn Grayson, Raymond Massey, Steve Cochran, Ray Collins, Dick Wesson, Allyn McLerie. Library of Congress Motion Picture Collection FGA 22702–2713.

11. The scandal that was Freud had indeed brought people to consider words they "never had heard of," and one of them was, of course, the *id*, the term that above all others captured the way "we are 'lived' by unknown and uncontrollable forces" (*General Selection* 214). There had been considerable debate about the translation of that key Freudian term. Joan Riviere chose to translate the 1923 *Das Ich und das Es* as "The Ego and the Id." The Nietzschean term for whatever in human nature is impersonal, *das Es*, should have been made into English "the It," or so John Rickman complained in a letter to Leonard Woolf (*Bloomsbury/Freud* 267). Woolf agreed with Rickman, but feared that a literal translation would be "bound to tell against the sale to ordinary readers" (307). Alix Strachey protested to her husband, James, "I hope to God the Es isn't really going to be the Id?" (176). Joan Riviere's translation appeared in 1927, just as Elinor Glynn was making It famous and *The Desert Song* was opening.

12. It is ironic, in view of the American solidarity with France and the acceptance of French overlordship in the 1943 and 1953 versions, that the United States was the last of the Western powers to accept France's position in Morocco—Theodore Roosevelt had helped keep Morocco relatively free of the European powers through the Algeciras Conference of 1906—and that Franklin Roosevelt is said to have suggested to Sultan Mohammed V in 1943 that foreigners should not be allowed to drain the wealth of Morocco and that the United States would aid Morocco after World War II. See the Introduction. For Teddy Roosevelt's part, see John Gable's correction of the impression given in the 1975 Metro-UA film *The Wind and the Lion* that Roosevelt had sent troops into Morocco to settle a dispute with a Riffian leader, 6. According to Gable, Roosevelt negotiated the release of an American held hostage in Morocco without firing a shot and shortly after negotiated the Algeciras Conference, "which both preserved Moroccan inde-

pendence and the Euoprean balance of power, thus for a time saving the peace in North Africa and Europe."

13. It is important to all versions that the Orientals are different in yet another way—in their religion. The men are all Muslims, and Islam, poorly understood in the West even now, is the butt of unpleasant, if obligatory, jokes. In the early versions, the Riffs engage in a rousing drinking song, guaranteed to offend Muslims, who believe that alcohol is prohibited. And in a very strange scene "at the edge of the desert," Act II, Scene 4 (Harbach 61) as the disgraced Red Shadow takes leave of his men, the men turn toward Mecca and pray. The stage directions reveal an unusual sensitivity to Islamic custom: "As the MEN kneel it is recommended that they are careful to cover the soles of their boots with their djeelabas." What the men then do is—one hopes unknown to the authors of the script—an incredible affront to a Muslim (an old anti-Muslim slander going back to the Crusades): they pray, not to Allah, but to Mohammed! It is important to note that there is no comedy intended in this. It is a moment of quiet intensity: the hero in disgrace, forced to leave his friends, with great emotion on both sides, and the prayer is supposed to increase the emotional involvement of the audience. They "pray" to "Mighty Mohammed, the King of Men,/ Look down upon us and keep us from sin." Later versions drop this scene, but add little gratuitous slams at "these Mohammedans" who do not drink anything, not even champagne (and thus represent a loss to the bistro owner) (1943), and at Allah, mainly for failing to save the people (1953).

14. Mulvey 412–28. In *Morocco* Von Sternberg "produces the ultimate fetish" by subordinating the male protagonist's gaze to that of the audience. "The beauty of the woman as object and the screen space coalesce; she is no longer the bearer of guilt but a perfect product, whose body, stylized and fragmented by close-ups is the content of the film and the direct recipient of the spectator's look" (426).

15. The importance of dialects or accents in these versions is greater than one might think, because in the film versions the dialects range in a hierarchy based on proximity to the audience, at least initially American. One kind of prestige is attached to Stage English; another kind is attached to British English (actually a form of RP or Received Pronunciation), usually for formal occasions; a very different prestige is allotted to dialects of American English, which immediately

breaks down barriers between the characters and the audience. "Frenchified" English—spoken with a stereotypical French accent—and "Germanized" English (in 1943) clearly mark the foreigner, the cultural other. Below those are the "Arabized" English accents that mark the great divide between East and West. Not surprisingly, Arabized English is not only different phonologically, but it occasionally—especially from the mouth of Azuri—is pidginized, and the character will use "bad grammar" in a way that diverges from the American vernacular. Especially in 1943, when being American was so important, vernacular American was a sign of solidarity—no matter what school grammarians might find objectionable about "poor usage."

16.　The 1927 script directs that the Red Shadow enter the scene wearing the sword in his belt, not in his scabbard. When he leaves his sword in the room, the directions tell Margot to talk to the sword "as though it were a doll which she holds" in her left hand (Harbach 58).

17.　Sagan emphasizes the point, since it accounts for the ambivalence of Freud toward morality, civilization, and women. The father becomes the ego ideal, whose values are interiorized in the superego. As Freud put it, "The superior being, which turned into the ego ideal [superego], once threatened castration, and this dread of castration is probably the nucleus round which the subsequent fear of conscience has gathered; it is this dread that persists as the fear of conscience" (*The Ego and the Id*, cited by Sagan 7).

18.　Harbach 66. Azuri is drunk, and she takes her reward "for being a traitor" with exceedingly bad grace. Azuri is bitter in her denunciation of her "white masters," who have taught her people "to sell *any-thing*—for silver." The general demands more than the bargain, and she finally relents. Revealing the identity of the Red Shadow is tied not only to jealousy, but to the conflict of cultures. "White men have hurt me— hurt me much. To-day I have been paid back for all my hurts."

CHAPTER 4. JANE BOWLES AND THE SEMI-ORIENTAL WOMAN

1.　Dillon, *A Little Original Sin* 397. For a brief chronology, see 427–28. On Jane Bowles's fiction, see also Dillon, "Jane Bowles: Experiment as Character" 140–47. Dillon has edited *Out in the World: Selected Letters of Jane Bowles, 1935–1970*. Ellen G. Friedman deals with modernism and postmodernism in Bowles, "Where Are the Missing

Contents?" 244–46. The Moroccan hotel figures in another text discussed here (chapter 7), and its reputation among Moroccans as a suspicious place where men and women can meet is confirmed. Elizabeth Fernea was living in Marrakech when the Hotel du Sud was opened in her neighborhood and increasingly irritated the women she was getting to know. By the end of her stay, the women, traditionally secluded from public life, had organized for political action—an astonishing novelty in that Moroccan city—to close the hotel. Fernea also recorded another episode involving hotels. A woman she knew in the neighborhood, Fatima Henna, took a job in one of the Western hotels in order to pay her brother's hospital bills. The other women who knew her were indignant. Fatima Henna had brought dishonor upon herself and her family. However desperate her situation, and however worthy the cause, Fatima Henna had violated traditional rules of conduct (*A Street in Marrakech* 191–92).

    2. Palmer, "Hermeneutics and the Postmodern" 7: "Modern man begins to dream of reducing everything to measurable terms, of making everything visualizable, i.e., spatial. And the mind, with its armory of mathematical symbols—better and more reliable than any ordinary languages—nominates man as the absolute monarch of the world."

    3. Dillon, *Original Sin* 210. The circumstances of the transposition reflect the complexities of their personal relationships. Her English publisher, Peter Owen, suggested a collection of Jane's stories, but she showed no interest in the project; indeed, she claimed to have no copies of her work. Paul produced copies, and still she balked, since she had published so little work. Changing "East Side: North Africa" into fiction was but one of a number of steps taken by Paul to put the volume together (367).

    4. "Everything is Nice" 319. *My Sister's Hand in Mine* (1978) is an expansion of the 1966 *Collected Works.* "Everything Is Nice" appeared in the 1966 edition, but "Emmy Moore's Journal" and "The Iron Table" were added to the expanded edition.

    5. The story does not comment further on the tattooes, which are common enough among Moroccan women. While the tattooes originally may have signified the tribe to which the woman belonged, they are now as often as not decorative, and the designs are invented by the women for their beauty.

6. However gross Jane makes Tetum out to be, she was "crazy mad about Tetum—a hopeless hopeless situation. I feel a kind of fever and I even wonder if she hasn't given me a gri-gri to eat—a gri-gri made for Europeans and which prompts them to give away everything they own" (172). More noteworthy is that the woman Jane became increasingly attached to, Cherifa, is not mentioned in the story. The Betsoul of the story was Cherifa's sister; and Zodelia was one of the "grain market group" who made Jane's life in Tangier so enticing.

7. *The Hidden Dimension* 155. Hall devotes a chapter to "Proxemics in a Cross-Cultural Context: Japan and the Arab World," 144–53.

8. Fernea ran into this question both in Iraq and in Morocco. The reaction was always the same, "Poor girl." "To be alone without any of one's womenfolk was clearly the greatest disaster which could befall any girl" (*Guests of the Sheik* 36).

9. The concepts of cultural differences in the handling of time are developed by Hall, for example, *The Silent Language* 19–21, 134–39, where he distinguishes American time and Arabic time, and in *Beyond Culture* 17, where he calls them "M-time" and "P-time."

10. On the "wa-wa" style, see Kaplan 6–10 and Yorkey 68–69, 80–82.

11. Jane Bowles elsewhere, in a letter to Paul, commented on a similar situation, where she had to eat "quantities of perfectly terrible tortilla-like bread soaked in rancid oil, flies and honey" with "the old yellow-faced mountain dyke," Tetum (Dillon, *Original Sin* 171). In the same letter she expresses her despair about learning Arabic: "I can speak a little. But understanding them, when they speak to each other, is another cup of *tea*" (172). Paul, in his autobiography, indicates that Jane studied Arabic in Paris before she went to Morocco, learned the local dialect quickly once she lived there, and preferred the Tangier dialect to the one Paul preferred, the dialect of Fez. While he appreciated the "medieval formality of Fez," which he felt was reflected in the dialect spoken there, she rather appreciated the "hybrid, seedy quality of Tangier." She came to love spending her time with Moroccans, he pointed out, "because of their sense of humor. Like Jews, they spent their lives with their families, distrusting, ridiculing, and reviling one another, and yet managed to laugh together betweentimes" (*Without Stopping* 284).

12. Moroccan Arabic, like English, distinguishes among several words for home and house (*'a'ila, le-ḍ-dar, maḥell*) such that different terms can be used for "My home is in Casablanca," "I have to go home," and "There's no place like home." See Sobleman and Harrell 100.

13. Dillon, in her biography of Jane, lists no fewer than fourteen hotels by name, at least four of which are in Tangier (457). Following the moves of the Bowleses through their houses and hotels in Tangier is a bewildering task for the reader, only partly because Paul and Jane lived apart much of their time in Tangier.

14. Published in *My Sister's Hand in Mine*, 465–67, but not in the earlier *Collected Works*. Dillon's version, "The whole civilization: notebook 22," appears in her biography of Jane Bowles 256–58.

15. It is a preoccupation in his short fiction and novels, such as, "Tea on the Mountain" in his *Collected Stories, 1939–1976* 15–25, or his novel *Let It Come Down*. The quotation is from the "Foreward" to his collection of essays, *Their Heads Are Green and Their Hands Are Blue* viii.

16. Dillon discusses the biographical context of "Emmy's Journal" (*Original Sin* 192–97) and includes a short passage (196) not included in the published version (*My Sister's Hand in Mine* 443–49); see also Lougy 159.

17. Dillon reads this as very thinly disguised autobiography. She sees in Emmy's agony the "little original sin" that haunted Jane Bowles for years, leaving her completely blocked. "For she is anchored by her sense of sin—not just the sin of her failure to write, but the opposing and even greater sense of sin that will be hers if she breaks through the block" (197).

CHAPTER 5. PENETRATING THE RAMPARTS

An earlier version of this chapter appeared in *The Atlantic Connection*, 245-58.

1. NY: Random House, 1963; rep. Ecco Press, (1984).

2. "The Music of Morocco" (L63-L64).

3. The full-length studies of Bowles to date are the critical biography by Lawrence D. Stewart, *Paul Bowles: The Illumination of North Africa* (1974); Johannes Willem Bertens, *The Fiction of Paul Bowles: The Soul is the Weariest Part of the Body* (1979); Wayne Pounds, *Paul Bowles: The Inner*

Geography (1985); and Richard F. Patteson, *A World Outside: The Fiction of Paul Bowles* (1987).

4. Stewart 101. See also Bailey 95–96 and Davis 103.

5. For an account, see Stewart 111–44, and Pounds, "Paul Bowles and *The Delicate Prey*: The Psychology of Predation" 620–21.

6. For Bowles and the storytellers, see Rountree, Lesser, and Rondeau, and Chapter 9.

7. The early work is considered at length by Stewart, Bertens, Pound (*Soul Is Weariest*), and Patteson (*World*); see also Hassan, "The Pilgrim as Prey: A Note on Paul Bowles"; Collins; Evans ("Interview" and "Paul Bowles and The 'Natural' Man"); and Joyce Carol Oates ("Aspects of Self: A Bowles Collage" 280–81).

8. *Midnight Mass* is discussed by Metcalf, Hibbard, Ditsy, Mottram, and Hauptman.

9. See Patteson, "The External World of Paul Bowles"; Gore Vidal, "Introduction" to the 1980 edition of *Collected Stories*; and Stewart, esp. 30–36, 75–79.

10. See Stewart 34–35.

11. "Tea on the Mountain" (1939) is the first story in *Collected Stories* 15–25.

12. Sartre 241–70. See also Lehman.

13. "Introduction" to the 1980 *Collected Stories* 9. The passage is found on 120–23.

14. For comments, see Vidal's "Introduction," and Paul Bowles's introduction to *Let It Come Down* 8.

15. Bowles, "A Man Must Not Be Very Moslem" 71–72. On the novel, see Halpern 162–63; Hassan, "Pilgrim" 28–30; Metcalf 36–37; Mottram 11–16; and the longer studies by Patteson, Pound, and Bertens.

16. "The Hyena," *Collected Stories* 291–93; also Bertens 199–200; Ditsy 68–70.

17. "The Garden," *Collected Stories* 363–65; also Ditsy 70; Rondeau 29.

18. "He of the Assembly," *Collected Stories* 313–25; also Ditsy 67; Mottram 26–27.

19. For a detailed discussion of the work, see Stewart 129–35.

20. *Collected Stories* 337–61. While the setting shares much with Bowles's stories of Morocco (or of the not-fully-localized settings in the

Sahara), the setting and the historical situation are Algerian, not Moroccan; see Ditsy 62–65.

21. As in "He of the Assembly" 318–19; Bowles considers Aisha Qandisha possibly Tanit or Astarte; see Bailey 94; Pounds, "Predation" 117.

22. Mohammed Mrabet, "El Fellah" and *"The Chest,"* The Chest, 9–13, 73–80. Daisy Hilse Dwyer records a version of "The Chest" that includes a number of significant variations. The main character in "The Murderer of Ninety-Nine Souls," *Images and Self-Images* 103–4, is not the pious Cheikh but the murderer himself. In his search for Allah, a transforming experience for the murderer, he finds, not Allah but "Saint Gabriel," who gives the man Allah's answer to his question.

23. *Midnight Mass* 151–62; also Pounds, "Predation" 134–37; Hauptman 72–73; and Metcalf 39.

CHAPTER 6. ELIZABETH FERNEA'S MOROCCAN PILGRIMAGE

An earlier version of this chapter appears in *MELUS, Journal of the Society for the Study of the Multi-Ethnic literature of the United States* 15 (1988): 67–81.

CHAPTER 7. INSIDER VIEWS

A segment of this chapter apppeared earlier in *The Maghreb Review* (1993).

1. For the place of cultural studies in, mainly, the American academy today, see Bathrick; Schor surveys work in feminist and gender studies in the same work. Evelyne Accad has pointed out that women writers in the Maghrib have generally been less radical in their views of society, in spite of their dismay at women's low status, than male writers. See her *Veil of Shame* and "Women's Voices from the Maghreb: 1945 to the Present" 18.

2. See, e.g., Burillo 35, 45. Not considered here, for reasons that have been explained above, are Moroccan writers who write in French, particularly expatriate writers such as Tahar Ben Jallūn and Driss Chraibi.

3. Roger Allen, for one, was disappointed that Abouzeid's narratives, though well written and forceful, are not really experimental, but

rather "belong to a period in the modern development of the genre that is long since over" ("Review" 677).

4. See Richard Palmer, "Postmodernity and Hermeneutics" 363–64; and the implications for at least one contemporary Arabic writer, Maier, "Walid Ikhlassy" 73–87. That four movements make up the modern is advocated by Stephen Toulmin 16. The fourth movement of modernity is postmodernism.

5. "A Stranger," Trans. John A. Haywood, *Modern Arabic Literature, 1800–1970* 269–74. The Arabic original, "Gharīb," appeared in *Wadī al-Dimā'* (Cairo, 1947); Rpt. Casablanca: Dar al-Thaqafy, 1989, 23–32.

6. Mohammed Barrada, "Life by Installments," Trans. Denys Johnson-Davies 128-34. The original appeared in *Salkh al-Jild* (Beirut: Manshurat Dar al-Adab, 1979), 25–33.

7. Hall, *The Hidden Dimension* 173. For a fuller treatment of the two time systems, see Hall, *Beyond Culture* 17–18, 158–59. The Arab world provides Hall with his most useful examples of P-time.

8. Eddijli's main theoretical work is derived from Goldman, *Towards a Sociology of the Novel*.

9. "Flower Crazy," Trans. Denys Johnson-Davies, *Arabic Short Stories* 143–48. The original appeared in *Majnūn al-Ward* (Beirut: Al-Ṭab'a al-Awwali, 1978); Rpt. Casablanca: Al-Ṭab'a al-Thania, 1985), 91–5.

10. Unpub. interview with Amina Hayani Fakhri, Tangier, spring 1990.

11. Leila Abouzeid, "Divorce," Trans. M. Salah-dine Hammoud, in Fernea, *Women and the Family in the Middle East* 84–88; rpt. *Year of the Elephant* 83–88. For the details of Moroccan family law, see Mernissi, *Beyond the Veil* 46–50. For Moghrebi or Moroccan Arabic, see Sobleman and Harrell; for Modern Standard Arabic, see Wehr, and *Al-Mawrid: A Modern English-Arabic Dictionary*.

12. Jilali El Koudia, "Rolling Rubber," *Collages & Bricolages* 2 (1990):71–76.

CHAPTER 8. TWO MOROCCAN STORYTELLERS

An earlier version of this chapter appears in <Postmodern Culture>, *An Electronic Journal of Interdisciplinary Criticism* 1 (1991): MAIER 591.

1. For the postmodern turn in Arabic literature, which also complicates the relationship between Western narratology and the East, see Maier, "A Postmodern Syrian Fictionalist." Anton Shammas's *Arabesques* (1986), written by a Palestinian whose first language is Arabic, but written in Hebrew (it caused no little controversy in Israel), is a postmodern novel that somehow manages to incorporate both traditional Arab storytelling and a distinctively Western narrative. Amulets, fortune-telling, and magical birds combine in the same work with the (apparent) autobiography of a Palestinian writer carefully set in a specific historical situation. In many ways the main narrator, Anton, measures himself against the man he could not be, his uncle Yusef, the storyteller rooted in Arab and early Christian traditions. Anton is more sophisticated, more Westernized, more modern—in all the ways suggested by Daniel Lerner, especially in his "psychic mobility"—than his uncle; the traditions are known to Anton, and fascinating, but they elude him:

> That's how Uncle Yusef was. One the on hand, he was a devout Catholic, who like Saint Augustine was utterly certain, as if the Virgin Mary herself had assured him, that the years of his life were but links in a chain leading to salvation. On the other hand, as if to keep an escape route open for himself, in case the only reality was dust returning to dust and the jaws of the beast of nothing gaped wide, he still could believe that the circular, the winding and the elusive had the power to resist nothingness. However, he did not judge between these and even conceived of them as a single entity in which the *djinni's* Ar-Rasad was one and the same as the cock that crowed at dawn when Saint Peter denied Jesus thrice. And here I am, his nephew, who served as an altar boy until I was twelve and since then have trod among the alien corn, here I am trying to separate myself from Uncle Yusef's circular pagan-like time and follow the linear path of Christian time, which supposedly leads to salvation, to the breaking of the vicious circles. (227–28)

2. What cannot be suppressed can be subverted by irony, as in Paul Bowles's story "The Eye," considered in Chapter 6, a brilliant study of a society that believes in the "evil eye," and of an intrusive Westerner, a kind of self-styled "private eye," who manages to get the Moroccans to talk to him about a bizarre event that happened in the past.

3. Palmer identifies the "movement beyond Western forms of reality" as an important feature of postmodernity. "For some, the way beyond modernity is the way *outside* Western forms of thought"

("Postmodernity and Hermeneutics" 373). To the examples Palmer gives could be added a most intriguing one from the Arab-Muslim world. In 1964 a court case was brought against the Lebanese writer, Layla Ba'labakki (1936–   ), who was charged with obscenity and harming public morality for a short story she published, "A Space Ship of Tenderness to the Moon." The case brought against Layla Ba'labakki by the Beirut vice squad rested on two sentences in the story. The case against her was dismissed by the court of appeals. The judges accepted Ba'labakki's claim to belong to the literary school of realism, but in doing so, the judges appealed to Islamic tradition (making a move that would certainly seem strange to, say, American jurisprudence):

> The court wishes to state that realism in human life can be traced to the most ancient period in our history, to be more precise, to the moment when man was created by God, in his naked reality, and, later, hid his nakedness with fig leaves. On the whole, the court believes that so-called realistic phrases used by the author are only a means to express a kind of example (*hikma*), as in the lessons or examples we receive from the following works of literature: 1. The myth of man receiving the Covenant from God, the rainbow in the heavens, and man's unworthiness to receive it 2. The legend of the isolated cave in the desert (Saw'ar), its walls stained red with blood which stained the entire land of Canaan 3. The tale of Egypt's Pharaoh, in which his loved one, tempting the Pharaoh to lust, writhes on a bed of Lebanese cedar wood, her naked body fragrant with the scents of the land of Ethiopia 4. The story of the virgin of Israel, guardian of a dying kingdom, bringing to old age and coldness the warmth of her body . . . 5. The legend of the rose of Sharun, the lily of the valley. . . . (Fernea and Bazirgan 288)

Arab realism is rooted in Arab-Islamic traditions, and the lower court's decision stood closer to those traditions than the higher court's. Overturning the lower court reflected the influence of more cosmopolitan and probably Western traditions.

4. Modern Standard Arabic is a grammatically simplified version of Classical Arabic, the language of the Qur'an, the most prestigious form of language in the Islamic—not just the Arabic-speaking—world. Originally designed for the media, Modern Standard has already made "diglossia" much too simple a notion to describe the sociolinguistic intricacies of Arabic. M. H. Bakalla prefers the term *spectroglossia* for that reason (87).

5. Jane Bowles's biographer, Millicent Dillon, includes much information about Ahmed Yacoubi (1931–   ) in *A Little Original Sin* (464). Paul Bowles discusses him in *Without Stopping* (esp. 308–33) and in *Five Eyes* (7, 144).

6. For the different kinds of Middle Eastern and North African folktales, see Bushnaq, esp. "Djinn, Ghouls, and Afreets, Tales of Magic and the Supernatural" (63–74) and "Magical Marriages and Mismatches" (153–57). One of the tales is discussed in Chapter 10.

7. For an explanation based mainly on Piaget's stages in the child's conception of the world, see Favat, *Child and Tale* 25–28 ("Magical Beliefs in Child and Tale") and 48–57 ("The Present Explanation"). According to this explanation, the child's interest in the fairy tale peaks between six and eight years and then declines rapidly. There is a resurgence of interest around eighteen and twenty years, and "in the adult there are vestiges of animism, magic, moralities of constraint, egocentrism, and the like" (56) that may account for continued interest in such stories long after the magical stage is abandoned.

8. Dillon and Paul Bowles offer insights into the life of Larbi Layachi:

> Paul and Jane had met Larbi while he was a guard at a cafe at Merkala Beach in Tangier. He had struggled since childhood to survive on his own and had spent a good deal of time in jail for minor infractions. Though he was illiterate, he had a remarkable gift as a storyteller, which Paul had immediately recognized. . . . Though Larbi had made some money from the sale of the book [*A Life Full of Holes*], he was quite content to work as houseboy for Paul in Arcila. (*Original Sin* 346)

Bowles fills in the background of Larbi's book, segments of which had already been published:

> At some point Richard Seaver had the idea of presenting the volume as a novel rather than as nonfiction, so that it would be eligible for a prize offered each year by an international group of publishers. . . . Larbi's book was defeated by Jorge Semprun's *Le Long Voyage* . . . Larbi made enough money from it to look for a bride. (*Without Stopping* 350)

Besides underscoring the prestige of the novel in the West, the story indicates the ease with which fiction and nonfiction slide into one another.

9. Bowles does not translate or explain a number of Moroccan terms and references, thus giving the narrative an exotic quality. Terms such as *ouakha* (rather like American OK 56), vocatives such as *auolidi* (my son 60), and exclamations (*Allah hiaouddi!* and *Ehi aloudi!* 64) really require no gloss. Common Moroccan terms such as *djellaba* (the hooded overgarment with sleeves 66), *qahouaji* (the coffee maker 74), *baqal* (grocer 59), and *tajine* (a Moroccan dish 56) are so common in Moroccan stories (and in Bowles's fiction) that they give the ordinary reader a sense of being an insider. Local references—Dar Menebbhi, Aqaba al Kasbah, the Monopolio, Bou Khach Khach, the Charf—work in largely the same way.

10. Note the (unremarked) presence in this Muslim world (where "Nazarenes" [Christians] at least upset the half-brother's father) of "the Jew" who buys things from Larbi: "There was a Jew who lived near the bull-ring, and he always bought everything I took him. Usually I sold him bones. He paid three gordas a kilo for them" (70–71). This time he sells things from the dump and gets twelve pesetas. There is no hint of animus: it is simply accepted that they are culturally other.

11. The most horrifying of the youthful stories is Bowles's account, given him by his grandmother, of his father's attempt to kill the six-week-old infant (*Without Stopping* 38–39). According to his grandmother, Bowles's father was jealous of the attention his son was receiving and exposed the infant to snow and cold. He was rescued by his grandmother. In a less dramatic gesture, the father beat him—only once—when Bowles was young and seized the boy's notebooks: "This was the only time my father beat me. It began a new stage in the development of hostilities between us. I vowed to devote my life to his destruction, even though it meant my own—an infantile conceit, but one which continued to preoccupy me for many years" (45).

12. See Patai's chapter, "The Endogamous Unilineal Descent Group" (407–36), added to the 3rd edition of his work. On paternal authority regarding the son—including beating—with examples from around the Middle East, see 412–17.

13. For the attraction of French surrealism, see Dillon, *Original Sin* 92–93. Wayne Pounds notes that "in Moroccan folk culture Bowles has found a mythology and an objective correlative to those concerns which have remained most important to him as a writer" (*Paul Bowles: The Inner Geography* 119)—e.g., in tales of the terrible mother such as one

finds in Yacoubi's story. Pounds elsewhere (50–51) distinguishes between "the primitive" of the anthropologists (i.e., "a shared symbolic ordering of experience") and of those who see it as a regression to older, pre-civilized thought. Eli Sagan gives a lucid account of Freud's argument against civilization 123–25.

14. Paul Bowles provides a good example of Barthes's "hybrid" author-writer—who is, according to Barthes, a characteristic literary figure of our time. Not only is it virtually impossible to separate life from fiction in Bowles's work, but nonfiction can be turned into fiction. A case in point is his revision of his wife's nonfiction piece, "East Side: North Africa," into fiction ("Everything Is Nice," discussed in Chapter 5). Stories in his *Collected Stories*, such as "Istikhara, Anaya, Medagan and the Medaganat" (401–4) and "Things Gone and Things Still Here" (405–9), were originally conceived as essays. "Unwelcome Words" (61–86), the title piece in a series of stories, consists of letters of "Paul" to another writer cast in fictional form.

CHAPTER 9. TENTED VISIONS

1. For the Orientalist painters, see Jullian 75–111; Rosenthal, 91, 123. On the intellectual history that ties ancient Near Eastern images and the Middle East to modernism, see Maier, "The Ancient Near East in Modern Thought."

2. A brief version of the interview with "Zahrah" appears in Fernea and Bezirgan 201–18. Susan Schaefer Davis has kindly permitted me to read the transcription of the entire interview in Arabic with an English translation. Here the letter *P* stands for the published text in Fernea and Bezirgan; *T* for the typescript; and *AE* for the Arabic and English transcription.

CHAPTER 10. IN THE SERVICE OF AISHA QANDISHA

1. Otto ix. While he does not take up Sufism or the demonic Aisha Qandisha directly, Otto does make this claim about Islam that in some ways captures the fascination and terror of the demoness:

> In Allah the numinous is absolutely preponderant over everything else. So that, when Islam for giving a merely "fortuitous" character to the claim of morality, as tough the moral law were only valid through the

chance caprice of the deity, the criticism is well justified, only "chance" and fortuitousness have nothing to do with the matter. The explanation is rather that the numinous in Allah, nay, even his uncanny and daemonic character, outweighs what is rational in him. (90–91)

2. Bernal, *Black Athena* II, 107, thinks that the heroic image of a club-carrying Herakles existed before 1750 B.C., when swords first appear in the Mediterranean.

3. Bouasla 236–40 is more hopeful that the trends in American anthropology he has detected, especially dynamic and interpretive anthropologies, will make increasingly important contributions to understanding if they are combined with a comprehensive analysis of social structure.

4. Mernissi, "Women, Saints, and Sanctuaries" 57–68. See *Doing Daily Battle* 213.

5. See the controversy in Kaplan's "Contrastive Thought Patterns—Yet Again" 1–2. The term *wa-wa style* was used by Yorkey 78–85.

CONCLUSION

1. Sarah Spence argues that Virgil was actually writing a subtext subversive of the public text, one that was sympathetic at least to Dido and critical of the exaggerated heroics of Aeneas. Dido, Spence claims, changes to a "sympathetic character guided by her emotions who is nonetheless not submissive," an anomaly and a threat to the "humanist rhetorical mode" that informs much of the work (and presents Aeneas as the hero of tradition), *Rhetorics of Reason and Desire* 31.

2. Georg Luck, trans. *Arcana Mundi: Magic and the Occult in the Greek and Roman Worlds* 372–78, provides a translation and comment on this important work.

3. Henry P. Laughlin, *The Ego and Its Defenses*, defines ego defense as "a specific defensive process, operating outside of and beyond conscious awareness. It is automatically and unconsciously employed in the endeavor to secure resolution of emotional conflict, relief from emotion tension, and to avert or allay anxiety. A given dynamism is evoked by the ego as an attempted means of coping with an otherwise consciously intolerable situation" (6). Among the "minor" defenses Laughlin discusses are concepts displaced from earlier religious contexts, such as,

"absolution" and "atonement and penance." The major and minor defenses (plus several "special reactions and combinations of dynamisms, e.g., the King David reaction) are listed in Table 1 (7).

4. David Bathrick devotes a section, "Cultural Theory as a Challenge to Literary Theory," in his overview of cultural studies, 323–29. "Central to the strategic evolution of cultural criticism," Bathrick notes, "has been a programmatic effort to challenge what it sees as the claim to universalism at the heart (or at least the practice!) of existing literary theory" (324).

5. Walter Burkert, *The Orientalizing Revolution; Near Eastern Influence of Greek Culture in the Early Archaic Age* 4–8.

> In the period at about the middle of the eighth century, when direct contact had been established between the Assyrians and the Greeks, Greek culture must have been much less self-conscious and therefore much more malleable and open to foreign influence than it became in subsequent generations. It is the formative epoch of Greek civilization that experienced the orientalizing revolution. (8)

6. The term is used by George Lakoff and Mark Johnson, 14–17, to mark the experiential ground that enables humans to organize a system of mainly spatial relations: up/down, in/out, front/back, on/off, deep/shallow, central/peripheral.

7. Stetkevych thinks that Standard Arabic has configured its syntax to modern, largely non-Semitic "thought-dynamics. The modern Arabic mind is becoming an offshoot of the modern Western mind and is retaining fewer and fewer of the rigidly Semitic thought-habits and thus fewer of the classical idiomatic molds and structural particularities" (*The Modern Arabic Literary Language; Lexical and Stylistic Developments* 119–20). The same could be said of the gap between a strictly regional Appalachian speech and Standard English, though the refiguration of American vernaculars as social rather than regional dialects complicates the picture.

8. The line ends a column of cuneiform text. The next column opens with the end of Enkidu's first speech. There we find that Enkidu will cry out, "I, I alone, am powerful./ I am the one who changes fates" (Gardner and Maier 81). Enkidu's early boast gives way to contending claims and emotions, which intensify once it becomes clear to Enkidu, midway through the story, that he must die. He uses language, the sym-

bolic order, in a powerful way to curse the woman who made him human. The god Shamash speaks to Enkidu in a persuasive way, arguing that Enkidu has been given much, the best that life has to offer, though he must die. Enkidu is convinced and blesses the woman he had just cursed (Tablet VII.iii–iv). Immediately the poem turns to a terrifying dream in which a demonic being seizes Enkidu and transports him to the dreaded land of the dead (see Gardner and Maier 172–80).

9. *Écrits* xi. Already for English-speaking critics in "Imaginary and Symbolic in Lacan: Marxism, Psychoanalytic Criticism, and the Problem of the Subject" Frederic Jameson emphasizes the isolation of objects in the visual field made possible in the mirror stage; with the category of container and contained, inside/outside, otherness is struggle, Lacan's "aggressivity" (356).

10. See Ong, *Orality and Literacy; The Technologizing of the Word*, esp. ch. 6, "Oral Memory; the Story Line and Characterization," and the journal *Oral Tradition*.

11. See Lilian R. Furst's "Introduction" to her collection of earlier and more recent views of realism (1–24).

> Aspects of all these approaches take us forward from earlier notions of realism as a direct and uncomplicated reporting of the truth of everyday life to a more differentiated understanding of the writer's partial relationship to his or her world, to the complexities, constraints and artifices involved in trying to depict it, including the role of literary form in a writer's options, and the dynamics of readers' responses to those strategies." (21–22)

12. The term *Prestige* is used throughout in the sociolinguistic sense that variations, like linguistic variables, are attached to the "social group with the most social status," as Jennifer Coates puts it (57), and usually involve a process of standardization (identification, acceptance, codification, and elaboration of uses) and often correctness. However, *stigma* is "attached to non-standard forms" (57).

13. Lerner 47–52. "It is a major hypothesis of this study that high empathic capacity is the predominant personal style only in modern society, which is distinctively industrial, urban, literate, and *participant*" (50).

Bibliography

Abouzeid, Leila. "Divorce." Tr. M. Salah-dine Hammoud. *Women and the Family in the Middle East*. Ed. Elizabeth Warnock Fernea. Austin: University of Texas Press, 1985. 84–88. Rpt. *Year of the Elephant: A Moroccan Woman's Journey Toward Independence*. Trans. Barbara Parmenter. Austin: University of Texas Press, 1989. 83–88.

Abrams, M. H. *A Glossary of Literary Terms*. 6th Ed. Fort Worth: Harcourt Brace Jovanovich, 1993.

Accad, Evelyne. *Veil of Shame: The Role of Women in the Contemporary Fiction of North Africa and the Arab World*. Sherbrooke: Naaman, 1978.

———. "Women's Voices from the Maghreb: 1945 to the Present." *Mundus Arabicus* 1 (1982): 18–34.

Allen, Roger. *The Arabic Novel: An Historical and Critical Introduction*. Syracuse: University Press, 1982.

———. Rev. of *Year of the Elephant* by Leila Abouzeid. *International Journal of Middle East Studies* 23 (1991): 676–78.

Allen, Virginia M. *The Femme Fatale: Erotic Icon*. Troy, NY: Whitson, 1983.

Allen, Walter. *The English Novel: A Short Critical History*. NY: Dutton, 1954.

Al-Mawrid: A Modern English-Arabic Dictionary. Ed. Munir Ba'albaki. Beirut: Dar El-Ilm Lil-Malayen, 1982.

Alster, Bendt. *Studies in Sumerian Proverbs.* Copenhagen: Akademisk Forlag, 1975.

Altoma, Salih J. "Westernization and Islam in Modern Arabic Fiction." *Yearbook of Comparative and General Literature* 20 (1971): 81–88.

Al-Udhari, Abdullah, ed. and tr. *Modern Poetry of the Arab World.* Harmondworth, England: Penguin, 1986.

Ammons, Elizabeth. *Edith Wharton's Argument with America.* Athens: University of Georgia Press, 1980.

"Aspects of Self: A Bowles Collage." Butscher and Malin. 259–300.

The Atlantic Connection, 200 Years of Moroccan-American Relations, 1786–1986. Ed. Jerome Bookin-Wiener. Rabat: Edino, 1990.

Auerbach, Erich. *Mimesis: The Representation of Reality in Western Literature.* Tr. Willard Trask. Garden City, NY: Doubleday, 1953.

Augustine. "Confessions." Mack 1: 692.

Baida, Jamaâ. "The United States and the Franco-Moroccan Conflict (1950-1956)." *The Atlantic Connection.* 183–96.

Bailey, Jeffrey. "The Art of Fiction LXVII: Paul Bowles." *Paris Review* 81 (1981): 63–98.

Bakalla, M. H. *Arabic Culture Through Its Language and Literature.* London: Kegan Paul International, 1984.

Bakhtine, Mikhail. *Esthetique et Theorie du Roman.* Trans. Daria Olivier. Paris: Gallimard, 1978.

Ba'labakki, Layla. "A Space Ship of Tenderness to the Moon." Tr. Denys Johnson-Davies. Fernea and Bezirgan. 273–79.

Barrada, Mohammed. "Life by Instalments." Tr. Denys Johnson-Davies. London: Quartet, 1983. 128–34. "Hayah b-al-taqsit." *Salkh al-Jild.* Beirut: Manshurat Dar al-Adab, 1979. 25–33.

Bassett, Mark T. "Imagination, Control and Betrayal in Jane Bowles' 'A Stick of Green Candy.'" *Studies in Short Fiction* (Newberry, SC) 24 (1987): 25–29.

Bathrick, David. "Cultural Studies." Gibaldi. 320–40.

Beauvoir, Simone de. *The Second Sex.* Tr. H. M. Parshley. NY: Knopf, 1952.

Benabdeljelil, Abdellatif. "Introduction." *The Atlantic Connection.* 1–4.

Ben Jallūn, 'Abd al-Majīd. "A Stranger." Tr. John A. Haywood. *Modern Arabic Literature, 1800–1970.* NY: St. Martin's, 1978. 269-74. "Gharīb," *Wadī al-Dimā'* Cairo, 1947; Rpt. Casablanca: Dar al-Thaqafy, 1989. 23–32.

Bernal, Martin. *Black Athena: The Afroasiastic Roots of Classical Civilization.* 2 vols. New Brunswick, NJ: Rutgers University Press, 1987, 1990.

Berque, Jacques. "New Fields of Meaning." *Cultural Expression in Arab Society Today.* Tr. Robert W. Stookey. Austin: University of Texas Press, 1978. 80–102.

Bertens, Johannes Willem. *The Fiction of Paul Bowles: The Soul Is the Weariest Part of the Body.* Amsterdam: Rodopi, 1979.

Bloomsbury/Freud: The Letters of James and Alix Strachey 1924–1925. Ed. Perry Meisel and Walter Kendrick. NY: Basic Books, 1985.

Blum, Virginia. "Edith Wharton's Erotic Other-World." *Literature and Psychology* 33 (1987): 12–29.

Bono, Barbara J. *Literary Transvaluation: From Vergilian Epic to Shakespearean Tragicomedy.* Berkeley: University of California Press, 1984.

Bouasla, Ettibari. "Moroccan Society and American Anthropology." *The Atlantic Connection.* 223–44.

Bowles, Jane. "East Side: North Africa." *Mademoiselle.* April, 1951: 134+.

———. *My Sister's Hand in Mine.* NY: Ecco, 1978.

———. *Out in the World, Selected Letters of Jane Bowles, 1935–1970.* Ed. Millicent Dillon. Santa Barbara: Black Sparrow, 1985.

Bowles, Paul. "Africa Minor." *Their Heads Are Green and Their Hands Are Blue.* 20–40.

————. "Allal." *Collected Stories.* 409–17.

————, tr. *The Chest.* Bolinas: Tombouctou, 1983.

————. *Collected Stories, 1939–1976.* Santa Barbara: Black Sparrow, 1979.

————. "The Eye." *Midnight Mass.* 151–62.

————, ed. and tr. *Five Eyes.* Santa Barbara: Black Sparrow, 1979.

————, "The Fqih." *Collected Stories.* 377–80.

————, "The Garden." *Collected Stories.* 363–66.

————, "He of the Assembly." *Collected Stories.* 313–26.

————, "Introduction" to William Betsch. The Hakima; A Tragedy in *Fez.* NY: Aperture, 1991. 8–9.

————, "Journal, Tangier 1987–1988." *Antaeus* (1988): 57–69.

————, LC 12,017A typescript. Archive of Folk Culture, Library of Congress. Washington, DC

————. *Let It Come Down.* 1952. Rpt. Santa Barbara: Black Sparrow, 1980.

————. *Midnight Mass.* Santa Barbara: Black Sparrow, 1983.

————. "New York 1965." *Unwelcome Words.* 15–26.

————. *The Sheltering Sky.* 1949. Rpt. NY: Ecco, 1978.

————. *The Spider's House.* NY: Random House, 1955.

————. "Tea on the Mountain." *Collected Stories.* 15–26.

————. *Their Heads Are Green and Their Hands Are Blue.* 1963. Rpt. NY: Ecco, 1984.

————. "The Time of Friendship." *Collected Stories.* 337–62.

————. "The Wind at Beni Midar." *Collected Stories.* 327–36.

————. *Unwelcome Words.* Bolinas: Tombouctou, 1988.

————. *Without Stopping, An Autobiography.* 1972. Rpt. NY: Ecco, 1985.

Brooke, Stopford, ed. *Life and Letters of Fred. W. Robertson, M.A.* London: Kegan Paul, Trench, Trubner, 1893.

Brooker, Peter, ed. *Modernism/Postmodernism.* London: Longman, 1992.

Burillo, Fernando de Agreda. *Encuesta sobre la literatura marroquí actual.* Madrid: Instituto Hispano-Arabe de Cultura, 1975.

Burkert, Walter. *The Orientalizing Revolution: Near Eastern Influence on Greek Culture in the Early Archaic Age.* Trs. Margaret E. Pinder and Walter Burkert. Cambridge, MA: Harvard University Press, 1992.

Bushnaq, Inea, ed. and tr. *Arab Folktales.* New York: Pantheon, 1986.

Butscher, Edward, and Irving Malin, eds. "Paul Bowles Issue." *Twentieth Century Literature* 32 (1986): 255–455.

Canetti, Elias. *The Voices of Marrakesh.* Tr. J. A. Underwood. New York: Farrar Straus Giroux, 1978.

Cassirer, Ernst. *The Individual and the Cosmos in Renaissance Philosophy.* Tr. Mario Domandi. NY: Harper, 1963. 125–30.

Cecil, L. Moffit. "Paul Bowles' Sheltering Sky and Arabia." *Research Studies* 42 (1974): 44–49.

Chedid, Andrée. *From Sleep Unbound.* Trans. Sharon Spencer. Athens: Ohio University Press-Swallow Press, 1983.

Chittick, William C. *The Sufi Path of Love.* Albany: State University of New York Press. 1983.

Chodorow, Nancy. "Family Structure and Feminine Personality." *Women, Culture, and Society.* Ed. Michelle Zimbalist Rosaldo and Louise Lamphere. Stanford: University Press, 1974. 43–66.

Chukri, Mohammed. "Flower Crazy." Tr. Denys Johnson-Davies. *Arabic Short Stories.* London: Quartet, 1983. 143–48. "*Majnūn al-Ward.*" *Majnūn al-Ward.* Beirut: Al-Ṭab'a al-Awwali, 1978; Rpt. Casablanca: Al-Ṭab'a al-Thania, 1985. 91–95.

————. Unpub. interview with Amina Hayani Fakhri. Tangier, Spring 1990.

Clausen, Wendell. *Virgil's "Aeneid" and the Tradition of Hellenistic Poetry.* Berkeley: University of California Press, 1987.

Coates, Jennifer. *Women, Men and Language: A Sociolinguistic Account of Sex Differences in Language.* London: Longman, 1986.

Cohn, Carol. "Sex and Death in the Rational World of Defense Intellectuals." *Signs* 12 (1987): 687–718.

Collins, Jack. "Approaching Paul Bowles." *Review of Contemporary Fiction* 2 (1982): 55–63.

Crapanzano, Vincent. "The Hamadsha." *Scholars, Saints, and Sufis: Muslim Religious Institutions in the Middle East Since 1500.* Ed. Nikki R. Keddie. Berkeley: University of California Press, 1972. 327–48.

————. *Tuhami: Portrait of a Moroccan.* Chicago: University Press, 1980.

Crosman, Robert. "How Readers Make Meaning." Staton 357–66.

Damis, John. *U.S.-Arab Relations: The Moroccan Dimension* Washington: National Council on U.S.-Arab Relations, 1986.

Davis, Stephen. "Paul Bowles in Tangier: An Interview." *Zero* 4 (1990): 98–113.

Davis, Susan Schaefer. *Patience and Power: Women's Lives in a Moroccan Village.* Rochester, VT: Schenkman, 1983.

————. ed. "Zahrah Muhammad: A Rural Woman of Morocco." Fernea and Bezirgan. 201–18. = P (for published text), vs. T (for the Davis typescript), both of which have page numbers, and AE (for Davis's Arabic and English transcription), which divides the conversation into utterances (stretches of conversation without a break).

Deleuze, Gilles and Félix Guattari. *Anti-Oedipus, Capitalism and Schizophrenia.* Tr. Robert Hurley, Mark Seem, and Helen R. Lane. Minneapolis: University of Minnesota Press, 1983.

Derrida, Jacques. "Structure, Sign, and Play in the Discourse of the Human Sciences." Tr. Alan Bass. Staton 390–409.

The Desert Song. 1927 Stage Version:
Otto Harbach, Oscar Hammerstein II, and Frank Mandel. *The Desert Song.* NY: Samuel French, 1932.

The Desert Song. Three Film Versions:
1929. Director Roy Del Ruth. Screenplay by Harvey Gates. Stars John Boles as the Red Shadow, Carlotta King as Margot, Louise Fazenda and Johnny Arthur were the comedians, with John Miljan, Edward Martindel, Jack Pratt, Otto Hoffmann, and Myrna Loy (as Azuri). Library of Congress Motion Picture Collection FCA 5143–45.

1943. Director Robert Florey. Screenplay by Robert Buckner. Stars Dennis Morgan, Irene Manning, Bruce Cabot, Gene Lockhart, Lynne Overman, Faye Emerson, Victor Francen, Curt Bois, and Jack La Rue. Additional lyrics and music by Romberg and Jack Scholl. Library of Congress Magnetic Recording Laboratory LWO No. 23111.

1953. Director Bruce Humberstone. Screenplay by Roland Kibbee. Stars Gordon MacRae, Kathryn Grayson, Raymond Massey, Steve Cochran, Ray Collins, Dick Wesson, Allyn McLerie. Library of Congress Motion Picture Collection FGA 22702–2713.

A Dictionary of Moroccan Arabic: English-Moroccan. Ed. Harvey Sobleman and Richard S. Harrell. Washington, DC: Georgeton University Press, 1963.

Dillon, Millicent. "Jane Bowles: Experiment as Character." Friedman and Fuchs. 140–47.

———. *A Little Original Sin: The Life and Work of Jane Bowles.* New York: Holt, Rinehart, 1981.

Ditsky, John. "*The Time of Friendship*: The Short Fiction of Paul Bowles." *San Jose Studies* 12 (1986): 61–74.

Donne, John. "The Ecstasy." *John Donne's Poetry.* Ed. A. L. Clements. New York: Norton, 1966. 29–31.

Dreiser, Theodore. *Sister Carrie.* New York: Doubleday, 1900.

Dryden, John. "An Essay of Dramatic Poesy." *18th Century Poetry and Prose.* Ed. Louis I. Bredvold, Alan D. McKillop, and Lois Whitney. NY: Ronald Press, 1956. 101–02.

Dwyer, Daisy Hilse. *Images and Self-Images: Male and Female in Morocco.* New York: Columbia University Press, 1978.

Eberhardt, Isabelle. *The Oblivion Seekers.* Trs. Paul Bowles. San Francisco: City Lights. 1975.

Eddijli, Hamid. *"Social Reality" in Mohamed Berrada and in Mohamed Chukri.* Unpub. thesis, Sidi Mohamed Ben Abdellah University, 1990.

Eickelman, Dale F. *Moroccan Islam: Tradition and Society in a Pilgrimage Center.* Austin: University of Texas Press, 1976.

Eisler, Riane. *The Chalice and the Blade.* NY: Harper and Row, 1987.

Eliade, Mircea. *Shamanism: Archaic Techniques of Ecstasy.* 1951. Tr. Willard R. Trask. Princeton: University Press, 1964.

El Koudia, Jilali. "Rolling Rubber." *Collages & Bricolages* 2 (1990): 71–76.

El Saffar, Ruth. "The Making of the Novel and the Evolution of Consciousness." *Oral Tradition* 2 (1987): 231–48.

Evans, Oliver. "Interview with Paul Bowles." *Mediterranean Review* 1 (1971): 3–15.

———. "Paul Bowles and the 'Natural' Man." *Critique* 3 (1959): 43–59.

Exum, J. Cheryl, and Johanna W. H. Bos, eds. *Reasoning with the Foxes: Female Wit in a World of Male Power.* Atlanta: Scholars Press, 1988. [= *Semeia* 42]

Fairclough, H. Rushton, ed. *Virgil.* 2 vols. Cambridge: Harvard University Press, 1965.

Favat, F. André. *Child and Tale: The Origins of Interest.* Urbana: National Council of Teachers of English, 1977.

Fernea, Elizabeth Warnock. *Guests of the Sheik.* Garden City: Anchor Doubleday, 1969.

————. *A Street in Marrakech*. Garden City: Anchor Doubleday, 1980.

————, ed. *Women and the Family in the Middle East*. Austin: University of Texas Press, 1985.

————, and Basima Qattan Bezirgan, eds. *Middle Eastern Muslim Women Speak*. Austin: University of Texas Press, 1977.

————. "An Account of the Trial." Fernea and Bezirgan. 280–90.

Fodor's North Africa 1986. Ed. Richard Moore. New York: Fodor's, 1985.

Fontaine, Carole. "The Deceptive Goddess in Ancient Near Eastern Myth: Inanna and Inaras." *Semeia* 42 1988): 84–102.

Foucault, Michel. *The History of Sexuality*. Tr. Robert Hurley. 1976. New York: Vintage, 1980.

Freud, Sigmund. *Moses and Monotheism*. 1939. Tr. James Strachey. *The Standard Edition of the Complete Psychological Works of Sigmund Freud*. Vol. 23. London: Hogarth, 1964. 3–140.

Friedman, Ellen G., and Miriam Fuchs. *Breaking the Sequence: Women's Experimental Fiction*. Princeton: Princeton University Press, 1989.

————. "Contexts and Continuities: An Introduction to Women's Experimental Fiction in English." Friedman and Fuchs. 3–51.

————. "Where Are the Missing Contents? (Post)Modernism, Gender, and the Canon." *PMLA* 108 (1993): 240–52.

Frymer-Kensky, Tikva. *In the Wake of the Goddesses: Women, Culture and the Biblical Transformation of Pagan Myth*. NY: Fawcett Columbine, 1993.

Fuchs, Esther. " 'For I Have the Way of Women': Deception, Gender, and Ideology in Biblical Narrative." *Semeia* 42 (1988): 68–83.

Funston, Judith E. "*In Morocco*: Edith Wharton's Heart of Darkness." *Edith Wharton Newsletter* 5 (1988): 1–3, 12.

Furst, Lilian, ed. *Realism*. Longman House, England: Longman, 1992.

Gable, John. Letter. *Variety*. 11 June 1975: 6.

Gallop, Jane. *Reading Lacan.* Ithaca: Cornell University Press, 1985.

Gardner, John, and John Maier, eds. and tr. *Gilgamesh: Translated from the Sin-leqi-unninni Version.* New York: Knopf, 1984.

Gargano, James W. "Edith Wharton's *The Reef:* The Genteel Woman's Quest for Knowledge." *Novel* 10 (1976): 40–48.

Geertz, Clifford. *Islam Observed: Religious Development in Morocco and Indonesia.* Chicago: Chicago University Press, 1971.

————. *Local Knowledge: Further Essays in Interpretive Anthropology.* New York: Basic Books, 1983.

————. "On the Nature of Anthropological Understanding." *American Scientist* 63 (1975): 47–53. Rpt. *Local Knowledge.* 55–70.

————. *Works and Lives: The Anthropologist as Author.* Stanford: University Press, 1988.

Geertz. Hildred. "The Meanings of Family Ties." *Meaning and Order in Moroccan Society.* Ed. Clifford Geertz, Hildred Geertz, Lawrence Rosen. Cambridge: University Press, 1979. 315–92.

Gellner, Ernest. *Muslim Society.* Cambridge: University Press, 1981.

A General Selection from the Works of Sigmund Freud. Ed. John Rickman. Garden City: Doubleday, 1957.

Gibaldi, Joseph, ed. *Introduction to Scholarship in Modern Languages and Literature.* 2nd. ed. NY: Modern Language Association, 1992.

Gimbel, Wendy. *Edith Wharton: Orphancy and Survival.* New York: Praeger, 1984.

Goldman, Lucien. *Towards a Sociology of the Novel.* Tr. Alan Sheridan. London: Tavistock, 1975.

Grant, Michael. *Myths of the Greeks and Romans.* NY: New American Library, 1962.

Grant, Robert M. *Gods and the One God.* Philadelphia: Westminster, 1986.

Greenblatt, Stephen J. "Shakespeare and the Exorcists." *Contemporary Literary Criticism*. Ed. Robert Con Davis and Ronald Schliefer. NY: Longman, 1989. 428–48.

Guthrie, W. K. C. *The Greeks and Gods*. Boston: Beacon, 1955.

Haberstach, Charles. "Paul Bowles' Fiction: Lost Directions." *Exploration* 1 (1973): 36–41.

Hall, Edward T. *Beyond Culture*. Garden City: Doubleday, 1977.

———. *The Hidden Dimension*. Garden City: Doubleday, 1969.

Halpern, Daniel. "Interview with Paul Bowles." *TriQuarterly* 33 (1975): 159–77.

Harbach, Otto, Oscar Hammerstein II, and Frank Mandel. *The Desert Song*. NY: Samuel French, 1932.

Hardie, Philip. *Virgil's Aeneid: Cosmos and Imperium*. Oxford: Clarendon, 1986.

Hardin, Richard F. "'Ritual' in Recent Criticism: The Elusive Sense of Community." *PMLA* 98/5 (1983):846–62.

Hassan, Ihab. "The New Gnosticism: Speculations on an Aspect of the Postmodern Mind." *boundary* 2 1 (1973): 547–69.

———. "The Pilgrim as Prey: A Note on Paul Bowles." *Western Review* 19 (1954): 23–36.

———. "Quest: Forms of Adventure in Contemporary American Literature." *Contemporary American Fiction*. Ed. Malcolm Bradbury and Sigmund Ro. London: Edward Arnold, 1987. 123–37.

Hauptman, Robert. "Paul Bowles and the Perception of Evil." *Review of Contemporary Fiction* 2 (1982): 71–73.

Hawthorne, Nathaniel. *The Scarlet Letter*. Ed. Harry Levin. Boston: Houghton Mifflin, 1960.

Haywood, John A. *Modern Arabic Literature, 1800–1970*. New York: St. Martin's, 1972.

Heath, Jeffrey. *From Code-Switching to Borrowing: Foreign and Diglossic Mixing in Moroccan Arabic.* London: Kegan Paul International, 1989.

Hernadi, Paul. "Doing, Making, Meaning: Toward a Theory of Verbal Practice." *PMLA* 103 (1988): 749–58.

Hibbard, Allen E. "Expatriation and Narration in Two Works by Paul Bowles." *Philological Papers* (West Virginia University) 32 (1986/87): 61–71.

Highet, Gilbert. *The Speeches in Vergil's "Aeneid."* Princeton: University Press, 1972.

Hirtzel, Fredericus Arturus, ed. *P. Vergili Maronis Opera.* Oxford: Clarendon, 1900.

Howells, William Dean. *The Rise of Silas Lapham.* NY: New American Library, 1963.

Hughes-Hallett, Lucy. *Cleopatra: Histories, Dreams and Distortions.* NY: Harper and Row, 1990.

Johnson, W. R. *Darkness Visible: A Study of Vergil's "Aeneid."* Berkeley: University of California Press, 1976.

Johnson-Davies, Denys, tr. *Arabic Short Stories.* London: Quartet, 1983.

Jullian, Philippe. *The Orientalists: European Painters of Eastern Scenes.* Tr. Helga and Dinah Harrison. Oxford: Phaidon, 1977.

Jung, Carl G., ed. *Man and His Symbols.* NY: Dell, 1964.

Kabbani, Rana. *Europe's Myths of Orient.* Bloomington: Indiana University Press, 1986.

Kaplan, Robert B. "Contrastive Thought Patterns—Yet Again." *Idiom* 19 (1989): 1–2.

Kassis, Hanna E. *A Concordance of the Qur'an.* Berkeley: University of California Press, 1983. 471–72.

Knight, W. F. Jackson, tr. *The Aeneid.* Harmondsworth: Penguin, 1956.

———. *Vergil: Epic and Anthropology.* Ed. John D. Christie. NY: Barnes and Noble, 1967.

Kramer, Samuel Noah. *The Sacred Marriage Rite*. Bloomington: Indiana University Press, 1968.

―――. and John Maier. *Myths of Enki: The Crafty God*. NY: Oxford University Press, 1989.

Kristeva, Julia. "Stabat Mater." 1974. Tr. Leon S. Roudiez. *Contemporary Literary Criticism*. 2nd. ed. Robert Con Davis and Ronald Schleifer. NY: Longman, 1989. 185–204.

Lacan, Jacques. "The Mirror Stage as Formative of the Function of the I." *Écrits: A Selection*. Tr. Alan Sheridan. NY: Norton, 1977. 1–7.

―――. "Seminar on 'The Purloined Letter' (with introductory note by Jeffrey Mehlman)." Trans. Jeffrey Mehlman. Staton 320–49.

Lakoff, George, and Mark Johnson. *Metaphors We Live By*. Chicago: University of Chicago Press, 1980.

―――. and Mark Turner. *More than Cool Reason: a Field Guide to Poetic Metaphor*. Chicago: University of Chicago Press, 1989.

Landau, Rom. *Moroccan Drama, 1900–1955*. San Francisco: American Academy of Asian Studies, 1956.

Laroui, Abdallah. "Colonizer Follows Colonizer." *The History of the Maghrib: An Interpretive Essay*. Tr. Ralph Manheim. Princeton: Princeton University Press, 1977. 27–89.

Laughlin, Henry P. *The Ego and Its Defenses*. NY: Appleton-Century-Crofts, 1970.

Layachi, Larbi. "The Half-Brothers." Paul Bowles, *Five Eyes*. 55–75.

Lehan, Richard. "Existentialism in Recent American Fiction: The Demonic Quest." *Texas Studies in Language and Literature* 1 (1959): 181–202.

Lerner, Daniel. *The Passing of Traditional Society: Modernizing the Middle East*. London: Free Press of Glencoe, 1958.

Lesser, Wendy. "Paul Bowles' *Collected Stories*." *Review of Contemporary Fiction* 2 (1982): 50–52.

Let's Go: The Budget Guide to Spain, Portugal and Morocco. Ed. Martha Hodes. NY: St. Martin's, 1985.

Lewis, C. Day, tr. *The Aeneid of Virgil.* Mack 1: 641–44.

Lougy, Robert E. "The World and Art of Jane Bowles." *CEA Critic* 49 (1986–87): 157–73.

Luck, Georg. Anima Mundi: *Magic and the Occult in the Greek and Roman Worlds.* Baltimore: Johns Hopkins University Press, 1985.

McCrum, Robert, William Cran, and Robert MacNeil. *The Story of English.* NY: Penguin Books, 1987.

Mack, Maynard, et al., eds. *World Masterpieces.* 2 vols. NY: Norton, 1965.

Mackenzie, John. *Orientalism: History, Theory and the Arts.* Manchester: University Press, 1995.

Maier, John. "The Ancient Near East in Modern Thought." *Civilizations of the Ancient Near East.* Ed. Jack Sasson. 4 vols. NY: Charles Scribner's Sons, 1995. I: 107–20.

———. "A Postmodern Syrian Fictionalist: Walid Ikhlassy." *Journal of South Asian and Middle Eastern Studies* 11 (1988): 73–87.

———. "Une catégorie de la littérature mondiale: La littérature archaïque." *Littérature générale/Littérature comparée* 6 (1992): 21–33.

Malin, Irving. "Drastic Points." *Review of Contemporary Fiction* 2 (1982): 30–32.

Mekouar, Hassan. "'Barbary' in Early American Literature." *The Atlantic Connection.* 259–68.

Mernissi, Fatima. *Beyond the Veil: Male-Female Dynamics in a Modern Muslim Society.* Rev. ed. Bloomington: Indiana University Press, 1987.

———. *Doing Daily Battle.* Tr. Mary Jo Lakeland. London: Women's Press, 1988.

———. "Women, Saints, and Sanctuaries." *The "Signs" Reader, Women, Gender and Scholarship.* Ed. Elizabeth Abel and Emily K. Abel Chicago: Chicago University Press, 1977. 57–68.

Metcalf, Paul. "A Journey in Search of Bowles." *Review of Contemporary Fiction* 2 (1982): 32–41.

Moffitt, Cecil L. "Paul Bowles' Sheltering Sky and Arabia." *Research Studies* 42 (1974): 44–49.

Moi, Toril. *Sexual/Textual Politics: Feminist Literary Theory.* London: Metheun, 1985.

Mottram, Eric. "Paul Bowles: Stacity and Terror." *Review of Contemporary Fiction* 2 (1982): 6–30.

Mrabet, Mohammed. *The Chest.* Tr. Paul Bowles. Bolinas: Tombouctou, 1983.

Mulvey, Laura Mulvey. "Visual Pleasure and Narrative Cinema." *Screen* 16 (1975): 6–18. Rpt. *Women and the Cinema: A Critical Anthology.* NY: Dutton, 1977. 412–28.

Nasr, Seyyed Hossein. "What Does Islam Have to Offer to the Modern World?" *Sufi Essays.* New York: Schocken. 1977. 164–70.

Nef, John U. *Cultural Foundations of Industrial Civilization.* New York: Harper, 1960.

Neumann, Erich. *The Great Mother.* 1955. Tr. Ralph Manheim. Princeton: Princeton University Press, 1963.

Newman, J. K. Rev. of *Literary Transvaluation*, by Barbara J. Bono. *The Classical Journal* 83 (1987–88): 166–69.

Nietzsche, Friedrich. "Ecce Homo." *The Philosophy of Friedrich Nietzsche.* New York: Random House, 1954. 809–946.

O'Leary, Joseph S. *Questioning Back: The Overcoming of Metaphysics in Christian Tradition.* Minneapolis: Seabury, 1985.

Ong, Walter J. *Orality and Literacy: The Technologizing of the Word.* London: Methuen, 1982.

Otto, Rudolf. 1958. *The Idea of the Holy.* Tr. John W. Harvey. New York: Oxford University Press.

Pagels, Elaine. *The Gnostic Gospels.* NY: Vintage, 1981.

Palmer, Richard. "Postmodernity and Hermeneutics." *boundary* 2 5 (1977): 363–93.

Patai, Raphael. *Society, Culture, and Change in the Middle East.* 3rd. ed. Philadelphia: University of Pennsylvania Press, 1969.

Patteson, Richard F. "The External World of Paul Bowles." *Perspectives on Contemporary Fiction* 10 (1984): 16–22.

———. Richard F. *A World Outside: The Fiction of Paul Bowles.* Austin: University of Texas Press, 1987.

Pöschl, Viktor. *The Art of Vergil.* Tr. Gerda Seligson. Ann Arbor: University of Michigan Press, 1966.

Pounds, Wayne. "Paul Bowles and *The Delicate Prey*: The Psychology of Predation." *Revue belge de philologie et d'histoire* 3 (1981): 620–33.

———. *Paul Bowles: The Inner Geography.* NY: Peter Lang, 1985.

Price, Alan. "Lily Bart and Carrie Meeber: Cultural Sisters." *American Literary Realism* 13 (1980): 238–45.

Putnam, Michael C. J. *The Poetry of the Aeneid.* Cambridge: Harvard University Press, 1965.

Quinn, Kenneth. *Virgil's "Aeneid": A Critical Description.* Ann Arbor: University of Michigan Press, 1968.

Rabinow, Paul. *Reflections on Fieldwork in Morocco.* Berkeley: University of California Press, 1977.

Reynolds, Dwight F. "*Sirat Bani Hilal*: Introduction and Notes to an Arab Oral Epic Tradition." *Oral Tradition* 4 (1989): 80–100.

Rondeau, Daniel. "Paul Bowles, Un Americano en Tanger." *Quimera* 48 (1986?): 27–33.

Rosenthal, Donald A. *Orientalism: The Near East in French Painting, 1800–1880.* Rochester, NY: Memorial Art Gallery, 1982.

Rountree, Mary Martin. "Paul Bowles: Translations from the Moghrebi." *20th Century Literature* 32 (1986): 388–401.

Sagan, Eli. *Freud, Women, and Morality: the Psychology of Good and Evil.* NY: Basic Books, 1988.

Said, Edward W. *Orientalism.* NY: Vintage, 1978.

Salim, George. *Al-Muqammara Al-Riwaya.* Damascus: Mansurat Ittihad al-Kutub al-'Arab, 1973.

Sartre, Jean-Paul. *Existentialism.* Ed. and tr. Walter Kaufmann. NY: Meridian Books, 1956.

Schechner, Richard. "The Future of Ritual." *Journal of Ritual Studies* 1 (1987): 5–34.

Schor, Naomi A. "Feminist and Gender Studies." Gibaldi. 262–87.

Schriber, Mary Suzanne. "Edith Wharton and the French Critics, 1906–1937." *American Literary Realism* 13 (1980): 61–72.

Servier, André. *Islam and the Psychology of the Musulman.* Tr. A. S. Moss-Blundell. New York: Charles Scribner's Sons, 1924.

Shah, Idries. *The Sufis.* Garden City: Doubleday, 1964.

Shales, Tom. "Warner's Musicals—Busby and Beyond." *The American Film Heritage.* Washington: Acropolis, 1972. 80–82.

Scholes, Robert, and Robert Kellogg. *The Nature of Narrative.* NY: Oxford University Press, 1966.

Schwab, Raymond. *The Oriental Renaissance.* Tr. Gene Patterson-Black and Victor Reinking. NY: Columbia University Press, 1984.

Shammas, Anton. *Arabesques.* Tr. Vivian Eden. New York: Harper and Row, 1988.

Shipler, David K. *Arab and Jew: Wounded Spirits in a Promised Land.* NY: Penguin, 1986.

Shir, Jay. "The Black Star: Paul Bowles' 'The Sheltering Sky.'" *Arbeiten aus Anglistik und Amerikanistik.* 8 (1983): 68–78.

Slyomovics, Susan. *The Merchant of Art: An Egyptian Hilali Oral Epic Poet in Performance.* Berkeley: University of California Press, 1987.

Sobleman, Harvey, and Richard S. Harrell. *A Dictionary of Moroccan Arabic: English-Moroccan*. Washington, DC: Georgetown University Press, 1963.

Spence, Sarah. *Rhetorics of Reason and Desire*. Ithaca: Cornell University Press, 1988.

Staton, Shirley, ed. *Literary Theories in Praxis*. Philadelphia: University of Pennsylvania Press, 1987.

Stetkevych, Jaroslav. *The Modern Arabic Literary Language: Lexical and Stylistic Developments*. Chicago: University of Chicago Press, 1970.

Stewart, Lawrence D. "Paul Bowles and 'The Frozen Fields' of Vision." *Review of Contemporary Fiction* 2 (1982): 64–71.

————. *Paul Bowles: The Illumination of North Africa*. Carbondale: Southern Illinois University Press, 1974.

Stivers, Richard. *Evil in Modern Myth and Ritual*. Athens: University of Georgia Press, 1982.

Talmor, Avital. "Beyond 'Wedlock' and 'Hierogamy': Non-Marriage in Modern Fiction." *The Durham University Journal* 77 (1984): 79–85.

Tannen, Deborah. *You Just Don't Understand: Women and Men in Conversation*. NY: Ballantine, 1990.

Terrasse, Henri. *History of Morocco*. Tr. Hilary Tee. Casablanca: Editions Atlantides, 1952.

Thornton, Agathe. *The Living Universe: Gods and Men in Virgil's "Aeneid."* Leyden: E. J. Brill, 1976.

Tindall, William York. *Forces in Modern British Literature, 1885–1956*. NY: Vintage, 1956.

Toulmin, Stephen. *Cosmopolis: The Hidden Agenda of Modernity*. NY: Free Press, 1990.

Turner, Frederick. "Performed Being: Word Art as a Human Inheritance." *Oral Tradition* 1 (1986): 66–109.

Ullah, Najib. *Islamic Literature*. NY: Washington Square Press, 1963.

Voltaire. *Candide*. Tr. Lowell Bair. NY: Bantam, 1959.

Waller, Margaret. *The Male Malady: Fictions of Impotence in the French Romantic Novel*. New Brunswick, NJ: Rutgers University Press, 1993.

Warwick, Henrietta Holm, ed. *A Vergil Concordance*. Minneapolis: University of Minnesota Press, 1975.

Wehr, Hans. *A Dictionary of Modern Written Arabic*. Ed. J. M. Cowan. Ithaca: Spoken Languages, 1976.

Wells, Linda A. "Paul Bowles: 'Do Not Appropriate *My* Object.'" *Review of Contemporary Fiction* 2 (1982): 75–84.

Westermarck, Edward. *Marriage Ceremonies in Morocco*. London Curzon Press, 1914.

———. *Ritual and Belief in Morocco*. 2 vols. New Hyde Park, NY: University Books, 1968.

———. *A Short History of Marriage*. NY: Macmillan, 1926.

———. *Wit and Wisdom in Morocco*. NY: Horace Liveright, 1931.

Wharton, Edith. *A Backward Glance*. NY: Appleton-Century, 1934.

———. *In Morocco*. 1920. Rpt. NY: Hippocrene, 1984.

Williams, John Alden, ed. *Islam*. NY: Washington Square Press, 1961.

Wolff, Cynthia Griffin. *A Feast of Words: The Triumph of Edith Wharton*. NY: Oxford University Press, 1977.

Wolkstein, Diane, and Samuel Noah Kramer. *Inanna: Queen of Heaven and Earth*. NY: Harper and Row, 1983.

Yacoubi, Ahmed. "The Night before Thinking." Paul Bowles, *Five Eyes*. 23-35.

Yorkey, Richard. "Practical EFL Techniques for Teaching Arabic-Speaking Students." *The Human Factors in ESL*. Ed. James E. Alatis and Ruth Crymes. Washington, D.C.: TESOL, 1977. 57–85.

Index